Warships in Profile

Warships in Profile

VOLUME ONE

General Editor
JOHN WINGATE, D.S.C.

With illustrations by:
T. Brittain
D. Cobb, R.O.I.R.S.M.A.
G. Davies
T. Hadler
D. Johnson
M. Trim
D. Warner
P. Warner

Published by
PROFILE PUBLICATIONS LIMITED
Windsor, Berkshire, England

Uniform with this volume

Aircraft in Profile Series
(3rd Edition)

Volume 1 (Part numbers 1–24)
Volume 2 (Part numbers 25–48)
Volume 3 (Part numbers 49–72)
Volume 4 (Part numbers 73–96)
Volume 5 (Part numbers 97–120)
Volume 6 (Part numbers 121–144)
Volume 7 (Part numbers 145–168)
Volume 8 (Part numbers 169–192)
Volume 9 (Part numbers 193–210)
Volume 10 (Part numbers 211–222)

History of the AFVs of the World Series
(1st Edition)

Volume 1 AFVs of World War I
Volume 2 British AFVs 1919–1940
Volume 3 British and Commonwealth AFVs 1940–1946
Volume 4 American AFVs of 1930–1950

Locomotives in Profile Series

Volume 1 (Part numbers 1–12)

© *Profile Publications Limited* 1971
SBN 85383 060 6

First published in England 1971, *by*
PROFILE PUBLICATIONS LIMITED
Coburg House, Sheet Street, Windsor, Berkshire, England

Printed in England by
Chichester Press Limited, Chichester, Sussex

Foreword

THE SHIP AND THE MAN

The launch of a ship is both an anxiety and a triumph. Months of work fuse in one dramatic moment. The chocks are knocked clear; a moment's suspense, as she hangs motionless, then slowly gathering momentum she slides down the slipway. Plunging into her element, she is afloat and viable: her life has begun.

So it was with the publication of the Warship Profiles: the launch gathered momentum and like the miracle of each new ship, the Series is now well and truly afloat. This book, the first Warship Bound Volume, is the direct result of the help and interest shown by that international phenomenon, the Ship-Lover and Ship-Modeller.

"A ship," it is said, "has a soul." A warship mirrors the nation that builds her. Added to national pride is that vital ingredient, the sailor who mans her—and he too is the product of the nation that forges the ship.

Therein lies the fascination: the man fashions his ship—and, because man is human, his ship assumes the mantle of the man.

The seafarer, schooled by the sea, it at heart an uncomplicated man. He remains apart from his land-reared cousin, which explains why the landsman cannot comprehend the ways of the seaman.

The shipman is disciplined by watch-keeping. He sleeps and wakes, day in, night out, sensitive to the mood of the weather: he wonders at the marvels of the deep, lives with the sea, combats the sea, is at peace with the sea, and, in the final analysis, he returns to the sea whence, aeons ago, his forbears originated when the earth was created.

The seafarer's ship must therefore be part of him: and, in these Islands, his ship has always been his mistress. To him his ship is like his woman: vital, responsive, fickle, capricious. But with all her contrariness, he can but love her. To the man of the sea, a ship is most definitely female.

The ships of every nation differ; the class of ship differs and each ship in that class varies. In the Warship Profiles, each ship has been described by a naval historian of that warship's nationality. Each ship, because she is unique, has her own story to tell; her record will therefore be differently presented by each author.

To this end, the broadest spread of canvas has been selected: the picture includes warships from the beginning of this century until those of the present day. Some of the authors have served in these ships; others, authorities in their special field, have viewed their subjects with contemporary judgement. But all, as far as it is humanly possible, have combined with the artists to provide historically accurate records of the ships which they have so faithfully described.

For all Ship-Lovers and Ship-Modellers throughout the world, these Warship Profiles will present an authoritative and indispensable record.

THE EDITOR

Contents

Acknowledgements

Profile Publications Ltd. are grateful to the Trustees, Directors and Head Librarians of the following authorities: The National Maritime Museum, Greenwich; The Imperial War Museum; The Public Record Office; The Ministry of Defence; The National Portrait Gallery; The Naval Library and Historical Section; The City of Southampton Public Library; The Hampshire County Library; The Winchester Library; The London Museum Library; The Illustrated London News & Sketch Ltd.; U.S. Navy; U.S. Air Force; The National Archives of the United States; Bibliothek für Zeitgeschichte, Stuttgart; Bundesarchiv/Militarchiv, Freiburg. Without the patience and unfailing courtesy of their historical and photographic staffs, the Warship Profiles could not have been produced. In addition, the Publishers wish to thank all those who have so generously given of their experience and time in the compilation of the Warship Series.

1906/7. Entering Portsmouth Harbour from Spithead. Probably post trials; note draught marks indicating light load. The first cutter is turned out for use as the sea boat.

HMS Dreadnought

John Wingate DSC

THE STATE OF THE NAVY: 1900

'What we have, we hold . . .' may be morally indefensible, but the supreme position which the Royal Navy held during the nineteenth century guaranteed this maxim. With the Royal Navy unchallenged, 'Pax Britannica' existed for nigh on a century, the nation's policy being expressed in Lord Palmerston's three *dicta*: first, the Navy must be more powerful than any combination of other navies; second, no foreign power should command the shores of the English Channel; and third, the continuance of the European balance of power.

The alarm bells rang in 1896. The Kruger Telegram alerted British suspicions of German hostility during the Boer War; in 1898 and 1900, the German Navy Laws confirmed German's aggressive and competitive policy. These Laws stated specifically that the German Navy was to be so strong that, if any other navy was to challenge it, the adversary would be at risk.

The challenge went not unheeded in the Mediterranean where Admiral Sir John Fisher was Commander-in-Chief of the Mediterranean Fleet from 1899 to 1902. It was here that the first stirrings of Naval Reform

germinated: Fisher had gathered about him a group of ardent and keen young officers whose ideals were to shake the Navy out of the lethargy into which it had lapsed since Trafalgar.

The 'Service' had passed through traumatic change, to the satisfaction of its erstwhile antagonists, the French, who had much to gain by innovation. The first sailing ship of the Royal Navy to be screw-driven and steam propelled, the *Agamemnon*, was built in 1852 at Bucklers' Hard from the oak of the Beaulieu woods, two years after the French *Napoleon*. Genéral Paixhans developed the explosive shell for naval armament and consequently introduced armour plating to ships' wooden hulls, the first 'iron-clad', the *Gloire*, being built in 1859. The British replied with *Warrior* in 1860, an all iron-built ship with additional armoured protection on her sides.

There followed the inevitable evolution from sail to steam; and from the muzzle-loaded gun to the interrupted screw-thread, breech-loading big gun mounted in armoured cupola-type turrets. HMS *Victoria* reached the pinnacle with twin 16·25-inch guns in an armoured turret forward and with protection of 18-inch compound

1

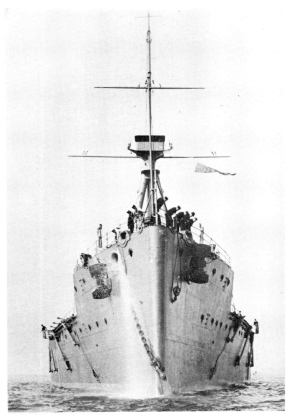

HMS *Dreadnought*, Battleship, eighth of the name, 1906. On trials and weighing anchor: the cable party is hosing down the cable as it is hove in. Note the leadsmen in the chains on both sides; the starboard leadsman is about to heave the lead.

armour. She was lost in collision with *Camperdown* in 1893, during fleet manoeuvres.

The development of the Whitehead torpedo and the appearance of the submarine had forced upon a reluctant Admiralty the provision of counter measures in the shape of the quick-firing gun and the fast torpedo boat destroyer. The water-tube boiler and triple-expansion machinery giving 17 knots; Harvey steel for armour and the final adoption of four 12-inch breech-loading guns was the point of development in 1895 which produced the Spencer programme of nine *Majestic* class battleships. Battle was still considered as an action in which battleships pounded each other at point-blank range. Such was the material state of the Navy whilst Fisher brooded in the Mediterranean and when an international incident erupted upon a complacent world.

THE BATTLE OF TSU-SHIMA

After the Sino-Japanese war of 1894–95, the Russians, in 1898, forced the Chinese to hand over Port Arthur so that, from this new naval base, her aspirations to annexing Manchuria could be achieved. In 1904 and 1905, the Russian fleet, after its long haul around the Cape of Good Hope from the Baltic, finally arrived at Port Arthur. The ships and their companies were in a parlous state, so that the final battle in the Straits of Tsu-shima could not be judged as representing a fight between equals. The Japanese fleet, ably led and handled by

Admiral Togo, annihilated the Russians during the battle of 27/28/29 May 1905. Analysis by the Admiralty of the British Naval Attaché's reports produced the following conclusions:

(**i**) The advantage of six knots speed in Togo's battle-fleet allowed the Japanese Admiral to choose his tactical position and to maintain a minimal rate-of-change of range.

(**ii**) Two 12-inch shells hit the leading Russian flagship, *Tzarevitch*, at a range of 14,000 metres. One shell killed the fleet navigating officer and wounded the Chief of Staff and Captain. Splinters from the second shell flew through the conning tower aperture to kill and wound all those inside. The coxswain fell dead across the wheel, jamming it hard-a-starboard. The flagship thus hauled out of line, the rest following to cause utter confusion in the Russian battle-line. The big gun, with only two hits, had decided the issue of the day.

These lessons of Tsu-shima did not, in fact, affect the thinking of Admiral Fisher. The results of the battle, however, helped to allay the bitter criticisms of the decisions which this man of genius was about to take.

JACKIE FISHER

Admiral Sir John Fisher was 61 when he became Second Sea Lord in 1902, fresh from the Mediterranean. Though old by today's standards, at the turn of the century, to reach this exalted position at his age was exceptional: because of stagnation in promotion, admirals of eighty years of age were not unusual. This state of affairs naturally bred inefficiency, as exemplified by the lethargy displayed throughout the Navy, not only in the appalling gunnery results at ranges of 2000 yards, but in the conditions of service for both officers and men.

Life on the lower deck remained harsh. Bad pay, discipline bred on fear and with no security after discharge, a seaman's life attracted only the dregs of society; yet the spirit in the Fleet was good, due, no doubt, to the morale inculcated by 'pride of ship' in appearance and drills. The same, however, could not be said for the Reserve Fleet where men lay rotting for years on end. 'Brightwork stations' usurped the sailor's function for which he was trained and this purposeless existence did not lead to high morale.

Officers were efficient enough in their peacetime role of 'showing the flag' and suppressing native risings, but there was little incentive in the thoughtful pursuit of the art of war. Until the German challenge in 1898 and 1900, there had been no threat to shake the Navy from its lethargy, until, that is, Sir John Fisher became Second Sea Lord.

Jackie Fisher had fought his way to the top. He had gathered in his 'Fishpond', as his adversaries termed his team of progressive thinkers, all those who cared passionately for the efficiency of the Navy. No new broom is popular and Jackie Fisher was certainly no exception. He was ruthless, arrogant and, when the need arose, devious to achieve what he knew to be right. He was deeply religious and frequently quoted The Scriptures to prove his point. He had the highest ideals and would brook no interference with his decisions, which in his view, he made for the good of the Navy.

THE FISHER REFORMS

The upheaval began when Fisher became Second Sea Lord. Responsible now for the manpower of the fleet, he at last possessed the power he needed. From June 1902, until his appointment as Commander-in-Chief, Portsmouth, on 31 August 1903, Fisher, against all conservative opposition in the Navy, instituted the following revolutionary reforms:

(**i**) He introduced the Selborne scheme which was designed to break down the 'snobbish' barriers between officer specialisations. The 'young gentlemen' were to enter the Navy at 13 years of age. They were to join the *Britannia* and *Hindustan*, who were moored in the Dart, and to attend the Royal Naval College at Osborne where the young cadets would mix in all branches of specialisations.

When Fisher became Commander-in-Chief at Portsmouth in 1903, he was able to keep a close eye on developments at Osborne.

(**ii**) He reorganised the conditions of service, promotion and advancement of both Wardroom and lower deck. To Fisher, as with Nelson, the man came before the machine.

(**iii**) He scrapped all obsolescent ships, to an outcry of dissent both inside and outside the Navy. He realized that it was the development of long range shooting and not the building of a new super-ship which rendered obsolete the existing Navy.

(**iv**) He reorganized the efficiency of naval gunnery by using the leadership of Captain Scott who was now the first Captain of the new Gunnery School at Whale Island, HMS *Excellent*.

(**v**) He introduced the 'Nucleus-Crew System' for the Reserve Fleet. This ensured the highest possible state of readiness for a peace-time reserve fleet.

(**vi**) When First Sea Lord, he disposed the Fleets throughout the world to achieve Mahan's maxim: the greatest concentration of effort at the right place and the right time. He instituted the Channel Fleet, based on Dover; and the Atlantic Fleet, based on Gibraltar, in addition to the existing Mediterranean Fleet.

Admiral of the Fleet, Sir John Fisher.

1907, after refit. Note short top-gallant mast has now replaced the original top-gallant mast on the foremast; a small secondary compass platform has been fitted on the quarter deck.

1907, after refit, dockyard coal-burning paddle tug alongside. Note three-masted sailing ship dressed overall in background.

April 1908. Leaving Portsmouth Harbour, Vice-Admiral's flag flying at the masthead. Note the screw flagmen on the quarter deck and the ship's company fallen in on the upper deck.

THE SUPER-SHIP

All these reforms were conducted against violent opposition. On 21 October, Trafalgar Day, 1904, he became First Sea Lord. He could now carry through his greatest achievement: the realization of a dream he had held for so long, the building of a super-ship, HMS *Untakeable*, as, in his imagination, she was known. This ship was to be 'like a hard boiled egg,' he said, 'unbeatable'.

In 1903, Mr Fred T. Jane published, in his *Fighting Ships*, an article by the Chief Constructor of the Royal Italian Navy, Colonel Vittorio Cuniberti. This brilliant designer had been responsible for the four revolutionary light battleships of the *Vittorio Emanuele* class which were

laid down in 1901 at Spezia and Castellamare. Cuniberti's genius went unrecognized by his Italian masters, so he crystallized his ideas on the ship of the future and, with Italian permission, submitted his paper, '*An Ideal Battleship for the British Fleet*', to Mr Fred T. Jane.

Cuniberti's proposals were startling. He advocated two essential qualities for his revolutionary battleship:
(i) twelve to sixteen 12-inch guns, thus exploiting the recent developments in gun manufacture and the new techniques of fire control by 'spotting' similar splashes in controlled salvoes. One ammunition size would also be an important advantage.
(ii) the vital importance of speed so that the ship could

choose her range and tactics. The ship should be considerably faster than any other projected battleships of the world.

The Italian designer's proposals galvanized the thinking of the world's navies. America and Japan reacted almost immediately: these two countries could welcome rendering their smaller fleets obsolescent and, psychologically, their officers were attuned to innovation.

Not so naval opinion in Great Britain whose fleets consisted of up-to-date battle squadrons. A revolutionary ship would render useless these monster ironclads which held such sinister appeal for the people of the United Kingdom. It was Cuniberti, however, who provided the spark of debate. It required the genius of Fisher to translate, against bitter opposition, the dream into practical reality.

Dreadnought: Germination

Fisher stated in his Memoirs that he first conceived the idea of *Dreadnought* when he was in Malta in 1900. There he had discussed his ideas with Mr W. H. Gard, the Chief Constructor in the Dockyard. When Fisher became Commander-in-Chief, Portsmouth 1903, Gard was the Manager of the Constructive Department in Portsmouth Dockyard. Fisher had been swayed by arguments in favour of the 10-inch gun (Design A) but by 1904, when, as First Sea Lord, he laid his proposals before the Cabinet, his thoughts had hardened upon an all-big-gun ship with eight 12-inch guns (Design B).

In submitting his case for HMS *Untakeable*, his imaginary ship, Fisher cleverly argued his case for the two designs. He included all that was novel and revolutionary, features now made possible by the advance of engineering technology. His arguments embraced much to serve as targets for his critics, arguments which, when demolished, would permit acceptance of the essential points:

HMS Untakeable

(i) A uniform armament of eight 12-inch guns. Six capable of firing a broadside at one time, from 60° before the beam to 60° abaft the beam. The long range of the big guns would enable her to exploit the accuracy of modern fire control.

(ii) She would have to fight other battleships and, with her superior speed, she could choose her range. Naturally she would shoot at long ranges and this would also eliminate the hazard of torpedo atack from the fleets of enemy torpedo boats.

The effect of a few well aimed guns would be devastating.

The argument for speed and accurate big guns would be unanswerable.

'. . . The fast ship with the heavier guns and deliberate fire should absolutely knock out a vessel of equal speed with many lighter guns, the very number of which militates against accurate spotting and deliberate hitting.'

'. . . Suppose a 12-inch gun to fire one aimed round each minute. Six guns would allow a deliberately aimed shell with a huge bursting charge every ten seconds. Fifty per cent of these should be hits at 6000 yards. Three 12-inch shells bursting on board every minute would be HELL!'

The new battleship would be not only a battleship but, because of her speed, would be superior to any modern first class cruiser.

1909/10. Prior to refit. Dressed overall; note the lower booms, the starboard gangway and the steam picket boat. The range-finder platform with hinged side extensions can clearly be seen over the midship control tower, for'd of the after funnel.

Circa 1910/11. Range clock has been fitted temporarily to fore control top but blast screen has not yet been added on 'A' turret.

'. . . highly placed guns which can see the enemy and fight in any weather is what is wanted.'

There would be no secondary armament.

The next quality would be speed. Twenty-one knots would be required and this meant a ship longer than any existing battleship.

She should also have excellent sea-keeping qualities, so her bows should be high ($24\frac{1}{2}$ feet) and she should have a light draught.

'. . . These two essential qualities of an eminently powerful armament and a high speed have been obtained without raising the displacement above that of existing ships. Economy is thus assured, a very important point.'

She would be virtually *unsinkable*, each compartment being self-contained with its own ventilation and ladders. There would be no watertight doors piercing the transverse bulkheads and there would be no half-measures in this policy: there would be no holes whatsoever in the bulkheads. The ship should, therefore, be safe from sinking by torpedo.

The ship should be protected to the limit by armour without affecting:
speed, stability and a maximum displacement of 16,000 tons.

The twin gun mountings were to be protected in 12-inch armoured redoubts extending down to the main deck. The armoured belt should also be of 12-inch armour plate.

Oil fuel was to be used as far as possible, thus obviating watertight doors in the coal bunkers. Coal to be used when making passages. Once the country had an assured oil supply the Navy should become oil furnaced, thus rendering watertight the inner skin of hulls.

The ship was to be commanded from a 12-inch steel protected conning tower sited forward. Below it would be the Signal House and above it the forward Control Position which would be directly above the main steering position. This arrangement meant simplicity of communication and control of the guns. There would be no other conning tower.

A tripod mast was to form the structure about which the above positions would be centred.

Boats were to be lighter (10 to 12 tons) and a novel system of derricks would be provided.

The ram bow was to disappear, this form of attack being impracticable as battle would be fought at long ranges. '. . . It is only extra length which will make it (the ram) more difficult to dock a ship, and more of a peril to friends in peacetime than of any probable use in war.'

Thirty Yarrow boilers working at 275 lb. pressure would supply steam to triple expansion engines turning twin screws. Horse Power would be 30,000 and revolutions 120.

6

1912/13. The blast screen has now been added abaft the QF guns on 'A' turret in order to protect the bridge personnel. Note the starboard bower anchor hanging a-cockbill and the seaboat's crew standing by to man the first cutter preparatory to coming to a buoy.

These, then, were Fisher's recommendations but the problem was how to obtain acceptance of these revolutionary proposals without creating overwhelming opposition. The new First Lord immediately attempted to solve the problem by taking the following action:

(i) He appointed to Admiralty his old friend, Mr Gard, as Assistant Director of Naval Construction with the commission to finalise the drawings and calculations from the original drafts.

(ii) He shrouded in secrecy the proposals for the All-

Big-Gun ship by appointing on 22 December 1904, a *Committee on Designs, 1904*. To conceal his own influence, he merely acted as Chairman of this Committee which he had filled with carefully selected members.

The Committee first convened on 3 January 1905. Its main problem was to decide the combination of 12-inch guns and their siting: and how to achieve a speed of 21 knots on a displacement of about 16,000 tons. Discussion swayed to and fro and, after prolonged arguments on the merits of 'End-on-Fire' as against

After refit, 1913. The main topmast has now been removed; W/T extensions have been fitted on the foremast below the fore control top and on the mainmast where the aerials are now led direct to the stern.

1913. Entering Portland Harbour. The W/T extension on the foremast is clearly visible.

'Broadside Fire', Fisher's will prevailed: 'End-on-Fire' it would be.

Five further plans were drawn up, considered and rejected until, on 13 January 1905, just a year since its first meeting, the Committee on Designs finally approved the Design for Battleship 'H'. The ship was to become HMS *Dreadnought*, the eighth ship in the Royal Navy to bear that name. The Battle of Tsushima was still four months in the future.

Dreadnought: Maturation

Design 'H' was discussed in detail and the following decisions made:

THE MACHINERY '. . . speed is armour.'—Fisher.

At Queen Victoria's Diamond Jubilee Naval Review at Spithead in 1897, a diminutive boat of 42 tons displacement outraged authority and the patrolling picket boats by weaving at over 30 knots in and out of the majestic lines of ships.

She was the *Turbinia*, a small vessel especially built to demonstrate the excellence of her revolutionary power unit which consisted of a marine turbine designed by the Honourable Charles Parsons. By 1905, only *Viper* and *Cobra*, two torpedo-boat destroyers, had been completed with turbines but they reached speeds of 36 knots. All other ships were still driven by triple expansion machinery, so Fisher and his Committee were staking all upon their decision to drive *Dreadnought* by turbine machinery.

Captain Reginald Bacon, a member of the Committee on Designs and Assistant to the First Sea Lord, has described the transformation in the Engine Rooms: 'When steaming at full speed in a man-of-war fitted with reciprocating engines, the engine-room was always a glorified snipe-marsh; water lay on the floor plates and was splashed about everywhere; the officers often were clad in oilskins to avoid being wetted to the skin. The water was necessary to keep the bearings cool. Further, the noise was deafening; so much so that telephones were useless and even voice-pipes of doubtful value. In the *Dreadnought*, when steaming at full speed, it was only possible to tell that the engines were working, and not stopped, by looking at certain gauges. The whole engine-room was as clean and dry as if the ship was lying at anchor, and not the faintest hum could be heard.'

Doubts as to *Dreadnought's* manoeuvring abilities were allayed by Sir Charles Parsons who promised a satisfactory performance: there were to be four propeller shafts, the inner shaft being placed close to novel twin rudders which were to be balanced and overhung, their weight being supported inboard.

THE MAST. The control position was to be high up above the foremost funnel. To reduce vibration and to provide rigidity and strength, a tripod mast was chosen.

WATERTIGHT SUBDIVISION. The only permitted piercing of bulkheads was to be for electrical leads, steam and hydraulic pipes.

TORPEDO-BOAT DEFENCE. Twenty 18 cwt. 12 pdrs. were to be mounted on the superstructure and turret roofs.

SHELL AND CORDITE ROOMS (MAGAZINES). Because the magazines could not be further inboard than 15 feet from the ship's side, the magazines would be protected by 2 to 2½ inch armour plate. To save this extra weight the redoubt, turret and conning tower protection was to be reduced from 12 to 11 inch armour.

The proposal to reduce the turret armour was made by Captain John Jellicoe, a brilliant gunnery officer and a member of the Committee on Design. He supported his argument by pointing out that the shock of a direct hit upon a 12 inch protected turret would almost certainly put the turret temporarily out of action anyway.

THE SHAPE OF THE BOW. Though originally designed for a clipper bow, Fisher preferred a modified underwater 'snout' stem for appearance. The Committee concurred with their Chairman's wish.

ACCOMMODATION. Because of the length of the ship, the officers were to be accommodated as near to the bridge as possible. The officers' quarters were to be forward, the messdecks to be aft.

Admiralty's Policy Decisions

(i) *Dreadnought* to be laid down immediately and completed within a year. Trials were to be executed swiftly to gain experience for future ships.

(ii) No further battleships were to be built until the results of the trials were analysed.

1914, after refit. Note searchlight re-sited low on fore tripod. Photograph taken shortly before the commencement of hostilities against Germany. Note that brightwork has not yet been painted over.

Dreadnought in floating dock. Her bottom has not yet been scrubbed—note the working party on the floating pontoon. The top-gallant mast has been struck and sheer legs have been rigged on the fo'c'sle. *Diadem* class cruisers are in the background.

1914. The last days before the Great War. Note the aerial deck fittings for the main W/T aerials in the eyes of the ship and leading to the fore topmast.

(iii) The battleships in the process of building were to be allowed to be completed. *Lord Nelson* and *Agamemnon* had progressed too far to replace their 9·2-inch guns by 12 inch.

Dreadnought: Fruition

The Royal Dockyard at Portsmouth was selected to construct the ship, Constructor J. H. Narbeth being in charge. He immediately drew a set of lines to bear the proposed displacement, with the suggested dimensions, in order to calculate the minimal horse power to achieve 21 knots. Seven models were built and tested in the tank at Haslar before Mr R. E. Froude, Superintendent of the Admiralty Experimental Works and a member of the Committee of Designs, was satisfied that 23,000 hp instead of 28,000 hp would suffice to drive a ship of this displacement and with Mr Narbeth's fullness of lines. The reduction of 5000 hp eliminated the necessity for one row of boilers and saved 25 feet in hull length, and, consequently, a great saving in weight. The following were the design specifications to which Mr Narbeth had to work:

Dimensions

Length (between perpendiculars)	490' 0"
(overall)	526' 0"
Beam	82' 0"
Mean draught	26' 6"
Displacement	17,900 tons
Deep load	21,845 tons
Load draught	18,110 tons
Hull	6100 tons
Designed load	11,700 tons
Sinkage	70 tons per inch

Armament

12" B.L. Guns/45 calibre	10
12-pdr. 18 cwt. Q.F. guns	27
Torpedo tubes (18" submerged)	4 broadside
	1 stern
Torpedoes: 18"	23
14" (boats)	6

Protection

Belt	11", 8", 6". 4"
Bulkhead	8"
Barbettes	11"–4"
Turrets	11"
Conning Tower	11" and 8"
Decks: main	$\frac{3}{4}$"
middle	3"–1$\frac{3}{4}$"
lower	4"–1$\frac{1}{2}$"

Machinery

Parsons turbines, 23,000 horse-power	21 knots
Boilers: Babcock & Wilcox	18,250 lb pressure
Propellers	4. 320 rpm

Fuel

Coal	900/2900 tons
Oil fuel	1120 tons
Patent fuel	120 tons
Complement	695/773

Radius

6620 m. at 10 kt. 4910 m. at 18.4 kt. (continuous sea-going speed)

Dreadnought: Building

Speed was also vital in building *Dreadnought*. The design was approved by the Committee on 13 January 1905. The speed of her construction was largely due to the efficiency of Mr J. R. Bond who, in the mould loft in Portsmouth Dockyard, saw to it that the laying-off and detail drawings were always well in hand. The efficiency with which she was built was also due to ordering standard plates, thus obviating the work of sorting and cutting out.

The following principal events in *Dreadnought's* construction indicate the speed with which she was built.

The details are taken from Captain Sir Charles Madden's notebook, Naval Assistant to The Controller at the time, and a member of the Designs Committee:

1905
Jan.	12-inch guns and hydraulic machinery ordered.
June 24	Main propelling machinery ordered.
July	First demands for structural materials forwarded from Yard, 2200 tons.
Aug.	Armour, principal ship castings and auxiliary material ordered.
Sept.	All principal ship castings delivered or cast; also 5000 tons of structural materials ordered.

On 2 October 1905, less than nine months since Design 'H' was accepted, *Dreadnought's* keel was laid down. Only ten weeks later, on 28 December, the centre line of her shafts were sighted in; four days later, on New Year's Day 1906, boring out commenced. Work certainly did not halt over the Christmas and New Year period.

It is difficult, in these days, to imagine with what devotion and energy the dockyard shipbuilders must have toiled, for, only five weeks after boring out, and 13 weeks from laying down, Jackie Fisher's proudest day dawned on 10 February 1906.

Launching Day, 10 February 1906

King Edward the Seventh christened *Dreadnought* with a bottle of Australian wine which refused to shatter until the second royal attempt. The King used a mallet fashioned from *Victory's* timber to strike the chisel which cut the last securing tie, then, with an imperceptible gathering of momentum, the steel leviathan slid majestically into the waters of Portsmouth Harbour.

At this instant, few of the thousands of official and unofficial onlookers could realize that history was being forged and that this was a most significant event and one which could have only one inevitable conclusion: a trial of strength between Britain and Germany.

GERMAN REACTION

Amongst the official guests on the bunting bedecked launching platform was Rear-Admiral Coerper of the German Imperial Navy who was representing Kaiser Wilhelm II, King Edward's brother-in-law. The secrecy in which *Dreadnought* was built had stimulated interest in the German naval mind; already much was known by the German Admiral and this knowledge had arrested the German Imperial Navy's building programme until the results of the *Dreadnought's* trials became evident.

Dreadnought's launch forced Germany to choose between the only two alternatives:

(i) Abandon her policy of competing with the Royal Navy; to accept instead a '*guerre de course*' policy which meant harassing the superior potential enemy's sea lanes across the oceans. The building emphasis would, therefore, be upon armoured cruisers,

Or

(ii) Emulate the British and, having learnt *Dreadnought's* secrets, to build even better and more battle-

February 10th, 1906. Launch of HMS *Dreadnought*. Sections of the cradle can be seen still floating forward and aft. The White Ensign and Union Flag are flying for the first time.

In dry dock—flooding up.

Battle practice targets streamed astern of HMS *Bellerophon*. These targets were used for gunnery exercise by the Fleet.

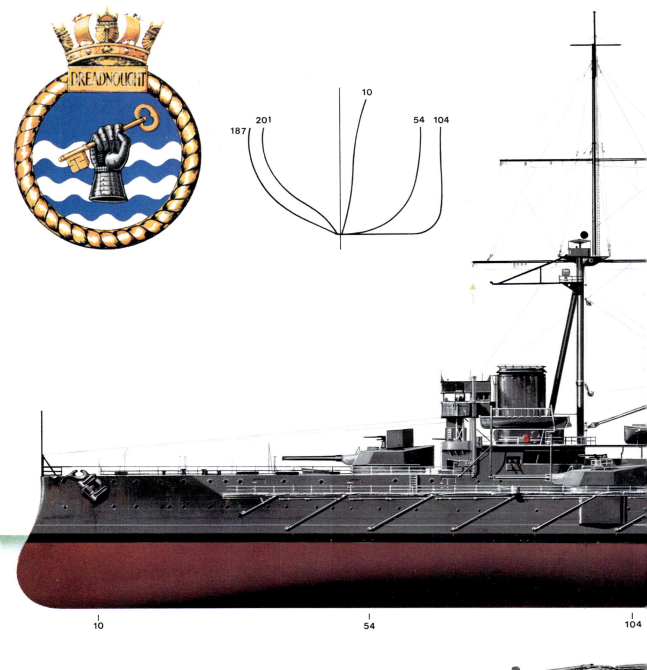

187 201   10   54 104

10   54   104

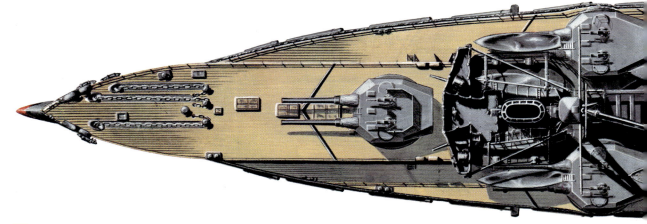

HMS Dreadnought 1906-1920

Ship's Badge
Per fesse: wavy blue and white ; two bars wavy blue.
Badge: a dexter gauntlet proper grasping a key in bend sinister ward to the dexter gold.
Motto: 'Fear God and dreadnought.'

Contours
It is interesting to compare the fullness of lines at section 104 with the clean entry of her bows at section 10. This fullness ensured a stable gun platform but it was still possible to reduce the Horse Power by 5000 to achieve the designed 21 knots.

Rigging
Dreadnought is here depicted as she was in 1914/15. Her yards are shown turned through ninety degrees in order to illustrate her rigging at that date.

T. Brittain/T. Hadler © Profile Publications Ltd.

187   201

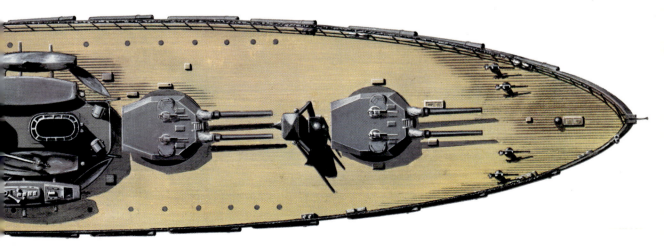

The Great War, 1915. Moored to a buoy. The port boats are turned out and the launch and picket boat are lying at the lower boom.

ships. This would entail widening and deepening the Kiel Canal; producing big guns and mountings, and constructing larger docks. This policy would require money and time, but, by the date when Germany was finally ready to build, *Dreadnought* and her immediate successors would be out of date. Germany could then build modern ships, blow for blow, with Britain.

The German Admiralty chose the latter course and so *Dreadnought* had unleashed the cataclysmic arms race.

DREADNOUGHT: COMPLETION

Five days after *Dreadnought's* launch, on 15 February 1906, it was decided to try and advance the completion date of the ship by 1 January 1907, instead of in the second week of February. The building programme then proceeded at break-neck speed as recorded in Captain Madden's notebook:
1906
2 Mar.   All boilers on board. 2000 tons of armour placed in position this month.
April   10,000 tons worked into ship (aggregate).
May   First shipload of Turbines arrived from Parsons. Weight of ship 11,500 tons.
June   Six 12-inch guns placed on board. All Turbines on board. Weight of ship 13,100 tons.
July   All 12-inch guns in position. Torp. Tubes and 12-pdrs. being shipped. Weight of ship 14,000 tons.
3 Aug.   2nd docking. 15,380 tons worked into the ship in the aggregate by the end of month.

1 Sept.   Commissioned with nucleus Crew.
8 Sept.   Inclined.
12 & 13   Preliminary Hydc. trials.
15 Sept. Ready for trials alongside.
17 Sept. Basic trials.
1 Oct.   Proceeded on Official Steam trials.
9 Oct.   Returned to prepare for Gun trials.
17 Oct.   Proceeded on Torpedo and Gun trials.
18 Oct.   All trials concluded. (22nd was programme date.)
19 Oct.   Returned to Yard. Opening out Machy. commenced.
28 Nov.   Completed examn. of Machy.
29 Nov.   Second Basin trial.
1 Dec.   Proceeded on 24 hrs. acceptance trial.
3 Dec.   Returned to Yard.
11 Dec.   Completed to full crew.

Dreadnought had been built in two months less than the time planned. This peace-time ship-building effort has never been surpassed.

CHARACTERISTICS

When her first crew 'slung their hammocks' in the after ends of the ship on 11 December 1906, their new home bore these characteristics:
HULL A long fo'c'sle, designed to keep the ship 'dry' in bad weather for efficient gun laying and fire control.

The Launch. Turning her in Portsmouth Harbour. Note the whaler under oars recovering floating debris and the two steam picket boats.

The Launch. Tugs are hustling alongside to take control. The Portsmouth Dockyard building shed and slipway derricks can be seen to the right.

The Launch under control; the tugs have now been secured alongside. Note her anchor cables and the shape of her bow.

'Cleared for action'. The ship is under rudder; guard rails and stanchions have been cleared away. This is not an action photograph—see 'goofing' party on quarterdeck. Note QF guns on turret roof.

'A' turret trained on a bearing of Green 120. Note that the tompions have been removed from the gun barrels.

The flare from the bows was taken as far aft as the midship section where she became slab-sided to resist rolling. The fo'c'sle decks and sides were especially strengthened to withstand the shock from the firing of the for'd and wing turrets.

The first broadside firing trials were critical. The tension mounted on board when the Director of Naval Construction, Sir Philip Watts, clambered below to the messdecks for the moment of the first broadside firing of the guns. One of his Constructors wrote:
'. . . He selected a position on the port side of the forward barbette (the guns fired to starboard). He looked very grave and serious and I am quite sure that he fully expected the decks to come down wholesale. Presently there was a muffled roar and a bit of a kick on the ship. The eight guns had been fired and scores of men between decks had no idea what had happened.'

WATERTIGHT SUBDIVISION
(i) Because the oil fuel was contained directly below the machinery spaces, no intricate subdivision of these large compartments was necessary. The ship's structure was thereby simplified and weight saved.
(ii) Because each compartment was self-contained, with no watertight doors in the bulkhead, each compartment had its own ventilating, pumping and drainage arrangements.
There was, therefore, no requirement for a main drain running the length of the ship.
Electrical pumps were used instead of being steam driven, which allowed for the washing down of the anchor cables before they descended the navel pipes. The cable was thus stowed in a clean condition in the lockers.
(iii) Passenger lifts were fitted in all machinery compartments.
(iv) The magazines were sited along the centre line of the ship, as far as possible from the ship's side.
ARMAMENT To save time, Lord Nelson's and Agamemnon's 12-inch guns were used. Weight was saved by using the latest design of mounting which reduced the outside barbette diameter from 34 to 29 feet. This allowed vast economies in weight for the construction of turn-tables and the barbette armour. Circular bulkheads were built to carry the roller paths for the gun mountings.
Eight guns could fire on either broadside.
Four or six guns could fire on ahead or astern bearings.

Gun heights above L.W.L.: forward	$31\frac{1}{2}$ feet.
amidships	$22\frac{1}{2}$ feet.
aft	23 feet.

Twelve 12-pdrs. were mounted on the superstructures:
two on each turret roof, five on the quarterdeck. (Initially, she mounted four on the fo'c'sle, and on the fore turret roof). Twenty-seven 12-pdrs. in all.
Later she mounted four HA 12-pdrs. and twenty 18 cwt. guns. The for'd and after guns were on disappearing mountings (1915/16).

ARMOUR Protection was subordinated to the essentials of the 'all-big-gun' and speed policy:
Turrets	11″ side, 3″–4″ roof.
Amidships	8″ and 11″
Bows	6″
Stern	4″
Upper deck-nil	(Long ranges and 'plunging fire' had not yet been developed).
Magazines	2″ below water
	4″ wing positions

Underwater Protection

Designed to be safe for up to two torpedo explosions.

STABILITY Because of a large metacentric height (5·07) enforced by the policy of unpierced bulkheads, the ship's period of roll was small. Period for double roll: $13\frac{1}{2}$ sec. This disadvantage was the price of safety.

On trials, when steaming at 19 knots across waves 500 feet long and 15 feet high, Dreadnought 'took it green' up to a few feet above the stem head, thus exposing her forefoot for 30 feet along the keel. The ship remained steady and dry.

List of Weights in Tons for LORD NELSON & DREADNOUGHT

	Lord Nelson	Dreadnought
Water for 10 days	67	60
Provisions for 4 weeks	44	40
Officers' stores	45	42
Officers, men and effects	95	82
Masts, yards and tops	105	113
Cables and anchors	112	115
Boats	52	48
Warrant Officers' stores	90	90
Torpedo net defence	40	60
Total general equipment	650	650

Armament (including turn-tables and turrets)		
Armament (including turn-tables and turrets)	3110	3100
Propelling and auxiliary machinery	1660	1990
Engineers' stores	60	60
Coal	900	900
Total:	6380	6700
Armour and Backing		
Vertical, on sides and citadel	2000	1940
Plating on sides	—	—
Protection to Magazines	—	250
Decks and gratings	1170	1350
Backing	120	100
Barbettes	800	1260
Casemates	—	—
Conning-tower	110	100
Total armour	4200	5000
Total load	10,580	11,700
Hull	5720	6100
Total weight required	16,300	17,800
Board margin or displacement weight	200	100
Total displacement required	16,500	17,900

MACHINERY Parsons marine turbines for all propelling machinery. A great saving in weight and, because of fewer working parts, much more reliable than triple expansion engines: *Dreadnought* steamed to the West Indies and back (7000 miles) at 17½ knots without mechanical defects.

Manouvreing: four astern turbines on all shafts; one H.P. and one L.P. astern turbine on each side.

The tripod mast and bridge. Note the QF guns beneath the flag deck and between the first cutter's davits. The outhauls for the booms of the anti-torpedo netting can be clearly seen.

Stopping Distance: 20 knots—1025 yards.
                        12 knots— 725 yards.
Full Power: 23,000 H.P. at 320 revs.
                        (trials: 26,350 H.P. at 328 revs. = 21·6 knots).

STEERING AND TURNING CIRCLE Twin balanced rudders, underslung, side-by-side and directly abaft the screws to give steerage way as soon as the propellers revolved, instead of waiting, as previously, for the ship to gather way before the rudder produced an effect. This design resulted in excellent manoeuvrability.

Tactical Diameter:

Dreadnought: length waterline, 490 feet.
                 35° rudder at 13 knots = 455 yards.

RIGGING Tripod mast abaft the foremost funnel. Funnel fumes affected personnel in control top.

When steering into the wind, the tripod became hot abreast the funnel top, thus making difficult access to the control top. In the next class, *Bellerophon*, *Superb* and *Temeraire*, the foremost funnel was abaft the tripod, the struts of which ran aft, instead of for'd.

The after or secondary control was mounted below the smoke line on a small tripod mast for'd of the after turret.

The 12-inch guns of HMS *Superb*, one of the first successors to *Dreadnought*. *Dreadnought's* 12-inch guns were identical.

The tripod mast and flagdeck. Heat from the funnel and its fumes made the ascent inside the legs of the tripod to the control top unpleasant and sometimes impossible.

The Monkey's Island. Dressed overall for a Japanese visit. Note the spreaders for the W/T aerials and the chain bridle for the main derrick topping-lift.

General

TORPEDO NETS The most comprehensive system yet devised. The nets led from right forward to aft and could be hoisted and lowered in one evolution, the nets being brailed up on themselves with brailing leads led from the heads of the booms. Hoisting the nets took but a few minutes; lowering, even less time.

The ship's trim could be assessed at deep load draught when the heels of the booms were awash.

APPEARANCE The most impressively functional appearance of any ship yet built. To quote the words of the late 'Doctor' Oscar Parkes, OBE, AssINA, who devoted 31 years of his life to produce the classic authority on *British Battleships* (published by Seeley Service & Co., through whose good offices and that of the Ministry of Defence the author of this Warship Profile has been permitted to quote several passages from *British Battleships*):

'In appearance the *Dreadnought* with her grim, awe inspiring sense of efficiency was something essentially British, outclassing anything else afloat, and unique in contrast to any other battleship. Her successors although bigger and better armed could never strike the same note of novelty and overwhelming power. The first sight of her completing in dock was an unforget-

table experience, and as flagship of the Home Fleet she dwarfed her consorts to an extent that mere difference in tonnage would never suggest.'

When *Dreadnought* slid down her Portsmouth slipway on 10 February 1906, the commotion that she caused spread much further than through the waters of Portsmouth Harbour. Controversy spread throughout the nation, discord that culminated with the acrid and undignified battle of words between 'Charlie B', Lord Charles Beresford, and Fisher.

The bitter dissension caused by the building of *Dreadnought* divided the Navy into two factions: Fisher's, 'The Fish Pond' versus 'The Syndicate of Discontent', led by Charlie B. There is no space in this first Warship Profile to record the controversy which, to students of naval history, is a tragic but fascinating story. Suffice to state that the feud culminated in Beresford being forced to strike his Admiral's flag in March 1909; and in Fisher's resignation on 25 January 1910.

The Life of HMS Dreadnought

| 1905–06 | Estimates: approval for construction of *Dreadnought*. |
| 2 Oct. 1905 | Keel laid down in Portsmouth Dockyard. |

18

10 Feb. 1906	Launched by King Edward VII.
1 Sept. 1906	Commissioned in Reserve with Nucleus Crew for trials.
3 Oct. 1906	Began trials from Portsmouth.
3 Dec. 1906	Trials completed.
11 Dec. 1906	First Commissioned with full complement.
5 Jan. 1907	Attached to Home Fleet for Special Duties. Proceeded to Mediterranean and Trinidad on experimental cruise. Near disaster in Strait of Bonifacio, Corsica, when steering broke down.
23 Mar. 1907	Returned to Portsmouth.
April 1907	Flagship, Nore Division, Home Fleet.
Mar. 1909	*2nd Commission* Flagship, First Division, Home Fleet (Flag to March, 1911).
1911	Refit, Portsmouth Dockyard.
June 1911	Coronation Review, Spithead.
May 1912	*3rd Commission* Relieved by *Neptune*, the first British Battleship to have superimposed turrets and all guns able to fire on one broadside. *Dreadnought* joined First Division, Home Fleet.
Dec. 1912	Flagship, Fourth Battle Squadron.

The Great War

Aug. 1914	Joined the Grand Fleet. Flagship, Fourth Battle Squadron.
18 Mar. 1915	Rammed and sank U-boat, U-29 in Lat. 58° 21′ N, Long. 01° 12′ E.

Copy of report from C.O. Dreadnought, Captain W. J. S. Alderson RN to Vice-Admiral Commanding Fourth Battle Squadron.

HMS 'DREADNOUGHT',
18 March 1915.

Sir,

I have the honour to report that on 18 March 15 at about 0–28 p.m. a periscope of a submarine was sighted by Lt. Commr. B. H. Piercy, R.N., the O.O.W., about one point on the port bow, distance about 1500 yards. The formation of the squadron at the time being Divisions in line abreast disposed astern, 'DREADNOUGHT' being port wing ship of the leading division, speed 15 knots, course W.S.W.

2. Commr. (N) H. W. C. Hughes R.N. and myself were on the bridge, syren was blown, red flag hoisted, course altered towards the submarine, and speed increased to full about 17½ knots.

3. The course of the submarine was altered several times, but her mean course appeared to be straight away from me. The periscope disappeared for a few moments but re-appeared almost at once, this was very shortly before she was rammed. One round only was fired, the periscope being very difficult to lay on.

The bridge and tripod mast. The downhaul and fore-guy of the anti-torpedo booms can be seen on the right.

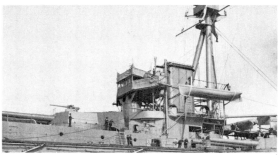
The bridge and tripod mast from the port side.

The after funnel from the port side. The 42′ launch is stowed in its seagoing position but the crutches for the 50′ steam picket boat are vacant. Note the side armour and the covers over the discharge outlets. The two midship QF guns are just visible.

The forward superstructure. The midship control tower and athwartship stowage of the whaler are clearly visible. Note the leadsmen in the starboard chains.

THE VICE-ADMIRAL COMMANDING, FOURTH BATTLE SQUADRON.
27 March 1915.

With reference to your minute No. 083 of 21st March, 1915, forwarding a diagram to indicate the approximate tracks of the ships of the Fourth Battle Squadron during the submarine attack of the 18th idem, assuming that 'MARLBOROUGH'S' signal 'Submarine ahead of you' was received at 0.15 p.m. in the position shown in the diagram. I am of opinion that your squadron should have been turned *away* by blue-pendant to the eastward.

Battleships should never be purposely taken into the proximity of submarines except when the danger is so close that the only safety lies in an attempt to ram the submarine.

The 'wheel' shown at 0.20 was decidedly risky, especially for the pivot ship, which was apparently ordered to reduce to ten knots. It is presumed that course was altered by compass-pendant and not by 9-pendant—as shown in the diagram, such a signal not being applicable to the formation given.

(*Signed*) J. R. JELLICOE,
Admiral.

4. At 0–35 p.m. I overtook and rammed the submarine apparently striking her on the starboard quarter. When struck the impact was plainly felt on the bridge by myself and others.

5. The conning tower did not appear at all so her present number was not seen, but when struck her bows came out of water at an angle of about 30° from the vertical showing about 30 feet of her fore part and the number 'U-29' was observed in 'relief' figures painted over, on her bow.

6. She immediately sank by the stern and a large oily patch was seen in the place where she disappeared. H.M.S. 'BLANCHE' visited the spot immediately after.

7. Force of wind was one to 2, sea smooth with a slight swell.

8. I submit that credit is due to Lt. Commr. Piercy who was the first to sight the periscope, and that the successful striking of the submarine is due to the extremely skilful way in which Commr. (N) Hughes conned the ship during the chase.

I have, etc,

(Signed) W. J. S. ALDERSON
Captain.

Spring 1916	Major refit.
May 1916	After the German raid on Lowestoft, transferred as Flag to Third Battle Squadron at Sheerness.
Mar. 1918	Rejoined Fourth Battle Squadron, Grand Fleet.
July 1918	Paid off to Reserve Fleet, Devonport.
Feb. 1919	In Reserve, Rosyth.
31 Mar. 1920	Placed on Sale List.
May 1921	Sold to T. Ward & Co. for £44,000.
2 Jan. 1923	Arrived Inverkeithing for scrapping.

1917. At sea and cleared away for action. Her turrets are trained abeam to starboard and she is steaming at speed.

1917. The torpedo nets and booms have been removed. The fore control top has been enlarged and the DCT added above. The bridge has been rebuilt and the navigating platform extended forward. Three searchlights have been resited on the mainmast.

The Battle Cruisers. 18.34 on 1st May, 1916, at the Battle of Jutland. When hotly engaged in close action with the German Fleet, a heavy shell struck the starboard midship 12-inch turret of HMS *Invincible*. The flash from this shell ignited the magazine of the two 12-inch turrets, which contained 50 tons of cordite. The ship broke in half and sank in 10 to 15 seconds with the loss of 1,025 officers and men out of a total of 1,031.

The Battle of Jutland, 31st May, 1916. The loss of the battle cruiser *Queen Mary*. Her destruction was due to the same cause as that which destroyed *Invincible*—a flash-back into the magazine.

The Battle Cruisers. HMS *Lion* being hit on 'Q' turret at Jutland, 31st May, 1916. She was saved from destruction by the prompt flooding of the magazines. Note the 13th flotilla of torpedo boat destroyers working ahead to attack the German battle fleet.

Stern view of *Dreadnought*. Note the 'gash-chute' over the port quarter.

Alterations to Dreadnought

1906–1907	Additional QF guns mounted to each centre line turret.
	Removal of lower pair of Searchlights (SLs) on superstructure amidships.
	Longer W/T yard fitted to mainmast.
	Range Finder Platform with hinged side extensions fitted over midship Control Tower.
	Short top-gallant replaced existing top gallant mast on foremast.
	A small compass platform was fitted at the after end of the quarterdeck.
1910–1911	Range clocks temporarily fitted to fore control top.
	Prominent blast screen added abaft QF gun on fore turret.
1913	Main topmast removed.
	W/T aerials led direct to stern.
	Similar extension fitted for'd below fore control top.
1914–1915	Bridge SL re-sited low on fore tripod, abreast the foremost funnel.
1915	Fore top-gallant mast removed.
	Topmast reduced to a stump.
1915–1916	Fore control top enlarged. DCT (Director Control Tower) added above. QF guns removed from fore A turret and each beam turret. All QF superstructure guns removed except two upper mountings in for'd superstructure. Two 3-inch and two 12-pdrs. H.A. mounted,

two at after end of quarterdeck, on disappearing mountings.

Siting of other pair unknown but probably on beam turrets. This re-distribution and siting of QF in the open was to meet the claim that one hit would not knock out a whole battery; and that, after the experience of the Russians and Japanese, a gun without a shield is less lethal than one protected by a thin shield.

The bridge was rebuilt and made longer to leave the Conning Tower clear.

The Navigating Platform was extended for'd.

The superstructure was built up below the bridge.

The Control Platform over the midship Conning Tower was removed.

1916–1917	After the disasters of cordite 'flash-backs' at Jutland in *Queen Mary*, *Indefatigable* and *Invincible*, the magazine internal protection was improved.
1917	Deflection scales painted on A and Y turrets.
1917–1918	The SL on the after superstructure and the remaining two SLs on the midship structure resited on large square platform on mainmast.

General Appearance Notes

1. The 4 QF quarterdeck disappearing mountings were still mounted during 1915/1916.
2. *1915/1918 Period*
   a) No main-topmast.
   b) W/T aerials taken to SL platform on mainmast.
   c) Battleship Grey paintwork.

The Battle Cruisers

The complement to Fisher's Battleship, *Untakeable*, (*Dreadnought*) was his other inspired dream, HMS *Unapproachable*, a swifter *Dreadnought* and therefore more lightly armoured.

To be classed as 'Battle cruisers', the first of this lineage, the *Invincible*, materialised in 1908, two years after *Dreadnought*. Because of insufficient protection around the magazines against plunging fire and because of inadequate anti-flash precautions, she blew up at Jutland when 'Q' turret was hit. Only two officers and three men out of a complement of 1031 were saved, a disaster to be repeated in World War II when *Hood* was sunk by *Bismarck*.

Invincible's sister ships, *Inflexible* and *Indomitable*, survived the Great War and were followed by the most graceful ships the world has seen: the 'Mighty *Hood*', *Renown* and *Repulse*.

Dreadnought's effect on World History

Dreadnought's successors numbered 177, for, emulating the British lead, the world's Greatest Powers were forced to compete. Germany had to widen her Kiel

Canal and could not build her *Dreadnought* until the Canal was finished which was much to Fisher's delight.

Foreign navies built for national prestige and, for most of the 60 years of their lives, the *Dreadnoughts* wielded their power from the mists of distant anchorages.

Dreadnought's descendents evolved majestically, through the 15-inch *Queen Elizabeth* and *Revenge* classes, to the inter-war 16-inch triple turret battleships, *Nelson* and *Rodney*. Then in World War II, the 14-inch *King George Vth* class, whose *Prince of Wales*, sunk by Japanese aircraft, sounded the knell of the *Dreadnoughts*: the new weapon, air power, had finally superseded the 'all-big-gun' battleship.

Our adversaries were forced to compete. The Italians: *Vittorio Veneto*; the Japanese: *Kongo* and *Yamato*; the Germans: *Graf Spee*, *Bismarck* and *Tirpitz*.

The United States closed the chapter. World War II ended when the Japanese signed their unconditional surrender aboard the quarter-deck of USS *Missouri* in 1945.

The last of the 'all-big-gun' ships was the most majestic of all. In *Vanguard* lay the acme of perfection: a beautiful ship with superb sea-keeping qualities.

Vanguard never fired a gun in anger: this may, perhaps, be the most fitting epitaph to be bestowed upon the last of the *Dreadnought* battleships. Fisher's *Dreadnought* has handed on her tradition to her successor, HM Nuclear Submarine, *Dreadnought*, the progenitor of a fresh epoch. Will she also bear the same record as *Vanguard*, the last of the *Dreadnoughts*?

HMS DREADNOUGHT

Built at Portsmouth

Laid down:	2 October 1905.
Launched:	10 February 1906
Trials:	3 October 1906
Completed:	December 1906
Cost:	£1,783,883
Dimensions:	490' (527') × 82' × 26.5' = 17,900 tons
	Deep load: 21,845 tons
	Load draught: 18,110 tons (sinkage: 70 tons per inch)
	Hull: 6100 tons
	Load, 11,700 tons (designed)
Armament:	Guns: 10 12-in./45; 27 12-pdr. 18 cwt.
	Tubes: (18-in. submerged): 4 broadside, 1 stern.
	Torpedoes: 23 18-in.; 6 14-in. (boats)
Protection:	Belt: 11", 8", 6", 4". Bulkhead: 8"
	Barbettes: 11"–4". Turrets: 11"
	C.T.: 11" and 8".
	Decks: main $\frac{3}{4}$"; middle 3"–1$\frac{5}{8}$"; lower 4"–1$\frac{1}{2}$".
Machinery:	Parsons turbines, 23,000 h.p., 21 knots
	Boilers: 18 Babcock and Wilcox, 250 lb. pressure
	4 screws, 320 rpm
Fuel:	900/2900 tons coal plus 1120 tons oil plus 120 tons patent fuel.
Complement:	695/773. Radius, 6620/10: 4910/18.4 knots (Continuous seagoing speed)
Constructor:	J. H. Narbeth

Legend of Weights

Freeboard: Forward	28' 0"
Minimum	16' 6"
Aft	18' 0"
Indicated Horse Power	Turbines equal to 23,000
Speed	21 (20$\frac{3}{4}$–21) knots
Coal: Tons at normal load draught	900 tons
General Equipment	650 tons
Armament	3100 tons
Machinery	2050 tons
Total weight of equipment	6700 tons
Total weight of Armour and Backing	5000 tons
Total weight of Hull	6100 tons
Board Margin	100 tons
Total Displacement at Normal Load Draught	17,900 tons
Cost per ton	£17.5

HM Nuclear Submarine *Dreadnought* on the surface. Ninth ship of the name.

'The Emperor of Abyssinia and his Suite.

THE DREADNOUGHT HOAX

Early one forenoon during the last of the summers before the Great War, a telegram for the Commander-in-Chief of the Channel Fleet arrived aboard HMS *Dreadnought* who lay at the head of the battle-line anchored in Weymouth Bay, where the Fleet was paying a courtesy visit to the town. Signed '*Hardinge*', the Permanent Under Secretary of State for Foreign Affairs, the telegram warned the Admiral of the imminent arrival of The Emperor of Abyssinia and his Suite to inspect the flagship.

The Fleet had three hours in which to prepare for the royal visitors: the civic dignitories in Weymouth were immediately warned and the Fleet was dressed overall.

The royal train arrived on time, at Weymouth station where the Emperor of Abyssinia and his dark-skinned entourage were greeted by cheering crowds. Protocol was rigidly observed and, after being welcomed by a senior naval officer, the party moved off along the red carpet to the waiting cars which transported the royal visitors to the picket boat waiting on the pier.

Aboard the *Dreadnought*, pride of the British Fleet, the Royal Marine Band crashed into a foreign national anthem as the Emperor clambered up the gangway to the quarterdeck where the Admiral and *Dreadnought*'s Captain waited in full dress to welcome the Emperor, his Suite and the seedy English interpreter in morning dress who accompanied the party.

After inspecting the Royal Marine Guard of Honour, the Captain took the Emperor round the ship. After a thorough inspection, including witnessing the training of the turrets and the elevation and depression of the 12-inch guns, the Emperor was ushered ashored again with all due pomp and ceremony.

The royal train departed back to London and the Emperor and his Suite were never seen again.

This hoax, carried out by a group of Cambridge students led by an undergraduate named Horace Cole, caused much mirth throughout the nation, but sadly discomfited the Navy.

The Author wishes to express his gratitude and to acknowledge the unstinted service given by The Directors and The Head Librarians of the following authorities:

The National Maritime Museum, Greenwich
The Imperial War Museum
The Public Record Office
The Naval Library and Naval Historical Section
The City of Southampton Public Libraries
The Hampshire County Library
The Winchester City Library
The Ministry of Defence.

Without the patience and the unfailing courtesy of their historical and photographic staffs, the first Warship Profile could never have been produced.

Bibliography
BRITISH BATTLESHIPS by Oscar Parkes, OBE, AssINA, Seeley Service & Co., Ltd
THE 'DREADNOUGHT' HOAX by Adrian Stevens, Hogarth Press
A HISTORY OF THE MODERN BATTLESHIP by Richard Hough, George Allen and Unwin, Ltd
HMS DREADNOUGHT—THE FIRST FIVE YEARS by Rolls-Royce and Associates Ltd
FROM DREADNOUGHT TO SCAPA FLOW, VOLUME I by Arthur J. Marder, Oxford University Press.

Acknowledgements
Profile Publications Ltd., are grateful for the permission of the Trustees of the National Maritime Museum, the Imperial War Museum and the National Portrait Gallery to reproduce the photographs in this Profile.

Painting of Cossack *going alongside the* Altmark *in Josing Fjord by Norman Wilkinson.*

HMS Cossack

David Lyon RNR MA

INTER-WAR DESTROYER DEVELOPMENT

At the end of the First World War, Britain had established a clear lead in destroyer design with the superb 'V and W' class which provided the classic layout for destroyers over the next 20 years. The main characteristics of the 'V and W's and all Royal Naval destroyers up to the 'I' class of the late thirties were:

  an ample freeboard;
  two funnels;
  four guns (4″ or 4·7″) in single mountings super-
    imposed fore and aft;
  two multiple torpedo tube mountings;
  and a displacement of about 1250 tons.

Though the 'I's' were of a good balanced design, were excellent seaboats, were very handy with good armament for their size, they were also completely outclassed in size, speed and armament by destroyers in service with several foreign navies.

In 1918 the Germans were building a class of extra-large destroyers armed with four 5·9-inch guns, with a displacement of 2400 tons and a design speed of 37 knots. The two which were completed by the end of the war (*S113* and *V116*) were taken over by the French and Italians respectively (as the *Admiral Senes* and *Premuda*). Both navies, with their Mediterranean responsibilities, were impressed by the design and the idea of a 'super-destroyer' which was capable of acting both as a 'destroyer of destroyers' and a high-speed short range raider.

The French took the lead in pushing the concept to its logical extreme, as exemplified by two classes in service

by 1939. The *Mogador* with eight 5·5-inch guns in twin mountings was almost a light cruiser, whilst *Le Terrible* of the *Fantasque* class established a world speed record (which still stands) of over 45 knots for eight hours. The Germans, Japanese and Americans were also building super-destroyers and, by the mid-thirties, the Admiralty was becoming worried by the individual inferiority of British destroyers.

Whether Their Lordships were right is another matter. Destroyers were essentially the largest type of light craft capable, if necessary, of being risked in a torpedo attack, and they were generally operating in groups. The numbers of vessels in a flotilla are more important than individual excellence and, should larger enemies be encountered, the Royal Navy could usually produce a cruiser or battleship in support e.g., the *Warspite* at the Second Battle of Narvik. However large and powerful the destroyer, she would stand little chance of winning a stand-up fight with a cruiser, even if both ships were armed with similar guns. The latter would be more seaworthy, a better gun platform, more strongly constructed, and with better fire control equipment. Very high speed in a destroyer was also of questionable value: 'There is doubt of the value of speeds above 35 knots. Weather and other factors (time, vibration, spray, efficiency of armament, sea room, etc.) seldom permit ships of this size to steam at more than 32 knots, and, if in company, 30 knots is likely to be the limit . . . '

The French and Italians have aimed at higher—and perhaps excessive speeds. In normal weather, good enemy reports, sound judgment and tactical handling

Tribal Class destroyer on the stocks. Sikh or Zulu at Stephen's yard, Linthouse, Glasgow. Stephen's Collection.

may well lead to an advantage of "position" greatly outweighing the benefits of such margins of speed . . ."[1]

Accurate long range fire from a destroyer, particularly at speed in a seaway was very difficult, so the most valuable characteristics of a destroyer gun were a high rate of fire and ease of working. The 4·7-inch gun was probably at the upper limit of efficiency for destroyers; heavier guns merely added to topweight and reduced the likelihood of obtaining hits as the German destroyers found when they attempted to engage the smaller but more seaworthy British vessels in heavy weather.

Therefore, at a time when the need for extra displacement to accommodate a powerful close-range A/A armament, radar and other electronic equipment was not yet apparent, the Admiralty seems to have been justified in spending its limited resources on numbers of smaller destroyers.

[1] This quotation from a memorandum written in 1935 by the Assistant Chief of Naval Staff is taken (as is much of the ensuing information) from the Tribal Class Ship's Cover (Adm. 138-732), now held by the National Maritime Museum.

Tribal Class destroyer with the Mediterranean Fleet: Mohawk taken on 27 September 1938. She has the red, white and blue recognition stripes on 'B' gunshield worn by destroyers serving with the Neutrality Patrol during the Spanish Civil War.

THE SUPER DESTROYER
Design of the Tribals

However, in late 1934, a staff requirement was put forward for a class of super-destroyer whose chief task was to carry a powerful gun armament for surface action[2]. The 'V' Leaders, as the class was originally known, were to carry out: *'patrol work, shadowing, screening, close support of destroyer flotillas, and, in conjunction with cruisers, reconnaissance and escort duties'*. The main requirements for fulfilling this role were considered to be: a low angle armament of ten 4·7-inch guns in twin mountings; good communications and plotting arrangements; a speed of 36 knots; endurance of 5500 miles at 15 knots and a light torpedo armament for use in bad visibility and at night. All this was to be achieved within the London Treaty limitation of 1850 tons (standard).

Secondary requirements included the ability to contribute to the A/A defence of the fleet, harbours and convoys. For long range A/A fire, some or all of the 4·7-inch mountings were to be given 40° elevation; and a close range armament of 4-barrelled pompoms and/or multi-barrelled 0·5-inch machine guns was to be fitted. The long range A/A requirement was held to be more important, because it would be easier to improvise a short range armament in wartime.

Communications equipment was to be similar to a flotilla leader's: a Type 49 Medium Frequency (M/F) and High Frequency (H/F) transmitter, and the smaller 43A and 51H transmitters as auxiliary and fire control sets respectively. One M/F receiver was to be fitted for each of the following requirements: Admiral's wave, Reconnaissance wave, routine signals. Auxiliary and fire control equipment would also be provided. *ASDIC*, later known as Sonar, was also a possible fitting.

The Designs

The alternative sketch designs produced by the Director of Naval Construction (DNC) in March 1935 included three with the basic layout of five twin 4·7-inch mountings: two forward, two aft and one between the funnels (an earlier proposal for three superimposed mountings forward had been dropped), and two multiple machine gun mountings. The differences were in speed and displacement (36 to 35 knots, 1870 to 1812 tons). Another design substituted a quadruple pompom for '*Q*' mounting; the fifth design also had only four 4·7-inch mountings, but a speed of 37 knots, a divided engine room and four machine gun mountings. All designs standardised on a single quadruple set of torpedo tubes (a quintuple mounting was ruled out on grounds of weight).

The discussion which followed saw the defeat of the gunnery faction who were demanding the five 4·7-inch mountings (despite a proposal to give only two of the mounts 40° elevation in order to save weight). It was held that the division of the engine room by a transverse bulkhead would entail unjustified increases in weight and complement. Other proposals which were rejected were for the fitting of an eight-barrelled pompom, and for a single funnel to improve the field of fire of the machine guns.

[2] The Tribals were specifically designed to deal with the Japanese FUBUKI Class (six 5-inch guns in twin mountings and nine 21in torpedo tubes).

Cossack *on trials flying the red ensign to show that her builders have not yet handed her over. This is one of the very few surviving photographs of the* Cossack.

The final sketch design, tentatively approved in August and finally approved on 28 November 1935 after detailed alterations, was for a ship with four 4·7-inch mountings, two quadruple pompoms on the centre-line and two machine guns on either side of the bridge. Dimensions were very slightly reduced from the original designs, and the displacement was to be 1850 tons. A shaft horse power of 44,000 was expected to produce 36 knots. The 4·7-inch were to be hand-worked, but the torpedo mounting was powered. Two stern rails were provided for six depth charges (soon changed to two depth charge throwers, one set of rails and twenty depth charges) and ASDIC was to be carried. The ship was to have a Director Control Tower and a separate rangefinder, though an H/A director could be fitted in place of the latter subsequently.

On 7 November, tenders were invited for the construction of a flotilla of seven 'V' Leaders as part of the 1935 Construction Programme. A day later, the DNC was congratulated: '*the staff requirements have been met in the most satisfactory manner in the face of severe treaty restrictions*'.

The number of seven new ships for the flotilla had been decided on because seven would cost about the same as eight conventional destroyers plus their flotilla leader (£3,360,000 as against £3,250,000). Another seven (later raised to nine) were to be ordered for the 1936 Programme. Later, seven (reduced to three) and another seven (increased to eight) were ordered by the Australians and Canadians.

Two of the contracts for the original seven ships were awarded to Vickers-Armstrong's High Walker Yard on the Tyne, and they were given the yard numbers 6 and 7. The second was to cost slightly less than the lead ship because there was no need to repeat weighing and inclining trials. The hull was to cost £149,630; the main machinery £174,875 and the auxiliary machinery £16,577.

Matabele *taken in early 1939.*

Sikh on trials in the Clyde in 1938. Stephen's Collection

THE COSSACKS

The problem of finding a name for the new ships had caused considerable debate, a situation reminiscent of the classification of the *Daring* class ten years later. Names suggested included 'scout', 'corvette' 'cruiser destroyer', but the final choice was 'Tribal Class Destroyer' (The previous Tribals were Fisher's class 30 years earlier of ocean going destroyers which had marked a substantial increase in armament and size of destroyers). Accordingly, suitable names were appropriated to the new flotilla: the Walker Yard's second ship was allocated the name, *Cossack*, by an order dated 27 February 1936.

The Cossacks were, strictly speaking, not a tribe at all, but were groups of fugitive serfs and other frontiersmen gathered on the steppe boundaries of Russia during the 16th and 17th Centuries when they founded their own independent communities. They probably took their name from the Kazakh tribes from whom they copied their cavalry tactics and way of life. The Cossacks were later absorbed into Tsarist Russia, but they have continued to provide much of the irregular light cavalry in the Russian army.

BUILDING AND TRIALS

Cossack's keel was laid down on 9 June 1936. She was launched on the 8th of the same month in 1937 and commissioned on 7 June 1938, but whilst she was building a number of alterations were made in the design.

The original straight stem was replaced by a French-type sharply raked bow, which would keep the fo'c'sle

Maori in 1939, mounting trained to starboard

Broadside view of Mohawk *taken on 27 September 1938*

drier, though paravanes could no longer be streamed from the bow. A proposal to exchange the positions of 'X' 4·7-inch mounting and the after pompom, which would have given a better defence against dive bombers attacking from aft (their favourite angle), was unfortunately turned down*.

Increase of topweight in the design caused the unfortunate decision to remove the forward pompom, and to substitute the two multiple machine guns in sided positions between the funnels. On the platform between their sponsons, the ring for the pompom remained for future eventualities. This position had already been strengthened to take an extra 4·7-inch mounting if required, in a last outburst of nostalgia for the ten-gun main armament.

A slight hold-up during fitting out was caused by delays in the delivery of the new 4·7-inch mountings from Vickers, though *Cossack* did not have to wait as long as some of her sisters.

Her trials performance was satisfactory, her six hours full power trial obtaining an average of 36·223 knots, 44,430 SHP* at 366·4 RPM† with a displacement of 2030 tons. The rest of her class achieved similar results: the fastest on the six hours trial was *Bedouin* with 37·457 knots.

DETAILS OF CONSTRUCTION

The *Cossack* was clearly a lineal descendant of the 'V and W's. She was larger, having substituted twin mountings for single guns, but on the other hand, she had only one torpedo mounting.

The basic layout was, however, still the same, with two funnels above three water tube boilers, though in the majority of 'V and W's the after funnel was the thicker of the two. Each boiler was in a separate compartment, a bulkhead separating the turbines from the gearing, but the engines were of the same type, Parsons single reduction geared turbines. These were very reliable, but, as they used steam at lower temperatures and pressures than foreign contemporaries, they were not as powerful or economical.

Slightly higher stresses were accepted than had been

the practice and upper deck girders were increased from four to five a side. Frames were spaced at 1ft 9in intervals before the boiler room bulkhead, and at 2ft abaft it. As a minor curiosity, the plating was overlapped (butt-lapped) instead of butt-strapped which had been the normal destroyer practice. It was left till the next class, the 'J's to use the weight-saving longitudinal method of construction which became standard in later construction*.

The only important innovation in the *Tribal's* design was the introduction of the twin 4·7-inch mounting. This had already undergone trials when fitted in 'B' position in the 'H' class destroyer *Hesperus* (and removed after successful completion of the trials in 1937). *Hesperus* also had the new form of bridge which was used in the *Tribals*. To give a clear view over the higher gunshield of the twin mounting, the wheelhouse was raised and set forward of the bridge, instead of being directly underneath, as in previous designs. The mounting proved very satisfactory, though its 40° elevation was to prove totally inadequate for A/A fire. It was proposed to fit the Mark XI 4·7-inch gun in this mounting, a weapon which fired a 62lb shell (heavier then the shell for the German 5·1-inch gun). Unfortunately, the gun was not ready in time, so the *Tribals* were fitted with the Mark XII instead, which only fired a 50lb shell.

* The *Ardent* built by Denny in 1913 had been longitudinally framed, but the experiment had not been repeated since.

Eskimo in early 1939 with Neutrality Patrol recognition marks on 'B' gunshield.

* The later Canadian improved *Tribals* repositioned their pompom where the 24in searchlight had been, thus gaining the necessary stern arcs of fire.

* Shaft Horse Power.
† Revolutions per minute.

Two pictures of Sikh *whilst still in her builder's hands. She is still flying the Red Ensign. NMM Stephen Collection*

ALTERATIONS DURING SERVICE

War soon demonstrated the deficiencies in the *Tribals'* A/A armament, particularly the inability of the 4·7-inch guns to provide high angle fire, and the inadequacies of the unreliable and inaccurate 0·5-inch as a close range weapon. During repairs after the Second Battle of Narvik, 'X' 4·7-inch mounting was removed and replaced by a twin 4-inch High Angle mounting, which immediately proved invaluable in action.

The after funnel was cut down by four feet to improve the field of fire of the light guns. The 0·5-inch machine guns and the useless empty pompom ring were moved from between the funnels and replaced by a single

20mm Oerlikon. Single Oerlikons were also installed in the sponsons on either side of the signal deck and on either side of the superstructure deck. These guns were replaced (probably in June 1941) by twin power-operated guns of the same type. The latter position had originally been occupied by the depth charge throwers which were moved down to a more exposed position on the upper deck. By early 1941 *Cossack* seems to have been fitted with single pompoms in the bridge wings and, possibly, on either side of the after deck-house as well, though still retaining the 0·5-inch guns amidships at that stage.

Protective plating was fitted around the after steering

Mashona *in March 1939. Note the rakish, slightly curving bow copied from the French*

position and all gun positions to supplement the bullet-proof plating already installed round the bridge, wheelhouse and plotting office.

The direction-finding aerial was removed from the masthead and replaced by a Type 286P radar aerial. A Type 285 radar office was placed on top of the crew's galley.

The mainmast and mechanical semaphore were removed and one 25ft motor boat and the 14ft sailing dinghy landed to reduce topweight. Another significant change was the addition of a portable salvage pump.

The *Tribals* were driven hard in the first years of the war, and this uncovered slight weaknesses in construction. The *Cossack* was persistently afflicted by leaks in the oil fuel tanks below the fo'c'sle break. An Admiralty signal dated 10 October 1942 drew attention to two/three inch long cracks in the plating at upper deck level in this position. This signal also required local strengthening to be installed as soon as possible, but *Cossack* sank before this could be done.

Ships of this class who survived to the end of the war were fitted with lattice masts, improved radars, and an H/F D/F (High Frequency Direction Finder) mast added aft. Canadian and Australian *Tribals* had all

Two Tribals seen from the quarter; Maori (*in 1939*) and Zulu (*1938*) both NMM. Maori's after mountings are in split control and the guns at high elevation

Another quarter view, this time of Mohawk. *The unusual original position of the depth charge throwers on the after superstructure (just under the searchlight position in the photograph) is clearly shown.*

the initial wartime modifications installed whilst building, and two (*Cayuga* and the second *Athabaskan*) were given a main armament entirely composed of 4-inch guns.

OPERATIONAL CAREER

Both *Afridi* and *Cossack* were fitted as flotilla leaders, though the latter was not used as such at first. After commissioning, she became divisional leader in the 1st Destroyer Flotilla with the Mediterranean Fleet, under the command of Captain D. de Pass. She was lucky to acquire a very good crew, most of whom remained with her throughout her career, as did the Maltese wardroom stewards and cooks (led by a notable character called, Spiteri). She seems to have been from first to last a happy and efficient ship.

The *Tribals* were the most powerful and modern destroyers in the Royal Navy, so it was not surprising that the officers and crew, '. . . regarded ourselves as the *crème de la crème*. The *Tribals* were the *Hoods* of the destroyer world'.

Cossack when new must have been a most attractive sight in light grey with a red band round her fore funnel. Her first pendant number was L.03 but this was changed in 1940 to G.03. However, in September, 1939, the polished brightwork of peace was abandoned as the 1st D.F. was recalled to home waters.

Cossack became part of the 4th Flotilla operating from Rosyth on convoy escort. Two abortive attacks on submarine contacts were followed by a collision with the s.s. *Borthwick* (7/11/1939) off May Island which put *Cossack* in dock till early January, but almost immediately afterwards she had another (fortunately minor) collision with a merchant ship. Later the same month, she was out of action because of an epidemic of influenza amongst the crew.

The flotilla leader, *Afridi*, was being repaired, so the new Captain (D) of the 4th Flotilla took over command

of the *Cossack*. His name was Philip Vian*, one of the greatest fighting seamen of the war: his name is very closely linked with the *Cossack*, as they achieved fame together. He was a brilliant and inspiring leader in action, and a tireless seeker after operational efficiency though not perhaps the outstanding ship-handler of legend. He may have been a hard man to cross at times, but his abrupt manner concealed a fundamentally shy man who had a deep concern for the welfare of the men under his command.

The Navy's Here!

At 2300 on 14 February 1940, her complement made up to scratch by temporary drafts from other ships, *Cossack* in company with two cruisers (*Arethusa* and *Penelope*) and the rest of the 4th Flotilla (*Intrepid, Ivanhoe, Sikh* and *Nubian*) sailed from Rosyth. The force was to carry out Operation DT, a sweep into the Skaggerak, the following night. The sweep was relatively uneventful, but at 1206 on the 16th the C-in-C, Home Fleet, ordered Vian to intercept the German supply ship *Altmark*.

This tanker, carrying British merchant seamen made prisoner by the *Graf Spee**, was making her way home through Norwegian territorial waters. The Norwegians had boarded her but, not having found the prisoners, they were escorting her with two old torpedo boats. These prevented the *Intrepid* from boarding later in the afternoon, and the *Altmark* prudently retreated into the fastnesses of Josing Fjord. The Admiralty retaliated by cutting through the diplomatic niceties of the situation and by giving Vian clear and unequivocal orders to search the *Altmark* with or without the Norwegians' consent, and using force if necessary.

That night, brilliantly handled by her navigator in the dark and narrow fjord, the *Cossack* approached the tanker. There was an indeterminate exchange with the captain of the Norwegian torpedo boat, *Kjell*. Then *Cossack* closed her enemy, dodged an attempt to ram which put the *Altmark* ashore, and boarded her in fine style. The Norwegians fortunately did not intervene, the prisoners being liberated to the famous cry, '*The Navy's here!*'. In a sporadic exchange of small-arms fire, several Germans were hit but only one member of the *Cossack*'s crew was wounded.

At a period of 'phoney war', this relatively minor exploit in the best cutting-out traditions of the Royal Navy was given perhaps rather more attention than it deserved. The crew of the *Cossack* resigned itself with a certain amount of distaste to becoming a 'Daily Mirror' ship; the Norwegians were left unhappily wondering which ship, *Cossack* or *Altmark*, had infringed their neutrality to a greater degree; and Hitler was possibly fortified in his resolve to invade Norway at the earliest possible opportunity.

After landing about 300 liberated prisoners, including one leper, at Leith, *Cossack* returned to escorting convoys. Vian took over the refitted *Afridi* and Commander R. St J. Sherbrooke, R.N., (later to win the Victoria

---

* Later, Admiral of the Fleet Sir Philip Vian, GCB, KBE, DSO. His autobiography '*Action This Day*' is a useful source of information for much of what follows.
* Warship Profile No. 4.

Cross defending a Russian Convoy) became the new C.O. She made another fruitless attack on a submarine on 1 April. Eight days later she was towing the *Kashmir* back to Lerwick after colliding with her.

THE INVASION OF NORWAY:
The Second Battle of Narvik

The German invasion of Norway, accelerated by the *Altmark* incident, included an assault on the northern port of Narvik. The German attacking force was carried in a group of ten large destroyers which remained in Narvik after the successful attack. Surprised on the morning of 10 April 1940 by Captain Warburton-Lee's gallant attack, the Germans lost two of their larger ships and five were damaged; two British

destroyers were lost and one damaged. The Germans were left low on fuel and ammunition as their ammunition ship had been sunk.

Cossack and eight other destroyers (*Bedouin, Eskimo, Foxhound, Forester, Punjabi, Hero, Icarus, Kimberley*) were sent on 13 April to Narvik Fjord to mop up the German force. To assist the destroyers, the battleship *Warspite* followed them up the fjord, the noise and effect of her 15-inch gun salvoes in these narrow waters being devastating. Even more important, she catapulted her Walrus floatplane, which spotted for her, warned of ambushes and sank a U-boat.

After exchanges of fire with enemy ships on the way up the fjord, *Cossack* entered Narvik harbour, where she promptly became engaged with a German destroyer

Two views of Mashona *in her pre-war guise*

at close range*. Both ships obtained hits; the German had probably exhausted her outfit of Semi-Armour-Piercing shell and was having to use High Explosive, so the *Cossack* soon transformed her opponent into a blazing wreck.

Cossack's own damage was not light. She had been hit forward several times, and one shell in the forward boiler room cut all leads to the steering engine. She

---

* For a superb account of this action, and much other information on the *Cossack* see her then First Lieutenant's autobiography '*Convoy Escort Commander*' by Vice Admiral Sir Peter Gretton, KCB, DSO**, OBE, DSC (by Cassell, 1964).

promptly went aground in the harbour, where she remained in this somewhat invidious position until late in the afternoon of the next day. Meanwhile, she silenced a howitzer which was unwise enough to bombard her from an exposed position, and she also methodically shelled all the shipping left in the harbour.

Local repairs were made with Norwegian help at Skjelfjord, under the constant threat of air attack. She sailed for Scapa, in company with the auxiliary, *War Pindari*, at 12 knots on 23 April. Until June she was repairing and refitting in Thornycroft's Northam yard at Southampton.

Back in service, Vian resumed command of *Cossack*, as *Afridi* had been sunk off Norway. On 6 July she was

Two views of Zulu, *just before and just after commissioning. NMM Stephen's Collection and NMM respectively*

sent with *Maori*, *Fame* and *Fortune* to help the damaged submarine *Shark*. They failed to find her, but were discovered themselves and heavily bombed by the Luftwaffe. The *Cossack* accidentally shot down one RAF Blenheim long range fighter which was unwise enough to venture too close to her in the middle of the attacks. Fortunately she rescued the crew and, just as ammunition was running low, she was saved from further attack by the providential appearance of a thick bank of fog.

The next few months were spent relatively quietly in escort work from Scapa Flow, but broken by a minor refit in September.

Somali with wartime modifications, including 4-inch guns and radar, but retaining mainmast.

Destroyer Raid off Egersund

On the night of 13/14 October 1940, she took part in what one officer described as, '*the best thing we ever did*'. Leading the *Ashanti*, *Sikh* and *Maori*, she intercepted a small convoy of three ships with two small escorts four miles off the Egero Light, at the southern tip of Norway. Two ships were sunk and the others damaged in a short and efficient action which went more smoothly and certainly faster than a peace-time exercise. The only damage to the flotilla was a hit in *Cossack's* tiller flat which slightly wounded one rating in the backside.

MAID OF ALL WORK

Early in November, a projected sortie to Jan Mayen Island to capture a German scientific expedition was called off. Later in the same month *Cossack* made a fruitless sweep north of Aalesund to attack German and Norwegian fishing boats. During the winter of 1940/41, a number of voyages were made in bad weather whilst escorting the 1st Minelaying Flotilla which was laying a barrage between Iceland and the Faeroes. Driving against the winter gales, *Cossack* corrugated her bottom and had to undergo another refit at Southampton to

Sikh entering Valetta harbour. Notice wartime alterations including twin 4-inch mounting in the 'X' position, single 20 mm. Oerlikons replacing the 0·5-inch multiple mountings between the funnels, radar and the mainmast removed

Matabele in wartime camouflage. Alterations include 4-inch mounting. The funnels abaft her stern belong to a 'V & W' class destroyer

HMS Cossack/Tribal Class Destroyer

0   32 Feet

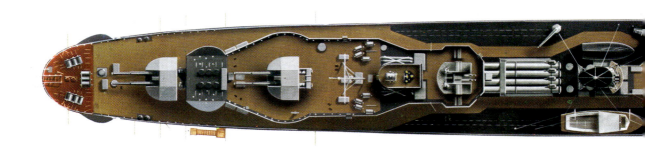

HMS Zulu
Late 1941 early 1942
wearing Intermediate
emergency camouflage.

HMS Ashanti
1941 wearing Admiralty
light disruptive type
camouflage.

HMS *Cossack* is here depicted as she appeared in 1938. 'B' gun shield has been painted with the colours of Britain and France who, in conjunction with other interested powers, instituted naval patrols off the Spanish coast, in accordance with the Nyon Conference, to protect British and French merchant ships from unprovoked Axis submarine attacks during the Spanish Civil War.

T. Hadler © Profile Publications Ltd

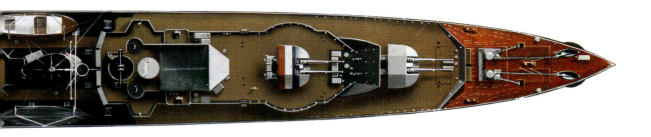

HMS Matabele
1941 Admiralty light mottle type camouflage.

HMS Eskimo
Late 1941/1942 wearing two-tone Western approaches scheme.

ARRANGEMENT
OF
MOUNTING

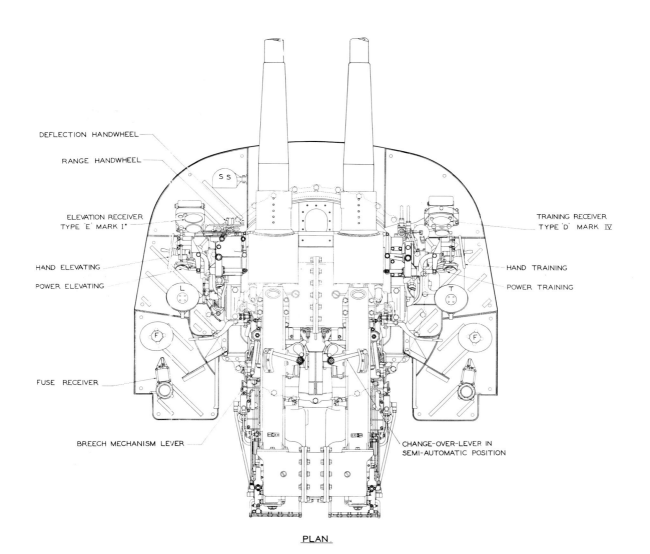

DEFLECTION HANDWHEEL

RANGE HANDWHEEL

S S

ELEVATION RECEIVER
TYPE 'E' MARK I*

TRAINING RECEIVER
TYPE 'D' MARK IV

HAND ELEVATING

POWER ELEVATING

HAND TRAINING

POWER TRAINING

L

T

F

F

FUSE RECEIVER

BREECH MECHANISM LEVER

CHANGE-OVER-LEVER IN
SEMI-AUTOMATIC POSITION

PLAN.

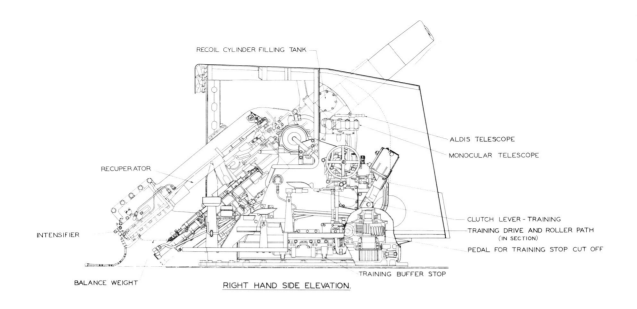

RECOIL CYLINDER FILLING TANK

ALDIS TELESCOPE

MONOCULAR TELESCOPE

RECUPERATOR

CLUTCH LEVER - TRAINING

TRAINING DRIVE AND ROLLER PATH
(IN SECTION)

PEDAL FOR TRAINING STOP CUT OFF

INTENSIFIER

TRAINING BUFFER STOP

BALANCE WEIGHT

RIGHT HAND SIDE ELEVATION.

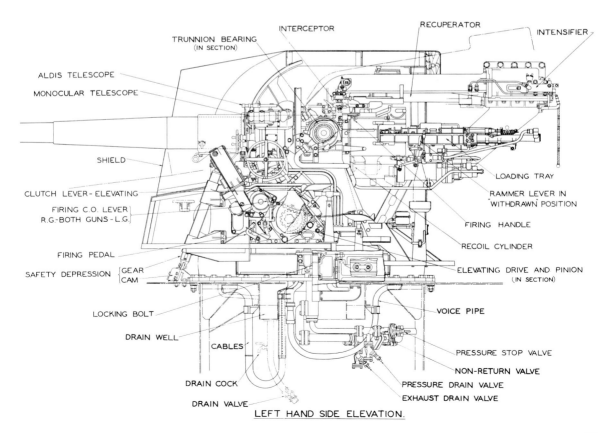

INTERCEPTOR

RECUPERATOR

INTENSIFIER

TRUNNION BEARING
(IN SECTION)

ALDIS TELESCOPE

MONOCULAR TELESCOPE

SHIELD

LOADING TRAY

CLUTCH LEVER - ELEVATING

RAMMER LEVER IN
WITHDRAWN POSITION

FIRING C.O. LEVER
R.G-BOTH GUNS-L.G.

FIRING HANDLE

RECOIL CYLINDER

FIRING PEDAL

ELEVATING DRIVE AND PINION
(IN SECTION)

SAFETY DEPRESSION {GEAR
{CAM

VOICE PIPE

LOCKING BOLT

DRAIN WELL

PRESSURE STOP VALVE

CABLES

NON-RETURN VALVE

DRAIN COCK

PRESSURE DRAIN VALVE

DRAIN VALVE

EXHAUST DRAIN VALVE

LEFT HAND SIDE ELEVATION.

39

rectify the defect in February 1941.

When returning from this refit, she sank a drifting derelict and heard a mysterious explosion which might have been an acoustic mine. On at least one occasion at this time, whilst escorting Atlantic convoys, the 4th Flotilla was temporarily renamed the 11th A/S Flotilla. During March, 1941, she screened the Home Fleet which was searching for the *Scharnhorst* and *Gneisau*, but no contact was made and the Flotilla was forced into Rejkjavik to fuel and reprovision.

THE HUNTING OF THE BISMARCK

The chance to engage a capital ship came on 26 May 1941. The Flotilla (*Cossack*, *Maori*, *Sikh*, *Zulu* and the Polish *Piorun*) was escorting the troop convoy, WS8B, when they were detached to join Admiral Tovey's battleships as a screen. The *Bismarck* was loose in the Atlantic and contact had been lost, when an RAF Catalina aircraft sighted her making for Brest.

Vian, on receiving this signal and without orders, immediately altered course to intercept, in the hope of slowing the enemy battleship by torpedo attack. He must have felt the *Tribals'* deficiency in torpedo armament keenly at this juncture. Fortunately, *Ark Royal's* Swordfish crippled the *Bismarck* just before dusk.

During this attack, the flotilla sighted *Sheffield* who was shadowing by radar, and almost simultaneously a heavy sea swept both *Cossack* and *Maori* round on opposite courses (they were steaming at 26 knots in very bad conditions). The two ships missed each other by feet and found that they had performed an involuntary change of station—'*but we were so keyed up at the time that we took little notice*'.

The *Bismarck* was sighted at about 2230. Vian quickly realised that she had been slowed down sufficiently for the Home Fleet battleships to catch her. However, he decided to separate the flotilla to make a series of harassing attacks. This was the prelude to a hectic night.

The *Bismarck's* armament was demonstrably still in working order, and the flotilla was lucky to escape with no more than splinter damage from near misses by 15-inch shells. The destroyers closed '*to about 6000 yards before she opened up; we then went away and hid for a while*'. In the middle of the night, the radar operator reported strange shapes on the radar screen which were moving between the *Bismarck* and the *Cossack*. The Signals Officer* realised that these were shells fired at the *Cossack*.

---

* Lieutenant, now Captain, Peter Hankey, DSC, RN, who very kindly gave the author much information, especially about the *Bismarck* action.

Maori *in 1939*

Zulu *in 1938*

Eskimo with Peter Scott's off-white camouflage scheme, which worked very well in making a ship less visible at night

Punjabi. A good view of the 4-inch mounting. She has masthead radar and Oerlikons in the bridge wings and between the funnels, but retains the mainmast and the after superstructure depth charge throwers; the after funnel has not been cut down

In this view, probably taken off Iceland, Ashanti *is sporting a very varied camouflage scheme. She would appear still to have her 0.5-inch close range but not her mainmast. The 4-inch mounting has replaced one 4.7-inch, and the after funnel has been cut down*

The *Cossack* had her aerials shot away, but not before she passed a series of reports to Sir John Tovey who found them of the greatest use. Both she and *Maori* may have obtained a torpedo hit apiece, though German sources deny that any resulted from the destroyer attacks. The next morning the flotilla delivered their large antagonist into the hands of the *King George V* and *Rodney*. *Cossack* reported two casualties in this action.

ESCORT DUTIES AND THE MEDITERRANEAN

Afterwards, she went back to the grind of escort work. For a time in June 1941, she operated from Plymouth, and on 6 July reported that she had spent 23 of the last 33 days with convoys. Captain Vian, promoted to Rear Admiral ahead of time, left her on 12 July for a mission to Russia.

Shortly afterwards, *Cossack* sailed to Gibraltar to reinforce Force H. She took part in Operation SUB-STANCE, a successful supply convoy to Malta. Heavy bombing attacks by high level, dive and torpedo bombers were fought off. During a night attack by E-boats, a torpedo passed right under *Cossack* without exploding (0250, 24/7/1941). She entered Valetta harbour with the convoy, but sailed for Gibraltar almost immediately.

She was detached from Force H on 1 August to carry out a night bombardment of Alghero in Sardinia. Her starshells revealed no shipping in the harbour, so she did not carry out the bombardment, though one of the starshells set fire to a building on the outskirts of the town.

The rest of the month was spent escorting *Renown* and *Pasteur* to the Clyde. She then returned to the Mediterranean as part of the escort for the aircraft

Tartar *with wartime modifications*

Aerial shot of Tartar *at speed. No mainmast, cut down after funnel and the 4-inch in 'X' position show that the picture was taken during the war. Black flag indicates that she is on gunnery exercises and is about to open fire*

carrier *Furious* and Convoy WS 11. This convoy was destined for Malta, and *Cossack* helped to escort it through the usual air attacks to the beleaguered island (Operation HALBERD).

FIGHT FOR LIFE

On 22 October 1941, she sailed from Gibraltar as part of the local escort for Convoy HG 75. At 2255 on the night of the 23rd, she was hit forward by a torpedo. Her position was 35° 36' North, 10° 4' West. The torpedo was probably fired by *U.563*. The torpedo removed the bow, foremast and most of the bridge; the explosion killed her Commanding Officer, Captain Berthen, as well as many of the ship's company, but the intact after part of the ship remained afloat. The destroyer *Legion* picked up 43 survivors, the corvette *Carnation*, 47, and the Free French sloop *Commandant Duboc*, 10.

The next morning the sea was fortunately slight. *Carnation* passed a tow, with some of *Cossack*'s survivors back on board her trying to raise steam and start the pumps, while *Legion* meanwhile stood by both ships. The tug *Thames* was sent from Gibraltar under the escort of the *Jonquil* to render assistance. The destroyer *Duncan* also left Gibraltar at speed with a surgeon and medical supplies for the survivors on board.

By nightfall on the 25th, the remains of *Cossack* were being towed at a steady three knots by *Thames* towards Gibraltar, with the *Carnation* and *Jonquil* as escorts. On the next morning, a Catalina from Gibraltar joined the escort. Unfortunately the weather worsened on the evening of the 26th, and *Jonquil* had to take off the remnant of *Cossack*'s crew who had been working so hard to save her. The position was critical, though further assistance was on its way (the tug *Rollicker* was sent from Gibraltar to replace the *Thames*, who had to be diverted to help the burning merchant ship *Ariguani*).

The fight to save *Cossack* ended in tragedy on the next day. Just after noon on 27 October 1941, the Admiralty received the laconic signal, '*Cossack has sunk*'.

SUMMARY: THE TRIBALS AS FIGHTING SHIPS

The *Tribals* were in the forefront of action throughout the war and a history of the class would be virtually a summary of the history of the Royal Navy's part in the war at sea.

Only four of the original sixteen *Tribals* survived till the end of hostilities. As the most powerful destroyers available, they were required wherever the fight was

With the advantage of hindsight it is easy to see that

Cossack (*nearest to the camera*) and other destroyers steam towards Narvik and action on 13 April 1940

Cossack, *aground in Narvik Fjord engages shore batteries. She is next to the wreck of a German transport, just beneath the bank of smoke in the foreground. These photos show distinct signs of touching up, and remain, unfortunately, very indistinct*

hottest. It was, however, as destroyers that they were operated, and not as the somewhat different type of warship specified in the original staff requirements. They were usually used in mixed flotillas with other classes of destroyers, and were completely compatible with their flotilla-mates. Compared with other British destroyers, they handled just as well, though their slightly greater size meant that their minimum turning circle was larger: they were, therefore, correspondingly handicapped in the anti-submarine role.

Greater gunpower and better communications and plotting facilities compensated for the smaller torpedo armament. The men who conned them had nothing to complain about in the *Tribals'* manoeuvrability and handling; they were good seaboats if not driven too hard. Because of the increase in size over other destroyers, they tended to ride through, rather than over, the waves. This made the upper deck correspondingly wet and dangerous in bad weather. *Cossack* lost several men overboard, including her 'Buffer' (Chief Boatswain's Mate) and First Lieutenant, though the latter was lucky enough to be washed back on board by the next wave.

With the advantage of hindsight it is easy to see that the *Tribals'* concentration on low-angle gunfire was a mistake. The dual purpose armament of 4-inch guns fitted to the last two Canadian *Tribals* would have served the earlier ships much better in beating off air attacks; these guns also would probably have been as useful as the 4·7-inch guns in a surface action because the volume of fire and ease of handling compensated for the smaller weight of individual shells.

In the light of knowledge available at the time of their design, a more valid criticism of the *Tribals* is that the funds spent on these 16 large destroyers would have been put to better use in building perhaps 20 of the standard British inter-war destroyers of the A to I classes. A large number of destroyers *of any kind* was what was required at the time.

However, it is hard to criticise the *Tribals* with their handsome and powerful profiles, and, above all, with their splendid and tragic record. They deserve their reputation as the most famous of all British destroyers on that ground alone, and the *Cossack* was a worthy representative of that class.

Cossack *aground at Narvik between the wreck of a German transport and the British destroyer* (*this latter is one of the* '*F*' *or* '*H*' *class destroyers present at the battle; either* Forester, Foxhound or Hero)

APPENDIX: THE OTHER TRIBALS

Seven vessels, including *Cossack*, ordered for the 1935 Programme.

Seven (later altered to nine) ordered for the 1936 Programme.

Seven '*Improved Tribals*' ordered for Canada (later increased to eight to replace the war loss).

Seven for Australia (four of which were later cancelled).

The R.N. *Tribals* served in most theatres of war in which the Navy was engaged, the four survivors participating in the final campaign against Japan. In the Far East theatre, their crews suffered in ships not properly equipped for service in tropical waters and, by that stage in the war, the *Tribals* were overcrowded with new equipment.

The Canadian *Tribals* were mainly active in Northern European Waters, whilst their Australian sisters served in the Pacific. After the war, the surviving *Improved Tribals* were reconstructed to a greater or lesser degree. One, the *Haida*, is now preserved as a Museum and War Memorial in Toronto.

The blazing wreck of one of the German destroyers sunk at Narvik. She is one of the '*Z1*' *class, the first German super-destroyers, and a good example of the type of foreign vessel that the Tribals were designed to combat. Their armament of five 5·1-inch guns and eight 21-inch torpedo tubes was achieved on a tonnage of about 2,200. They were designed for a top speed of 38 knots, but had continuous trouble from their very high pressure steam installations*

Zulu early in the war. She has been fitted with the twin 4-inch, and with single 2-pdr. guns in the wings of the bridge and the superstructure positions from which the depth charge throwers have been removed. She still retains the 0·5-inch mountings between the funnels

A puzzle picture showing a Tribal refitting during the war. Can anyone identify the ship or her background? She has a 4-inch mounting in 'X' position, has lost her mainmast and the top of her after funnel, and appears to have Oerlikons in the bridge wings. (Gladstone Dock, Liverpool?)

Eskimo *with wartime modifications*

Name Pendant Number and Builder	Launch	Fate
AFRIDI 07 Vickers-Armstrong (Newcastle)	8/6/1937	Bombed and sunk by German aircraft off Namsos, 3/5/1940.
GURKHA 20 Fairfield	7/7/1937	Bombed and sunk by German aircraft off Stavanger, 9/4/1940.
MAORI 24 Fairfield	2/9/1937	Bombed and sunk by German aircraft in Valetta harbour, 12/2/1942. Hulk scuttled after the war.
MOHAWK 31 Thornycroft	5/10/1937	Torpedoed by Italian destroyer *Tarigo* off Cape Bon during raid on convoy; had to be sunk by *Janus*.
NUBIAN 36 Thornycroft	21/12/1937	Scrapped 1949.
ZULU 18 Stephen	23/9/1937	Foundered in tow after bombing by German aircraft off Tobruk, 14/9/1942.
ASHANTI 51 Denny	5/11/1937	Scrapped 1949.
BEDOUIN 67 Denny	21/12/1937	Torpedoed by Italian aircraft whilst in tow, after damage from gunfire of Italian cruisers, Central Mediterranean, 15/6/1942.
ESKIMO 75 Vickers-Armstrong (Newcastle)	3/9/1937	Scrapped 1949.
MASHONA 59 Vickers-Armstrong (Newcastle)	3/9/1937	Bombed and sunk by German aircraft S.W. of Ireland, 28/5/1941.
MATABELE 26 Scotts	6/10/1937	Torpedoed by German *U.454*, Barents Sea, 17/1/1942.
PUNJABI 21 Scotts	18/12/1937	Rammed by battleship *King George V*, North Atlantic, 1/5/1942 (her depth charges severely damaged the battleship).
SIKH 82 Stephen	17/12/1937	Sunk by gunfire from German shore batteries at Tobruk, 14/9/1942.
SOMALI 33 Swan Hunter (Wallsend yard)	24/8/1937	Foundered in tow South of Iceland, 24/9/1942, after torpedo from *U.703*, on 20/9/1942.
TARTAR 43 Swan Hunter (Wallsend yard)	21/10/1937	Broken up in 1948.
Australian		
ARUNTA I.30 Cockatoo Yard (Sydney)	30/10/1940	Scrapped at Taiwan 1968.
BATAAN (ex-*KURNAI*) I.91 Cockatoo Yard (Sydney)	15/1/1944	Scrapped, Japan 1962.
WARRAMUNGA I.41 Cockatoo Yard (Sydney)	6/2/1942	Scrapped, Japan 1962.
Canadian		
ATHABASKAN ex-*IROQUOIS* G.07 Vickers-Armstrong (Newcastle)	18/11/1941	Torpedoed by German torpedo-boat, *T.27*, off N.W. coast of France, 29/4/1944.
HAIDA G.63 Vickers-Armstrong (Newcastle)	25/8/1942	Museum at Toronto from 1964.
HURON G.24 Vickers-Armstrong (Newcastle)	25/6/1942	Broken up, Italy 1965.
IROQUOIS ex-*ATHABASKAN* G.89 Vickers-Armstrong (Newcastle)	23/9/1941	Broken up, Spain 1966.
CAYUGA R.04 Halifax Shipyard (Canada)	28/7/1945	Broken up, Faslane 1964.
MICMAC R.10 Halifax Shipyard	18/9/1943	Broken up, Faslane, 1964.
NOOTKA R.96 Halifax Shipyard	26/4/1944	Broken up, Faslane, 1964.
ATHABASKAN (*II*) R.79 Halifax Shipyard	4/5/1946	For disposal (1970).

Machinery:
  By builders except *Eskimo* and *Mashona* who were engined by Parsons. *Somali* and *Tartar*, by Wallsend Slipway.

Pendant numbers:
  The actual numbers stayed the same throughout, but the Royal Naval ships' flag superior changed from 'L' to 'F' in 1939, and then again to 'G' in 1940.

SPECIFICATION:

Dimensions:	Length (between perpendiculars) 355½' (load water line) 364' 8" (overall) 377' Beam: 36½' Depth: 21½'
Draught:	Light: 9', Full Load: 13' (by 1941 this had crept up to 13' 5")
Displacement:	Design (Standard): 1854 tons (hull-910, machinery-585, hydraulic machinery-11, armament-254, equipment-94) As built (Standard): 1959 tons (as above except: armament-254, equipment-174)
Armament:	*Guns:* 8-Mk. XII 4·7" Q.F. guns firing 50lb shell, on 4-twin C.P. Mk. XIX mountings. (maximum elevation 40°). 200 rounds per gun (low angle ammunition) plus 50 rounds of star shell and 50 rounds of high angle shell.

Ashanti during the war in Peter Scott's camouflage scheme. Notice the Oerlikon in the bridge wing

The last Cossack, the 'Co.' class destroyer of 1944. A typical wartime destroyer, the hull and single funnel are taken from the 'J' class, the heavy A/A armament the result of wartime lessons, but the basic layout of gun and torpedo armament is still that of the 'V & W' class, though the 4·5-inch dual-purpose gun has replaced the old 4·7-inch

Cossack and other destroyers steaming up Ofot Fjord towards Narvik on 13 April 1940

1-quadruple-barrelled Mk. VII two pounder pompom (14,400 rounds)
2-quadruple 0·5″ machine gun mountings
2-mountings for single 0·303″ Lewis machine guns on signal deck.
Note: This armament was as built. Later changes are described in the text.
Torpedoes: Single mounting (power worked) of 4 tubes for 21″ Mk. IX torpedoes.
Depth Charges: Single set of stern rails, 2-Depth Charge Throwers, 20 depth charges (30 in wartime).

Machinery: Two sets of Parsons single reduction geared turbines. 44,000 shaft horse power
(contract speed 36 knots)=32½ knots in deep condition
Three Admiralty 3-drum water tube boilers. Working pressure 300lb per sq. in at 620°F.
Oil Fuel: 524 tons
Endurance: 5700 nautical miles at 15 knots
3200 nautical miles at 20 knots

Complement: 219. *Cossack* carried a larger crew because she was fitted as a leader. Her sisters being built as private ships carried only 190. Wartime complement would be perhaps one third greater. Accommodation was better than in earlier destroyers, but spartan by today's standards.

Acknowledgements:
*I wish to thank Vice Admiral Sir Peter Gretton, K.C.B., D.S.O.**, O.B.E., D.S.C., and Captain P. Hankey, D.S.C., for giving so generously of their time and memories.*
I wish to thank also the Directors and Staff of the Admiralty Historical Branch and Imperial War Museum and particularly Mr Martin Brice and Mr John Wingate for their help. I especially wish to thank my friend and colleague, Antony Preston, for much assistance and many happy hours of discussion; and also Lt. Cdr. A. H. Waite, Mr P. G. W. Annis and Mr A. Raven for their helpful suggestions.
All the faults and errors of judgment are, however, mine alone.

Select Bibliography:
J. J. Colledge: SHIPS OF THE ROYAL NAVY, VOL. 1. (*David & Charles*).
S. W. Roskill: THE WAR AT SEA, VOL. 1 (*H.M.S.O.*).
Sir Philip Vian: ACTION THIS DAY (*Muller*).
Sir Peter Gretton: CONVOY ESCORT COMMANDER (*Cassell*).
H. T. Lenton: BRITISH FLEET & ESCORT DESTROYERS, VOLS. 1 & 2 (*Macdonald*).
E. J. March: BRITISH DESTROYERS (*Seeley Service*).

Acknowledgements
Profile Publications Ltd., are grateful for the permission of the Trustees of the National Maritime Museum, the Imperial War Museum and the National Portrait Gallery to reproduce the photographs in this Profile.

USS Hornet *after commissioning prior to fitting of armament and radar. Wartime camouflage scheme was applied in February 1942.*

(Photo: U.S. Navy)

USS HORNET (CV8) Aircraft Carrier

by Commander W. H. Cracknell, USN

Destined for a short life, 372 days from commissioning to sinking, *Hornet* and her crew earned themselves a firm place in United States history. The last carrier commissioned in the U.S. Navy prior to the attack on Pearl Harbor, *Hornet* was rushed into service to make her combat debut by launching Jimmy Doolittle's B-25 bombers on their famous Tokyo raid, an unprecedented feat. She next made a hurried transit to the South Pacific where she just missed the Battle of the Coral Sea; then an equally quick trip back to Pearl Harbor and on to participate in that pivotal engagement of the Pacific War, The Battle of Midway. It was at Midway that *Hornet's* Torpedo Squadron Eight made its supreme sacrifice, losing all but one of its pilots.

Hornet was then assigned to the Guadalcanal Campaign, that series of 'meat-grinder' operations mounted in an attempt to contain the Japanese advance until the full impact of United States mobilisation efforts could be brought to bear. It was during those hectic months of late 1942 that, for a period of over a month, *Hornet* had to carry the burden of being the only operational carrier the United States had in the Pacific; and it was here, in The Battle of the Santa Cruz Islands, that she came to her end.

Forebears

It is the practice in the U.S. Navy to name fast carriers after battles, famous men or famous ships in, U.S. history. It is from the latter that USS *Hornet's* (CV-8) name was derived; she was the seventh ship in American naval history to be named after this insect whose sting is very severe. Her predecessors were:

USS Hornet

1. Sloop *Hornet*: 10 gun.
   Chartered in 1775 to serve in the Continental Navy. Fitted out in Baltimore, she patrolled the Delaware Bay and convoyed merchantmen to Charleston. Apparently captured by the British off the South Carolina coast in the summer of 1777.

2. Sloop *Hornet*: 10 gun.
   Formerly merchant ship *Traveller* built in Massachusetts in 1802. Purchased by the U.S. Navy in Malta in late 1804 or early 1805, joining the U.S. Squadron off Tripoli in April 1805. After participating in the Barbary Wars she was sold in Philadelphia on 3 September 1806 for $1090.

3. Brig *Hornet*: 18 gun.
   Built by William Price of Baltimore, she was commissioned 18 October 1805. She sailed with the

USS Yorktown (*CV-5*). *The class leader of* Hornet's *class. This 19,800 ton aircraft carrier operated in both the Atlantic and Pacific before WWII. She was commissioned in September 1937 and lost in the Battle of Midway in June 1942. Note canvas covered, unshielded 5-inch mounts, two forward and two aft in this prewar photo.* (Photo: U.S. Navy)

USS Enterprise (*CV-6*). *Commissioned May 1938 and scrapped June 1958. One of* Hornet's *two sisters, she accompanied* Hornet *in all her major engagements. This photo, taken in 1944, shows addition of extensive radar antennae and 40 mm guard gun mounts.* Enterprise *was the only* Yorktown *class ship to carry 40 mm.* Dauntless *dive bombers are parked on the flight deck.* (Photo: U.S. Navy)

United States Squadron in the Mediterranean in 1806-07 and returned to home waters to assist in enforcing the Embargo Act in 1809-10. The Washington Navy Yard rebuilt her as a 'ship' in 1811. Service in the War of 1812 saw her capturing the privateer *Dolphin* 9 July 1812, HMS *Peacock* 24 February 1813 and several British merchantmen. She captured HMS *Penguin* 23 March 1815, both ships being unaware that the war had ended nearly three months earlier. She then joined the U.S. Squadron operating against pirates in the West Indies and spent most of the next ten years in this pursuit. She foundered with all hands in a gale off Mexico 29 September 1829.

4. Schooner *Hornet*: 5 gun.
   Purchased at Georgetown, District of Columbia in 1813 for $2200, she was commissioned 15 March 1814. She was used as a dispatch ship and to survey the coasts and harbours along the Atlantic. She was sold in Norfolk, Virginia in 1820.

5. Side-wheel steamer *Hornet*: 8 gun.
   Built originally as a Confederate blockade runner named *Lady Sterling* at Blackwall, England in 1864. She was captured and sold to the U.S. Navy by the New York Prize Court in November 1864 for

$135,000. Commissioned 24 April 1865 and named *Hornet* 17 June 1865; decommissioned at Philadelphia 15 December 1865 and sold 26 June 1869 for $33,000.

6. Gunboat *Hornet*: 5 gun.
   The former yacht *Alicia*, built by Harlan and Hollingsworth, Wilmington, Delaware in 1890, was purchased 6 April 1898 for $117,500 and commissioned 12 April 1898 for duty in the Spanish-American War. She participated in the blockade of Spanish Cuba and in several attacks on Spanish ships and fortifications on the Cuban coast. She was decommissioned 18 October 1898, loaned to the North Carolina Naval Militia and finally stricken from the Navy List 18 March 1910, being sold for $5100.

U.S. Navy Carrier Classifications

From 1931 C.Vs. were classified as 'Aircraft Carriers'. The classification C.V.E., 'Escort Aircraft Carrier' was adopted 15 July 1943 for those small carriers built on merchant ship class hulls who were previously known as A.V.G., 'Aircraft Escort Vessel' and A.C.V. 'Auxilary Aircraft Carrier'. The designation C.V.L., 'Small Aircraft Carrier' was also assigned 15 July 1943 to those fast carriers (most were built on cruiser hulls) that were smaller than C.Vs.

On 15 April 1945 the classification C.V.B., 'Large Aircraft Carrier' was introduced to denote the 45,000 ton *Midway* Class. C.Vs. and C.V.Bs. were redesignated C.V.As., 'Attack Aircraft Carriers', on 1 October 1952.

On 8 July 1953 various C.V.As. were reclassified C.V.Ss., 'Anti-submarine Warfare Aircraft Carriers'.

The classification L.P.H., 'Amphibious Assault Ship', was adopted 27 October 1955 for those carriers assigned as Marine Helicopter Carriers. C.V.A. (N), 'Attack Aircraft Carrier' (nuclear powered) was assigned 29 May 1956.

Other carrier classifications used in the past were: C.V.U., 'Utility Aircraft Carrier'; A.V.T., 'Auxiliary Aircraft Transport'; C.V.T., 'Training Aircraft Carrier'; C.V.H.E., 'Escort Helicopter Aircraft Carrier'; C.V.H.A., 'Assault Helicopter Aircraft Carrier'; and A.K.V., 'Cargo Ship and Aircraft Ferry'.

A.C.V.	Auxiliary Aircraft Carrier
A.K.V.	Cargo Ship and Aircraft Ferry
A.V.G.	Aircraft Escort Vessel
A.V.T.	Auxiliary Aircraft Transport
C.V.	Aircraft Carrier
C.V.A.	Attack Aircraft Carrier
C.V.A. (N)	Attack Aircraft Carrier (nuclear powered)
C.V.B.	Large Aircraft Carrier
C.V.E.	Escort Aircraft Carrier
C.V.H.A.	Assault Helicopter Aircraft Carrier
C.V.H.E.	Escort Helicopter Aircraft Carrier
C.V.L.	Small Aircraft Carrier
C.V.S.	Anti-submarine Warfare Aircraft Carrier
C.V.T.	Training Aircraft Carrier
C.V.U.	Utility Aircraft Carrier
L.P.H.	Amphibious Assault Ship

DEVELOPMENT

The United States, along with Great Britain and Japan, pioneered aircraft carrier development and tactics. The first U.S. carrier, USS *Langley* (CV-1), converted from the collier USS *Jupiter*, was commissioned 20 March 1922. Although not ideal for carrier operations, with her small flight deck and 14 knot top speed, she proved most valuable as a laboratory in developing the future requirements for naval carrier aviation. The tactical use of the carrier with the fleet, ship and aircraft characteristics, island location, flight and hangar deck arrangement, location of aircraft elevators and aircraft handling techniques were several of the many problems which *Langley* helped to solve.

When the Washington Naval Treaty was signed in 1922, the U.S. Navy was building its first two battle cruisers. Under the terms of the Treaty (which also limited the United States to 135,000 tons in carriers) these two ships were to be scrapped, but a clause of the

Douglas Dauntless *SBD-3 taking off a* Yorktown *class carrier. Large national insignia indicates photo was taken in early 1942. 'Pri-fly' juts out over the flight deck at right. White flag flying means deck is clear for flight operations. Note detail of forward elevator and just beyond the stowed wind fence. Seven cross-deck pendants of the forward arresting gear can be seen in this view.*
(Photo: U.S. Navy)

Hornet's *hangar deck looking aft. Superstructure foundation is at left. The hangar deck was 3-inch armor plate. More than 80 aircraft could be stored in this space. Fire curtains were installed to isolate fires.* *(Photo: U.S. Navy)*

Lt. Col. 'Jimmy' Doolittle takes off from Hornet 18 April 1942 enroute to bomb Tokyo. Fifteen additional U.S. Army B-25s are crowded aft awaiting their turn.
(Photo: U.S. Navy)

Squadron commanding officer's F4F-3 from Hornet's VF-8. Small fuselage insignia and squadron identity mark indicate photo was taken before Hornet departed for the Pacific. This model Wildcat did not have folding wings. (Photo: U.S. Navy)

An SBD-3 releases its bomb. The Dauntless could carry either a 500 or 1000 pound bomb on the centerline and one 100 pounder on each wing. The perforated, combination flaps and dive brakes are evident in this view.
(Photo: U.S. Navy)

A TBD-1 Devastator of VT-6 dropping its 'torpecker'. The aerial torpedoes, used the first year of the war, were Mk. XIII Bliss-Leavitts, 15 feet long, 2000 pound. They were generally undependable being slow, fragile and erratic. Only a pilot and gunner were usually carried in combat.
(Photo: U.S. Navy)

Treaty did permit their conversion to carriers. The latter course was chosen.

After much debate between the Navy's General Board and the various bureaus concerned with fundamentals such as armor plate, armament, arresting gear, elevator and catapult design, the sister ships USS *Lexington* (CV-2) and USS *Saratoga* (CV-3) were commissioned 14 December and 16 November 1927, respectively. With a standard displacement of 33,000 tons, 901 feet in overall length, a beam of 111 feet, 9 inches, eight 8-inch guns, and a 33-knot speed using 16 boilers, these ships would prove to be the largest carriers in operation in the world, up through the completion of World War II.

It was during the *Fleet Problems* of the late twenties and thirties that these first three carriers provided yeoman service in formulating fleet doctrine: improving carrier operation techniques and training the naval aviators who were destined to become the tacticians that led the fast carrier task groups across the Pacific in World War II. Ironically, as early as 1928, in *Fleet Problem VIII*, aircraft from *Langley* made a surprise attack against Pearl Harbor. Such attacks against Pearl and the Panama Canal were to occur with disconcerting regularity during exercises over the next decade.

THE FIRST PURPOSE-BUILT CARRIER

On 4 June 1934, over ten years after the British and Japanese had designed and built a carrier from the keel up, the U.S. Navy commissioned its first wholly designed carrier, USS *Ranger* (CV-4). She was built in the midst of the Great Depression when budget dollars for armaments were hard to come by. In addition to cost problems, the General Board was influenced by several other considerations before finally approving plans for the 14,500 ton carrier.

The Treaty tonnage limitations were a concern— the bigger the carriers, the fewer that could be built within the limitations (69,000 tons were left out of the original 135,000 tons). *Lexington* and *Saratoga* totalled 66,000 tons, but *Langley*, classed as 'Experimental', was excluded.

There also was disagreement in the Navy as to size. One school felt that more aircraft could be carried per ton of ship on smaller carriers; greater numbers of small carriers could obviously be in more places at sea at any one time. Thus the 'all the eggs in one basket' philosophy could be minimised in case of damage.

The other school of naval aviators, however, felt that the optimum size carrier must be established by the dictum that each carrier had to be a self-contained unit. It had become obvious that the main offensive and defensive armament of a carrier was her aircraft. The carrier should be able to operate enough aircraft to launch an effective strike, while keeping enough fighters for defense of the ship. She needed deck and hangar space to operate and maintain aircraft swiftly and efficiently, as well as space for aviation stores and bunker fuel to give her endurance in battle.

Ranger was the result of the former school of thought. A small carrier with maximum speed of 29 knots and a maximum load of 75 aircraft, she was destined to serve throughout World War II in Anti-submarine warfare (ASW), close support and training roles. But even before *Ranger* was completed, the General Board had become convinced that the minimum effective size for carriers was 20,000 tons.

Captain Marc A. Mitscher, first captain of Hornet, was soft-spoken, bald and slight, but tough and wiry. At age 29, in 1916, he was Naval Aviator No. 33. He earned the Navy Cross in 1919 by participating in the Navy project to fly the Atlantic. He was executive officer of old Langley and made the first landing on old Saratoga, as well as being successively her air operations officer and executive officer. From Hornet he was promoted to Rear Admiral as a Carrier Division Commander; he went on to become, as a Vice Admiral, Commander Fast Carrier Force, Pacific Fleet and, after the war, Deputy Chief of Naval Operations (Air). He died in February 1947. Considered by many to have been the U.S. Navy's greatest carrier admiral.
(Photo: U.S. Navy)

Grumman TBF-1 Avenger torpedo planes. This aircraft replaced the Devastator in all air groups in June 1942. Used also as a bomber and later a rocket carrier. Armament included a fixed forward firing 30 cal m.g., a single 50 cal m.g. in the power turret topside and a single 30 cal m.g. in the step aft of the bomb bay.
(Photo: U.S. Navy)

SBD drops bean bag message container. This system was used to pass reports when radio silence was being maintained. Note port forward 5-inch mounts at high elevation. (Photo: U.S. Navy)

A North American B-25B Mitchell medium bomber of the type used for the tests on Hornet in February 1942 and on the Tokyo Raid in April 1942. This particular aircraft is an exact replica of Doolittle's plane down to the registration number; it now resides in the U.S. Air Force Museum, Wright-Patterson Air Force Base, Ohio.
(Photo: U.S. Air Force)

YORKTOWN CLASS CARRIERS

After much consideration, a request for two 20,000 ton carriers was submitted in 1932 to be included in the Building Program of 1934. These were authorised and were to be paid for by the Public Works Administration, an agency established to finance federal projects to assist the nation out of the Depression. USS *Yorktown* and USS *Enterprise* were subsequently commissioned 30 September 1937 and 12 May 1938, respectively. Sister ship *Hornet* was authorised five days after *Enterprise*'s commissioning. All three ships of this class were built by Newport News Shipbuilding of Newport News, Virginia. The years of experience in the operation of carriers and the numerous studies and conflicts within the Navy, as to what an aircraft carrier should be, now took definitive form. A Bureau of Aeronautics (BUAER) memorandum dated 15 May 1931 indicates the considerations devoted to these new carriers:

The Department (of the Navy) has approved a new building program with two aircraft carriers similar to the *Ranger* but before embarking on this new construction, it is suggested that a careful examination may show many design changes are desirable.

The particular improvements in *Ranger* design that should be considered are: speed increase to 32·5 knots; addition of underwater subdivision to resist torpedo and bomb explosions; horizontal protective deck over machinery, magazine and aircraft fuel tanks; improvement in operational facility (this includes hangar deck devoted exclusively to plane storage, four fast elevators, complete bomb handling facilities, possible use of two flying-off decks, and improved machine gun anti-aircraft defense).

DESIGN

The *Yorktown* class carriers were the epitome of carrier design, compared to their contemporaries of the late 1930s.

They had a standard displacement of 19,800 tons, a length overall of 809·5 feet, a beam of 83·1 feet, extreme width of flight deck of 109·5 feet and a draft of 28 feet. Designed to carry an air group of 80-100 aircraft these ships were highly manoeuverable and could generate a maximum speed of close to 33 knots, greatly assisting the launching and landing of aircraft.

Machinery, W.T. Subdivision and Armor

Their general design became the format for future U.S. Navy carriers. The boiler rooms, located amidships, contained nine boilers. The engine rooms located aft of these contained geared turbine (vice turbo-electric drive previously favoured on USN. capital ships) driving four shafts. The total output of the turbines was 120,000 shaft horsepower. Three main uptakes were routed to the starboard side, culminating in a single large funnel integrated into the island structure. A high degree of watertight integrity was obtained by extensive compartmentation of the hull. A main belt of four-inch armor plate protected her vitals at the waterline; main bulkheads also were constructed with four-inch armor.

Hangar deck

Three high speed, centreline elevators, more than previously installed in a U.S. carrier, expedited the movement of aircraft between hangar and flight deck. The main deck was the hangar deck and was built of three-inch armor plate. Certain areas of the lower decks were also armored with one to three-inch armor where required. The hangar deck ran the full length of the ship with five large openings on the starboard side and six similar openings on the port. These openings, which were equipped with roller type overhead doors, allowed the loading of supplies and spares as well as venting and natural lighting of the hangar deck spaces when opened. The larger openings were also designed to allow the use of athwart-ships catapults to launch aircraft from the hangar decks—a feature never used in practice.

Flight deck

The flight deck was built up from the hangar deck to a height of 55 feet above the water. It was covered over with six-inch wide hardwood planks laid athwartships. It was not until the introduction of the *Midway* battle carrier class (CVB) in 1945 that U.S. carriers were equipped with armored flight decks, a discrepancy which cost dearly during World War II. Metal aircraft tie-down strips were installed at four-foot intervals, running the full width of the deck and flush with it. Two wind fences were installed to protect aircraft on the flight deck. These were constructed of a series of 7 foot planks mounted flush in the deck and pivoted so that they could be raised to the vertical to form a picket fence effect across the full width of the flight deck. One of these fences was located immediately forward of the forward elevator and the other, adjacent to the forward 1·1-inch gun tub.

Arrester gear

Yorktown class carriers were equipped with arresting gear for landing aircraft on both the after section and the forward section of the flight deck, thus making it possible to take aircraft aboard from either end. In practice, because of the relative wind generated over the flight deck, aircraft were landed over the stern; later classes of carriers did not carry arresting gear forward.

Each set of arresting gear consisted of eight to ten arresting cables, or *cross-deck pendants* as they were often called, backed up by two to four twin cable barriers to protect the aircraft parked beyond. The pendants were flush mounted in the deck and were attached to hydraulic self-compensating machines at each end.

When landing operations were underway the pendants were elevated several inches above the deck by shaped metal tube supports called 'pies'. The wire barriers located just beyond the pendants were also flush mounted in the deck and connected to hydraulic self-compensating machines. The barriers were raised to a height of five to six feet above the deck by a metal hinge on each side of the flight deck. Thus, if an aircraft did not hook one of the pendants, it would usually be forcibly stopped by one of the barriers beyond. The introduction of the angled deck by the Royal Navy in the post war period would eliminate the requirement of permanently installed barriers.

The Island

The island superstructure was relatively large: it was located slightly forward of amidships on the starboard side and partially overhanging the hull. The funnel, which occupied the after half of the island rose to a height of 103 feet above the water and the mast head topped out at 143 feet. *Hornet* was lightly rigged with a tripod foremast carrying a large crosstree topped by a small pole mast. The pole mainmast with small crosstree and gaff was abaft the funnel. The design and location of the island and the height of the funnel kept to a minimum, when underway, the turbulence across the flight deck which was generated by such a structure and the stack gases. Since the U.S. Navy used a left-hand landing pattern, aircraft coming on to the final approach for landing did not have to fly through the trailing stack gases.

The island is, of course, the nerve centre for aircraft and ship operations, as well as for task group operations when an admiral is aboard. The *Yorktown* class established the general pattern of future U.S. carriers in the island arrangement. The first level housed the flight deck officer who managed the spotting and movement

James H. Doolittle, Lt. Col., USAAFR, pictured here on the deck of Hornet *attaching Japanese medals to a 500 pound bomb to be dropped on Tokyo. The medals were awarded to U.S. Navy personnel before the war. Doolittle joined the U.S. Army Air Service in 1917 resigning in 1930. He was the first man to fly across the U.S. in less than 12 hours, first to fly an outside loop and pioneered blind flying. He won the Schneider, Bendix, Thompson, Mackay, Harmon, Guggenheim and Wright Brothers trophies. He held a doctors degree in aeronautical engineering. Called to active duty in 1940 as a major, he rose to the rank of Lieutenant General before reverting to inactive status after the war. He commanded the 12th, 15th and 8th Air Forces during the war. For leading the Tokyo Raid he received the Medal of Honor and was promoted directly from Lt. Col. to Brig. General.*
(Photo: U.S. Air Force)

of aircraft on the flight deck. The next deck up was 'Admiral's Country' where the flag bridge and flag plot were located. Above were the pilot house and the captain's navigation bridge. Immediately behind was the primary flight control overlooking the flight deck from which the ship's air officer directed flight operations. Also located in the island was the signal bridge, air plot, communications and aerology. The vital areas in the island were protected by light armor splinter shields.

The Gallery deck

Below the flight deck and suspended from it was the gallery deck. Here were a rudimentary combat intelligence centre, squadron ready rooms, and other air department offices.

Pilots of 'Special Aviation Project No. 1' checking short field take-off performance at Elgin Field, Florida in March 1942. None of the Tokyo Raiders had ever made an actual carrier take-off prior to their launch from Hornet. *Left to right Lts. Knoblock, McElroy, Joyce and Farrow. Lt. Farrow was one of the three raiders executed by the Japanese.*
(Photo: U.S. Air Force)

U.S. Navy blimp L-8 *rendezvous with* Hornet *on 3 April 1942 and lowered two boxes, containing special ordered glass navigators' windows. Note the forward wind fence in the up position just beyond the B-25.*

(Photo: U.S. Navy)

Cranes and Derricks

For handling boats and heavy lifts a crane was located on each side aft at the hangar deck level and two derricks were provided on the flight deck—one abaft the island and the other on the starboard side of the island just forward of the funnel. The latter was removed from all three ships after 1941.

ARMAMENT

The armament specifications in 1942 for the *Yorktown* class allowed for the following:

Air Group

The real 'main battery' on an aircraft carrier is her air group. The standard organisation of the *Yorktown* class in 1941 was one fighter squadron (VF), one scout-bombing squadron (VSB), one bombing squadron (VB) and one torpedo squadron (VT), each with 18 aircraft plus spares. Types: *Wildcat, Dauntless, Avenger, Devastator.* In practice, the number of aircraft in each squadron was never exact. Extra fighters were usually carried and, as the war progressed, the need for greater numbers of fighters was immediately recognised. By the time *Hornet* entered her final battle in October 1942 she had embarked 36 fighters. By 1945, an *Essex* class air group would have 72 fighters and fighter-bomber type aircraft on its roster.

5-inch guns

Eight single, open mount, dual purpose 5-inch/38 calibre (calibre × the diameter = barrel length) guns. They were located in pairs on splinter shielded sponsons just below the flight deck level forward and aft on each side. The 5-inch gun fired semi-fixed ammunition with the shell and powder casing weighing a total of 60 pounds. Two high angle gun directors were fitted—one on top of the navigation bridge just forward of the tripod mast and one on the same level abaft the funnel. It was on top of these that the carriers' first radar antenna were located at the outbreak of war.

1.1-inch guns

Sixteen 1·1-inch machine guns, nicknamed 'Chicago Pianos' or 'pom-poms', located in four splinter shielded gun tubs. The locations varied on the various ships of the class. *Hornet* had two mounts on the flight deck forward of the island, one stepped behind the other. One mount was on the flight deck abaft the island and one was further aft on the starboard side at the gallery deck level.

20 millimetre guns

Sixteen 20mm Oerlikon machine guns mounted at the gallery deck level and arranged in splinter shielded half tubs along the flight deck edge. As the war progressed, 20mm mounts proliferated with *Enterprise* adding 40mm quad mounts after 1942. When *Hornet* entered the war zone she mounted twenty-three 20mm guns: two in an oblong tub on the fo'c'sle under the flight deck overhang, one at each corner of the after end of the flight deck, two groups of five each on the port side over the large hangar deck openings, four on the starboard side over the large hangar deck opening forward, three abaft of the after 1·1-inch mount and two more singly arranged just forward of the after 5-inch mounts on the starboard side.

HORNET'S BEGINNING

With the authorisation to build *Yorktown* and *Enterprise* in 1933, the U.S. Navy was still 14,900 tons below its maximum carrier limitations established by the Washington Conference. Since another carrier of the *Yorktown* class would exceed the limit, a scaled down design following the general plan of that class was ordered on 27 March 1934. As a result, USS *Wasp* (CV-7) was launched 4 April 1939 displacing 14,700 tons.

On 31 December 1936, the treaties of the Washington Conference of 1922 and London Conference of 1930 were terminated when Japan abrogated. The threat of war was increasing in Europe and the Pacific, and since there was no longer an international agreement on total tonnage limitations to which it must adhere, Congress passed the Naval Expansion Act of 17 May 1938. Included in this Act was the authorisation to increase aircraft carrier tonnage by an additional 40,000 tons. USS *Hornet* (CV-8) and USS *Essex* (CV-9) were the result. *Essex* was to be the progenitor of a long line of aircraft carriers and these were the keystone to the building blocks on which the Japanese defeat was built. Twenty-four ships of the *Essex* class or its variations were to be built and an additional eight authorised but never built.

The keel of *Hornet* was laid on 25 September 1939

in Newport News, Virginia. Construction progressed rapidly compared to her earlier sisters. Europe was at war and the United States was increasingly aware that its years of isolation, as far as international affairs were concerned, were rapidly coming to an end. The fleet exercises of the late thirties and the opening naval operations of World War II in Europe convinced more and more naval planners that the aircraft carrier was replacing the battleship as the capital ship of the fleet (a fact the proponents of naval aviation had been preaching for over a decade). The Royal Navy's Fleet Air Arm attack against the Italian fleet at Taranto and the Imperial Japanese Navy carrier strike against Pearl Harbor were to establish the role of the carrier beyond a shadow of a doubt.

Hornet was launched 14 December 1940. Her place on the same building way was then taken by the keel of *Essex*. The Secretary of the Navy, Frank Knox, commissioned her on 20 October 1941 in Norfolk, Virginia. Her cost was $45,000,000.

Hornet's skipper was Captain Marc Mitscher, destined to become the Commander of Task Force 58, the greatest concentration of carrier striking power ever assembled. Mitscher will go down in history as one of the greatest carrier admirals. An early naval aviator, he participated in the U.S. Navy's attempt to be the first to fly the Atlantic Ocean in 1919 (his NC-1 went down at sea but NC-4 was succesful) and he made the first landing on *Saratoga*. Quiet and unimpressive looking, he was a seaman as well as an aviator and he would quickly forge *Hornet* into an effective, happy fighting ship.

Hornet was the last carrier to be commissioned by the Navy before the United States' entry into World War II. Old *Langley*, redesignated AV-3, had been relegated to seaplane tender duties on 15 September 1936. But, four months before *Hornet* was to join the fleet, the first of the escort carriers, USS *Long Island* (AVG-1), was placed in commission. Later redesignated CVE-1, *Long Island* was converted in just three months from the motor cargo ship *Mormacmail*. Thus, the total carriers in commission in the U.S. Navy was eight on 7 December 1941.

SHAKEDOWN

Under orders to join the Pacific Fleet, and with tensions rising during the seven weeks between her commissioning and the attack on Pearl Harbor, *Hornet's* fitting out was intensive and abbreviated. She left Hampton Roads on 26 December 1941, gathered in her escort and her air group, and departed on a combined shakedown and work-up cruise. This was to enable her to steam to the Pacific as soon as possible. Much work had to be done: her crew consisted of 75 per cent 'green' personnel. In fact, 700 had reported only two hours before she was commissioned direct from the Great Lakes Naval Training Station, 'Boot Camp'.

Hornet Air Group was new also; over half the aviators had just completed flight training. Her squadrons— Fighting Eight (VF-8), Bombing Eight (VB-8), Scouting Eight (VSB-8) and Torpedo Eight (VT-8) were all newly commissioned at Naval Air Station (NAS) Norfolk, Virginia, in the late summer of 1941. The practice of naming air groups after their carrier was dropped in August 1942 and *Hornet* Air Group became

Crew No. 1 on deck of Hornet: *left to right Lt. Henry A. Potter, Navigator; Lt. Col. James H. Doolittle, Pilot; S/Sgt. Fred A. Braemer, Bombardier; Lt. Richard E. Cole, Co-pilot; S/Sgt. Paul J. Leonard, Engineer-gunner. Thunderbird patch on jacket is the insignia of the 17th Bombardment Group from which the volunteer crews and planes came.* (Photo: U.S. Air Force)

Group Eight. Although the squadrons were new, the aircraft in which they trained were not necessarily so. Although VF-8 was equipped with the new Grumman F3F-3 *Wildcats*, VB-8 and VSB-8 had to make do with biplane Curtiss SBC-4 *Helldivers* and VT-8 had to soldier on with obsolete Naval Aircraft Factory SBN-1.

By the time *Hornet* sailed on her shakedown cruise, most of the SBCs had been replaced by the new Douglas *Dauntless* SBD-1, 2 and 3 variants. All but eight of the SBNs had been replaced by the ill-fated Douglas TBD-1 *Devastator*.

Hornet headed south through the submarine infested waters toward the warmer temperatures of the Caribbean. No time was wasted as the crew commenced an immediate routine of work and training. Captain Mitscher ordered that no neck ties need be worn and proceeded to set a hectic pace for his crew to follow. Watch and Battle Bills had to be tested and modified to achieve the ultimate in efficiency. Each piece of equipment and machinery was intimately learned by its

Lt. Farrow's B-25, the last to take off from Hornet, *is shown protruding over the fantail. Navy Seaman Robert Wall lost an arm when blown into the propeller of this plane; its crew was captured and two of them executed. Destroyer* Gwinn *in the background.*

(Photo: U.S. Navy)

Crew No. 8: left to right, Lt. Nolan A. Herndon, Navigator-bombardier; Capt. Edward J. York, Pilot; S/Sgt. Theodore H. Laban, Engineer; Lt. Robert G. Emmons, Co-pilot; Sgt. David W. Pohl. This was the only crew to land safely after the Tokyo Raid. Interned in the Soviet Union they escaped over the Iranian border in May 1943. Note detail of tie-down strips, cross-deck pendant and barrier cable troughs in deck. (Photo: U.S. Air Force)

Lt. Col. Doolittle, revving his engines on Hornet's wet deck waiting for Lt. Osborne to drop the checkered flag sending him on his way to Tokyo. After-portside 20 mm gun mounts can be seen in the background.
(Photo: U.S. Navy)

The Tokyo Raiders' B-25 Mitchells enroute to Japan on Hornet flight deck. Four SBDs are visible among the B-25s. Prior to launch all 16 of Doolittle's planes were spotted aft in only a little more space than can be seen in this view. Note the center elevator detail and the two stowed wire barriers of the arresting gear just beyond.
(Photo: U.S. Navy)

operator. All the peculiarities that give each ship its own personality had to be mastered—which equipment was dependable, which had to be given special attention, which needed to be replaced or modified.

SHIP'S ROUTINE

The myriad details required in shaking down and working up a large combatant not only had to be effected in five weeks' time, but also had to be done under the conditions of wartime readiness. The Plan of the Day called for 'flight quarters' to be blown at 0400 hours by bugle in Officers' Country and by bo's'ns pipe and loud speaker in the crew's quarters. 'General quarters' were sounded an hour before sunrise and secured an hour after. The procedure was repeated in the evening with battle condition being set one hour before sunset and secured an hour after. 'Darken ship' was maintained at night with only the blue battle lanterns lit in exposed areas.

As morning twilight occurred, the air officer would call, 'Prepare to start engines'. Then in fast succession, 'Pilots, man your planes', 'Stand clear of propellers', and finally, 'Start engines'. The flight deck would then come alive with noise and smoke as the starter cartridges popped and the engines began turning. After warm-up the air officer would switch on the green light. As each plane lined up for take-off, the flight officer would give the pilot a final check before giving him the chequered flag to commence his take-off roll. The aircraft took off according to types, the nimble fighters first, the scout bombers next and the heavy torpedo planes last; the sequence was dictated by the distance required to become airborne.

Hornet's aircraft were flown almost continuously during daylight hours—patrolling for submarines, doing target practice, making dry runs at their own ship and learning the intricacies of carrier aircraft operations. At night the 'airdales' (ground crews) took over and prepared the planes for the next day's flights. All flight operations had to be carried out under conditions of radio silence, a situation that caused real hardship for the talkative aviators.

The ship's gun crews practised daily by firing at helium balloons and towed target sleeves, or simulated firing at their own aircraft. Skeet shooting was also carried out in order to sharpen the gunners' aim.

It was with this gruelling seven-day-a-week routine that the crew of the *Hornet* was to live for the next year. When she returned to Norfolk on 31 January 1942, she was in fighting shape, but the Navy planned an odd chore for her before she was to sail for the Pacific.

ARMY BOMBERS ON NAVY CARRIER

After their hectic shakedown, the crew of *Hornet* was looking forward to liberty in Norfolk, but, as the ship was warped to the pier, no order for shore leave came. Instead, on 2 February 1942, a dock-side crane hoisted aboard two North American B-25B Mitchell bombers. This new type of twin-engined bomber was much larger than any of the carrier aircraft of the period and rumours as to their purpose on *Hornet* ran through the mess decks. Many crewmen thought they had worked *Hornet* into fighting trim only to be relegated to aircraft ferry duty.

The B-25s were on *Hornet* as a result of a 'crash' program designed to bolster morale on the home-front and to strike a blow at the growing feeling of Japanese invincibility. President Roosevelt was anxious to mount some sort of combat operation against Japanese home islands. It was Captain Francis S. Low, a submariner on Chief of Naval Operations Ernest J. King's staff, who suggested flying army bombers off the deck of an aircraft carrier to bomb Tokyo. The idea came to him on 10 January 1942, while watching army bombers make passes at a naval air strip painted with the outline of a carrier deck.

Captain Donald B. 'Wu' Duncan, King's air operations officer, analysed the various aspects of the problem and decided that the project was possible if the B-25 was used. Of the other bombers considered, the B-18 could not carry enough payload for the distance required, the B-23 had too wide a wingspan for flight deck take-offs and the B-26 required too long a distance to become airborne.

General Henry H. 'Hap' Arnold, Chief of the Army Air Forces, was most enthusiastic when presented with the plan. He selected Lieutenant Colonel James H. 'Jimmy' Doolittle, a world renowned aviator only recently recalled to active duty, to organise the Army Air Corps participation in the plan. Surprise was of the utmost importance for such an operation to be successful. Only seven officers would know the complete details of the plan, right up until launch time.

To prove Captain Duncan's paper calculations, three B-25s, with Lieutenant John E. Fitzgerald in charge, were sent to Norfolk in January. A number of test flights were conducted with different aircraft weights from one of the auxiliary fields. The results were satisfactory. It was two of these aircraft that were placed aboard *Hornet* on the morning of 2 February. Even Captain Mitscher did not know the purpose of this test—only that his ship was to attempt to launch these aircraft once at sea.

That same day, as the *Hornet* steamed just out of sight of the Virginia Capes, preparations were made to launch the B-25s. In the midst of the pre-launch activity a periscope was sighted. The escorts rushed to the datum and proceeded to depth charge the spot. Only on closer investigation of the oil slick was it discovered that the 'periscope' was the topmast of a sunken tanker.

Doolittle's B-25 just prior to lift off. The two white lines painted on the deck were a guide for the pilot, allowing him six feet clearance between his wing and the island.
(*Photo: U.S. Navy*)

Both B-25s subsequently took off with room to spare; the test was an unqualified success. Ironically, unknown to the planners of the Tokyo raid, tests had been conducted with the Navy's twin-engined, tricycle landing geared XJO-3 on 29 August 1939 aboard *Lexington*.

TOKYO RAID PREPARATIONS

To best summarise the preparations for the raid, the following is the planning memo drafted by Jimmy Doolittle:

Subject: B-25 SPECIAL PROJECT
To: COMMANDING GENERAL, ARMY AIR FORCES.

The purpose of this special project is to bomb and fire the industrial center of Japan.

It is anticipated that this will not only cause confusion and impede production but will undoubtedly facilitate operations against Japan in other theaters due to their probable withdrawal of troops for the purpose of defending the home country.

An action of this kind is most desirable now due to the psychological effect on the American public, our allies and our enemies.

The method contemplated is to bring carrier-

Jimmy Doolittle with flaps fully extended lifts clear of Hornet *with yards to spare, 0820 18 April 1942. He made one low pass down the flight deck, then headed for Tokyo. The other 15 B-25s await their turn on the after half of the flight deck.*
(*Photo: U.S. Navy*)

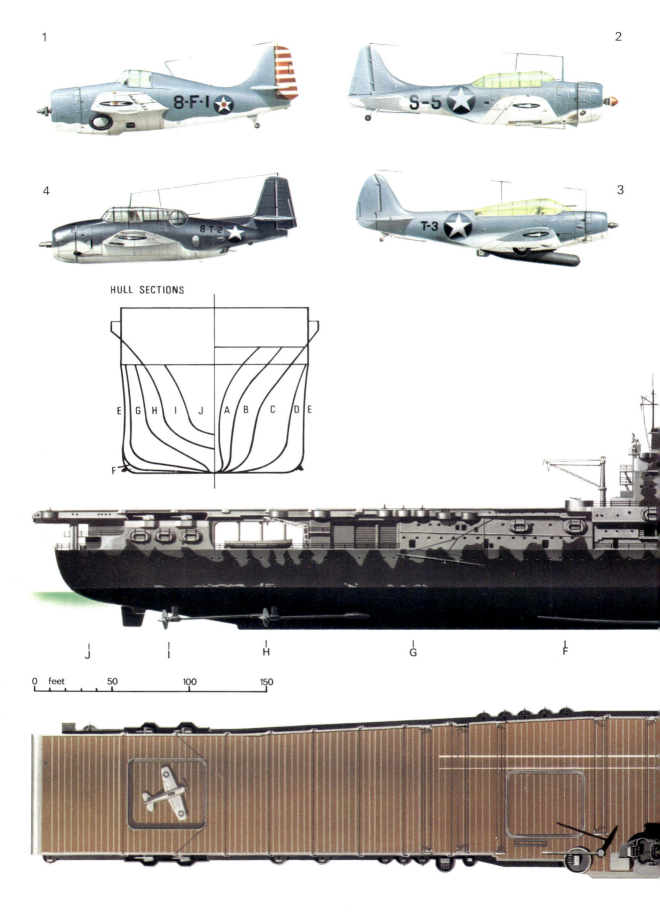

HULL SECTIONS

E G H I J A B C D E

F

J   I   H   G   F

0 feet   50   100   150

USS Hornet (CV-8) 1941-1942

Paint Scheme

Hornet is depicted as she appeared in April 1942 when she launched the Tokyo Raiders. This camouflage scheme was carried throughout her Pacific campaigns and was unique to U.S. carriers. Later in the war most U.S. carriers were camouflaged with the 'crazy guilt' pattern. Note the two white lines on the flight deck used as wheel guides for the B-25s.

1. F4F-3 Grumman *Wildcat* fighter, VF-8, color scheme used from October 1941 to January 1942. *Hornet* carried both fixed wing F4F-3 and folding wing F4F-4.

2. SBD-3 *Dauntless* scout and dive bomber, VS-8, color scheme used from January 1942 to May 1942.

3. TBD-1 Douglas *Devastator* torpedo bomber, VT-8, color scheme used from May 1942 to February 1943. All of VT-8s Devastators were lost at Midway. Squadron was reformed with Avengers and subsequently served aboard *Saratoga*.

4. TBF-1 Grumman *Avenger* torpedo bomber, VT-6, this squadron joined *Hornet* in June 1942 as a replacement for VT-8. A detachment of VT-8 operated six TBFs from Midway Atoll during the Battle of Midway.

5. B-25B North American *Mitchell* medium bomber, color scheme used by Tokyo Raiders in April 1942. This particular airplane was flown by Lt. Col. Jimmy Doolittle.

David Warner/T. Brittain © Profile Publications Ltd.

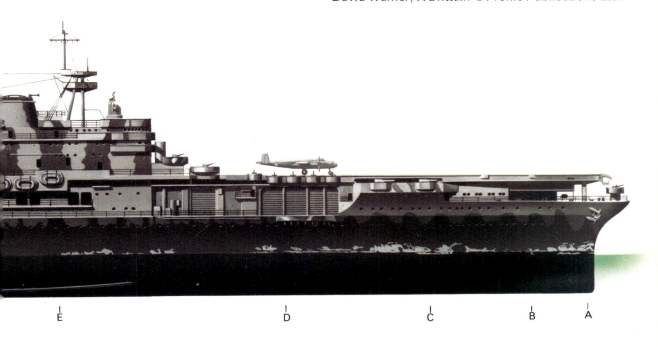

E   D   C   B   A

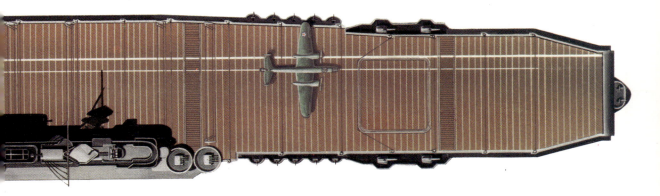

Photo of Yokosuka Naval Base taken by Lt. Richard A. Knoblock just before bombs were released. The dock yard area and a drydocked aircraft carrier were damaged.
(Photo: U.S. Air Force)

borne bombers to within 400 to 500 miles (all distances mentioned will be in statute miles) of the coast of Japan, preferably to the south-south-east. They will then take off from the carrier deck and proceed directly to selected objectives. These objectives will be military and industrial targets in the Tokyo-Yokohama, Nagoya and Osaka-Kobe areas.

Simultaneous bombings of these areas is contemplated with the bombers coming in up waterways from the south-east and, after dropping their bombs, returning in the same direction. After clearing the Japanese outside coastline a sufficient distance, a general westerly course will be set for one or more of the following airports in China : Chuchow, Chuchow (Lishui), Yushan and/or Chienou. Chuchow is about 70 miles inland and 200 miles to the south-south-west of Shanghai.

After refuelling, the airplanes will proceed to the strong Chinese air base at Chungking, about 800 miles distant, and from there to such ultimate objective as may, at that time, be indicated.

The greatest non-stop distance that any airplane will have to fly is 2000 miles.

Eighteen B-25B (North American Medium Bomber) airplanes will be employed in this raid. Each will carry about 1100 gallons of gasoline which assures a range of 2400 miles at 5000 feet altitude in still air.

Each bomber will carry two 500lb demolition bombs and as near as possible to 1000lb of incendiaries. The demolition bombs will be dropped first and then the incendiaries.

The extra gasoline will be carried in a 275-gallon auxiliary leakproof tank in the top of the bomb bay and a 175-gallon flexible rubber tank in the passageway above the bomb bay. It is anticipated that the gasoline from this top tank will be used up and the tank flattened out or rolled up and removed prior to entering the combat zone. This assures that the airplane will be fully operational and minimizes the fire and explosion hazard characteristic of a near empty tank.

In all other respects the airplanes are conventional. The work of installing the required additional tankage is being done by Mid-Continent Airlines at Minneapolis. All production and installation work is progressing according to schedule and the 24 airplanes (6 spares) should be completely converted by March 15th.

Extensive range and performance tests will be conducted on Number 1* article while the others are being converted. A short period will be required to assemble and give special training to the crews. The training will include teamwork in bombing, gunnery, navigation, flying, short take-off and at least one carrier take off for each pilot.

If the crews are selected promptly from men familiar with their jobs and the B-25B airplane, the complete unit should be ready for loading on the carrier by April 1st.

General operational instructions will be issued just before take-off from the carrier.

Due to the greater accuracy of daylight bombing a daylight raid is contemplated. The present concept of the project calls for a night take-off from the carrier and arrival over objectives at dawn. Rapid refuelling at the landing points will permit arrival at Chungking before dark.

A night raid will be made if, due to last minute information received from our intelligence section or other source, a daylight raid is definitely inadvisable. The night raid should be

* The first Mitchell to be modified.

Hornet at the Battle of Midway, with F4Fs aft on her flight deck. To the right is heavy cruiser Vincennes and in the foreground anti-aircraft cruiser Atlanta. A new class, Atlanta could do better than 40 knots and carried 16 5-inch/38 cal guns for her main battery.
(Photo: U.S. Navy)

made on a clear night, moonlight if Japan is blacked out; moonless if it is not.

All available pertinent information regarding targets and defenses will be obtained from A-2, G-2 and other existent sources.

The Navy has already supervised take-off tests made at Norfolk, Va., using three B-25B bombers carrying loads of 23,000lb, and 26,000lb and 29,000lb. These tests indicate that no difficulty need be anticipated in taking off from the carrier deck with a gross load of around 31,000lb.

The Navy will be charged with providing a carrier, (probably the *Hornet*), loading and storing the airplanes and with delivering them to the take-off position.

The Chemical Warfare Service is designing and preparing special incendiary bomb clusters in order to ensure that the maximum amount that limited space permits, up to 1000lb per airplane, may be carried. Forty-eight of the clusters will be ready for shipment from Edgewood Arsenal by March 15th.

About 20,000 U.S. gallons of 100 octane aviation gasoline and 600 gallons of lubricating oil will be laid down at Chuchow and associated fields. All other supplies and necessary emergency repair equipment will be carried on the airplanes.

1st Lt. Harry W. Howze, now with the Air Service Command and formerly with the Standard Oil Company of New Jersey, will be charged with making arrangements for the fuel caches in China. He will work through A-2 and A-4 and with Col. Claire Chennault, a former Air Corps officer and now aviation advisor to the

TBDs prepare to launch against the Japanese carrier force off Midway. Out of a total of 41 launched on 4 June only four returned. Note wing folding operation on foremost aircraft and large wingspan. (Photo: U.S. Navy)

Pilots of Torpedo Squadron Eight, who all, except Ens. George Gay, lost their lives in the Battle of Midway. Gay viewed the remainder of the attack on the Japanese carriers by floating under his seat cushion and was picked up by a PBY the next day. From left to right: standing; Ltjg. Owens, Ens. Fayle, Lt. Cdr. J. C. Waldron, R. A. Moore, U. M. Moore, W. R. Evans, G. W. Teats, and H. J. Ellison. Kneeling; G. M. Campbell, W. W. Ambercrombie, H. R. Kenyon, G. H. Gay, J. D. Woodson, W. W. Creamer, and R. B. Miles. (Photo: U.S. Navy)

The only surviving TBF from VT-8's detachment on Midway Atoll. Riddled with holes, one crewman dead, and the pilot and other crewmen wounded, this plane managed to limp back to Midway. This was the first time in combat for the TBF and a number of different models would serve into the early 1950s with the fleet.

(Photo: U.S. Navy)

Chinese government. Col. Chennault should assign a responsible American or a Chinese who speaks English to physically check and assure that the supplies are in place. This man should also be available to assist the crews in servicing the airplanes. That the supplies are in place can be indicated by suitable radio code signal. Work on placing supplies must start at once.

Shortly before the airplanes arrive the proper Chinese agencies should be advised that the airplanes are coming soon but the inference will be that they are flying up from the south in order to stage a raid on Japan from which they plan to return to the same base.

Radio signals from the bombing planes immediately they drop their bombs may be used to indicate arrival at gassing points some six or seven hours later.

Care must be exercised to see that the Chinese are advised just in time as any information given to the Chinese may be expected to fall into Japanese hands and a premature notification would be fatal to the project.

An initial study of meteorological conditions indicates that the sonner the raid is made the better will be the prevailing weather conditions. The weather will become increasingly unfavourable after the end of April. Weather was

Japanese heavy cruiser Mikuma *sunk by SBDs from* Hornet *and* Enterprise *off Midway, 6 June 1942.*

(Photo: U.S. Navy)

considered largely from the point of view of avoiding morning fog over Tokyo and other targets, low overcast over Chuchow and Chungking, icing and strong westerly winds.

If possible, daily weather predictions or anticipated weather conditions at Chungking and the coast should be sent, at a specified time, in suitable code, in order to assist the meteorologist on the carrier in analysing his forecasts.

Lt. Col. J. H. Doolittle, Air Corps, will be in charge of the preparations and will be in personal command of the project. Other flight personnel will, due to the considerable hazard incident to such a mission, be volunteers.

Each airplane will carry its normal complement of five crew members; pilot, co-pilot, bombardier-navigator, radio operator and gunner-mechanic.

One crew member will be a competent meteorologist and one an experienced navigator. All navigators will be trained in celestial navigation.

Two ground liaison officers will be assigned. One will remain on the mainland and the other on the carrier.

At least three crew members will speak Chinese—one in each of the target units.

Should the Russians be willing to accept delivery of 18 B-25B airplanes, on lease lend, at Vladivostok, our problem would be greatly simplified and conflict with the Halverson† project avoided.

The Seventeenth Bombardment Group and its attached Eighty-Ninth Reconnaissance Squadron were selected to furnish the aircraft and crews for the Tokyo mission. It was decided that a total of 24 aircraft and crews were required to assure the availability of the estimated 15 or 16 B-25s *Hornet* could carry. The call for volunteers for an '*extremely hazardous mission*' was answered by practically every man in the Group.

The selected men and aircraft were ordered to Eglin Field, Florida, under instructions that absolute secrecy must be maintained concerning all aspects of their training. Lieutenant Henry L. Miller, USN, was attached to the group to train the army in carrier take-off technique and a period of intensive training followed. As the training progressed the aircraft received their required modifications: extra fuel tanks, bottom turrets removed, two broomsticks inserted in the tail to simulate a gun position, a $0.75 'nuts and bolts' gunsight to replace the still secret Norden sight, fine tuning of engines and close calibration of instruments. Never given an official squadron number, Special Aviation Project No. 1 departed Eglin for the West Coast of the United States on 23 March 1942. Twenty-two B-25s made the trip, two of the original 24 being damaged in training.

HORNET TO THE PACIFIC

The *Hornet* spent the rest of February in Norfolk. The minor problems revealed during shakedown were

† *A plan to base heavy bombers in China.*

remedied; the air group replaced the last of its SOCs and SBNs with SBDs and TBDs; she was given her wartime camouflage and additional 20mm guns were installed. She sailed for the Panama Canal in late February in company with a convoy destined for Australia. Torpedo Squadron Eight left behind a detachment to take delivery of the first Grumman TBF-1s, the first squadron to receive the new torpedo bomber. It would be in the waters off Midway that some of the members of the detachment were destined to rejoin their squadron mates.

After clearing the Canal, 'The Happy *Hornet*', as her crew now called her, headed along the Pacific coast accompanied only by her escorts. She spent a number of days off California training air crews for other carriers before tying up on 1 April at NAS Alameda in San Francisco Bay where Doolittle's group also arrived on the same day. The first 16 B-25s that were checked in without any mechanical problems were towed to the quayside and hoisted on board *Hornet*. All 22 crews and some ground support personnel were sent aboard, including 70 officers and 64 enlisted men. To the crew, appearances were that of an aircraft ferry mission—evidently the planners hoped the assumption would be the same to anyone else seeing *Hornet* packed with army bombers. *Hornet's* own aircraft were crammed below on the hangar deck.

TOKYO BOUND

Hornet was underway from San Francisco at 1018 Thursday, 2 April 1942. She steamed under the Golden Gate Bridge accompanied by two cruisers, four destroyers and an oiler in bright sunlight. The *Hornet* group, designated Task Group 16.2, set a zigzag course towards a rendezvous with Admiral William F. 'Bull', Halsey's *Enterprise* group north of Hawaii. Immediately the battle drill started again, now with the added problem of the bombers. If an emergency arose, the army crews had to be prepared to fly their aircraft off or assist in pushing them overboard.

On the afternoon of 2 April, Mitscher announced over the loud speaker system and by semaphore to the other ships of the group, '*This force is bound for Tokyo.*' Cheering could be heard throughout the ship, morale reached a new high, and the previously close-mouthed 'alien' army men were now accepted as part of the crew by the navy personnel. The Air Corps crews had only been told that morning of their destination, although many had correctly guessed it during their training.

On the second day out, Jimmy Doolittle was sitting in the cockpit of a B-25 with Hank Miller and gazing down the deck toward the bow.

'That distance looks mighty short to me, Hank,' said Doolittle pointing toward the bow.

'You know it, Colonel Doolittle,' Miller answered, 'this is a breeze. You see that tool kit that is away up the deck there—that's where I used to take off in fighters.'

Doolittle pondered a moment—then, smiling at Miller, said, 'Hank, what do they call 'baloney' in the Navy?'

Miller, with Lieutenant Dick Joyce, USA, was scheduled to take the sixteenth B-25 off *Hornet* that day and fly back to California—just to prove to all the army flyers it could be done. In the afternoon Captain

Captain Charles P. Mason, second and last captain of Hornet, *was a strong, fiery officer. Naval Aviator No. 52, he served in France during WWI. Spending his early years in patrol bombers, he served on* Saratoga, *was executive officer of* Langley *and* Yorktown. *He came to* Hornet *from being Commanding Officer of NAS Jacksonville, Florida. Promoted to Rear Admiral after* Hornet *sunk, ill health would keep him out of the front line for the rest of the war.* (Photo: U.S. Navy)

Mitscher called Miller to the bridge and, after discussing the chances of a successful take-off, Mitscher informed Miller that the sixteenth plane would remain aboard for the raid.

Doolittle's men spent their time profitably while crossing the Pacific. Navy maintenance personnel assisted the army crews in keeping the B-25s in condition. Target folders were studied, courses plotted, and lectures attended on first aid and Japanese and Chinese geography. Chuchow, China was to be their recovery airfield. One aircraft each was slated to bomb Kobe, Nagoya and Osaka; the rest were assigned targets in the Tokyo-Yokohama area. Doolittle repeatedly admonished his crews that no bombs were to fall on the Emperor's Palace. During periods of relaxation, Army played Navy at poker—it is still being disputed as to who won that 'battle'.

On the morning of 13 April, in foul weather and poor visibility, the *Hornet* and *Enterprise* rendezvoused at 38°00' North—180° 00' and headed west at 16 knots. *Hornet* now had the protection of *Enterprise's* aircraft and from this point any vessels or aircraft encountered would be assumed to be the enemy. The U.S. Navy was following the same general course in reverse that the Japanese had used in attacking Pearl Harbor.

TASK FORCE 16

The following was the task force organisation:

TASK FORCE 16
Vice Admiral William F. Halsey

	TG 16.1	TG 16.2
CARRIERS:	*Enterprise*	*Hornet*
CRUISERS:	*Vincennes*	*Northampton*
	Nashville	*Salt Lake City*
DESTROYERS:	*Gwin*	*Balch*
	Grayson	*Benham*
	Monsson	*Ellet*
	Meredith	*Fanning*
OILERS:	*Cimarron*	*Sabine*

Enterprise, *a destroyer, and battleship* South Dakota *under attack at the Battle of the Santa Cruz Islands.*

(*Photo: U.S. Navy*)

In addition to the above, submarines USS *Trout* and USS *Thresher* were operating off the Japanese coast where they were watching for any countering fleet movements from the enemy and from whence they were to report the weather.

As Task Force 16 steamed west, *Enterprise* maintained air patrol during daylight hours, dawn and dusk search flights being flown out to 200 miles in an arc 60 degrees off each bow. Final plans were made. On the afternoon of 15 April Halsey signalled the following message to the force:

INTENTION FUEL HEAVY SHIPS 1000 MILES TO WESTWARD X THENCE CARRIERS AND CRUISERS TO POINT 500 MILES EAST OF TOKYO LAUNCH ARMY BOMBERS ON HORNET FOR ATTACK X DDS AND TANKERS REMAIN VICINITY FUELLING POINT REJOIN ON RETIREMENT X FURTHER OPERATIONS AS DEVELOPMENTS DICTATE.

Because of their lack of high-speed fuel endurance, the destroyers had to be left behind; the larger ships were going to make the dash to the launch point.

The B-25s were spotted for take-off; Doolittle's lead plane had 467-feet of clear deck. Fuel tanks were topped off and all ordnance loaded. Ten five gallon cans of gasoline were loaded in the after station of each plane to bring the total fuel load to 1141 gallons. By evening of 17 April, all was ready but the weather remained foul.

The plan was to launch Doolittle's plane first, about 400 miles from the closest Japanese landfall. He would arrive over Tokyo at sunset, followed three hours later by the rest of the B-25s, to permit a night attack. This gave the attackers the advantages of escaping under cover of darkness and the possibility of landing in China in daylight the next morning.

If the Force was detected Halsey and Doolittle had agreed on an alternative plan. The planes would be launched immediately—it was calculated, given the prevailing winds, that the B-25s could launch 550 miles out and still make their destination in China.

'ARMY PILOTS MAN YOUR PLANES'

At 0558 on the morning of 18 April 1942, Lieutenant O. B. Wiseman in an SBD sighted a small patrol craft 42 miles from the Force. He immediately dropped the contact report by bean bag message container on the deck of *Enterprise* and the Force altered course. At 0738 a lookout on *Hornet* sighted another small patrol boat, *No. 23 Nitto Maru*. She was subsequently sunk by *Nashville* but not before she had sent off her report to Japanese Naval Headquarters.

At 0800 Halsey flashed to Mitscher:

LAUNCH PLANES X TO COL DOOLITTLE AND GALLANT COMMAND GOOD LUCK AND GOD BLESS YOU.

On *Hornet* the klaxon sounded and over the loudspeaker came, '*Army pilots man your planes.*'

A gale of more than 40 knots was blowing, churning the sea and causing the ship to pitch violently. Lieutenant Edgar G. Osborne stood near the bow with a chequered flag. His timing had to be calculated to start the B-25s on their take-off rolls so they would reach the end of the flight deck just as the carrier's bow started its next plunge.

At 0820 Jimmy Doolittle opened his throttles and kept his wheels on the guide lines painted on the deck to maintain a six foot clearance between his starboard wing and the island. As the *Hornet* cut through the top of a wave at full speed, Doolittle lifted off with yards to spare.

The rest of the B-25s took off at approximately four minute intervals with the last plane off at 0920. Two incidents marred the launching. One plane cracked a nose glass panel when it rammed the tail cone of the one ahead of it. Seaman Robert W. Wall got blown into an idling propeller by prop blast and lost an arm. Its part of the mission completed, Task Group 16 turned around and sped toward Hawaii. It was later established that by nightfall on 18 April, units of the Force had made contact with 17 enemy patrol vessels and one submarine.

ENEMY REACTION

The Japanese were not in complete ignorance of what was developing. On 10 April they intercepted radio traffic and radio experts deduced that an American task force with two or three carriers was heading west. No additional intelligence was received, however, until No 23 *Nitto Maru* had flashed her contact report. Vice Admiral Matoi Ugaki, Commander-in-Chief of Combined Forces, estimated the American force had to transit for another 24 hours before it would be within carrier strike range of Japan and he planned accordingly. He was in for a rude shock.

Even as the B-25s were dropping bombs on Tokyo, the Japanese high command thought the army bombers must have been launched from some land base. It was felt this was a co-ordinated attack and the carrier planes would soon follow and plans were made to attack the exposed carriers. But it would be 33 months before carrier planes would again attack Japan—led by Vice Admiral 'Pete' Mitscher.

THE RAIDERS

Each of Doolittle's planes departed *Hornet* independently and each crew would have its own tale to tell of the events that followed. Tokyo was enjoying beautiful spring weather on the afternoon of 18 April.

At 1230 Doolittle dropped his bombs, followed sporadically for the next 30 minutes by the other B-25s. All aircraft departed the shores of Japan safely. Fourteen hit their targeted cities while one dropped its bombs on its secondary target at Nagoya. One aircraft jettisoned its bombs when jumped by fighters.

The raiders' luck ran out as they approached China. The mainland area for which they were heading was 'weathered in'. Only one of the B-25s landed safely and it had to divert to the Soviet Union because of poor fuel consumption. Landing near Vladivostok the crew and aircraft were interned by the Russians. Of the other 15 bombers, four crash-landed and the crews of those remaining were forced to bail out in the darkness over China.

Eighty men took off from *Hornet* on the Tokyo Raid—one was killed when he bailed out, two were killed in a crash landing, five were interned, eight were captured and the rest managed to reach Chungking and safety. Of the eight that were captured three were executed, one died and four were freed at the end of the war.

The news of the attack on Tokyo gave a great boost to American and allied morale: only defeat had been experienced in the Pacific since 7 December 1941. The raid, however, had the opposite effect on the Japanese. Although the material damage was relatively light, the effect on their morale was great. It would be months before the complete story of the Tokyo Raid would be made public. President Roosevelt, when asked from where the B-25s had been launched, referred to James Hilton's novel *Lost Horizons* and replied, 'They came from *Shangri La*'.

BATTLE OF MIDWAY

Hornet spent only five days in Pearl Harbor after her return from the Tokyo Raid. She got underway for a fast transit to the South Pacific with the *Enterprise* on 20 April. The Japanese were pushing towards Port Moresby and the Allies were determined to stop this advance. *Hornet* again filled the role of a ferry as each carrier had 12 Marine F4Fs and their pilots aboard. These were to be flown off to Espiritu Santo near New Caledonia.

The two carriers were still 1000 miles away when Task Force 17, with *Lexington* and *Yorktown*, stopped the Japanese at the Battle of the Coral Sea. Old 'Lady Lex' was lost on 7 May but the Japanese paid dearly. Their carrier *Shoho* was lost, *Shokaku* was heavily damaged and

Zuikaku's Air Group lost so many planes that she missed the Battle of Midway. *Enterprise* and *Hornet* returned to Hawaii.

Hornet and her crew had now spent five months on the move at a tremendous pace, with only several days liberty, but she had yet to fire a shot in anger. The liberty haunts of Honolulu were a welcome change. But *Hornet* was to get no rest—only two days in port when the word was passed, 'All liberty cancelled. Report at once to the ship.' The rush was on for the message was meant for the whole fleet. The Japanese Navy was steaming towards Midway Atoll at the far western end of the Hawaiian chain; other elements were heading for the Aleutian Islands off the tip of Alaska.

THE ADVERSARIES

Hornet and *Enterprise*, as part of Task Force 16, departed Pearl on 28 May. They were under the command of Rear Admiral Raymond A. Spruance. TF-16 consisted of two carriers, six cruisers, eleven destroyers and two oilers.

Yorktown had limped into Pearl Harbour with battle damage from the Coral Sea battle on 27 May. Originally it was estimated it would take 90 days to put her in battle trim again. The shipyard civilians and her crew dry-docked her and hurriedly repaired the vital damage, allowing her to sortie three days later on 30 May. She was part of Task Force 17 under Rear Admiral Frank J. Fletcher. TF-17 consisted of one carrier, two cruisers and six destroyers.

In addition, 19 submarines were deployed in the battle area. Based on Midway were 38 naval aircraft, 54 marine planes and 23 army bombers.

Arrayed against the United States forces in four separate groups, the Japanese had six carriers, three seaplane carriers, 11 battleships, 14 cruisers, 46 destroyers, 16 submarines and a number of support ships. These, plus the transports of the invasion force, made the odds formidable.

Hornet's newly appointed commanding officer, Captain Charles P. Mason, was aboard; but in the rush to sea the change of command had not taken place. Thus 'Pete' Mitscher remained in command. *Hornet's* squadrons and their losses during the Battle of Midway were as follows:

Air Group Commander: Lt. Cdr. Stanhope C. Ring
VF-8   27 F4F-4

Lt. Cdr. Samuel G. Mitchell	12 lost

VB-8   19 SBD-2 and 3

Lt. Cdr. Robert R. Johnson	5 lost

VS-8   18 SBD-1, -2, -3

Lt. Cdr. Walter F. Rodee	5 lost

VT-8   15 TBD-1

Lt. Cdr. John C. Waldron	All lost

A plane from Hornet *took this photo of Task Force 17 manoeuvering at the Battle of Santa Cruz.* Hornet *is just to left of center.*
(Photo: U.S. Navy)

In addition, six new TBF-1s of the VT-8 detachment had just arrived on Midway from the United States, and five of these were lost.

FIRST SIGHTING

At 0603 on 4 June, as *Hornet* and her two sisterships steamed westward about 325 miles northeast of Midway, a Catalina search plane flashed the position of the Japanese carrier force. The Japanese had just launched a strike against Midway and soon were warding off the attacks of the Midway based aircraft. At 0702 *Hornet* commenced launching 35 dive bombers and 15 torpedo planes with fighter escort. *Enterprise* launched a somewhat smaller group at the same time while *Yorktown*, who had to recover the morning search aircraft, launched her air group at 0838.

At 0728 Admiral Nagumo received a message from one of his search planes reporting the position of the U.S. carrier force. As soon as he recovered his Midway strike, he changed course 90 degrees at 0917 to place him in a better position to attack. The Japanese carriers' flight decks were loaded with planes being rearmed and refuelled, their most vulnerable posture, when U.S. carrier aircraft found them.

Torpedo strike

The *Hornet's* and *Enterprise's* TBDs, flying slower and at a lower altitude, became separated from their air groups and each other. When VT-8 'skipper', Lieutenant Commander John Waldron, did not locate the Japanese where anticipated, he took his squadron north and became the first unit of the carrier strike force to encounter the enemy. The TBDs lumbered in low over the water at 120 knots. Swarms of Zeros pounced the

Hornet *takes first near misses at approximately 0911. List is due to hard port turn. This sequence of photos taken from* cruiser Pensacola.
(Photo: U.S. Navy)

Damaged Japanese Val dive bomber making a suicide dive on Hornet *at 0913. Smoke and damage of bomb hit on after portion of flight deck can be seen as two Kate torpedo planes fly past.*
(Photo: U.S. Navy)

Val crashes into island and continues through flight deck seconds later. Kate, seen in previous photo on left continues at right; the aircraft probably dropped one of the torpedoes that hit Hornet *seconds later. Another Val presses in above* Hornet's *bow.*
(Photo: U.S. Navy)

attackers who were then met by a tremendous barrage of anti-aircraft. Only a few planes survived to drop their antiquated torpedoes, without gaining a hit. All 15 of the TBDs were eventually shot down and out of 30 aircrew only one survived, Ensign George Gay. But 'Torpedo Eight's' sacrifice was not to have been in vain.

Enterprise's TBDs attacked at 0940, a few minutes after *Hornet's*, with much the same results—10 of 14 shot down and no hits. Next came *Yorktown's* TBDs at 1000—again no hits and 10 of 12 shot down. Thus, out of 41 TBDs launched from the three carriers, only six returned. These uncoordinated attacks were catastrophic but fortunately they did serve the purpose of drawing the Japanese fighters down to low altitude. The attention of the Japanese Fleet was focused on the horizontal when the first dive bombers started their near vertical drops that would decide the battle.

The Dive Bombers

Hornet's SBDs and F4Fs unfortunately turned south when they did not locate the enemy fleet where expected. Most either ditched or recovered at Midway, missing out on the battle that day. *Enterprise's* dive bombers made a wide swing to the north, finally locating the enemy by flying the same course on which a lone Japanese destroyer was sighted steaming.

By a fortunate coincidence, *Enterprise's* two squadrons of dive bombers, having come the long way around, arrived over the Japanese Carrier Force at the same moment as *Yorktown's* single squadron, which took off an hour later. The first two squadrons attacked *Kaga* and *Akagi*, while the latter dived on *Soryu*. All three carriers received fatal hits.

That afternoon, *Hiryu's* aircraft dealt *Yorktown* a mortal blow and *Enterprise* launched her remaining SBDs, along with some 'refugees' from *Yorktown*, to reciprocate against *Hiryu*.

With his heavy carriers gone, Admiral Yamamoto, the Combined Fleet Commander, elected to withdraw. The Battle of Midway, the first smashing defeat for the Japanese in modern times, was to be recognised as the turning point in the Central Pacific. The Japanese were to advance no further in that area. *Hornet's* Air Group participated in the pursuit of Japanese stragglers on 5-6 June. Her SBDs, in company with those from *Enterprise*, participated in the attacks that sunk and heavily damaged heavy cruisers *Mogami* and *Mikama*, respectively.

TO THE SOUTH PACIFIC

Hornet arrived back at Pearl on 13 June 1942. Captain Charles P. Mason took over as commanding officer and *Hornet* took aboard her first 'flag', Rear Admiral George Murray, the recently promoted former 'skipper' of *Enterprise*. *Hornet's* Air Group was reformed to replace the losses at Midway and was officially designated Air Group 8. Her new torpedo squadron was VT-6, reformed around the few survivors left from the squadron's Midway experience while on *Enterprise*. 'Torpedo Six' was equipped with the new TBF-1 Grumman Avenger—so named to avenge the torpedo squadron losses at Midway.

New radar was installed and, after the completion of her upkeep and training period, she departed on 17 August to participate in the Solomon Islands Campaign.

The latter part of 1942 was a hectic period for the U.S. forces in the South Pacific. The Marines had invaded Guadalcanal 7 August and for the next six months the major efforts of the Pacific War by both sides would be in the Solomons area. At times it appeared the Marines would be pushed into the sea and the Navy was to lose 24 ships in the numerous

Damage to Hornet's *funnel and signal bridge moments after the Val smashed into it.* (Photo: U.S. Navy)

Destroyer Russell *alongside damaged* Hornet, *assisting in fire-fighting and removing injured and surplus personnel.* (Photo: U.S. Navy)

Heavy cruiser Northampton *attempting to get tow line aboard* Hornet *as a destroyer stands by.* Hornet *has fires under control, holed flight deck and is holding an eight degree list. A third torpedo and several more bombs, later in the afternoon, would seal her fate, however. She sunk early the next morning.* (Photo: U.S. Navy)

New Hornet (CV-12) *of the* Essex *class carries on for her namesake. Launched 30 August 1943 and commissioned 29 November 1943, she became part of the fast carrier attack force that swept across the Pacific in 1944-45. Ammunition ship* Lassen *alongside.*

(Photo: U.S. Navy)

battles fought over 'King Solomon's Isles'. *Hornet* was to be one of those ships.

Hornet again played the ferry role by carrying Marine F4Fs for delivery to Henderson Field in Guadalcanal. After this chore was completed, she joined the task groups of *Wasp* and *Saratoga* patrolling west of the Solomons on 29 August. On 31 August *Saratoga* was forced out of the war for a second time by a torpedo from a Japanese submarine. On 15 September *Hornet* and *Wasp* were supporting a convoy with reinforcements for Guadalcanal, when *Wasp* was hit by three torpedoes fired by Japanese *Submarine 1-19*. Damage by fire and explosion was extensive and she had to be abandoned and sunk by her own destroyers. *Hornet* recovered *Wasp's* airborne aircraft: she now was the only operational attack carrier left in the Pacific. *Enterprise* had been damaged by dive bombers earlier in August.

Her supplies exhausted, *Hornet* retired to Noumea, New Caledonia, arriving 26 September. She departed Noumea on 2 October on a mission that was to take her up the dreaded 'Slot' through the Solomon chain to hit airfield and shipping targets in the vicinity of the Shortland and Bougainville Islands. With an escort of four cruisers and six destroyers, Admiral Murray took his force up the slot on the night of 4 October. On the morning of 5 October *Hornet's* aircraft attacked shipping and airfields in the Bougainville area. Several cargo ships were sunk and the Japanese dispersed their shipping for the next few weeks.

On 16 October *Hornet's* aircraft hit the Japanese float-plane base at Rekata Bay where they fired two transports, sunk 12 float-planes and shot up the base. Her Air Group then spent the rest of the day attacking Japanese positions on Guadalcanal while Navy Seabees worked frantically to get Henderson Field operational again. In ten months of flight deck operations *Hornet* had registered 6619 landings by 15 October 1942.

THE BATTLE OF THE SANTA CRUZ ISLANDS

Hornet went back to the task of providing distant cover for the supply line of ships running into Guadalcanal. On 18 October she was once again joined by *Enterprise*. *Hornet* celebrated her first birthday on 20 October and the crew was treated to roast chicken, potatoes and cake—a welcome relief from the block beef and dumplings that had been their fare for two months.

On 24 October *Hornet* and *Enterprise* moved east of the Santa Cruz Islands to intercept the Japanese Combined Fleet steaming south to reinforce their land forces.

Task Force 61, under Rear Admiral Kinkaid, was comprised of *Enterprise*, one battleship, two cruisers, and eight destroyers. Task Force 17 under Rear Admiral Murray was comprised of *Hornet*, four cruisers and six destroyers. *Hornet's* Air Group was as follows:

Air Group 8, 1 TBF-1:		Cdr. Walter F. Rodee
VF-72	36 F4F-4	Lt. Cdr. Henry G. Sanchez
VB-8	18 SBD-3	Lt. James E. Vose
VS-8	18 SBD-3	Lt. Cdr. William J. Widhelm
VT-6	15 TBF-1	Lt. Edwin B. Parker, Jr.

The opposing Japanese Guadalcanal Supporting Force was comprised of four carriers, four battleships, ten cruisers, thirty destroyers and twelve submarines.

In the early morning of 26 October, *Hornet* launched two strikes toward the enemy carriers 200 miles away which had been reported at 0730 by *Enterprise* search planes, 15 SBDs, six TBFs and eight F4Fs and at 0815 nine SBDs, nine TBFs and seven F4Fs. Shortly after take-off, *Hornet's* planes informed her that they were passing a sizeable group of enemy planes heading her way. As the two air groups passed, each eyed the other, wondering who was going to have a flight deck to return to.

DIRECT HIT

At 0910 'Val' dive bombers and 'Kate' torpedo planes attacked the American ships through a curtain of F4Fs and anti-aircraft fire. *Hornet* took the first bomb hit of her short life on the starboard side of the flight deck aft and suffered two near misses off the starboard bow. At 0913 the Japanese squadron commander, his 'Val' damaged by a shell burst, crashed his plane into *Hornet*, glancing off the stack and through the flight deck. He was carrying one 500 pound and two 100 pound bombs. The first 100 pounder detonated on impact with the stack and signal bridge; the other went off as it passed through a ready room below the flight deck; the 500 pounder was a dud.

Next, two torpedoes exploded in the engineering spaces. Three more 500 pound bombs struck—one detonated on impact with the flight deck and two penetrated to the fourth deck before exploding. A 'Kate' made a suicide run at 0917 into the port forward gun gallery. *Hornet* lay dead in the water with an eight degree list to starboard; 25 of the estimated 27 planes that attacked her were lost. *Hornet's* aircraft managed to damage heavily the carrier *Shokaku* and cruiser *Chikuma* but those that returned had to recover on *Enterprise*.

Herculean efforts were underway aboard *Hornet* to save her. The fires and flooding were brought under control and efforts were made to get three boilers on the line. Cruiser *Northampton* made three attempts to take her in tow but additional Japanese raids frustrated these efforts. Over 800 excess personnel and 75 wounded were transferred to destroyers. At 1520 another six Japanese 'Kates' appeared and at 1523 *Hornet* took another torpedo on her starboard side. The list slowly increased to 18 degrees and at 1550 the order to abandon ship was passed. The accompanying destroyers took on survivors and the final count revealed 111 *Hornet* men killed and 108 wounded.

The decision was made to sink *Hornet*, as the Japanese force was bearing down fast from the north. Destroyers *Mustin* and *Anderson* took on the task. Nine more torpedo hits and nearly 300 rounds of 5-inch shells failed to sink her. By 2040 *Hornet* was ablaze throughout her whole length and the two destroyers headed south. At 2120 two Japanese destroyers, *Makigumo* and *Akigumo*, closed *Hornet* and fired four big 24-inch torpedoes into her.

At 0135 on 27 October Japanese sailors watched as *Hornet* sank in 2700 fathoms off the Santa Cruz Islands,

the last large carrier the United States would lose in World War II.

HORNET LIVES ON

Hornet was sunk but her name would haunt the Japanese again before the war was over. The U.S. Navy honoured her memory by naming two new *Essex* class carriers after her. USS *Hornet* (CV-12), commissioned in 1943, and USS *Shangri La* (CV-38), commissioned in 1944, were included in the large carrier task force that was to lead the victory drive across the Pacific. Both these carriers would return to the same shores where their namesake first entered the war by launching Jimmy Doolittle's B-25s against the island Empire.

Hornet's Progress

1. Loads Doolittle's B-25s and departs San Francisco, 2 April 1942.
2. *Hornet* Task Group rendezvous with Vice Admiral Halsey's *Enterprise* Task Group, 13 April 1942.
3. B-25s launched on Tokyo Raid, 18 April 1942.
4. *Hornet* and *Enterprise* rush to join *Lexington* and *Yorktown* but are too late to participate in the Battle of the Coral Sea, 8 May 1942.
5. *Hornet's* VT-8 and other carrier squadrons defeat Japanese carrier force in the Battle of Midway, 4 June 1942.
6. Upkeep and retraining in Pearl Harbor from 13 June to 17 August 1942.
7. After spending two months operating in the Solomons area *Hornet* is sunk 27 October 1942.

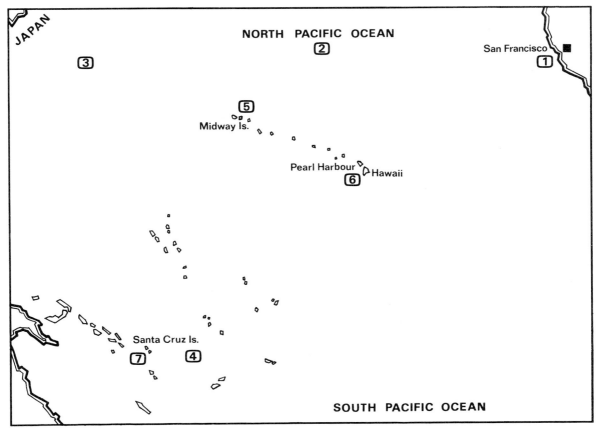

Hornet (*CV-8*) *just after commissioning before armament was added.* (Photo: U.S. Navy)

A port quarter view of Hornet (CV-8) showing flight deck overhang and large crane stowed in the small boat area. (Photo: U.S. Navy)

HORNET SPECIFICATIONS

Builder:	Newport News Shipbuilding and Dry Dock Co., Newport News, Virginia
Displacement:	19,800 tons—standard
Length:	809·5 ft—overall
	761 ft—waterline
Beam:	83 ft
Extreme width:	114 ft
Draft:	21·75 ft—mean
	29 ft—maximum
Height:	55 ft to flight deck
	103 ft to top of funnel
	143 ft to masthead
Machinery:	Nine Babcock & Wilcox Express boilers, driving Curtiss-Parsons geared turbines with total output 120,000 s.h.p. through four shafts.
Speed:	32-33 knots
Fuel:	7400 tons fuel oil
	187,000 gals of aviation gasoline
Complement:	160 officers, 1729 enlisted—peacetime
	306 officers, 2613 enlisted—wartime
Aircraft:	85-100
Aircraft type:	Wildcat, Dauntless, Avenger, Devastator
Armament (1942):	8 5-in/38 cal., single mounts
	16 1·1-in m.g. 4 quad mounts
	23 20mm m.g. single mounts
Armor:	4″ waterline belt girdling the machinery spaces amidships, 4″ on primary bulkheads, 3″ on the hangar deck, splinter protection around the vital spaces on the island and the gun mounts
Radar:	two of the latest SC type radar with antenna located on top of the two director control towers
Camouflage:	Entered service with standard dark gray battle paint. When she sailed for the war zone she was painted with an irregular wavy band of dull steel gray reaching from waterline to almost the level of the hangar deck in places. Irregular broad vertical bands of the same paint were painted at intervals on the island. This scheme remained until she was sunk.

TABLE OF YORKTOWN CLASS

As is often typical of class ships, where each is not necessarily built like the last, the three *Yorktown* class ships had differences. The greatest change was in *Hornet* which was built four years after her sisters and her design benefitted from their experience. The major external differences were: a wider flight deck (which *Enterprise* was to have later in her service) 114 feet compared to 109 feet in her sisterships, a different arrangement of her secondary armament, and an additional 100 tons in displacement.

	Yorktown (CV-5)	Enterprise (CV-6)	Hornet (CV-8)
Authorised:	Act of 16 June 1933	Act of 16 June, 1933	Act of 17 May, 1938
Builder:	Newport News	Newport News	Newport News
Laid down:	21 May 1934	16 July 1934	25 Sept 1939
Launched:	4 April 1936	30 Oct 1936	14 Dec 1940
Commissioned:	30 Sept 1937	12 May 1938	20 Oct 1941
First Commanding Officer:	Capt. E. D. McWhorten	Capt. N. H. Whiting, Jr.	Capt. M. A. Mitscher
Sponsor:	Mrs F. D. Roosevelt, wife of the President	Mrs C. A. Swanson, wife of the Sec. Navy	Mrs F. M. Knox, wife of the Sec. Navy
Battle Stars:	3	20	4
Final disposition:	Disabled by Japanese carrier aircraft on 4 June, torpedoed by *Submarine I.168* on 6 June. Sunk 6 June 1942	Decommissioned 17 Feb 1947. Sold to Lipsett Inc. 27 June 1958, arriving at Kearny, N.J. for scrapping 21 Aug 1958	Disabled by Japanese carrier aircraft 26 Oct torpedoed by destroyers *Mukigumo* and *Akigumo* on 27 Oct Sunk 27 Oct 1942

The Author wishes to express his gratitude and acknowledge the following:

United States Navy Department, Office of the Chief of Naval Operations, Naval History Division (OP-09B9)
The Imperial War Museum
The London Museum Library
The National Archives of the United States
Mr Edward H. Wiswesser for his ship drawings
Francis Rogers, Duke University, Durham, North Carolina.

Acknowledgements

Profile Publications Ltd. are grateful for the permission of the U.S. Navy, the U.S. Air Force and the Imperial War Museum to reproduce the photographs in this Profile.

Bibliography

DICTIONARY OF AMERICAN NAVAL FIGHTING SHIPS Office of the Chief of Naval Operations, Naval History Division, Department of the Navy.
DOOLITTLE'S TOKYO RAIDERS by Carroll V. Glines, Lt. Col., U.S.A.F., D. Van Nostrand Co., Inc.
EVOLUTION OF AIRCRAFT CARRIERS by Scot MacDonald, Office of the Chief of Naval Operations Department of the Navy.
THE FAST CARRIERS, THE FORGING OF AN AIR NAVY by Dr. Clark G. Reynolds, McGraw-Hill Book Co.
HISTORY OF UNITED STATES NAVAL OPERATIONS IN WORLD WAR II by Samuel Elliot Morrison, Rear Admiral U.S.N.R. (Ret), Little, Brown and Co.
A SHIP TO REMEMBER, THE SAGA OF THE HORNET by Alexander R. Griffin, Howell, Soskins Publishers.
U.S. NAVY DIVE AND TORPEDO BOMBERS by J. V. Mizrahi, Sentry Books.

Admiral Graf Spee at Montevideo after the battle. The hole from a direct hit on the port bow has been plated over by the ship's staff

KM ADMIRAL GRAF SPEE / Pocket Battleship

by Kapitän zur See Gerhard Bidlingmaier (Ret'd)

THE DESIGN CONCEPT OF THE PANZERSCHIFFE

When, in 1926, the German Navy could at last think of replacements for its long-since outmoded ships of the line, the Navy was limited under the Versailles Treaty to a mere 10,000 tons displacement and a maximum calibre of 28 cm. In such circumstances how could one build a 'battleship', when the Washington Agreement (1922) permitted maximum figures for this type, under the same headings, of 35,000 tons and 40·6 cm.? At first sight it seemed that nothing more than an armoured coastal patrol vessel could be considered. Soon, however, a better idea gained acceptance: the new ship was to be, '*stronger than anything faster and faster than anything stronger*'.

Panzerschiffe 'A': a political ship

The adoption of this building target had the immediate effect of devaluing the widely popular Washington cruiser, which was outclassed both in fire-power and strength of armour by Panzerschiffe 'A', as the first replacement was initially named in the Budget. The

efforts made by the Washington Powers to try to prevent Germany building these ships were therefore understandable. Indeed Germany would have been prepared, so a communication of the German Admiralty (Document AI a VI) dated 25 January 1930 asserts, to abandon the Panzerschiffe in the interests of world peace, but in return demanded admission to the circle of signatory powers as an equal member, where it would have been content to accept the ratio of approximately 1·25. This would have been tantamount to a revision of those clauses of the Versailles Treaty applicable to the Navy.

The Washington Powers could not agree to this proposition. Whereas the Anglo-Saxon Powers were inclined to make certain advances to the Reich, France was strictly opposed to any concession. Since the Panzerschiffe infringed none of the provisions of the Versailles Treaty, the Washington Powers had to accept its construction. Only France sought to restore the balance by having recourse to her permitted battleship tonnage and building two ships of the *Dunkerque* class, each of 26,500 tons, which she armed with eight 33 cm. and sixteen 13 cm. guns, a consider-

Launch of the pocket battleship Admiral Graf Spee *on 30 June 1934, at the Naval Yard, Wilhelmshaven.*

The Admiral Graf Spee, *after commissioning (6 Jan 1936), on her trials in the North Sea.*

able number of lighter guns, and equipped with a catapult and four aircraft; these battleships had a speed of 30 knots. At the London Conference of 1930, France also opposed a five-year extension of the pause in battleship building as well as a limitation on cruiser tonnage, in both cases on account of the German *Panzerschiffe.*

Significant dates for the Panzerschiffe class

This is how the half-derided, half-feared 'pocket battleships' came into being:
Deutschland laid down 5 February 1929, launched 19 May 1931, commissioned 1 April 1933.
Admiral Scheer laid down 25 June 1931, launched 1 April 1933, commissioned 12 November 1934.

Admiral Graf Spee[1] laid down 1 October 1932, launched 30 June 1934, commissioned 6 January 1936.

The *Deutschland* was built in the Deutsche Werke at Kiel; the other two were produced in the Naval Yard at Wilhelmshaven.

Armament

Their armament consisted of six 28 cm. guns arranged in two turrets, eight 15 cm. guns individually mounted,

---

[1] On 15 September 1917 the *Admiral Graf Spee* (35, 300 tons) had already been launched as a battle-cruiser of the *Mackensen* Class, but her construction was halted shortly after the launching. For simplicity, however, we propose to use from this point the shorter name *Graf Spee* for the pocket battleship; in any case this is normal practice in the German Navy.

The Admiral Graf Spee *secured to a buoy in Kiel Harbour; forecastle and ship's coat-of-arms.*

six 10·5 cm.[2] and eight 3·7 cm. anti-aircraft guns, together with eight 53·3 cm. deck-mounted torpedo tubes in two sets; finally, two seaplanes and an aircraft catapult completed the ship's armament—up to 1939 the planes were Heinkel He-60 biplanes and subsequently Arado Ar-196 monoplanes. The *Admiral Scheer* and *Admiral Graf Spee* initially carried, abreast the second port 15 cm. quick-firing gun, a canvas landing mat which could be swung outboard to pick up the aircraft (see page 77). Both ships were also fitted with active roll-damping equipment. The general design principles mentioned earlier were achieved by savings in weight resulting from the use of welding instead of rivetting, the extensive application of light metals and similar methods but, above all, by fitting a completely unorthodox main engine and propulsion equipment.

MACHINERY:
Revolutionary Design

The main propulsion equipment consisted of eight double-acting 9-cylinder two-stroke Diesels produced by the Maschinenfabrik Augsburg-Nürnberg, delivering 56,000 hp via two Vulcan reduction gearboxes and two shafts, and giving the ships a maximum speed of 26 knots; in fact, the *Graf Spee* attained 28·5 knots on her trials. Of the more powerful ships, only battle-cruisers could have been faster and therefore dangerous; but the only two then in existence belonged to the Royal Navy and, in the strategic thinking of the German Admiralty at that time, did not figure as potential enemies.

The advantages of Diesel engines

Diesel engines were more quickly operational, less demanding of manpower and space than steam turbines and, thanks to their economic fuel consumption, increased the operational range to 20,000 nautical miles at a cruising speed of 18 knots, roughly three times that of steam-driven vessels.

Tactical benefits were also linked with this operational advantage. Motor-driven vessels do not normally make smoke that might betray their presence at long range; moreover they can accelerate to maximum speed almost immediately and in any case in a much shorter time than any steamship. In this way, even if they encountered cruisers, the Panzerschiffe were assured of a margin of speed for up to fifteen minutes and therefore of freedom of decision. A further point was that, with Diesels, the steam hazard in battle was avoided.

Armour and Underwater Protection

The *armour-plate* was set at an angle to the sides of the hull, thus increasing the degree of protection. This effect was supplemented by 20 mm. thick longitudinal bulkheads between the armoured and upper decks. The protection below the waterline, a torpedo bulkhead, also arranged at an angle, reached as far as the inner bottom in the case of the first two ships.

² The *Deutschland* and the *Admiral Scheer* were equipped with this calibre only in the autumn of 1939, having previously been fitted with 8·8 cm. anti-aircraft guns.

Foretop of the Admiral Graf Spee *in its original form. One distinguishing feature, as compared with the* Admiral Scheer, *is the short support legs for the mast abaft the funnel, reminiscent of a tripod mast.*

SPECIAL FEATURES OF THE ADMIRAL GRAF SPEE

Armour Plate

The *Graf Spee* had more protection than her sister-ships in that the hull was plated with armour (60–80 mm.) one deck higher and the torpedo bulkhead (40 mm.) extended to the shell plating. The deck armour-plating was 45 mm. thick, that of the heavy-gun turrets 85 to 140 mm. and of the control tower 150 mm. thick.

Radar

The *Graf Spee* was the first German warship to be fitted with radar in 1938 (then known as '*De Te-Gerät*' = 'Deutsches Technisches Gerät' = 'German Technical Equipment'). Though it could determine the range of a target, direction was, however, very inaccurate. Though for this reason unsuitable for fire control, the radar was nevertheless of considerable use at night and in poor visibility. During the Spanish Civil War its effective range was increased from 5 to 15 km. The aerial array, popularly known as the 'mattress' among seamen on account of its shape

Unlike the Admiral Scheer, *the* Admiral Graf Spee *had from the start heavy cargo-loading gear on both sides abaft the funnel.*

a spar mast mounted aft of her tower mast and, in addition, short support legs for the mainmast and always two large cargo derricks aft of the funnel (see pages 78 and 79).

When the tower mast was modified in 1938, the two searchlight platforms were removed from the side and replaced by a single platform on the forward face (see page 75).

PANZERSCHIFF ADMIRAL GRAF SPEE

Armament: six 28 cm. quick-firing guns L/54·5, in twin-turrets; eight 15 cm. quick-firing guns L/55, singly mounted, with armoured shields; six 10·5 cm. anti-aircraft guns; eight torpedo tubes, calibre 53·3 cm., in two sets, one aircraft catapult and facilities for housing two aircraft (up to 1939, He-60; after that, Ar-196).

Engines: eight double-acting 9-cylinder Diesels, manufactured by Maschinenfabrik Augsburg-Nürnberg, 56,000 h.p.; four electric generating sets, with a total capacity of 3,360 kW at 220 V; two Vulcan gear sets, two shafts, one rudder.

(see page 87), was fitted to the revolving cupola on the foremast and coupled to the optical range-finder. A further installation, peculiar to this ship, consisted of a radio-monitoring unit that constantly swept the horizon and indicated any transmission, enabling it to be intercepted.

The Ship's Company

The crew consisted of 44 officers and 1080 petty-officers and men; included among them, in addition to the flying personnel, was a radio monitoring and decoding group and also, as Naval Reserve officers, a few officers of the Merchant Marine provided to take command of prize-crews. The ship served as Fleet Flagship from 1936 to 1938 and attended the Coronation Review at Spithead in 1937, in addition to being repeatedly in service in Spanish waters.

Identification

The *Graf Spee* could easily be confused with the *Admiral Scheer*, but differed from her sister-ship in having

ADMIRAL GRAF SPEE IN THE SOUTH ATLANTIC

At the outbreak of the war Hitler ordered the German Navy to engage in '*a trade war on the shipping lanes, with the main weight directed against England*'. To achieve sudden and repeated successes immediately in the Atlantic while tension was mounting, the Naval Staff has already dispatched the pocket battleships *Deutschland* and *Graf Spee* to their operational areas. They had orders to do all in their .power to disrupt the enemy's sea communications: in this they were to observe strictly the prize regulations, i.e. stop and search every ship and—in the event of seizure—to ensure the safety of the crew; battle with enemy naval forces, even if inferior, was to be avoided and the pocket battleships were to change their area of operation at frequent intervals.

This was the lesson that Raeder had learned from the naval raids on merchant shipping in the First World War; in those days almost all cruiser captains

The Graf Spee *after launching, in the fitting-out basin in Wilhelmshaven naval dockyard. First the heavy gun-turrets are fitted*

had had very little thought for anything other than military trials of strength which consequently contributed to the premature curtailment of their operations, just as the Commander of the Far Eastern Squadron, Admiral Graf von Spee, had done.

The purpose of this early deployment was not realized, because Hitler did not give the final word to bring his pocket battleships into action: he hoped it would be possible to negotiate peace with the Western Powers after a speedy overthrow of Poland.

The Graf Spee *in the fitting-out basin. Now the medium guns are already in position and funnel and tower-mast are erected.*

OUTWARD BOUND: PREPARING FOR WAR

The *Graf Spee* sailed on the evening of 21 August 1939 from Wilhelmshaven under the command of Captain Hans Langsdorff and on 1 September the German Naval Staff achieved a successful rendezvous between their battleship and its supply ship, the *Altmark*, south-west of the Canaries. To lighten his ship, while Langsdorff awaited his operational orders, he transferred superfluous equipment, such as riding and stern booms, heavy boats, canvas landing-mat, etc., to the *Altmark*, together with unnecessary items, inflammable paints and the like. He also gave two of his 20 mm. anti-aircraft guns to the *Altmark*, so that only eight were still left aboard the *Graf Spee*. At the same time he had the lighter boats so stowed that he could, depending on weather conditions, send out a boat from either side of the ship.

The waiting period was not without incident. On 11 September the battleship was preparing to transfer provisions from the *Altmark* (see page 86). As a security measure the ship's plane was launched. Very soon the observer spotted a fast naval vessel just altering course and heading directly for the *Graf Spee*. Immediately he flew back, gave visual warning and had his plane shipped aboard. Thus Langsdorff succeeded in evading his opponent, *HMS Cumberland*, by slipping off at high speed.

The tower-mast after the 1938 refit: above the optical range-finder rises the revolving canopy for the radar equipment, the flat surface on the front being provided for the aerial array; in place of the two searchlights at the sides, only one is now attached on the forward face. Over the barrels of the gun-turret the armoured fighting bridge can be discerned; above the 15-cm gun to the right of the gangway, the canvas landing-mat for the ship's aircraft.

The tower-mast in its original form: on each side a searchlight, the Admiral's bridge below, and beneath that the peace-time navigating bridge and wheelhouse.

The Graf Spee *differed from her sister-ship the* Admiral Scheer *in having, behind the tower-mast, a pole-mast rising from the signal-deck level (the* Scheer *only had a short pole-mast on the foretop gallery), and further in having her mainmast supported by short support-legs to the funnel. The conspicuous tower-mast was completely rebuilt on the* Scheer *in the light of the* Graf Spee's *experience.*

The Arado seaplane returning from a reconnaissance flight—Courtesy, Sir Eugen Millington-Drake, K.C.M.G.

THE FIRST DAYS OF WAR

When, on 26 September, the pocket battleships finally received permission to begin operations, as a result of Raeder's insistence, the *Graf Spee* was experiencing her first problems. In the first place, the engines were getting dangerously close to the total of running-hours at which regulations laid down dockyard overhaul. How long could the ship's engineers manage to keep the machinery in good running order after the expiry of this period, simply with the means available on board? Another worry was the shortage of carbon dioxide and Arctic oil for the refrigeration plant, which prohibited a prolonged stay in tropical waters.[3]

THE FIRST SUCCESS

On 30 September a steamship was sighted at 1300. Soon however, she altered course while still 14 miles distant. Langsdorff launched his plane which halted the ship but, armed with only one machine-gun, could not prevent the latter sending out the alarm. Langsdorff had the Master and Chief-Engineer brought aboard, sent a radio message to the Pernambuco station to ensure the safety of the rest of the crew, who had taken to the boats, and sank the ship, the British SS *Clement* (see page 83). In accordance with Admiralty instructions, the British captain had destroyed all important papers. Moreover, his behaviour in other respects, as his interrogation showed, corresponded strictly to Admiralty orders. These required British ships, if stopped by a warship, to transmit by radio as long as possible without any regard to orders to the contrary. This would force the raider to fire on them, giving the crew an excuse to take to the boats which was calculated to delay the search of the vessel. The use of the prize as a supply ship was to be prevented by putting the engines out of action. In future, therefore, *Graf Spee* would have to approach her victims as far as possible unrecognized, so that this procedure would not be effective.

When the British Admiralty heard of the *Clement's* fate, a warning was immediately issued to merchant

---

[3] The Naval Staff saw to it that supplies did get through.

Round the Cape of Good Hope Langsdorff picked up the scent of very little traffic so long as the Mediterranean represented a safe route from Gibraltar to Suez. So he pressed on to the waters off Pernambuco, leaving the *Altmark* behind in the waiting zone. On the eve of his first success, the Naval Operations Staff reminded Langsdorff that he must avoid fully committing his ship.

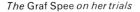
The Graf Spee *on her trials*

shipping and counter-measures introduced. The Admiralty did not exclude the possibility that the raider was a pocket-battleship, but only received confirmation of the fact when the *Clement's* crew reached a South American port on 1 October. Thereupon, in agreement with the French Ministry of Marine, the Admiralty distributed eight hunter groups in the Atlantic on 5 October and authorized the Commander-in-Chief, South Atlantic, Vice-Admiral G. H. d'Oyly Lyon, to retain four destroyers that he was due to detach to the Home Fleet.

SUCCESSFUL STRATAGEM

Langsdorff now turned his attention to the Cape route. While sailing to this area, he painted the for'd and side walls of his tower-mast a light colour and their edges dark, to give the impression of a tripod mast (see page 86).

At 0700 on 5 October a steamship hove into view over the horizon. The Captain set his approach course to ensure that he only presented his bows to the steamship's view. At a distance of 1950 yards he ran up signals calling on her to heave-to and imposing radio silence. The steamship, the *Newton Beech*, transmitted in spite of this, but very weakly. The prize-crew were just in time to prevent the destruction of a secret instruction in the radio-room. The Master had destroyed all other papers. He had interpreted the 'tripod mast' as belonging to a French ship and spotted the deception only when the *Graf Spee* swung to. The warship's captain wanted to use the steamship for housing the prisoners, and handed her over to a prize-crew.

The captured secret instruction was used henceforth to transmit bogus alarm calls, for which purpose Langsdorff also commandeered the prize's Marconi transmitter. He also discovered that each British ship had its own prescribed route laid down.

A further point of difference: in contrast to the Admiral Scheer, *the* Graf Spee *had heavy loading gear on both sides (the* Scheer *only on the port side).*

TWO FAVOURABLE OPPORTUNITIES MISSED BY THE BRITISH

The *Newton Beech's* SOS had been picked up by only one ship. Shortly after, she encountered the *Cumberland* and informed her. Because the distress call had not been an RRR, the cruiser decided against breaking radio silence, believing that the alarm must have reached the Commander-in-Chief. Four days later, *Ark Royal's* aircraft sighted a ship stopped west of Cape Verde, who claimed to be the American steamship

The Graf Spee *in Kiel Harbour; behind the funnel can be seen the wings of the ship's aircraft, an* He-60 ; *just before she slipped out into the Atlantic, the* Graf Spee *received urgent delivery of the first* Ar-196, *a monoplane.*

The Graf Spee, *like her sister-ships, had good sea-going qualities, riding easily and having excellent manoeuvrability; when heading into the sea, however, she was too wet. This latter drawback was to a large extent remedied on the* Admiral Scheer *by appropriate modifications to the bow section.*

Delmar. The aircraft-carrier was steaming without destroyer escort, so she refrained closing the vessel to investigate. Only when it was too late was it learned that the real *Delmar* was lying at New Orleans that day.

Two more successful deceptions with the 'tripod mast'

Against his next victim, sighted at 0825 on 7 October, Langsdorff used the same procedure. This time the radio-room was seized before the alarm had been sent out: the Master had assumed he was dealing with a French vessel. Langsdorff seized important provisions and stores, transferred the crew to the *Newton Beech* and sank the ship, the *Ashlea* (see page 86).

A logbook that had been discovered, containing large numbers of ships' positions, strengthened Langsdorff in his belief that, after each success, he must seek another area because no two ships would follow the same course. Hence he found it particularly frustrating that a crack had formed in the cylinder-block of the ship's aircraft and that he must forgo aerial reconnaissance until the spare engine had been fitted. Now, and again later, the price had to be paid for equipping the *Graf Spee* with the first Ar-196 off the production-line before adequate testing had been completed. It not only suffered from teething troubles but also proved less suitable for reconnaissance purposes than the slower He-60. Langsdorff also found himself held

up by the slow *Newton Beech* and her poor coal. So, on 8 October, he transferred the prisoners to his own ship and sank the prize.

On 10 October the *Graf Spee* seized the British steamship *Huntsman*, who only sent out a distress call at the last minute, because her Master had assumed a French warship. The battleship captain could not sink the ship immediately because the 84-strong crew could not be accommodated aboard his own vessel. He sent the prize off two days later to wait at a pre-arranged rendezvous.

The last three successes were scored in the area to the north of St. Helena. Langsdorff anticipated counter-measures and left this area. He announced his successes to the Naval Operations Staff and his intention to rejoin the *Altmark*. He also reported his evaluation of the captured secret documents and closed with the hint that the strong security measures to be expected from now on at the junctions of the main sea-lanes might require his ship to be fully committed. With this part of his report he wanted, as his war-diary states, to urge the Naval Operations Staff to relax the restrictions—*no full commitment*—if greater successes were desired.

Rendevous with Altmark

Delighted, Langsdorff received the report on 12 October that his plane was once more airworthy. In the morning of 15 October he rejoined his supply-ship, not without giving the *Altmark* captain a fright: he too mistook the pocket battleship for a French warship. The *Graf Spee* refuelled and the *Altmark* was made ready to accommodate the prisoners. By transferring the prisoners, Langsdorff thought to insure the captain of the *Altmark*, should his ship be detected by an enemy warship, against being sunk without the crew being saved.

Meanwhile the two ships set course for the rendezvous with the *Huntsman*, and found the prize during the morning of 16 October. Two days were spent transferring quantities of raw materials from the *Huntsman*, and all the prisoners to the *Altmark*, before the prize was sunk on the evening of 17 October. A captured code enabled them to decipher every radio message from the British Admiralty to its merchant shipping. The engineer personnel had meanwhile carried out an engine overhaul.

The Graf Spee *and, behind, the pocket battleships* Admiral Scheer *and* Deutschland, *together with three small cruisers, in Kiel Harbour firing a salute to Hitler (1936)*

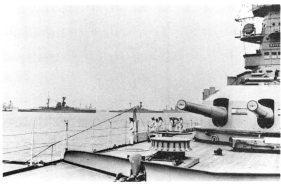

The Graf Spee *at the Coronation Review at Spithead* (*1937*).

The Graf Spee *at Spithead in 1937.*

DELIBERATIONS OF THE CAPTAIN AND THE NAVAL OPERATIONS STAFF

To reach a decision as to his best course of action, Langsdorff relied on the details of the distribution of enemy naval forces as supplied to him three days before by the Naval Operations Staff. So long as he was not permitted fully to commit his ship, he considered convoys to be '*one hundred per cent safe*' under the protection of these forces. At heart, he rebelled against the fundamental order that forbade him to commit the full fighting potential of his ship. Since the sinking of the *Clement* he reckoned on busier traffic round the Cape, especially as *Huntsman*, out from Calcutta, had only been diverted round the Cape from Suez. He therefore decided to make for the Cape route and, if necessary, to slip away into the Indian Ocean. How closely this line of thinking matched the conclusions of the Naval Operations Staff is shown by an order dated 22 October, in which they directed Langsdorff to move into the Indian Ocean as soon as the concentration of enemy forces made commerce-raiding impossible without full commitment of his ship.

MEAGRE SUCCESS AND HIGH RISKS OFF WALVIS BAY

On 19 October Langsdorff learned from Berlin that a French task force had joined up with a British unit off the West Coast of Africa. Nevertheless, he held course and on 22 October was off Walvis Bay. In the morning the ship's plane sighted a ship. Only when, at 1420 the *Graf Spee* swung away at a distance of 350 yards, did the ship put out a distress call; the radio operator remained undeterred by fire from the 20 mm. guns, but the position given was not clear and the name was missing. Langsdorff had sunk the MV *Trevanion*.

The next morning Simonstown called on all ships that had picked up a distress call from an unknown ship to repeat the call. Two repetitions were given, but with different positions, neither of them correct. One of them corresponded to the pocket battleship's position at that moment. The *Graf Spee* therefore ran at full speed westwards. It was indeed high time, for the Commander-in-Chief of the South Atlantic Station had already thrown all his forces into the hunt. These included, among others, an aircraft-carrier, HMS *Renown* and the *Strasbourg*, whom France had built specifically to be able to bombard the relatively slow-moving pocket battleship with her heavier armament,

without coming within range of the German guns.

On the afternoon of 24 October the Senior Naval Officer, Simonstown, issued a U-boat alarm, timed 1130, for a position where the *Graf Spee* had been at that time. Obviously it was based on a mistaken observation, but came at an opportune moment for the Captain; the hunting zeal of his pursuers would be damped by the U-boat danger.

ADMIRAL GRAF SPEE IN THE INDIAN OCEAN

On 28 October, revictualling was being completed from the *Altmark*, west of the Cape of Good Hope. Since the sinking of the *Trevanion*, the radio monitoring section had noted signs of anxiety and a considerable increase of wireless traffic among the enemy. To intensify this, Langsdorff now considered it appropriate to put in an appearance south of Madagascar. In this way he also hoped to mask his intention of returning to his home base, for the dockyard overhaul of his main engines could not be postponed beyond the end of January. His ship had now covered almost 30,000 miles, equal to nearly one and a half times the circumference of the earth !

The *Altmark* was directed to a waiting zone south-west of the Cape of Good Hope and, at midnight on 28/29 October, the *Graf Spee* set out on her voyage eastwards. On the following day the engine overhaul,

The Graf Spee *after her tower-mast was rebuilt (1938): above the optical rangefinder can be seen the aerial array of the radar apparatus, disguised by a sail-cloth cover. The photograph must have been taken shortly before she slipped out into the North Atlantic, for the Arado Ar-196 is already on board.*

The Captain of the Graf Spee, *Kapitän zur See Hans Langsdorff, born 20 March 1894 in Bergen auf Rügen, entered the Imperial Navy on 1 April 1912.*

The Captain addresses the crew at the outbreak of war.

The Altmark, *the* Graf Spee's *supply ship, disguised as a Norwegian vessel.*

begun on 24 October, was completed. Soon they ran into bad weather, which hardly hindered them at first, as the wind was blowing from astern. However, in this new area the weather did not permit any searching of steamships sighted. For two days the pocket battle-ship was forced to heave to and then the subsequent swell prohibited the use of the plane.

When flying-off was again possible, the flight produced no reconnaissance results but, on alighting on the water, cracks appeared in the seaplane's cylinder-block. So the plane was out of action once more; for good, in fact, as a worried Langsdorff thought, because no other spare engine was now available. Two days later Langsdorff tried his luck on the shipping lanes from India, which skirt Madagascar to the east. Again in vain. So he pushed on into the Mozam-bique Straits; as an extreme measure he contemplated attacks on the South African coastline. Since the flying personnel had in the meantime sealed the crack in the cylinder-block with a metallic sealing compound and strapped it tight with a steel band, he even weighed the pros and cons of a bombing-raid on the oil-tank installations at Durban, as a final mission for his aircraft.

Early on the morning of 14 November the *Graf Spee* lay north-east of Lourenço Marques. But it was only after nightfall that she sighted a small Dutch coaster; but even then weather conditions did not permit any search to be carried out. At last, at about noon on 15 November, *Graf Spee* sank the British motor tanker, *Africa Shell;* while the crew were able to row ashore (7 miles), Langsdorff took the Master on board as a prisoner. Even before the small tanker had sunk, the Japanese steamship *Tihuku Maru* came into sight. Without stopping her, the *Graf Spee* ran on an apparent north-easterly course out of sight of land.

The Captain was not satisfied with such an insigni-ficant result, but considered he had achieved his purpose of sowing alarm in the Indian Ocean. He soon had confirmation of this view when, on 16 November, the Senior Naval Officer, Durban, issued a warning of a 'German raider'. Langsdorff reported this success, and his intention of rejoining the *Altmark*, to the Naval Operations Staff. He concluded this report with detailed arguments in support of a renewed plea for relaxation of the burdensome restrictions placed upon him.

After weathering a heavy storm for days, the *Graf Spee* rejoined the *Altmark* and carried out an engine overhaul from 23 to 30 November.

ADMIRAL GRAF SPEE BACK IN THE SOUTH ATLANTIC

The *Graf Spee* had returned to the Atlantic just in time. After the disappearance of the *Trevanion*, nothing more had happened there. The British Admiralty did not exclude the possibility that the alarm had been simulated by a German auxiliary and therefore hoped that no pocket battleship was still away from base. The sinking of the *Africa Shell* corrected that miscon-ception. So Force H and Force K received the order to intercept the *Graf Spee*; between 27 November and 2 December they were cruising south of Cape Town. But by then, as reported, the pocket battleship was with its supply ship far to the west.

Refuelling from the Altmark.

Revictualling from the Altmark.

During the period while taking on provisions, Langsdorff had erected on the forecastle a raised dummy second gun-turret, and on the superstructure deck an extra funnel, to give his ship a silhouette close to that of an enemy cruiser (see pages 86 and 88).

VITAL DECISION: CHANGE OF POLICY

On 24 November the Captain called the junior officers together. He revealed to them that the ship must return to her home base for an engine overhaul; in contrast to his tactics to date, he would not try to evade enemy forces, but—committing his ship fully—'take with him' anything that came along. With this Langsdorff had released himself, on his own authority, from the order forbidding him to commit his ship fully. In his war diary the reasons for this decision are set out in full detail. He was convinced that, with his heavy armament, he would, at the least, so damage any opponent except the *Renown*, that such a vessel would be eliminated as a shadower. Hitherto, nevertheless, it had been right to avoid battle, because even insignificant hits might have forced the *Graf Spee* to give up her commerce raiding. But this reason lost its validity now that the ship was on course for home. In fact, in his opinion, it was essential to score an objectively outstanding success before the *Graf Spee* left the South Atlantic, because it was uncertain whether or when a second commerce raider would be able to operate in the area.

SUCCESSES ON THE CAPE ROUTE

On 30 November the *Graf Spee* was out on the hunt once more. On 1 December the ship's plane took off, admittedly without result, but at least the patched-up cylinder-block held! At noon the following day, after its second take-off, the plane had flown off due south-west, when the foretop lookout sighted smoke at over 28 miles to the northward. At high speed the battleship set course in that direction. As masts and a funnel came up over the horizon, those in *Graf Spee* were surprised that there was still no sight or sound of the ship's plane, which should have been back by now. Breaking with his tactics to date, Langsdorff stopped the ship by firing shots across its bows from a range of 14 miles. Did he wish to speed up the capture out of anxiety over the fate of his air crew, or was he aiming to bring about contact with the enemy?

His behaviour allowed the stopped ship, the *Doric Star*, to send out repeatedly an RRR distress call with

The first prize, the British steamship Clement.

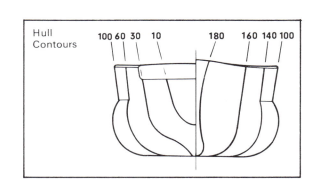

Hull Contours

100 60 30 10   180 160 140 100

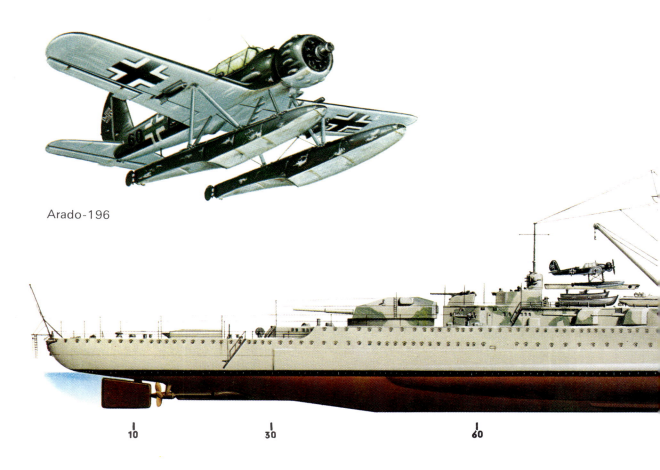

Arado-196

10   30   60

5 10   25   50   75   100

FEET

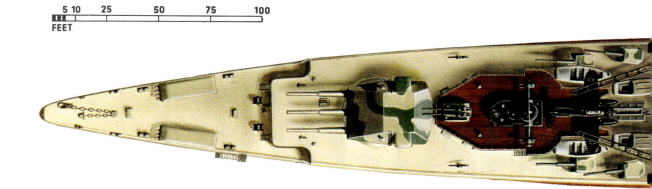

KM Admiral Graf Spee/Pocket Battleship 1932-1939

Admiral Graf Spee as she appeared during the last days of her commerce-raiding in the South Atlantic. The false high-speed bow and midship waves were painted to deceive an enemy's first-sighting estimation of speed.

The Arado-196 spotter reconnaissance sea-plane was the first machine of the type and consequently suffered many teething troubles.

The ship's crest was that of the von Spee family, Admiral von Spee being the victor of The Battle of Coronel, twenty-five years earlier.

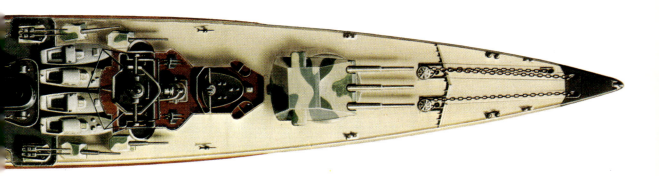

To deceive possible victims, the Captain had had the tower-mast painted in such a way that, at a distance, it looked like a tripod-mast

the addition of '*battleship*'. This call was repeated in rapid succession by six ships, one of them a warship, and now there came an SOS from the ship's plane. For the sake of its cargo Langsdorff would gladly have taken the ship with him, but he was forced to sink her because the Chief Engineer had put the engines out of action. After the crew had been transferred on board and the prize sunk, the battleship steered towards the plane's signals thereby reaching the aircraft just in time. The aircrew had not heard the ship's message about the change of course and so had not found their way back on reaching the end of their sortie. Lacking the smoother water in the lee of their ship, they landed hard in rough seas. As a result the port float sprang a leak and slowly filled. Consequently the machine swung across wind, the waves breaking higher and higher over the port wing. Meanwhile the aircrew had discovered a fault in the accumulator, which explained why they had heard nothing from the *Graf Spee*. They switched on their emergency transmitter and sent out homing signals. In the gathering dusk they fired white Verey lights which were sighted from the *Graf Spee*.

During the night, the pocket battleship steamed steadily SW and sighted a steamship at first light. She hove to but transmitted in spite of orders not to do so. She was the *Tairoa* and was sunk after the crew had been transferred. About noon on 6 December the *Graf Spee* made contact with her supply ship and handed over 140 prisoners, Langsdorff retaining on board his own ship only the officers and radio operators.

MEASURES TAKEN BY THE BRITISH

When news of the sinking of the *Doric Star* was received, the Commander-in-Chief, South Atlantic, halted the hunt south of Cape Town and allocated fresh search areas to his forces. Commodore Henry Harwood, in command of the South American Division, concluded, from the fact that the *Graf Spee* had steamed 170 miles SW between the sinkings of the *Doric Star* and the *Tairoa*, that the next target of the commerce raider would be the South American coast: she should be off Rio de Janeiro by 12 December, off the River Plate by about 13 December and in the Falklands area on 14 December. In the event, it was mere chance that actually brought the *Graf Spee* off the Plate, but more of that later.

As the Commodore considered this area the most important, he concentrated his effective forces, HMS *Exeter*, HMS *Ajax* (flagship) and HMNZS *Achilles*, off the Plate estuary and issued the following instructions:

'*My policy, with three cruisers in company versus one pocket battleship. Attack at once by day or night. By day act as two units, 1st Division (Ajax and Achilles) and Exeter diverged to permit flank marking. First Division will concentrate gunfire . . .*' He practised this procedure with his formation on the eve of the battle.

THE LAST SUCCESS

The *Altmark* was given a new rendezvous and the *Graf Spee* set course westwards. On the evening of 7 December her last victim crossed her path, the British freighter *Streonshalh*. Her Master was in doubt up to the last moment whether he had an enemy vessel before him. When the pocket battleship turned up into the wind he would not allow any radio transmission, to avoid endangering lives unnecessarily. Langsdorff transferred the crew and sank the freighter. Of the two bags of secret documents which the Master had thrown overboard, the prize-crew managed to salvage one. It gave information regarding focal points to which ships were to head.

The Ashlea *goes down.*

Dummy guns are constructed.

The tower-mast has its painted disguise renewed. Note the radar 'mattress' aerial.

The Ar-196 *is taken aboard after a reconnaissance flight* (*for lack of an original photograph, the author has chosen one of the* Admiral Scheer).

HMS Ajax, *flagship, flying Commodore Harwood's broad pendant—Courtesy, Sir Eugen Millington-Drake, K.C.M.G.*

Commodore Harwood, on taking command of the South American Station in 1936; a photograph supplied by Lady Harwood—Courtesy, Sir Eugen Millington-Drake, K.C.M.G.

Commodore Harwood's original rough diagram on a signal pad of his plan of attack on the Admiral Graf Spee.

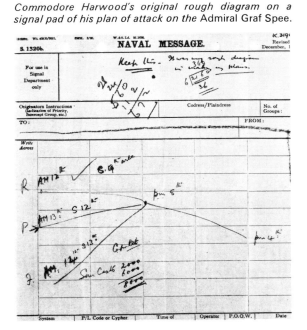

The Graf Spee, *with a raised second dummy gun-turret on the forecastle; on the extreme left, behind the ship's aircraft, the framework for the dummy funnel can be made out; the great bow-wave is painted on the ship's side.*

Sinking of the Doric Star.

The Graf Spee *makes smoke.*

The Graf Spee *at anchor in Montevideo*

If, hitherto, Langsdorff had intended to make for Santos Bay, now he hurried towards his fate, by altering course towards the focal point off the River Plate which he had gleaned from the newly-acquired documents. A communication from the Naval Operations Staff on 9 December also raised his hopes: a British convoy of four ships was reported to be leaving Montevideo under the protection of an auxiliary. At first however, the search was fruitless, in spite of reconnaissance flights. On 11 December, the engine of the ship's plane finally expired and broke down on its return from a sortie and the machine was jettisoned after salvaging all useful items. Further, the disguise (second turret on the forecastle, second funnel) was removed, in case it proved a hindrance in battle.

During the night of 12/13 December the *Graf Spee* was patrolling some 300 miles to the east of the Plate estuary. If Langsdorff found nothing on 13 December, he intended to try his luck in Lagos Bay. As the pocket battleship was steaming on a south-easterly patrol line at 0530, shortly before she was due to alter to the reciprocal course, two mast-heads were sighted on the starboard bow. For a few minutes they disappeared against the bright dawn sky, but the *Graf Spee* had turned on to the bearing and picked up the target once more at 0550. The navigation officer pointed out, in accordance with his duty, that operational orders required them to avoid engagements even with inferior forces but Langsdorff was counting on the convoy reported to him, and expressed his opinion that the escort would provide them with '*some fine target practice*'.

At 0552, however, *Exeter* could be made out and, near her, what Langsdorff took to be two destroyers, but shortly afterwards recognized as cruisers of the *Achilles* class. The Captain now considered it hopeless to try to elude the three cruisers. He gave orders to clear for action and increased to full speed, to be able to attack before the enemy had worked up to maximum speed, since he could not then himself have closed the range for effective engagement.

THE BATTLE OF THE RIVER PLATE

According to Commodore Harwood's report of the battle, his formation was steaming at 14 knots on a course of 060° in line ahead, with *Ajax* in the van and followed by *Achilles* and *Exeter*, when smoke was reported NW shortly after 0600. This was the smoke momentarily produced by the *Graf Spee's* Diesels as they were suddenly stepped up to maximum power. The *Exeter* was ordered to break away and reconnoitre.

Direct hit on the port side near the third 15-cm gun

HMS Exeter *arriving in her home port of Devonport, 15 February 1940. Note damage and absence of topmasts—Courtesy, Sir Eugen Millington-Drake, K.C.M.G.*

The Graf Spee *after being blown up on 17 December 1939*

Admiral Graf Spee : *Diagram of hits—Courtesy, Sir Eugen Millington-Drake, K.C.M.G.*

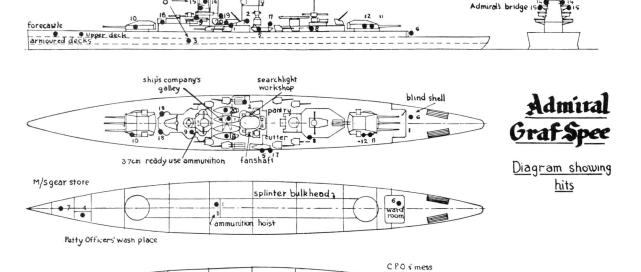

Diagram showing hits

Nos 3 & 15 are 8" hits
The remainder are 6"

The Graf Spee *after being blown up*

At 0616 she reported a pocket battleship. Exactly one minute later *Graf Spee* opened fire with both turrets on the *Exeter* and, with her medium armament, on the *Ajax*. As it had exercised the day before, the British formation split up. At high speed the light cruisers tried to reach *Graf Spee's* opposite flank, while *Exeter* set course to the west. At 0620 *Exeter* opened fire; *Ajax* joined in one minute, the *Achilles*, three minutes later.

EXETER: THE MAIN TARGET

Within half an hour the *Graf Spee* scored at least three hits on the *Exeter*, which put out of action the aircraft catapult, both forward turrets and the bridge, and started serious fires. To relieve the hard-pressed ship, the light cruisers, who had also received repeated hits, tried to close at top speed. Langsdorff who, as a former torpedo-boat commander, feared most the light cruisers' torpedo attacks, altered course and briefly put up a smoke-screen (see page 88), hoping thereby to present them both with a more difficult target, their shooting at the start having been very accurate. About 0640, as he out-manoeuvred a desperate torpedo attack delivered by *Exeter* using her port set of tubes, the first reports began coming in to Langsdorff of battle-damage in his own ship. His action station should have been the armoured conning bridge, but for a better all-round view, he exercised command from the unprotected foretop gallery and was twice wounded in the battle, and once deafened for several minutes by a near-miss.

The *Exeter* had ceased firing after making her torpedo attack, and turned away. Instead of following her, Langsdorff now turned on the light cruisers to the north-east. The latter attempted, with evasive action and the use of smoke-screens, to escape the accurate fire of the *Graf Spee*. As a result the battleship was forced into repeated changes of target and constantly recurring need for ranging shots. At 0700 the *Exeter*, coming in from the south and firing only from her stern turret, intervened once more in the battle so that the *Graf Spee* turned on her again. Soon the *Exeter* was firing from only one barrel. At 0715 she turned away, with a list to port, having suffered repeated severe hits, and withdrew under cover of a smoke-screen.

ATTACK BY THE LIGHT CRUISERS

Meanwhile Harwood had moved in, in echelon, with the 1st Division, to relieve pressure on the *Exeter* by means of torpedo attacks. In spite of the evasive action the *Graf Spee* was forced to take, she scored several 28 cm. hits on the *Ajax*, one of which put both stern turrets out of action at 0725. Since Harwood shortly afterwards received a report that only three guns remained in action in his flagship, and that eighty per cent of his ammunition had been used, he broke off the engagement by altering course to the east, and retiring behind a smoke-screen.

THE DECISION TO RUN FOR SHELTER

The *Graf Spee's* casualties in the battle were 36 dead, six seriously wounded and 53 slightly wounded. The battle damage was so severe in the Captain's opinion, that it seemed necessary to him to render his ship seaworthy again in a neutral harbour. In view of the weather conditions to be expected at this season in the North Atlantic, the most serious limitation on the ship's seaworthiness was a hit in the forecastle. Because

After the scuttling, Admiral Graf Spee *in flames off Montevideo.*

the filtration equipment for fuel and lubricating oil was also destroyed, it seemed doubtful whether her jaded engines could be relied upon to hold out with this particular failure. Langsdorff decided to put into Montevideo, requesting and obtaining the authority of the Naval Operations Staff to do so.

When Harwood divined the enemy's intentions he ordered both cruisers to shadow the battleship. Shortly before sunset they opened fire once more. The *Graf Spee* replied but with restraint, because of her ammunition stocks. She had used up well over half but, at only the second salvo, she forced the enemy to sheer off. This procedure was repeated, after which only one ship followed, and she—so they thought aboard the *Graf Spee*—soon also lost contact. At midnight, the pocket battleship anchored off Montevideo. Aboard the *Achilles* every detail had been observed, for the *Graf Spee* was clearly visible to her against the bright western sky and the lights of the city, whereas she had remained unseen, lost against the night-sky to the east.

IN MONTEVIDEO: DIPLOMATIC WAR

In Montevideo, Langsdorff requested permission for a long enough stay to make his vessel seaworthy. The expert committee that visited the ship on behalf of the Uruguayan Government considered 14 days would be necessary, but the Government would only grant 48 hours; in response to protests by the German Ambassador, the Council of Ministers extended this to 72 hours.

The *Graf Spee's* prisoners were released, the wounded transferred to hospital and the dead buried on 15 December, watched by large and sympathetic crowds. For the most part, even the freed prisoners attended the funeral ceremonies.

Aboard *Graf Spee*, prompted by enemy propaganda, but more particularly as a result of their own faulty observation, strong enemy opposition was anticipated, including the *Ark Royal*. In reality, as sole reinforcement for *Ajax* and *Achilles*, *Cumberland* had reached the scene during the night of 14/15 December. The British Ambassador, Mr Millington-Drake, who had fortified the Uruguayan Government in their intention to grant only a 48-hour stay, now strove to delay the *Graf Spee's* departure until such time as Harwood had assembled adequate forces off the River Plate. This was easy to achieve: if he sent out—as indeed happened on 16 December—an English or French freighter, under the terms of the laws regarding neutrality, the warship could only put to sea 24 hours later.

THE END

Langsdorff, as he admitted to himself, was now in a dilemma: to restore his ship to a seaworthy condition required time, but, the longer he stayed in Montevideo, the more forces the enemy could assemble off the Plate estuary. The *Graf Spee*, however, was only allowed to make herself seaworthy with neutral help, not restore herself to complete battle-readiness, for she had suffered in this respect too. Therefore, taking into account his reduced stock of ammunition, Langsdorff feared his ship '*would have to get herself shot to pieces*,

The Captain at the funeral of the ship's dead in the cemetery at Montevideo.

while more or less defenceless'. And, in this event, the comparatively shallow waters of the Plate estuary meant that there was a distinct risk *'that important secret equipment might fall into enemy hands'*, without the crew being able to prevent the calamity. He therefore instituted conferences to discuss how best to ensure complete destruction of all target-ranging and gun-laying equipment and guns, together with the effective blowing up of the ship. After he was refused a renewed request for an extension of stay, Langsdorff gave orders at 0300 on the morning of 17 December 1939 for the destruction of all important equipment and for preparations to be made for blowing up his ship.

At 1820 the *Graf Spee* put out to sea with her Captain and 40 men aboard. The rest of the crew followed aboard the German steamship *Tacoma*. At about 1900 the pocket battleship reached her anchorage outside territorial waters. Langsdorff had ordered that the remaining ammunition should be distributed about the ship at the most vital points for his purpose: blasting cartridges were to detonate the six torpedo-heads, the explosions of which were to supply the initial detonations for the individual stacks of ammunition. This destructive network was to be triggered electrically by a chronometer.

After the boats carrying the scuttling-charge crew had sheered away, exactly at sunset and simultaneously with a mighty clap of thunder, a jet of flame shot skywards. The flames changed to a squat black pillar and, shortly afterwards, an enormous ball of fire welled up from the stern. A second and much stronger explosion rent the air, and the smoke-cloud from this spread out like some giant brown stone-pine over the red evening sky. Then the *Graf Spee* was lost to view under a pall of thick smoke, further explosions being only dimly discerned. Even on the following day great oil-fires were still raging in the hull; in places the plating glowed red-hot. The fires persisted until 19 December.

After the ship was blown up the *Graf Spee's* crew climbed into tugs and lighters and were ferried across to Buenos Aires in Argentina; they arrived there at 1100 on 18 December and were interned in the course of the next few days.

Early on 20 December Kapitän zur See Langsdorff was discovered dead in his room. He lay in full uniform on his ship's battle-ensign. He had shot himself. The crew just could not take in the news of the death of their captain. Only the day before, calm and relaxed, he had expressed his satisfaction at knowing his crew were in safety, and told them he could do no more for them or for Germany. Whatever opinion one may hold on suicide, one must admit that Langsdorff, who had decided to avoid the risks he foresaw in renewing the battle, could not demonstrate to the world in any other way that his decision was based, not on cowardice, but on careful appraisal of the situation and its implications. He himself, in a farewell letter, gave the reasons for his action as follows: *'. . . any attempt to fight our way out to open, deep water with the remnants of our ammunition, was doomed to failure. But only in deep water could I, after firing off the ammunition, scuttle the ship and deny her to the enemy . . . The responsibility for my decision to blow up the ship is mine alone. For the*

After their arrival in Buenos Aires, the Captain (centre), the First Officer, Fregattenkapitän Kay (right), and Navigating Officer, Korvettenkapitän Wattenberg (left), study the newspapers

risk to the honour of the flag implicit in this, *I am gladly prepared to answer in my own person . . .'*

SUMMARY: FINAL ANALYSIS

The operations of the *Graf Spee* had shown that the pocket battleship, however, unorthodox a type she might appear, was outstandingly suitable as a weapon to employ against the shipping lanes. She had astonishing cruise endurance, could quickly change her operational zone, thanks to the high cruising speed that her Diesel engines made possible, and proved to be a handy ship at sea, riding comfortably and with excellent manoeuvrability. She was too wet a ship when heading into the seas (see page 80), but this failing was remedied in 1940 in the *Admiral Scheer* by widening and giving a greater overhang to the forecastle.

The results, expressed in tonnage—9 ships representing 50,089 GRT—would have been attainable by a U-boat in a shorter time and at less cost. To the Naval Staff, what mattered in the deployment of heavy ships against shipping was less the large number of sinkings than the creation of '*continuous, ceaseless unease and disturbance to English trade*'. The fragmentation of the enemy forces could better be attained by big surface ships than by U-boats, by which means it was hoped to relieve pressure on the home front. The Naval

Operations Staff regarded it a vital prerequisite that their commerce-raider should as far as possible keep clear of engagement with the enemy. This had been the constant theme of their reminders to Langsdorff whenever he suggested they allow him to commit his ship fully. That the desired effect was attainable with these evasive tactics has been proved by the operations of all surface raiders up to the *Bismarck*.

There is no doubt that Langsdorff conducted his war on shipping very skilfully. On reading his war diary one cannot help admiring the astuteness displayed in reaching his decisions and the care and skill he brought to the analysis of each capture and to the application of what he had learned to the next encounter. But it was a fateful decision for him and for his ship, at the end of his voyage, when he repudiated the obligation '*to avoid full engagement*' and sought contact with the enemy.

THE VERDICT OF HISTORY

We know today that the enemy first sighted the *Graf Spee* at least 20 minutes after they themselves had been identified. The pocket battleship could therefore have slipped away unnoticed. When the Naval Operations Staff were able to piece together a clearer picture of the course of the battle, from materials captured after the fall of France and from information received from

The supply ship Altmark *on the homeward voyage in Jössingfjord*

the *Graf Spee's* crew in their internment camp, the conclusion of a detailed inquiry into the battle was that:

> the fatal overestimation of the torpedo risk had severely reduced the potential effectiveness of Langsdorff's heavy armament and been the cause

of his reluctance to move in on the *Exeter* as well as the smaller cruisers.

Harwood's verdict was similar: he considered that after Langsdorff eased the pressure on the *Exeter*, he lost his former initiative and did not follow up his advantage.

THE LIFE OF ADMIRAL GRAF SPEE

1 Oct 1932	Laid down
30 June 1934	Launched
6 Jan 1936	First commissioned
1936-1938	Fleet Flagship,
	Spanish Civil War, Non Intervention Patrol
20 May 1937	Attended Coronation Review at Spithead.
21 Aug 1939	Sailed from Wilhelmshaven and proceeded to South Atlantic
Sept 1939 to	Commerce raiding in South Atlantic and Indian Ocean
12 Dec 1939	Nine ships sunk totalling 50,089 tons
13 Dec 1939	Battle of River Plate
17 Dec 1939	Scuttled outside Montevideo
1942	Wreck finally blown up

PANZERSCHIFF ADMIRAL GRAF SPEE

Built at Naval Yard, Wilhelmshaven.

Laid down:	1 October 1932
Launched:	30 June 1934
First commissioned:	6 January 1936
Cost:	£3,750,000 (85,000,000 Reichsmarks)
Cost per ton:	£375
Dimensions:	593' (609·25') × 69·5' × 21·66' = 12,100 tons (approx)
Armament:	six 28 cm. quick-firing guns L/54·5, in twin-turrets; eight 15 cm. quick-firing L/55, singly mounted, with armoured shields; six 10·5 cm. anti-aircraft guns; eight torpedo-tubes, calibre 53·3 cm., in two sets; one aircraft catapult and facilities for housing two aircraft (up to 1939 He-60; after that Ar-196); 28 cm. guns by Krupps, firing 670 lb. shell, with range 39,000 yd. at 45° elevation
Protection:	Turrets: 4" bases 5·5" faces 2-3" sides Belt: 4", with 1·5" internally Control Tower: 5" sides 2" roof Decks: 1·5"-2·25" 3" over magazines External anti-torpedo bulges
Machinery:	8 double-acting two-stroke 9-cylinder Diesels, manufactured by Maschinenfabrik Augsburg-Nürnberg, 56,000 h.p. at 450 r.p.m. Each bank of four Diesels drove a single propeller shaft through a Vulcan gear set, which reduced the revolutions to 250 per minute. Weight of main engines: 17·6 lb. per b.h.p., excluding propellers and shafting, Vulcan drive and air reservoirs. Total weight of machinery: 48·5 lb. per b.h.p. Frames: electrically welded.

HMS Exeter, *8-in gun Cruiser, lying at a buoy. The second cutter is being lowered to the water line.*

HMNZS Achilles, *6-in gun Cruiser; her Osprey spotter—reconnaissance sea-plane is on the catapult.*

Admiral Graf Spee *at the Coronation Review, Spithead, in 1937.*

Sources and bibliography
The sources used by the author were principally war diaries and documents of the Naval Operations Staff, the war diary of the pocket battleship *Admiral Graf Spee; Graf Spee*–Battle Summary N° 26, Naval Staff, Admiralty, London SW1, November 1944, and Supplement to the London Gazette, Tuesday, 17 June 1947, His Majesty's Stationery Office.

Acknowledgements
The author's thanks are due above all to the Historical Section of the Admiralty, London, SW1., for access to this material up to 1964, and in particular to the late Cdr M. G. Saunders, RN, and Cdr H. C. Beaumont, RN; also to Mr J. D. Lawson and the late Senior Civil Servant Mr W. Pfeiffer. The author also expresses his thanks to the Bundes-archiv, Militär-archiv, Freiburg i. Br., and the Bundes-archiv, Koblenz, for their willingness to cooperate in supplying material and photographs, and also valuable suggestions: at this point thanks are expressed in particular to Herren Archivräte Dr Maierhöfer and Regel. For further photographs the author is also grateful to the brother of the *Graf Spee's* captain, Herr Landgerichtsdirektor Dr Reinhard Langsdorff (retired); the Director of the Bibliothek für Zeitgeschichte, Stuttgart, Herr Dr J. Rohwer; the former navigation officer of the *Graf Spee*, Kapitän -zur-See a.D. J. Wattenberg (retired) and Fregatten-kapitän H. Dau, son of the *Altmark's* captain.

The author and publishers are also grateful for the kindness of Sir Eugen Millington-Drake, KCMG, MA (Oxon), and Peter Davies Ltd., the publishers, for their permission to use material in Sir Eugen's excellent book, *The Drama of Graf Spee and the Battle of The Plate.*

For the details of the history of the ship's construction, the following books were consulted:

Erich Gröner, *Die deutschen Kriegsschiffe 1815–1945*, 2 vols., München (J. F. Lehmanns Verlag), 1964 and 1968; Siegfried Breyer, *Schlachtschiffe und Schlachtkreuzer 1905–1970*, München (J. F. Lehmanns Verlag), 1970. For details of the British story, the author is indebted to S. W. Roskill: *The War at Sea*, vol. 1, Her Majesty's Stationery Office, 1954. For further literature, reference should be made to the comprehensive book by Sir Eugen Millington-Drake, KCMG, MA (Oxon), *The Drama of Graf Spee and the Battle of the River Plate*, London (Peter Davies), 1964, which con-tains an almost complete bibliography on the *Graf Spee.*

Gerhard Bidlingmaier.

Profile Publications Ltd., are grateful for the permission of the following persons to reproduce the photographs in this Warship Profile:

The Directors of the Bibliothek für Zeitgeschichte, Stuttgart
The Bundesarchiv/Militärchiv, Freiburg im Breisgau
Fregattenkapitän H. Dau.
Landgerichtsdirektor a.D. Dr jur. Reinhard Langsdorff
Kapitän-zur-See a.D. Jürgen Wattenberg.
Sir Eugen Millington-Drake, KCMG, MA(Oxon)
Peter Davies Ltd.

Table of number of 28 cm. and 15 cm. shells mostly with high explosive fuse fired by the GRAF SPEE
Shells fired by the *Graf Spee:* Total complement being 200 of each type :

200-28 cm. shells with high explosive fuse	Remainder Nil
184-28 cm. shells with bottom fuse	Remainder 16
30-28 cm. armour-piercing shells (against the light cruisers because the other ammunition was nearly exhausted)	Remainder 170
414-28 cm. shells	Total remaining : 186

      Hits : 8 on the *Exeter*
             2 on the *Ajax*

             10 = 2·7%
15 cm. and 10·5 cm. :
257-15 cm. shells with high explosive fuse
120-15 cm. shells with bottom fuse
80-10·5 cm. anti-aircraft shells with time fuse against
        the light cruisers on short distance

377-15 cm. shells
80-10·5 cm. shells   No hits
  It will be seen that the total number of 11-inch shells remaining in the *Graf Spee* as she lay in Montevideo harbour was 186, viz. 31 each for her six 11-inch guns and so only sufficient for an action of some 40 minutes; and this was a powerful consideration in Captain Langsdorff's decision not to attempt a break out.
From Sir Eugen Millington-Drake's book 'The Drama of Graf Spee and the Battle of The Plate'. Published by Peter Davies.

HMS Campbeltown (*ex USS* Buchanan (*DD-131*)). *On arrival on 29 September 1940 at Devonport after her Atlantic crossing*　　　　　　　　　　　　　　　　　　　　　　　　　　　　(*MOD*)

HMS Campbeltown (USS Buchanan)
John Wingate DSC

HMS CAMPBELTOWN
(ex-USS Buchanan)
World War I Building Programme

It was at the time of Jutland that the United States Navy decided to expand their destroyer building programme to the maximum. It is interesting to note that the tactical thinking of American Naval Officers agreed with their British allies. The Staff requirements for the torpedo boat destroyers were listed in the following priorities:
1. To attack the enemy with torpedoes.
2. To fight off attacking enemy torpedo boats.
3. Anti-submarine work.

The American destroyers were built as cheaply as possible and in large numbers to combat speedily the unrestricted U-boat warfare which was already raging. The American Navy department by 1 July 1919 had already ordered 166 destroyers of unusual design: with no break in the fo'c'sle and with a low freeboard aft, their appearance, though functional, was unattractive. With their four funnels, there was a stark fighting quality about their appearance but it was inevitable that these ships should be affectionately known as 'flush-deckers' or 'four stackers'. Though too late for World War I, these maids-of-all-work, produced so quickly and in such numbers, were to make a vital contribution to the war at sea in World War II. It is not exaggerating to surmise that, without the four-stackers, World War II may well have ended very differently and with fatal consequences for mankind.

THE FLUSH DECKERS
The different classes of these ships were generally named after the shipyards in which they were built, *Caldwell* being the first flush-decker to begin on the stocks in 1916. It is of interest that the first of the flush-deckers were at sea at about the same time as the first British 'V and Ws' were undergoing trials.

97

THE FIRST USS BUCHANAN

The Navy Department ordered DD-131 from the Bath Iron Works at Maine and her keel was laid on 26 June 1918. The shipyard went bankrupt in 1935, but not before having produced a ship whose fame would become renowned throughout the world.

On 2 January 1919, less than two months after the Armistice, Mrs C. P. Wetherbee, sponsor and wife of the Vice-President, launched DD-131 in the presence of the State Governor, Mr Cobb. The ship was commissioned on 20 January 1919, her first Commanding Officer being Lieutenant H. J. Bensen, USN. The ship whom he was to command had been well-built.

USS Buchanan (DD-131)

Dimensions

Length between perpendiculars	310'
Length overall	314' 4½"
Length of straight keel	268' 11½"
Beam	30' 11¼"
Camber of main deck in 30'	1' 3"
Draught	9' 1¾"
Ratio, length to beam	10' 1"
Area of rudder	65·3 sq. ft
Displacement (normal)	1154 tons
Tons per inch	15·4 tons
Number of frames	177
Frame spacing	1' 9"
Centre of buoyancy above bottom of keel	5·5'
Transverse metacentre above C.B.	8·93'

Heights above waterline

Top of main stub mast	50'
Bridge at centre line	22' 7¾"
Rake of mast and funnels	⅞" per ft
Top of main deck at stem	17' 2¾"
Top of main deck at stern	8 2¾"
Top of for'd funnel	39' 7⅞"
Centre of range finder	32' 9¼"
No. 1 gun (for'd)	19' 5¼"
Nos. 2 & 3 guns (amidships)	24' 8¼"
No. 4 gun (after)	20' 0"

Armament

4" guns 50 cal	4
21" Triple torpedo tubes	4
3" HA gun 23 cal	1
30 calibre machine guns	2

Depth Charges and Mines

Depth charge rails	fitted
Mine laying rails	fitted

Ammunition

4"	400 rounds
3" HA	400 rounds
Torpedo warheads	12

Machinery

Parsons Marine steam turbines fitted with reduction gear to propeller shafts	4
Shaft HP at 430 rpm	24,200
Steam at High Pressure turbine	240 lb/sq. in

Boilers

Normand, return flame type	4
Steam pressure	260 lb per sq. in
Furnace volume each	718 cu. ft
Heating surface each boiler	6500 sq. ft

Propellers

2 3-bladed dia.	110"
Pitch of blades	122"
Tip of blades below keel	21·43"

Fuel

Total tank capacity	86,295 gal net (US)

Ship's Boats

	No.	Crew	Total capacity
24' motor launch	1	2	17
26' motor whale boats	1	2	10
24' whale boat	1	7	27
10 punt	1	—	—

Complement

Peace-time	102
War-time	139

THE FIRST BUCHANAN: Days of Peace

The wife of the Vice-President of the shipyard, Mrs C. P. Wetherbee, named the first *Buchanan* on 2 January 1919. The ship's name was honouring Franklin Buchanan who had served both as a Captain in the United States Navy and as a Ranking Officer of the Confederate States Navy. He had served his country with distinction, but he will be remembered particularly as the first Superintendent of the Naval School at Annapolis and for his great interest in that academy.

After trials and work up, USS *Buchanan* reported to Commander, Destroyer Force, at Guantanamo, Cuba, the American naval base. She was attached temporarily to Destroyer Squadron 2, until she was sent in July

USS Buchanan (DD-131). This is the only known photograph of this flush-decker as she was from 1919-1940. Awnings are spread and the ship's company are in 'whites'. Her motor launch is being lowered and she is about to anchor   (USN)

1919 to the Pacific Fleet where she joined Destroyer Flotilla 4. She was paid off on 7 June 1922, when she was placed in care and maintenance at San Diego until 10 April 1930.

In commission once again, she joined Destroyer Division 10, Destroyer Squadrons, Battle Force, when she operated on the west coast on normal peace-time duties. Then, in the summer of 1934, after a cruise to Alaska with ROTC units on board, she was placed in reduced commission and attached to the Rotating Reserve Squadron 20 at San Diego.

She was fully commissioned again in December 1934, when she resumed operations with Division 5, Destroyers, Battle Force. However, she was again out of commission at San Diego from 9 April 1937 until 30 September 1939.

HITLER'S WAR: 1939

USS *Buchanan* was immediately refitted for action with Division 65, Destroyer Squadron 32, Atlantic Squadron and, from December 1939 until 22 February 1940, she operated with the Antilles Detachment of the Neutrality Patrol.

Buchanan was sent to patrol the Gulf of Mexico where she was based at Galveston, Texas; later she patrolled off Key West and the Florida Straits. On 2 September 1940 she was ordered to report to the Boston Navy Yard. She then proceeded to Halifax, Nova Scotia where, on 2 September 1940, she was de-commissioned.

Our darkest hour

At the outbreak of war, the Royal Navy had 184 destroyers. A year later, the total was only 171 though 21 new destroyers had been built to replace the 34 ships who had been sunk. Of the remaining 171, however, nearly half were in dockyard hands because of casualties from mines, U-boats, E-boats, the Luftwaffe and the common enemy, the weather. Seventeen had been damaged during the Norwegian campaign, sixteen during the Dunkirk evacuation.

While Britain regained her breath, Mr Churchill and President Roosevelt strengthened the ties of common blood. At this critical moment, on 3 September 1940, the first anniversary of the war, President Roosevelt made one of the most trusting gestures ever to be made. He dispatched across the Atlantic shiploads of ammunition and of old, but effective, rifles with which to re-equip the disarmed British Expeditionary Force: in addition, he ordered that 50 of the older destroyers in the United States Navy should be handed over to the Royal Navy in exchange for leases of naval and air bases in Newfoundland and the West Indies. These 50 over-age destroyers were the 'flush-deckers' who, from time to time, had been laid up since the end of the first World War.

The Grand Gesture

There steamed into Halifax, Nova Scotia, on 6 September 1940, the first of the four-stackers. On 9 September, the Royal Navy formally accepted the first of the American ships. The Stars and Stripes were hauled down, the White Ensigns hoisted. On the next day, 10 September 1940, the Admiralty ordered that the class should be known as the 'Town' Class, because each ship would bear the name of a town common to both America and Great Britain.

The Launching Platform. Behind Governor Cobb can be seen the stem which was to destroy 23 years later German aspirations to the command of the Atlantic through the power of its heavy ships (Bath Iron Works)

The first eight ships to be handed over were:

American name	British name
Herndon	Churchill
Abel P Upshur	Clare
Welborn C Wood	Chesterfield
Welles	Cameron
Aaron Ward	Castleton
Crowninshield	Chelsea
Hale	Caldwell
Buchanan	Campbeltown

The Crossing

Five days later, the first five of a flotilla of eight crossed the Atlantic on the appointed day:

Clare, Castleton, Caldwell, Chelsea and *Campbeltown*. They arrived at Belfast on 26 September and at Devonport three days later.

Commander R. E. D. Ryder, VC, RN. Naval Force Commander (C. E. Lucas Phillips)

Lieutenant-Colonel A. C. Newman, VC. Military Commander   *(C. E. Lucas Phillips)*

Lieutenant-Commander S. H. Beattie, VC, RN. Commanding Officer of HMS Campbeltown   *(Admiralty)*

HMS CAMPBELTOWN Four-Stacker

Commanding Officers:

Lieutenant T. W. T. Beloe, R.N.	October 1940
Lieutenant-Commander Lord Teynham, R.N.	October 1941

Campbeltown took her name from the fishing port in Kintyre, close by the Mull, and from her American sister-town in Florida.

Her pendant numbers were I-42 and her war-time complement numbered 146. During her refit in Devonport she was fitted with two 0·5-inch close-range weapons, two strip-Lewis and four Oerlikons. She was in Devonport on 29 September 1940, where her first

Commanding Officer, Lieutenant T. W. T. Beloe, R.N., carried out the shake-down. She joined the 7th Escort Group, Liverpool, and from Londonderry played her part in the Battle of the Atlantic.

Barely six weeks later, on 3 December 1940, she was in a collision at Liverpool where she was repaired until March 1941.

A year of cruel and bitter warfare at sea

She was then allocated to the Royal Netherlands Navy which had now formed in these islands; the Dutch wished to name her *Middleburg* but the Admiralty

Able Seaman W. A. Savage, VC RN, (posthumous). Pom-pom gunlayer of MGB 314   *(Admiralty)*

Sergeant T. F. Durrant, VC, RE, 1 Commando (posthumous)   *(Admiralty)*

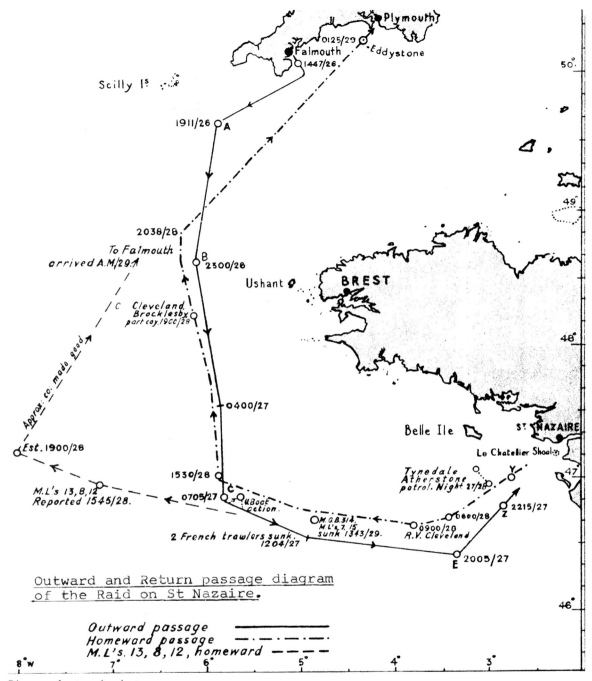

Diagram of outward and return passage

could not agree to this suggestion, as there was no Middleburg in America, and so *Campbeltown* reverted to her original name and was, for a time, manned by a Polish ships' company. However, she reverted to the Royal Navy in September 1941, a year after the Battle of Britain.

She took her place amongst the escorts of the Atlantic convoys and was attacked several times by U-boats and aircraft. She survived, however, and on 3 August 1941 she was part of an escort group that was on passage to meet convoy SL.81, when the destroyers, *Wanderer* and *St Albans*, and the corvette, *Hydrangea*, of the same escort group sank U.401 in position 50° 27′N, 19° 50′W.

On 15 September 1941, she recovered the survivors of *Vinga*, a Norwegian oil tanker who had been bombed in position 58° 01′N, 13° 20′W. 1942 began auspiciously for her when, on 25 January, she shot down a German aircraft which was probably laying mines. At the beginning of 1942, *Campbeltown* was, therefore, one of a vast number of ships employed solely on ensuring that freedom's lifeline across the Atlantic remained intact.

'B' Class Fairmile Motor Launch with Hotchkiss gun. In spite of their petrol tanks and wooden hulls, these were, never-theless, the only craft available for the raid. They were excellent sea boats for their size   (*C. E. Lucas Phillips*)

THE SEED IS SOWN: July, 1941

In July, a meeting under the chairmanship of Captain Godfrey French, C.B.E., of the Admiralty Planning Staff, was held to discuss raids on the Channel and Brittany coasts. Captain French, however, had been deliberating on Mr Churchill's proposals for landing a large force on the Brest peninsular and to catch *Scharnhorst* and *Gneisenau* in that port. The assault was to be a landing on the grand scale, with the committal of large numbers of soldiers.

At this meeting was Lieutenant-Commander George Gonin, R.N., of the French section of the Naval Intelligence Division. Gonin realised that, if *Tirpitz* could be prevented from dry-docking on the western Atlantic coast, she would be forced to return to her home ports. He also knew that at St Nazaire was the Normandie Dock, the only graving dock large and deep enough to take *Tirpitz*, Germany's remaining battleship, *Bismarck* having been sunk two months earlier. Lieutenant-Commander George Gonin submitted his ideas to Captain French who passed them to the Prime Minister.

The Frustrations

A docket was immediately started by Plans Division who recommended that the attack should take place. The scheme quickly grew into firm planning and a secret letter was sent to the Commander-in-Chief, Plymouth, Admiral Sir Charles Forbes, instructing him to prepare

MTB 74, a Vosper boat modified especially for firing her torpedoes over enemy nets. The torpedo tubes are mounted high on the fo'c'sle. She is here camouflaged as she was during the raid on St Nazaire   (*Vosper Ltd*)

for the raid. Gonin quietly set about his side of the house.

Firstly, he arranged for Medmenham (the Centre of Interpretation of Air Photographs) to construct a model of St Nazaire and the dry dock.

Secondly, he twice visited Medmenham and persuaded the staff to write a detailed report which was to be backed up by first-rate air photos. The whole concept was then enlarged to the size of a table and upon this a model was built. Not only the gun positions, but the buildings, and even the doors which led to the emplacements, were shown. It was upon this model that the raid was planned.

Thirdly, Gonin used the SOE for advice on how to place explosive charges. SOE co-operated magnificently and produced a scheme to blow up the large main lock gate of the Normandie Dock.

On 15 September 1941, a further meeting was held at the Admiralty, the Chief of Staff, Plymouth, being there. At this meeting, a rough plan of the raid was approved, except for the date. Two dates in October could have been suitable, one being Trafalgar Day. Sir Charles Forbes, however, after due consideration decided that the raid was not feasible: it was too hazardous because the expedition would have to sail from the West Country two or three hours before dark, and would, therefore, be certain of discovery by the enemy's reconnaissance aircraft. Surprise, the vital ingredient for the success of the enterprise, would be lost.

The Admiralty was, by now, very keen on the concept but the Director of Plans rightly insisted that the man on the spot, the Commander-in-Chief, Plymouth, must not be ordered to carry out an enterprise against his judgement. As an alternative, SOE were ordered to destroy, if they could, the locks by sabotage, but all knew this was an impossible task because of the size of the locks and the very strong guard the Germans had placed around them.

Obstacles overcome:
Admiral Mountbatten,
Chief of Combined Operations

It was now early 1942, the moment when Admiral Mountbatten became Chief of Combined Operations; he immediately began searching for targets. Gonin seized this opportunity and took the docket on St Nazaire and the big photographs to Mountbatten's Staff Officer, Intelligence. The new CCO took up the case and asked Admiral Forbes to attend a meeting. Admiral Mountbatten succeeded in persuading Admiral Forbes to change his mind with the result that C-in-C, Plymouth, was once again embued with enthusiasm and planning was restarted. The Intelligence was handed over to Mountbatten's staff and final plans were drawn up. One difficulty was a last minute request from the Sappers for detailed information* of the underground pumping machinery. This problem was resolved by sending the Sappers down to the King George V Dock at Southampton which was similar.

---

* Furnished most kindly from an old copy of 'The Proceedings of the Institution of Civil Engineers'.

MGB 314 photographed at sea immediately after the raid but before being scuttled on the return passage. She is flying the flag signal, 'Starboard engine out of action. Disregard my motions.' The pom-pom on the fo'c'sle is the gun at which Able Seaman Savage, VC, was killed. Note the power-operated 0·5-inch guns amidships and the splinter mattresses. MGB 314 became the Naval Force Commander's Headquarters on approaching St Nazaire
(C. E. Lucas Phillips)

Diagram of the port and docks at St Nazaire. The Normandie Dock (Forme Écluse) could dock an 85,000 ton ship
(C. E. Lucas Phillips)

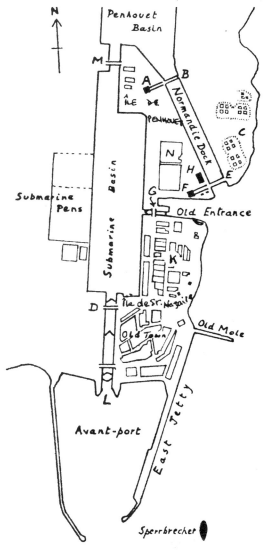

The port of St Nazaire photographed by the Royal Air Force before the raid   (C. E. Lucas Phillips)

THE FINAL PLANS
St Nazaire

St Nazaire is on the north bank of the river Loire and is an entirely artificial port, containing an 'avant port' and two large basins. The water level of these basins is maintained through two locks which unite to form a wide expanse of water. There are three entrances to this area:

1. Through the Southern entrance. Used by ships of 10,000 tons.
2. The small Eastern entrance, a small lock.
3. A large, new entrance which could be used as a dry dock, the Normandie Dock.

The sheltered submarine pens were to the westward of the basin which was 650 yards long and to the north of the 'avant port'. The main entrance to the basin was from the south lock of the 'avant port' which was crossed by two swing bridges. From the river at the Old Entrance, small craft could enter the basin through the East lock.

Objects of the Raid (in priority)

1. To destroy the entrance to the large lock, thereby preventing it from being used as a dry dock. This Normandie Dock was the only dry dock on the coast of France capable of taking the *Tirpitz*. It was unlikely that the ship would venture into the Atlantic to attack our convoys without the facilities of a dry

HMS Campbeltown *at Devonport Dockyard, March 10/19 1942. A 12 pdr. gun and gun shield have replaced the American 4-inch gun. 10 lb. NMBP protective plating has been fitted around the bridge wheel house. On the port side two stacks of protective mattresses are heaped, preparatory to being fitted to the exposed positions* (Captain Ryder, VC RN)

HMS Campbeltown *at* Devonport Dockyard, March *10/19* 1942. *The flag deck, starboard side, aft. The protective plating over the Degaussing coil and steering wire can be clearly seen. Two Carley floats have been stowed in the well-deck*
(Captain Ryder, VC, RN)

dock upon which to rely in case of damage. The destruction of the dock would immobilise the *Tirpitz*. This target was the over-riding objective of the intended raid.

2. To destroy any one complete set of lock gates, thereby rendering St Nazaire tidal. This would have the effect of severely hampering the U-boats, if not of denying them the use of the port altogether.

The Operational Plan
1. A destroyer was to ram the outer caisson of the large lock at the entrance to the Normandie Dock.
2. An MTB was to torpedo the lock gate of the small entrance.
3. Demolition parties were to land at the Old (Vieux) Mole and blow up all four pairs of lock gates of the southern entrance.

The Graving Dock
Connected with St Nazaire basin on the north was the Penhouët basin, at the north-eastern corner of which were three graving docks. Since 1932, the south-east corner of this basin had direct access to the river through a large lock which could, itself, be used as a large dock, known as the Normandie Dock, after the 83,400 ton liner for whom it had been specially built. At each end of the dock was a huge caisson which was opened and shut by hydraulic machinery.

The Normandie Dock, which was also known as the *Forme-Écluse*, was the largest dock in the world: 1148 ft long and 164 ft wide. It could dock a ship of over 85,000 tons. The caisson measured 167 ft long, 54 ft high and 35 ft thick.

The Expendable Destroyer
The four-stacker, *Campbeltown*, was selected for the operation. She was so to ram the lock gate at the southern end of the Normandie Dock and she would become immobile. Having on board a high explosive charge of 24 depth charges, she would be scuttled. The depth charges would be fused to blow up $2\frac{1}{2}$ hours later.

The Commandos
The Commandos were to leap ashore on to the lock from the bows of *Campbeltown*; and simultaneously to land from the Motor Launches (MLs) at the Old Mole and the Old Entrance.

Assault parties of Commandos were to land as covering forces, in order to allow the Sappers to reach their objectives. The second party of Commandos was to hold the area east of the St Nazaire basin, the locks, and the two small islands, Île de Penhouët and Île de St Nazaire, until the re-embarkation into the MLs was ordered.

Military Force

Group	Transport	Objective	Landing place
1	MLs (Port column)	(1) Silence Old Mole and East Jetty batteries.	N side of Old Mole
		(2) Destroy Southern Entrance lock gates (L and D).	
2	MLs (Stb'd column)	(1) Silence Île de St Nazaire batteries (K)	Both sides of Old Entrance.
		(2) Destroy installations (A, B, M, N) and hold Southern lock lifting bridge (G).	
3	HMS *Campbeltown*	(1) Silence Normandie Dock batteries (E & C).	Normandie Dock S gate.
		(2) Destroy pumping and winding gear (H & F).	

HMS Campbeltown *at Devonport Dockyard, March 10/19 1942. 10 lb. DIHT protective plating has been fitted around the bridge and a 0·5-inch Browning machine-gun has been re-sited on each side of the flag deck. The rectangular case to the left of the 10" signalling lantern is a flag locker*   (*Captain Ryder, VC, RN*)

HMS Campbeltown, *Devonport Dockyard, March 10/19 1942. Nos 1, 2, 3 and 4 Oerlikon guns have been fitted to replace the original Nos 2 and 3 American 4-inch guns. The Oerlikons are fully protected with 10 lb. NMBP plating. Nos 3 and 4 funnels have been removed; Nos 1 and 2 funnels have been modified to resemble those of a German Möwe-class torpedo boat*   (*Captain Ryder, VC, RN*)

The Plan of Attack

The Naval Force should reach well into the estuary before being detected, and, once the alarm had been given, it was hoped that the plan was so bold as to bluff the enemy for long enough to allow *Campbeltown* to reach the lock gates.

It was realised that the return to England was secondary to the object of the exercise but it was hoped that the use of smoke screens would help the embarkation.

The Forces taking part

Naval Force Commander and Senior Naval Officer:
  Commander R. E. D. Ryder, R.N.
Military Commander:
  Lieutenant-Colonel A. C. Newman
Headquarters Boat:
  MGB 314 Lieutenant Dunstan M. C. Curtis, R.N.V.R.
HMS *Campbeltown*:
  Lieutenant-Commander S. H. Beattie, R.N.
MTB 74:
  Sub-Lieutenant R. C. M. V. Wynn, R.N.V.R.
Escorts:
  HMS *Atherstone*: Lieutenant-Commander R. F. Jenks, R.N.
  HMS *Tynedale*: Lieutenant-Commander H. E. F. Tweedie, R.N.

MLs:

1st Flotilla
ML192	1	Lieutenant-Commander W. L. Stephens, *RNVR* (SO, MLs)
ML262	2	Lieutenant E. A. Burt, *RNVR*
ML267	3	Lieutenant E. H. Beart, *RNVR*
ML268	4	Lieutenant A. D. B. X. Tillie, *RNVR*
ML156	5	Lieutenant L. Fenton, *RNVR*
ML177	6	Sub-Lieutenant M. F. Rodier, *RNVR*
ML270	7	Lieutenant C. S. B. Irwin, *RNR*
ML160	8	Lieutenant T. W. Boyd, *RNVR*

2nd Flotilla
ML447	9	Lieutenant T. D. L. Platt, *RNR* (SO, 2nd Flotilla)
ML341	10	Lieutenant D. L. Briault, *RNVR*
ML457	11	Lieutenant T. A. M. Collier, *RNVR*
ML307	12	Lieutenant N. B. Wallis, *RANVR*
ML443	13	Lieutenant K. Horlock, *RNVR*
ML306	14	Lieutenant I. B. Henderson, *RNVR*
ML446	15	Lieutenant H. G. R. Falconar, *RNVR*
ML298	16	Sub-Lieutenant R. Nock, *RNVR*

Military Force
22 Officers 134 Other ranks	No. 2 Commando
16 Officers 74 Other ranks	Special Service Brigade Demolition Party
2 Officers 1 Other rank	Medical Service (No. 2 Commando)

The motor launches and *Campbeltown* were to carry the Commandos. The Hunt destroyers, *Atherstone* and *Tynedale*, were to escort the force but not to enter the Loire.

Security

Falmouth, the port selected for training and departure, was reputed to be harbouring enemy agents. If surprise was to be achieved, secrecy was vital to the enterprise and, as yet, no Commanding Officers had been let into the secret of the raid. Commander Ryder, therefore, instituted a deception plan which worked admirably.

All vessels taking part were named the '10th A/S Striking Force' and all training programmes were carried out beneath this banner. The issuing of tropical clothing to ML crews lent an air of reality that things were not entirely normal.

HMS Campbeltown, *Devonport Dockyard, March 10/19 1942. Nos 5 and 6 Oerlikon guns and 'bandstands'; the box-like armoured Sick Bay and the temporary ensign staff. The 15 lb. DIHT protective plating, fitted as steel fences, are clearly visible. The Commandos laid prone behind these fences during the final stages of the attack* (Captain Ryder, VC, RN)

It was 'leaked' that an exercise was shortly to be carried out to test Plymouth's defences, the exercise being code-named 'Vivid'. The exercise much annoyed the '10th A/S Striking Force' because of interference with its programme!

The Force returned on 23 March to Falmouth where it was kept at short notice, no leave being granted and all contacts being severed with the shore. Officers and key ratings were informed of the details of the operation but even now no-one knew of the final destination.

TRAINING AND PREPARATION

The final date for the raid was to be 27/28 March 1942. The following navigational data applied:

Sunset, 27 March 1931; end of nautical twilight, 2040
Sunrise, 28 March, 0701; beginning of nautical twilight, 0553
Moonrise, 27 March 1405 } 1st quarter, 25 March
Moonset, 28 March 0452 }
Low Water, 27 March 1944; High Water, 28 March 0123
Height 13½ ft
All times, BST

The training was to be carried out between 12 and 25 March 1942 at Falmouth.

Protection

Both the Naval and Military Force Commanders agreed that *Campbeltown*, the key to the whole attack, should have every advantage: the MLs were, therefore, to lead her in and support her with every available gun. This decision was reached after discussing the alternative of sheltering the wooden MLs in the lee of *Campbeltown*, a steel ship and more able to bear the weight of the German guns.

Demolition Parties

Captain W. H. Pritchard, R.E., an extremely efficient soldier, took his men to train on the King George V Dock at Southampton. They worked in the dark for weeks on end to perfect their knowledge of the working of the machinery, the winding and pumping gear. When the time came, their pre-training proved to be

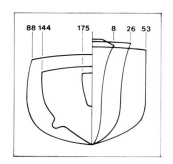

88 144   175   8   26   53

131

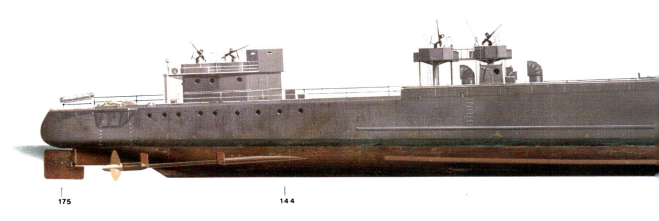

175   144

5   0   30´

HMS Campbeltown (USS Buchanan)

In fifteen days, HM Dockyard, Devonport, converted the original '*4-stacker*' into the expendable explosive destroyer who was to ram the lock gates at St Nazaire and affect the course of World War II.

Her two after funnels were removed and the two foremost modified to resemble those of a *Möwe*-class German torpedo boat. *Campbeltown's* 4-inch guns were replaced by eight 40mm Oerlikons; her torpedo armament was removed; and protective steel plating was fitted around the bridge and, as fences, along the upper deck behind which the Commandos could shelter during the last stage of the attack. Scaling ladders, for gaining the shore, were stowed on the fo'c'sle.

The ship was painted 'Mountbatten Pink' (Plymouth Pink), the colour adopted by ships of the Royal Navy operating in the Channel at that time.

Profile of USS *Buchanan,* on handing over to the Royal Navy in 1940 when she became HMS *Campbeltown.*

Brittain/Hadler © *Profile Publications Ltd*

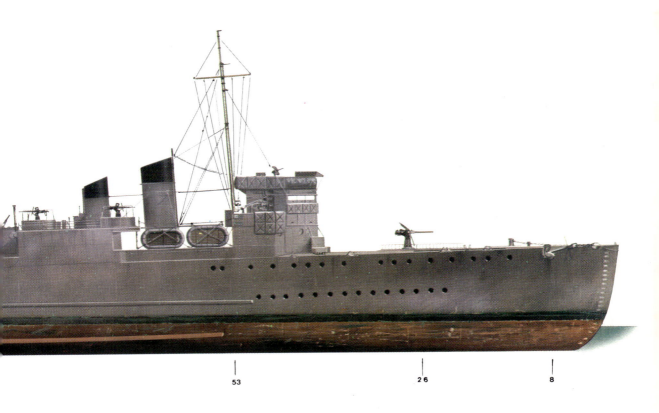

53   2 6   8

HMS Campbeltown, *Devonport Dockyard, March 10/19 1942. Nos 7 and 8 Oerlikon guns. 10 lb. NMBP protective plating has been fitted around the after steering position and over the Degaussing coil and steering wires. Two dockyard ordnance artificers are fitting No 7 Oerlikon, the shield of which can be seen. A compass repeater and the after binnacle are visible inboard of the protective plating forward of these two men. The ammunition ready-use lockers are sited outside the gun sponsons. Note the shaped rails for the guns' safety arcs*

(Captain Ryder, VC, RN)

HMS Campbeltown, *Devonport Dockyard, March 10/19 1942. The circular modifications to Nos 3 and 4 funnels can be clearly seen. The two line-throwers have been re-sited on top of the cover plate of No 3 funnel. The ship's boats have been removed; the midship steel fences have been fitted* (Captain Ryder, VC, RN)

of the highest order. In addition, the Commando assault, medical service and other demolition parties worked incessantly to reach a high state of training.

MODIFICATIONS TO HMS CAMPBELTOWN: 10 to 19 March 1942

Campbeltown was fitted out at Devonport, where she arrived on 10 March, only 17 days before the raid was due.

If *Campbeltown* was to clear the shallows in the Loire estuary, it was essential to reduce her draught aft from 14 ft to $10\frac{1}{2}$ ft. However, 4 tons 42 lb of high explosive would have to be added to her weight.

All unnecessary ammunition and fittings were removed and only sufficient fuel and water for the outward passage to St Nazaire were left in the tanks.

Armament

Plymouth Dockyard removed the four triple torpedo tubes and the main armament of four 4-inch guns. The depth charges, the depth charge throwers and traps and all ammunition were disembarked.

For close-range attack, eight Oerlikons were fitted on light stages (bandstands) and a 12 pdr. HA light automatic gun was transferred to the fo'c'sle.

Armoured Protection

Four rows of '10 lb NMBP' protective plating were fitted on deck to shield the soldiers who would be lying on the deck during the final approach.

Protective plating was also fitted around the bridge

HMS Campbeltown, Devonport Dockyard, March 10/19 1942. Two Carley floats and cork scrambling nets are being stowed on the quarter deck. The steering wires are plainly visible as are also both propeller guards. The protective plating over the Degaussing coil has left clear the quarter deck fairleads. This photograph must have been taken early on in the refit as the after draught mark still shows 13ft.
(Captain Ryder, VC, RN)

The Attack Disposition (*C. E. Lucas Phillips*)

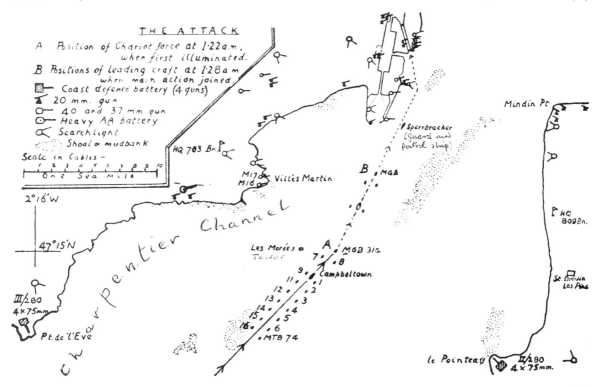

Action is joined. The raiders are illuminated and attacked by shore guns and by the guard ship who is engaging MGB 314
(Captain Ryder, VC, RN)

but slits were left through which the Captain, Lieutenant-Commander Beattie, could conn and the Coxswain, steer the ship. This plating was not more than ¼ in thick so that the weight of the ship could be kept to a minimum. The plating was of case-hardened steel and reputed capable of withstanding direct hits from 20 mm enemy guns positions along the water front of the assault area.

Appearance

The two after funnels were removed and the top of the two foremast funnels cut at an angle in order to resemble the Möwe-class enemy torpedo boats who were known to be operating at that time from the Biscay ports. The ship was painted 'Mountbatten (Plymouth) Pink', the customary colour for ships operating in the Channel, in order to minimise detection by searchlights.

The Explosive Charge

Lieutenant N. T. B. Tibbets, R.N., a Torpedo Officer appointed as Demolition Officer (awarded the DSC, although killed in the raid) gave much thought to the fitting and fusing of the explosive charge. He was assisted by Captain W. H. Pritchard, R.E., and together they solved the many problems.

The explosion of four tons of TNT, when it did occur, would hazard our troops ashore as well as the MLs in the vicinity. The idea of a delayed fuse to work after the withdrawal was discarded because the ship might be captured intact and the enemy might remove the fuses.

Lieutenant Tibbets suggested that the ship should be scuttled after ramming the dock and that the main

Last stage of the attack. Bogus Nazi ensigns have been hauled down and white ensigns run up. MGB 314 is about to haul out of line for Campbeltown's *final run-in to the lock gate (Drawing by Captain Ryder, VC, RN. Courtesy of Illustrated London News)*

charge should explode with the ship when she was on the bottom, thus providing a tamping effect. Once the ship had been scuttled, a long delay before the explosion would give the personnel time to leave. There was one vital condition: there must be alternative fusing arrangements to make certain that at least one scheme worked. Tibbets carried out this work and even produced one fuse which was certain to work under water. The charge was therefore built permanently into the ship.

Twenty-four depth charges were placed in a special tank which was built into the top of the fuel compartment. This tank was abaft the for'd gun support where it was hoped that the ship's structure would remain undamaged because of the strengthening in the hull.

The depth charges were fused with Cordtext, an instantaneous water-proof fuse. This arrangement would ensure simultaneous detonation and two different types of fuse were built into the system so that the whole charge would explode after 2½ hours. As a last precaution, an eighteen-hour delay pencil was to be placed in every third charge before the ship entered the Loire.

The Fuses

These were eight-hour delay fuses to be activated two hours before the ramming of the gate. They were army fuses of the acid-eating copper type and were guaranteed to within 25% of their specified time, i.e. they might go off after six hours or they might take ten. Eight of these fuses were fitted and each would explode a charge.

Without Tibbet's thoroughness, confidence would have been lost and, even if the charge failed to explode, the ship would be sunk across the entrance and therefore would immobilise the dock.

Devonport Dockyard

Under Mr R. C. Grant of the Constructive Department, the dockyard hands worked swiftly and well. Beattie, therefore, had time to exercise his new command and to carry out gunnery exercises with his new armament. It is interesting to read of *Campbeltown's* handling qualities:

'The 4-stackers were not so easy to handle as their contempories, the "V & Ws". *Campbeltown* had been lightened so that she drew 6 ft for'd and 10 ft 6 in aft and this made her skid when manoeuvring'.

Beattie took her out to Cawsand Bay for degaussing

A German photograph of HMS Campbeltown *taken a few hours after the ramming of the caisson. Her fo'c'sle projects about a foot over the empty dock. In the right background are the warehouses where the Commandos fought their dockyard battle. This photograph must have been taken a short time before she exploded because of the state of half-tide as seen in the background* (Courtesy of Illustrated London News)

trials, where he discovered that at 12 knots *Campbeltown* had an enormous turning circle. He also learnt that she would not handle like an ordinary destroyer until she reached about 16/17 knots: this was to affect his decision during the final run-in to the lock gate which he carried out at 20 knots. He knew, during those last few minutes, that she would handle like a conventional destroyer and, therefore, he would not have to think about making allowances for her peculiarities. *Campbeltown* had out-turning propellers.

Communications
Communications between bridge and engine room were similar to those of a British destroyer and presented no difficulties.

Opening fire: a bell on the bridge was wired up to the various mountings.

The Draught
In spite of lightening the ship to such an extent, the draught could not be reduced below 11 ft and she settled another foot when steaming at over 15 knots, her draught then being 12 ft. Even so, careful calculations were made with her fuel and boiler feed-water for her last journey. Both these commodities were reduced to a minimum. If, half-way across, the operation was cancelled, *Campbeltown* would have to return under tow.

THE OUTWARD PASSAGE
At 1400 on 26 March 1942, the 10th A/S Striking Force sailed from Falmouth. During daylight, the MLs were in open order at two cables, ahead of the three destroyers, thereby simulating an A/S sweep for the benefit of any prowling enemy aircraft. *MTB 314* was towed by

Atherstone and *MTB 74* by *Campbeltown*. The force gave the Lizard a wide berth and then altered course to follow the passage plan as closely as possible.

The weather could not have been more perfect on the afternoon of 26th: Wind force 4, E.N.E. and with considerable haze .At sunset on 26th, a Hurricane flew low over them as escort, then disappeared to the north in the gathering dusk.

The force altered course to clear the minefield of Ushant, then stood down to the Bay of Biscay, the hunting grounds of Hawk and Cornwallis. The wind eased, the sea became calm and a hazy moonlight night followed. Fourteen knots was maintained so that a speed reduction could be made the next day: at slow speed, a wash was not so visible to reconnaissance aircraft. Lieutenant A. R. Green, R.N., the Force Navigating Officer, had estimated that a speed of $11\frac{1}{2}$ knots was required to arrive at their ETA at the lock gate on time.

The 27 March dawned with the worst possible conditions: maximum visibility and a cloudless sky. At 0700 in position 11 miles S by W of Ushant, speed was reduced to 8 knots and course altered SE. At 0705 *Tynedale* attacked a U-boat (U-593) but failed to sink her. Shortly before noon two French trawlers were boarded, the crews were taken off and the ships sunk. At sunset, course was altered to the NE for position 'Z' where HM Submarine *Sturgeon* was acting as a beacon. At 2200 that night, *Sturgeon's* light was sighted right ahead and the force, at 2314, passed close enough to thank her through the loud hailer.

The destroyers turned away to proceed on their patrol line and the raiding force continued. The lights of fishing craft were away to port and starboard, which was of considerable help as the force might be able to slip through undetected because of the confusion to the enemy's radar.

Another German photograph of HMS Campbeltown *rammed into the Normandie Dock gate shortly before her end. More Germans have joined the inquisitive fo'c'sle party. Gun position M70 is visible on the far side* (*IWM*)

THE APPROACH UP THE LOIRE

Visibility decreased to about two miles as the mist came down. Shortly after midnight on 28 March, there was considerable flak to the north-eastward which indicated to the attackers that the Royal Air Force bombers were over the city as planned. Unfortunately, the R.A.F. did not drop their bombs because of strict orders not to bomb French towns unless the targets could be seen. This order had not been rescinded. The R.A.F. attack, therefore, merely alerted the defences without in any way causing distraction. Thus it was that when the attackers finally reached their destination, all gun emplacements were manned and all troops had stood to.

When in the vicinity of Le Chatelier Shoal at 0045, the northern shore could be dimly seen. The force was now only 7½ miles from St Nazaire and *Campbeltown*,

HMS Campbeltown *wedged securely into the caisson. Note the shell damage and the German inspection party on the fo'c'sle* (*IWM*)

now acting as guide, was given a course to steer by the S.N.O. who was now free in *MGB 314* to manoeuvre ahead in order to take soundings or to obtain radar ranges of the shore.

A considerable northward tidal set was experienced and *Campbeltown* grounded lightly twice, at 0045 and 0055. There were no accurate charts and it was only through the incredible skill of Lieutenant Green that the Force managed to reach its destination.

The Estuary

At 0125 Les Morées tower was passed. The weather was now perfect for the raiders: overcast, with low cloud; misty, with a light drizzle; and with a full moon behind the clouds, so that the night was not too dark. The Force was still undetected by the time it had passed Les Morées tower; everyone was elated and there was much chi-akking amongst the troops.

Discovery

Suddenly, however, an enemy searchlight beam was switched on astern of the force. The cone of light swept up towards the last ML in the line and then, just as detection was inevitable, the light went out. Ryder was able to see against the beam, the silhouette of a vessel patrolling the swept-channel entrance to the north-west.

The raiders were now only 1¾ miles from the lock gates. They were still undetected and apparently had not encountered mine fields, booms or any other obstructions. The greatest triumph was their luck in having crossed the flats of the estuary without stranding any vessel of the Force.

The Run-in

At 0122 the searchlight from No. 3 Heavy Coastal Battery suddenly illuminated the Charpentier Channel. A host of searchlights from both banks of the river opened up. The entire raiding force was illuminated.

Sub-Lieutenant Micky Wynn, now Lord Newborough, DSC, in MTB 74 attacking the lock gate of the Old Entrance. (Artist Brian de Grineau's painting of 1942. Courtesy Messrs Vospers Ltd and Illustrated London News)

The Force had been painted a dark colour; the dirtiest and most tattered ensigns, emblazoned with the crooked swastika, fluttered from the gaffs; and *Campbeltown*'s funnels resembled closely those of a Möwe-class torpedo boat. Each vessel, with her silvery bow-wave, stood out, starkly silhouetted, clean and bright; and *Campbeltown*, a giant amongst pigmies, was, judging by her funnel smoke, obviously increasing speed.

Precious Minutes
The force was challenged from the shore: first, by a coastal battery and later, from somewhere in the dock-yard. Signalman Pike, who was standing next to Commander Ryder, made bogus signals to the Shore Signal Stations; he succeeded, by brilliant deception, in staving off the enemy's fire for another precious four minutes.

Action is joined
Then a heavy fire was suddenly opened on the raiders and general action was joined. Commander Ryder wrote later: 'It is difficult to describe the full fury of the attack which was let loose on both sides: the air became one mass of red and green tracer, most of it going over'.

From the head of the line, it did not appear that any of the shore batteries opened fire but, as the action began, a flak ship, who was sighted ahead, opened fire with her automatic guns. Able Seaman Savage in MGB 314 silenced her but the ship had to be passed unpleasantly close. This guard ship was anchored in the river abreast the South entrance and in the search-lights was easily seen. She received the fire of every ML in turn as they passed and finally the German battery opened fire on the unfortunate ship who finally scuttled herself.

The only known photograph of the end of Campbeltown: the eruption, recorded a minute or so after the explosion
(C. E. Lucas Phillips)

German photograph of a sole survivor, covered in oil and slime, who is waiting on the next morning, to be picked up from his Carley float which is surrounded by wreckage
(C. E. Lucas Phillips)

After three to four minutes of this brisk action, the enemy slackened fire, a triumph for the Coastal Forces gun-layers and for those in *Campbeltown*. The duel was a straight fight between the enemy shore flak emplacements, protected by concrete and steel, against our gunlayers handling short-range weapons on the exposed decks of small, moving and lively craft. Only *Campbeltown* had steel protection but she was the most conspicuous target and so received most of the fire.

This was a short-lived triumph but a fine feat of arms of the British guns' crews and of the Officers and gunners' mates who stood beside the guns directing the fire. The slackening in the enemy's fire came miraculously at the precise moment when Lieutenant-Commander Beattie, on the bridge of *Campbeltown*, was aiming for the dock gate.

FINAL ATTACK

The Old Mole was passed by MGB 314 at a distance of 1½ cables. She then sheered off to starboard to keep clear of *Campbeltown* who had increased to 19 knots for her final run-in.

With only 500 yards to go, Beattie concentrated upon ramming his objective. It is best to recall his recollections:

'The original armaments had been removed and light stages had been built for the Oerlikons which were now in local control and directed by the First Lieutenant, Duff, who had to select the targets. He fired on the searchlights while the stewards and the cooks carried out a brisk fire into the fo'c'sle 12-pounder.'

Campbeltown, having mistaken the East Jetty and nearly run in through the South lock, altered to starboard as her captain fortunately saw a searchlight lighting up the Old Mole. Beattie now had his aiming mark. He was already swinging hard-a-starboard and reached 045°.

Beattie had worked out courses from the Old Mole lighthouse to the centre of the lock, calculations based on *Campbeltown* being half a cable off the Old Mole, when the course should have been 345°. If he was a cable off, he would steer 340° and so on, until he was out to 2 cables. He altered round the Old Mole with 25° of port wheel and ordered Tibbets to steer 340°.

As Beattie passed the Mole, he altered his estimation of his distance-off and so gave Tibbets a new course of 345°. Beattie thought he was nearer half a cable than a

cable. Tibbets did not have time to alter to 340° before Beattie had altered once more to 345°. His guess was good.

Beattie was on the bridge with Tibbets and Captain Montgomery for most of the run-in. Beattie sent Tibbets down to the wheel-house to take charge a few minutes before ramming the lock. The enemy's fire on the bridge had now become extremely hot, so Montgomery and Beattie retired to the wheel-house because they saw no point in being killed: the wheel-house had bullet-proof sheeting around it but the Captain could see adequately.

The soldiers were lying on the deck behind the special steel fences, although some men were in the after superstructure and on the mess decks for'd. Everyone was wearing a Mae West and the gun crews their tin-hats, but not their anti-flash gear.

Campbeltown neared the Old Mole. There was a slight check as she cut through the torpedo nets and then Beattie, concentrating as hard as he could, steered her straight for the lock gates. At the last moment he put his wheel hard-a-port in order to swing her stern clear of the Old Entrance. The wheel-house personnel braced themselves, because no-one knew the effects of a collision at this speed.

There was a rapid de-celeration as she struck and many of those on board did not even know she had hit. Beattie had propped himself against the front of the wheel-house but this was not really necessary. As the crash came, he turned to those around him and remarked: 'Well, there we are'. The impact was four minutes after the Expected Time of Arrival, the crash being at 0134.

In the engine room they were uncertain whether she had, in fact, struck. Though repeatedly hit throughout her length by bullets and shells of about 4-inch calibre and downwards, no essential part of the ship had been damaged. The Coxswain had been wounded in the wheel-house so Tibbets took over the wheel.

Campbeltown's fo'c'sle was ablaze. A vast hole appeared in the fo'c'sle and down this several Commandos fell and were injured. Every Oerlikon was firing at the gun emplacements ashore. The enemy was concentrating his fire upon *Campbeltown* whose bows had run about 35 ft into the 34 ft wide lock. The stem buckled and the fo'c'sle deck ran over the top of the lock to project a foot or so over the other side. This position brought the explosive charge, the foremost end of which was 36 ft from the stem, into an excellent position.

Campbeltown enjoyed a brief relief when ML 160, No. 8 and the torpedo carrier at the head of the starboard column, opened fire accurately with her 3-pounder and silenced flak positions to starboard of the four-stacker.

Objective Achieved

Campbeltown was now wedged in the lock with her charges waiting to explode. The main object of the raid had been achieved. It now seemed that the lock gates would be blown apart: no more could be done and so the secondary objectives were now concentrated upon. Only 40% of the troops, however, were put ashore because of the severe opposition encountered by the ML's. These small craft were set ablaze by the merciless fire from the German guns. Petrol driven and wooden-hulled, the small ships had no chance.

The Commandos

The assault troops and demolition parties, though they carried out their tasks with extreme gallantry and in face of overwhelming opposition, encountered impossible odds. They successfully achieved the following:

1. Inner caisson.	Severely damaged by hand-placed charges.
2. Withdrawing machinery for opening the outer and inner caissons.	Both destroyed by demolition charges; in one case the building also collapsed.
3. The power station.	Not destroyed, as it was situated in the Île St Nazaire.
4. The pumping machinery.	Entirely destroyed, together with many of the culverts and conduits deep down and into which heavy charges were dropped.

The Explosion

At 1135 (local time) on the morning of 28 March, a gigantic explosion shook St Nazaire. *Campbeltown* had blown up, taking some inquisitive 300 German officers and men with her.

The effect of her explosion was interesting:

After impact, the 4-ton high explosive charge must have been within 5 ft of the face of the caisson.

The explosion took place at 1135 (local time) which was at half tide. The Dock was empty and the explosion bent the caisson sufficiently to free it. Under the weight of water outside, the caisson pivoted through 90° into the Dock.

The forward half of *Campbeltown*, as far aft as the foremost funnel, disintegrated. The after part of the ship, however, was later discovered in the middle of the Normandie Dock, where she had been carried by the surge of water. Two merchant-ships, in dock at the time of the explosion, were also swept forward by the rush of water, but they remained afloat.

MTB 74†
Withdrawal and Return

Sub-Lieutenant Micky Winn, now Lord Newborough, D.S.C., reported to the Naval Force Commander who was in MGB 314 and supervising the embarkation of the troops from the Old Mole.

† See Warship Profile No. 7

Wynn's words speak for themselves:

'MTB 74 was especially built for independent operations and was originally brought into being for the purpose of entering Brest with the object of destroying the *Scharnhorst* and *Gneisenau*.

It will be seen from the photographs that the torpedo tubes were mounted unconventionally on the foredeck, as distinct from amidships, the object being that instead of firing torpedoes as such they were, in actual fact, torpedoes stripped of all machinery but each was rammed tight with 1100 lb of aminol, which in those days was considered to be of great potential explosive power. They were fired by compressed air but with a far higher charge than in normal use: the purpose being to propel these explosive monsters a distance of 150 ft, at a minimum height of 3 ft above the water, so that they would be capable of going over the top of the boom protecting these ships and coming to rest on the bottom underneath them. A special fuse was designed which in the case of the adventure at Brest, would have exploded the device within two minutes. The vessel was equipped for cutting booms or, in the case of a light boom, being able to lift it and slide underneath them. The hazardous adventure for entering Brest did not materialise due to the ships escaping just one week before we were due to enter.

MTB 74 was then chosen to go to St Nazaire, with the object of entering the inner basin through the lock gates, which should have been secured and opened by the Commandos. Gaining entry, we were then to proceed to the submarine base and discharge our weapons at this target. Failing this, our secondary object was to blow the small lock gate into the inner basin, which was situated near to where the *Campbeltown* blew the dry-dock gates.

For the St Nazaire operation, new fuses had to be hurriedly designed and it was literally only by a matter of minutes that these were delivered to us to fit in our weapons just before the flotilla was due to leave Falmouth. There had not even been time for them to be tested and we had to fit them ourselves while at sea, which was an unpleasant job, to say the least!

As we could not carry enough petrol for the return trip, we were towed the whole way until we got to

The British character: survivors of ML 306 under guard at the quay side (German photograph). On the left, Swayne (back to camera), Landy (in white submarine sweater); centre, standing, Private Eckmann; kneeling, Corporal Evans; on right, Telegraphist Newman, Stoker Butcher, Ordinary Seaman Batteson, Stoker Ritchie

(C. E. Lucas Phillips)

The Normandie Dock still out of action 10 months after the raid. HMS Campbeltown, her bows blown off, lies half way down the Normandie Dock where she was carried by the surge of water after the destruction of the lock gate. German engineers have sealed the outer entrance with sand to prevent the dock flooding   (IWM)

the estuary. We then took up our position, last in line, giving us a wonderful view of what took place while the little ships and the *Campbeltown* proceeded up the estuary. All seemed to be going extremely well until suddenly hell was let loose. As the Commandos were unable to secure the main lock gate and open it for us, we were ordered to blow the small gates into the inner basin.

While waiting to fire our monsters*, we had picked up 26 survivors. One engine, which had been damaged, had been repaired and so, when Commander Ryder gave us the order to return home, we went at high speed down the estuary, not realising that the German shore batteries had picked us up and were firing with the shells passing astern of us. One was suddenly faced with having to make a very quick decision, as right across our bows were two survivors on a Carley float. It seemed too inhuman to either run them down or pass so close to them and wash them off their means of survival. So, having managed to stop right alongside them and pick them out of the water, the German gunners, unfortunately, put three shells into us and set us on fire.

I was blown from the bridge into the bottom of the boat and my survival was due to P.O. Master Mechanic Lovegrove, who came to look for me and, although he found I was badly wounded, pulled me with him back on deck and into the sea, swimming with me until reaching a Carley float and lashing me to it.

I always feel it an honour to have served with such happy and brave men and it has always been a sad thought that out of a total of 36 only three of us survived, amongst them Lovegrove, to whom I owe my life, and who is still employed by Vospers, who are the builders of the boat.

It has also been a vivid memory in which Commander Ryder so brilliantly and courageously led those who followed him, which made one feel it an honour to be with him.'

Withdrawal and Return

There is not space to record in this Profile the details of the Commandos' battle ashore; the story of the ML's and the withdrawal of the battered craft; the destroyer action between *Atherstone* and *Tynedale* and the five Möwe torpedo boats.

The survivors struggled to their rendezvous in the Loire estuary at 0600 on that historic morning, 28 March 1942, and, meeting *Brocklesby* and *Cleveland* at noon, proceeded at slow speed back to Falmouth.

---

* Wynn fired his torpedoes at the lock gates of the Old Mole. The torpedoes leapt from their tubes, struck the gates, then sank in silence. The torpedoes exploded later; the lock gates were severely strained though not destroyed. The locks, unfortunately, were not rendered tidal.

The Cost

NAVAL: Of the 18 ML's who had set out on the raid, only four returned to Falmouth. MGB 314 had to be sunk by our own gun-fire during the return passage. MTB 74 was sunk by enemy gunfire.

One 'Town' class destroyer had been expended.

34 officers (55%) and 157 ratings (53·5%) were missing or killed.

MILITARY: The surviving troops became prisoners of war, but five succeeded in reaching Gibraltar, with the help of shelter and succour from the French Underground.

Returned to England	109
Prisoners of war	109
Killed or Missing	59

Verdict of History

The Raid achieved its strategic objectives:

(i)   The German heavy ships could no longer dock on the West Coast of France and therefore were withdrawn to home waters for the remainder of the war.

(ii) Because of the spontaneous rising of the French citizens, who erroneously believed that the raid heralded the beginning of the Second Front; and because of fear of repetition of raids of this magnitude, the German army was disproportionately diluted to man the coastal defences along the length of the French seaboard.

The Awards

The Victoria Cross:

Lieutenant-Commander S. H. Beattie, R.N., (HMS *Campbeltown*) ('in recognition not only of his own valour but also that of the unnamed officers and men of the very gallant ships' company').

Sergeant T. F. Durrant, Royal Engineers, 1 Commando (posthumous).

Lieutenant-Colonel A. C. Newman, Essex Regiment, 2 Commando.

Commander R. E. D. Ryder, R.N.

Able Seaman W. A. Savage, R.N.V.R. (posthumous), MGB 314.

Distinguished Service Order:	4 awarded
Distinguished Service Cross:	17 awarded
Military Cross:	11 awarded
Conspicuous Gallantry Medal:	9 awarded
Distinguished Service Medal:	24 awarded
Military Medal:	15 awarded
Mentioned in Dispatches:	51 awarded

HMS *Campbeltown* has become a legend. Her name is synonymous with man's highest endeavour and sacrifice.

Acknowledgements:

The author wishes to express his gratitude and to acknowledge the unstinted service given by The Directors and the Head Librarians of the following authorities:

The National Maritime Museum, Greenwich.
The Imperial War Museum.
The Public Record Office.
The Naval Library and Naval Historical Section.
The City of Southampton Public Libraries.
The Hampshire County Library.
The Winchester City Library.
The City of Plymouth Public Library.

Without the patience and unfailing courtesy of their historical and photographic Staffs, this Warship Profile could not have been produced.

In addition, special thanks are due to Mr R. E. Squires, Head of Photographic Department; and to Mr Roderick Suddaby, Documents Department, The Imperial War Museum, for their forbearance and help.

My gratitude is due to Rear-Admiral Kent W. Loomis, USN, Director of Naval History, Washington, and to his Staff for their co-operation in researching the earlier days of USS *Buchanan;* to Messrs Vosper-Thornycroft Ltd, and to the Bath Iron Works, Maine.

I am deeply indebted to Commander George Gonin, R.N. (Ret'd) and to Lord Newborough, D.S.C., for their invaluable contributions.

Finally, I wish to thank *The Illustrated London News* and *Sketch Ltd* for their kind permission to reproduce Brian de Grineau's picture of MTB 74 attacking the lock gates.

The reproduction of HMS *Campbeltown's* badge is 'Crown copyright'.

Bibliography:

Commander R. E. D. Ryder, V.C., R.N.: THE ATTACK ON ST NAZAIRE. (*John Murray*).

Brigadier C. E. Lucas Phillips, O.B.E., M.C.: THE GREATEST RAID OF ALL (*Heinemann*).

Sampson Low, Marston & Co: JANES FIGHTING SHIPS, 1919 (*David & Charles (Publishers) Ltd*).

The Naval Historical Branch: A SHORT HISTORY OF THE AMERICAN '4-STACKER' DESTROYER (*Admiralty*).

Series Editor: John Wingate, DSC

Appendix

EYE-WITNESS ACCOUNT OF THE AFTERMATH OF THE RAID ON ST NAZAIRE
28TH MARCH—3RD APRIL 1942

The following information as to events subsequent to the raid was obtained from a French electrical mechanic employed at the main electrical and radio workshop in the dockyard. The day after the raid, 28/3, he was unable to work, as the whole port area was closed to the public; but from a house in the town he heard firing punctuated with explosions till about 1000, when there was quiet for a couple of hours. About noon a particularly violent explosion shook the whole city and broke every window within a very large radius.

The next day, 29/3, was a Sunday, and the informant remained at home. A BBC broadcast to which he listened gave the story of the lock gate and the *Campbeltown* (who was said to have exploded in the early morning), but made no mention of the explosion at noon.

On 30/3 he proceeded to work as usual, but instead of

German guard of honour for British dead. Filing past, r to l, are Sergeant Bayliss, Lieutenant Purdon, Sergeant Jones, Private Whelon (?), Lieutenant Roderick, Sergeant Rodd
(C. E. Lucas Phillips)

The Run-In: Campbeltown *has hoisted her battle ensign and increased to 19 knots for the final run-in. The lock gates of the Normandie Dock can be seen on the right. In the foreground is MGB 314 who has moved clear. The artist, Captain Bryan de Grineau, re-created this dramatic moment immediately after the raid* (*Courtesy The Illustrated London News*)

entering the workshop, which was situated just east of the large lock, he passed on to look at the lockgate reported destroyed. No one stopped him as he walked on beyond his factory.

The lockgate was certainly destroyed, and there was no sign of HMS *Campbeltown* beyond some metal debris, but what surprised him most was the surrounding carnage. The whole of the corner on both sides of the lock was littered with legs, arms, heads and entrails. From the scattered pieces, he could see that they belonged to Germans. Military working parties were shovelling the remains together and scattering sand over the ground in a dazed, disorganised way.

He returned to his workshop, where he learned what had happened from some of the German workmen employed there. The *Campbeltown* had crashed into the main gate and was firmly lodged there. She was still there at daybreak, and later a strong cordon of troops had been thrown round the area on both sides of the lock. Meanwhile an inspection party of some 40 senior officers, including the S.N.O. (informant thinks an Admiral), had boarded the ship to see how best she could be moved. Many German soldier

HMS Castleton *(four-stacker) dressed over-all* (MOD)

sightseers had swelled the numbers round the ship. When she went up, they were all wiped out, including the officers on board. Apparently the officer death toll had been heavy on shore as well as on board, and this had a large bearing on subsequent events. The most conservative estimate put this death roll at 300, but many people believed that the figure was nearer 400. Informant believes the higher figure judging from the vast quantity of human remains which on Monday morning still covered the ground.

Work in his factory continued haltingly that day, and in the afternoon informant went over to a ship south of the graving docks to do some W/T repairs. At 1630 hours the port area was shaken by another heavy explosion and everyone rushed back towards the lock to see what had happened. A friend of informant had been working on an electric pylon near the old harbour entrance, and had been thrown off his perch into the water by the explosion. He guessed that a delayed action torpedo had gone off in that lockgate. (*MTB 74*.)

At 1730 hours a second explosion shattered the remains of this entrance. Pandemonium broke out. Together with all the other workers in his area, informant rushed to the bridge over the remaining lockgate. It was packed full of workmen, both French and German, but the exit was barred by sentries. The workmen overpowered them and rushed on to the bridge throwing bicycles over the barrier. The German sentries opened fire, and this was the signal for general firing to break out all over the port. Machine guns were turned on to the crowds of Frenchmen trying to leave the port. In all 280 French workmen were killed in this indiscriminate slaughter.

Informant had his mate killed by his side, and himself succeeded in taking cover in a trench 100 yards to the north-west of the bridge. Here he stayed till nearly midnight waiting for the fire to die down. He lay there in the centre of it all. Every kind of gun was being fired at a non-existent enemy. The German soldiers, having lost so many of their officers in the Saturday mid-day explosion, completely lost their heads and saw British commandos round every corner. Especially they picked on anyone dressed in khaki.

In the port area there was a great number of O.T. (Todt Organisation) men employed on various building jobs. These Germans joined the general panic and were mowed down by machine guns. Their khaki uniforms were mistaken for British battle-dresses. Many were killed under our informant's eyes as they ran. Many others were killed in the Penhouët neighbourhood as they left their work. When informant some days later visited this area he found all the houses facing the Avenue de Penhouët—the road north of Penhouët basin—pockmarked by bullets and shell holes. A heavy battle had obviously been fought here against the imaginary enemy and German O.T. (labour parties) casualties were severe. After darkness the battle continued between the German soldiers themselves, who returned each others fire to good effect. When after several days, things returned to normal, informant gathered that some 300-400 Germans, O.T. workmen and soldiers had been killed in this evening battle.

Launch in Kiel on 22nd August 1938
General-Field Marshal Keitel, Vice-Admiral Horthy (Reich Administrator for Hungary), Grand Admiral Raeder,
Adolf Hitler, after the launch.

Kriegsmarine Prinz Eugen

by Paul Schmalenbach *Fregattenkapitän a.D.*

HISTORICAL BACKGROUND TO THE HEAVY CRUISERS:

The Versailles Treaty, 1919

The Versailles Treaty allowed the German Reich a small navy: six armoured vessels and two reserve units, from which there later stemmed the well-known 'pocket-battleships'. These ships were not permitted to exceed 10,000 tons, their armament being limited to a maximum calibre of 28 cm. (See Profile No 4). In addition, there was an allowance of six cruisers of 6000 tons maximum; two reserve ships; 12 destroyers of 800 tons; 12 torpedo-boats of 200 tons and a few reserve boats, minesweepers and training ships. Manning was restricted to a maximum force of 15,000 on a 12-year service engagement, including at the most 1500 officers, serving for a period of 25 years. Submarines were prohibited, as was any type of aircraft.

Section V of the Versailles Treaty signed in 1919 had read:

'In order to facilitate the introduction of general limitation of armament for all nations, Germany undertakes strictly to observe the conditions specified in respect of land and sea forces and air navigation.'

Viscount Harold Rothermere, former director of the Press Office of the British Ministry of information and newspaper proprietor, wrote in his book, 'Warnings and Prophecies', the following sentences:

'Germany felt, rightly, that it had been cheated at Versailles. On the pretext that this was the first step to World Disarmament, it had been forcibly disarmed.'

The overwhelming majority of Germans thought like Rothermere and the German Government acted accordingly.

The Naval Staff, under its Chief, Admiral Dr h. c. Raeder, was in no doubt that, should the terms of the Versailles Treaty be relaxed, the details of international naval agreements would have to be observed qualitatively. This would mean that, in the construction of battleships and heavy cruisers, the limits of 35,000 tons and 10,000 tons respectively must not be exceeded. The limits of calibre for main armament would be 38·1 and 20·3 cm. respectively.

The Admiral Hipper Class:

the first guns ordered, 1934

The Naval Staff in 1934 issued contracts to the Friedrich Krupp AG in Essen for the construction of 38 and 20·3 cm. guns and double turrets for both calibres. These contracts were a start for the armament of the eventual *Bismarck* Class battleships and of the heavy cruisers of the *Admiral Hipper* Class. But before the construction of these ships could be started there was still some way to go, a way signposted by two dates:

After the launch. In the background the tower of Kiel Town-hall

April 1941 at Kiel

Steaming at over 33 knots. Notice clean entry of the bows and the height of her wash

16 Mar. 1935   By a law re-introducing general conscription, the German Reich re-established its military sovereignty.

18 June 1935   The Anglo-German Naval Agreement laid down, *inter alia*, that German Naval strength could amount to 35% of that of the Royal Navy, each class of ship being considered separately.

Germany was therefor entitled, on the basis of the Royal Navy's current 146,800 tons, to build heavy cruisers to a total of 51,380 tons. At a maximum displacement under previous Naval Agreements (Washington 1922, London 1930) of 10,000 tons, this gave Germany the right to build five heavy cruisers, with an armament limited to a maximum calibre of 8 inches (20·3 cm.).

With the signature of the Anglo-German Supplementary Agreement on 17 July 1937, Germany was granted the right to build further vessels of this type, in addition to the three cruisers already under construction. This addition was occasioned by the Soviet Union's declaration of her intention to build seven cruisers with an armament of 18 cm. calibre.

On 9 July 1935 the German Government announced a building programme that, in addition to two battleships (each of 26,000 tons and armed with 28 cm. guns), 16 destroyers and 28 submarines, also included two heavy cruisers. The two cruisers, planned in detail between 1934 and 1936 by the Design Section of the Naval Staff and first designated, *G* and *H*, were later named *Blücher* and *Admiral Hipper*. The *Admiral Hipper* was laid down in 1935 in the yard of Blohm & Voss AG, Hamburg, and launched on 6 February 1937, her name being used to designate the whole class. Her sister ship was only begun in 1936 at the Deutsche Werke, Kiel (successors to the former Imperial Shipyard), and launched on 8 June 1937.

PRINZ EUGEN: building and launching

In the autumn of 1936, the Krupp Germania Shipyard, Kiel, started work on the third heavy cruiser, originally designated, *J*.

The launch took place on 22 August 1938 during the period of a State visit by the representative of the King of Hungary, Vice-Admiral Nikolaus Horthy de Nagyhanya, Madame Horthy naming the ship.

In 1866, the Austrian Navy was one of the two navies then in existence in the German Federation. Together with the Prussian navy, the Austrian squadron under Commodore Tegetthoff had fought off Heligoland in 1864. So it was very natural to think of choosing a name for a new ship from their common history in order to emphasize the historical links with the Eastern March. The choice fell first on the victor of Lissa, Rear-Admiral

Prinz Eugen camouflaged before the Bismarck *operation. Her reconnaissance aircraft is ready for launching on the catapult*

Wilhelm von Tegetthoff, who without any doubt was the outstanding leader of the former Austrian Navy (the Tegetthoff family originated in Westphalia). The heavy cruiser then being built in the Germania yard was to receive this name. But having regard to the possible injured feelings of their Axis partner, Italy, the Reich Government decided to specify the name, *Prinz Eugen*.

The Three Heavy Cruisers:
Admiral Hipper, Blücher and Prinz Eugen

At first glance, the three cruisers were externally so similar as to be almost identical. This applies in particular to the hulls, the armour-plating and the propulsion units. The *Prinz Eugen* was however 6·6 m longer, 0·6 m wider, had 0·2 m greater draught and correspondingly 200 tons greater displacement.

Prinz Eugen: Design specifications

The ships were of longitudinal-frame, band-steel construction with 18 main watertight compartments and a double bottom over 72% of the total length.

Dimensions:

Length, waterline	199·5 m
Length, overall, before modification	207·7 m
Length, overall, (Atlantic stem)	212·5 m
Beam	21·9 m
Draught maximum	7·94 m
Draught full load	6·37 m

Displacement:

Full load	16,230 tons
Maximum load	18,400 tons
Official standard, officially quoted	10,000 tons

Costs:
(in millions of Reichmarks)

Admiral Hipper	87·8
Blücher	85·8
Prinz Eugen—extra cost due to more modern fire-control system	104·5

The mainmast from aft and looking forward. The extensive aerial network, the two after searchlights and the port after 10·5cm AA mounting are clearly shown

Prinz Eugen: *port side, after the new radar has been fitted*

Prinz Eugen: *starboard side, before fitting of new radar*

Torpedoed by HM Submarine Trident (*Commander G. M. Sladen*). Prinz Eugen, *her stern nearly blown off, steams into Trondheimfjord and manoeuvres by using her propellers to steer*

Engine Performance:

Contract specification	132,000 s.h.p. = 32 kt.
Admiral Hipper	134,000 s.h.p. = 32·5 kt.
Prinz Eugen	132,000 s.h.p. = 33·4 kt.

Range and Speeds

The cruising range was initially 6300 nautical miles at 20 knots; later, after conversion of a few bunkers and the filling of the roll-damping installation with fuel-oil instead of water, it reached 8000 nautical miles at 20 knots. For this, at type displacement, the ship could carry 1460 cu.m. of oil; at maximum displacement, 3250 cu.m. oil, and after refit, 4250 cu.m.

Range at 4250 tons, with all oil-bunkers 85% full:

2050 nautical miles at 32 knots
    = 64 hours = approx. 2·6 days
5500 nautical miles at 18 knots
    = 305 hours = approx. 12·8 days
6100 nautical miles at 15 knots
    = 400 hours = approx. 16 days

Using only 2 shafts:
6750 nautical miles at 15 knots
    = 450 hours = approx. 19 days

Using centre shaft alone:
7600 nautical miles at 12 knots
    = 633 hours = approx. 26 days

Speeds

Maximum speed over a period with three shafts, at 290 r.p.m. of the screws, 32·5 knots.
With the two outer shafts in use 27·0 knots (280 r.p.m.).
With centre shaft alone 22 knots (259 r.p.m.).
The reversing turbines could be used continuously for 30 minutes. They delivered 15,000 s.h.p. at 150 r.p.m. The highest speed attained was 33·4 knots at 133,631 s.h.p.

The stern is dismantled. Assistance is provided by the repair ship

The Mine Boom, Blisters and Underwater Fittings

The three ships had side-blisters to increase stability and unsinkability, and a bow blister that carried a passive underwater listening device. In the midships plane of the forecastle was located a tube, angled forwards and down at approximately 45°, with an internal diameter of some 20 cm. Into this the mine-boom (or 'asparagus' as the crew called it) could be withdrawn when not in use; the lower end of this served as a point of attachment for the mine-deflecting devices. Hawsers or chains, hammered to a sharp edge, served as shearing lines to the ends of which were attached the 'Otter' paravanes with their quick-release mountings near the forward turret. To bring this device into operation the boom was extended forward and down, the drive being electric.

The ships had bilge keels and one rudder. There were a great many perforations of the outer shell, by far the largest being the intakes and outlets for cooling water.

Armour Protection

The three cruisers had extensive armour protection. The thickness of the upper deck armour was 12 mm, or 30 mm in the area of the four heavy gun-turrets; the thickness of the actual armoured deck, 20, 30, 40 and 50 mm, depended on the importance of the space beneath to be protected. For this purpose Krupp supplied their Wh-material, whereas 20 mm Ww-material was used for the torpedo bulkhead. Kc-material of Krupp manufacture was used for the hull side armour plating (70 and 80 mm), as well as for all the following protective armour:

Control Tower—horizontal	50mm
vertical	150mm
After-conning tower—horizontal	20mm
vertical	30mm
Optical range finding apparatus	20mm
Foretop platform	20mm
Spherical segments of the anti-aircraft command-posts	17mm
Main armament turrets—top	70mm
front faces	105mm
side walls	70mm

All cable runs of importance for navigation and fire-control were laid in square trunking of splinter-proof material; this trunking was easy to open.

Draught and Sinkage

The moulded depth of the hull at the main bulkhead was 10·15 m for type-displacement and 12·45 m for maximum displacement.

With the ship lying at the designed waterline, the addition of a weight of 14·12 tons caused a general increase in submersion of one centimetre below that level.

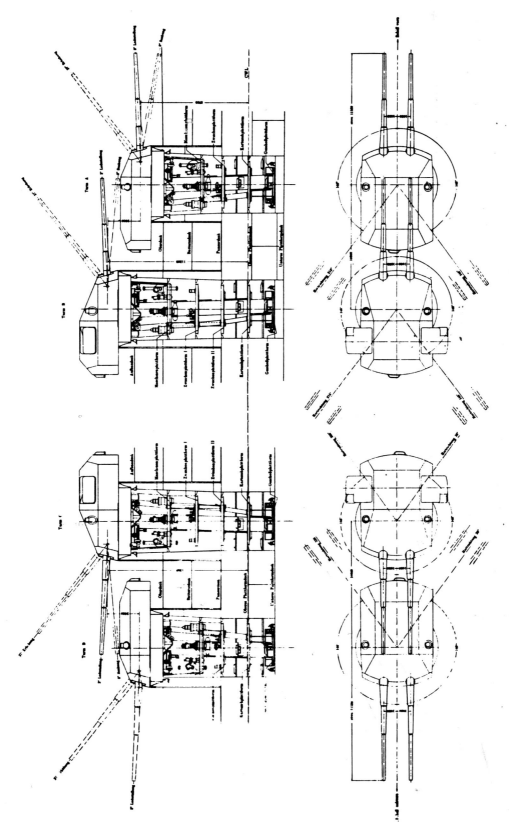

The 20·3cm quick-firing guns and turrets

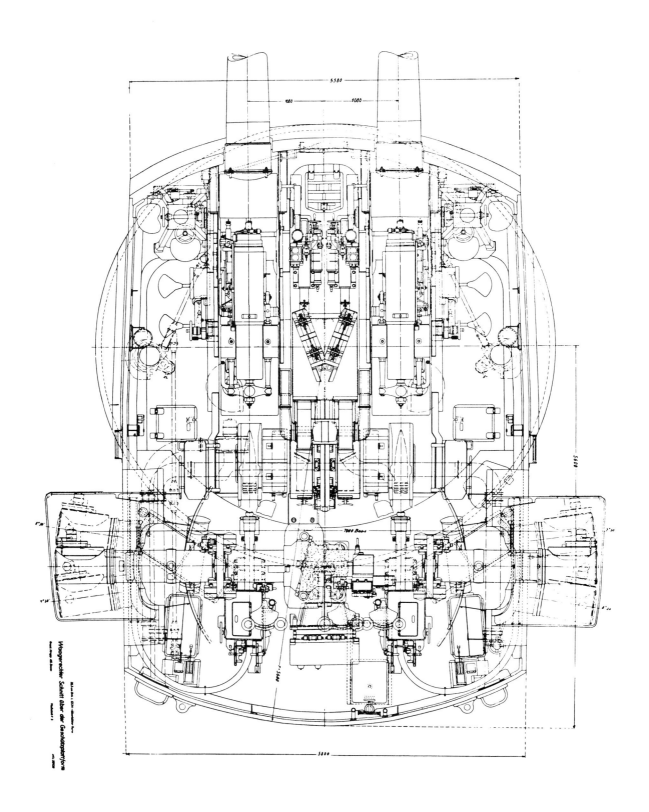

Plan view of a 20·3cm gun turret

The Propulsion Installation

The installation comprised 12 (only nine in the *Seydlitz* and *Lützow*) very high pressure boilers operating at a temperature of 450°C and at varying working pressures (*Blücher* and *Prinz Eugen* 70 atmospheres, *Admiral Hipper* 80, *Seydlitz* and *Lützow* 60 atmospheres). Depending on load, the boilers delivered from 35 to a maximum of 50 tons of steam per hour. The boilers were designed to fundamental ideas by Wagner but, for the *Admiral Hipper* and *Prinz Eugen*, as boilers with forced circulation in accordance with the La Mont principle. These latter used, at maximum load, 0·320 kg. of fuel oil per h.p. per hour.

The 12, or nine, boilers were installed in three boiler-rooms arranged one behind the other, and supplied three sets of geared turbines, each arranged in three housings. (Primary revolutions, with high- and medium-pressure stages fully loaded, 3840 r.p.m., with low-pressure stage fully loaded, 2820 r.p.m.)

Each set of turbines drove a propeller-shaft carrying a three-bladed propeller of 3·15 m external diameter. The centre engine was in the after engine-room, the port and starboard engines in the room immediately forward of it. The main suppliers were Deschimag, but for *Admiral Hipper* the Blohm & Voss shipyard and for *Prinz Eugen* Brown, Boveri & Co. The propulsion installation was highly refined and demanded of the engine-room crew very good training and constant close attention. (When the *Prinz Eugen* was finally

Torpedoed by HM Submarine Trident: *the damaged stern*

handed over to an American crew one of its 12 boilers was out of action; on arrival in Honolulu only one of the ship's boilers was reputed to be in action.)

The installation of the *Admiral Hipper* produced many problems and repeatedly gave cause for complaint. In the case of the *Prinz Eugen*, after the ship had parted from the *Bismarck* and was operating alone, admittedly in more southerly latitudes, it became obvious that the cooling of the condensers with sea-water was not adequate. The positioning and cross-section of the cooling-water inlets were respectively wrong and inadequate.

Side elevation of a 20·3cm gun turret

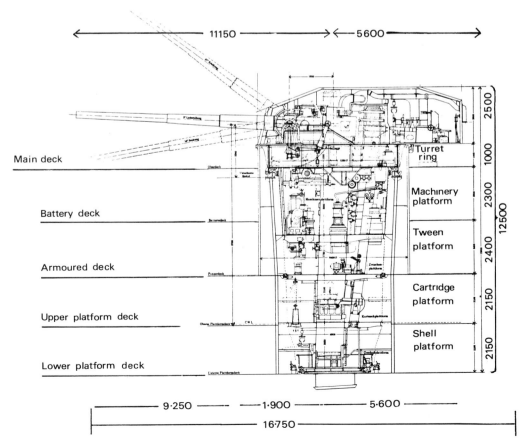

Huascaran. *Two emergency rudders are constructed, fitted and operated through the stern capstan*

ARMAMENT
The 20·3 cm Quick Firing Gun

The main armament was represented by the eight Krupp 20·3 cm guns in four twin-turrets, two forward and two aft, and designated A, B, C and D from the forward turret aft. The heavy guns thus corresponded to the standard introduced into almost every navy. The official description ran:

20·3 cm quick-firing gun C/34 in turntable mounting C/34, where 'C/34' signified start of construction 1934.

The 20·3 cm quick firing gun:

Barrel elevation	45°
Barrel depression	10°
Rate of fire	3 shells/min
Maximum range	39,400 yards

Ammunition:

Armour-piercing shell, with sensitive nose fuse,	
or with base fuse	960 rounds
1944 modification	1060 rounds
Starshell	80 rounds

FIRE CONTROL

Fire-control was exercised by four target-directors, two of which were to port and starboard high up in the foretop and one each in the forward and after command posts. These target directors were replaced at night by four special night target columns on each side of the forward command-post on the bridge, and on each side of the after command-post, and reinforced by two particularly good night-glasses on either side of the lower bridge-structure.

The turrets and guns could be fired individually. The turrets could be remotely controlled together, in groups (forward or aft), or individually, or directed from the control tower.* Fire-control and gun-laying equipment were linked with the turrets by a comprehensive cable-network, which radiated from the main junctions in the two gunnery control-centres. The deflection calculations were made in the two firing-data computers C/38 K, where K designated the version produced for 'kreuzers'.

The computers were installed in the forward and after surface-target computing centres respectively. Here, as also in the three command-posts and four turrets, auxiliary gear was provided to enable fire to be maintained independently in the event of a breakdown in fire-control or rupture of the cable connectors. This equipment comprised the EU/SV indicator (rate-of-range-difference and lateral-deflection indicator), course and a speed indicator for calculating range settings and a wind speed and direction indicator.

The Turret Machinery

The 20·3 cm turrets were traversed electrically. The elevation of the barrels, the opening and closing of the breeches, the loading of the shell and main cartridge (the detonating charge pushed home by hand!) and the ammunition feed were all operated hydraulically. The hydraulic pump was driven electrically.

The Target Directors

The target directors and range-finding equipment were stabilised in laying and training by a centrally operated 'master stabilising unit' which was duplicated as a stand-by. This made it possible to engage two targets simultaneously, each under complete fire-control.

However, a land-target computer was available only in the forward surface-target computing-centre. This particular equipment enabled land-targets to be bombarded even when they were not visible from the ship. A prior requirement, however, was that the geographical bearing and distance of the target relative to an auxiliary target, visible from the ship, should be known.

Primary Action Control

In battle, the control of the heavy armament was normally exercised from the foretop by the First Gunnery Officer, using one or other of the target selectors located there. Two other Gunnery Officers were in the forward and after command-posts, ready to take over control in case of breakdown or sighting difficulties, and at night to control fire from the night target indicators.

Searchlights

Behind the two night-target columns, two searchlight-training units were arranged on either side for the remote control of the five searchlights, each with 200 cm diameter mirrors. Even the striking and dousing of the arc, as well as the opening and closing of the blind-shutters, was controlled from these training units.

One searchlight was attached to the forward side of the fighting mast below the foretop, two others on either side of the funnel and two on the searchlight platform aft. In the case of the *Blücher*, the searchlights were retained but, in the *Admiral Hipper* and the *Prinz Eugen*, the forward searchlights were removed and replaced by light anti-aircraft guns. In the *Prinz Eugen*, the forward searchlight was replaced in Brest (January 1942) and the two on the funnel in Kiel in June/July 1942; in the *Admiral Hipper* this was carried out during the end of spring, 1941.

RANGE DETERMINATION: two methods

For daylight engagements, the determination of range became increasingly important as the range increased. For this reason, from as far back as 1932, no pains were spared to ensure maximum accuracy for this important gun-laying parameter. To this end two distinct paths were followed:

* The barrels of the turrets could be freed from each other, i.e., the barrels could be elevated independently of each other, thus compensating for different losses of muzzle velocities. This factor explains the high accuracy of bombardment.

Steering the ship by operating the jury rudders by capstan power. The wires leading through leading-blocks to the rudder yokes can be clearly seen

The repaired stern, showing the new bulkhead and two jury rudders

1. Optical range-finders

The first was the extension and improvement of the method employed hitherto, by increasing the performance of the optical measuring-instruments with a considerable lengthening of the measuring base. So the ships acquired, in addition to two extremely high-intensity instruments with 3 m base on either side of the bridge, five instruments with 7 m base. Two were fitted in the upper turrets, B and C, the turret roofs being suitably modified. Three similar instruments were installed in so called 'swivelling cupolas', mounted on the roofs of the foretop control-post, and the forward and after control-posts respectively.

The instruments in the turrets could be deflected by some 10° relative to the line of fire, since they had to be directed at the target rather than along the line of fire. The swivelling cupolas had unlimited freedom or lateral movement. All instruments were stabilised in respect of elevation, to facilitate gun-laying when the ship was rolling.

2. The first radar

The second method was the use of electromagnetic waves, the time taken for these waves to travel from ship to target and back being measured. This was a fundamental concept first brought to practical realisation on 20 March 1934, in Kiel (48 cm wavelength): the first successful attempt at radar.

After further development and experience, the heavy cruisers were equipped with two radar installations of 80 cm wavelength, changed to 50 cm in 1943. The sets were installed, one on the foretop rotating cupola, the other on the cupola of the after control-post. The range thus measured was initially passed on by telephone; later it was fed in automatically by remote control in the fire-control for the heavy armament.

Radar Search Receivers

In the *Prinz Eugen*, a third set was installed on the main-mast in the summer of 1943. The aerial array stood, free to rotate, at a considerable height, while the associated crew were housed in an extra cabin below. At the same time, receiving aerials were fitted on the four sides of the protective plating round the main anti-aircraft command-post in the foretop, to give warning of enemy radar transmissions.

A.A. Gunnery Fire Control

Under the overall responsibility of the First Gunnery Officer, the Second Gunnery Officer exercised control over the heavy, medium and light anti-aircraft armament. The heavy anti-aircraft guns consisted of 12 10·5 cm guns in twin mountings, the medium originally of 12 3·7 cm guns and the light of eight 2 cm machine guns. All three types of mounting had movement for laying in three axes, the third being designed to counter the ship's rolling motion (parallel to the deck plane in the line of fire).

Prinz Eugen *from right ahead. Note the new radar aerial complex and the two large range finders*

The new radar seen from the fo'c'sle

The ship's boats: motor boat and cutter shown on the crane and at the davits

The 10·5s

The 12 heavy anti-aircraft guns could, depending on the particular conditions of attack, be massed in four groups with up to four twin mountings, that is up to eight guns, into batteries under the control of an officer or senior petty officer.

The A.A. Directors (Command Posts)

The officer sat in one of the four stabilised anti-aircraft command-posts; these were such a typical feature of German battleships and heavy cruisers, the spherical upper section being gimbal-mounted and enclosing the stabilised gun-laying and ranging platform. Externally these command-posts were identical. The *Prinz Eugen*, like the *Bismarck* and the *Tirpitz*, had the later version, in which the stabilisation was governed by a system of small gyroscopes, whereas the older version still operated with heavy gyros.

The Computers

The rate-of-change of target-bearing and elevation, together with the measured range, were fed into one of the four computers for calculating the deflection and control of the guns (azimuth, elevation and roll angles) and for conversion in the fuse-setting machines to the appropriate time-setting on the shell-fuses. The four anti-aircraft computers were installed in pairs in the forward and after anti-aircraft computer centres respectively.

The 10·5 cm guns also served as medium armament,*

* The port battery of 10·5 guns fired at *Prince of Wales* at ranges from 1500 to 1800 yards.

for use against marine targets. Their maximum range amounted to 19,240 yards, their supply of ammunition 400 rounds per gun, making a total of 4800 rounds.

Target Selection

The four battery-controllers had the targets for attack allotted to them by remote indication from the two anti-aircraft command-posts. Target bearing and elevation angles were indicated by one of the target selector units, installed two each in the main command-post (gallery surrounding the foretop command-post) and the reserve post aft (behind the main mast), via remote-controlled slave dials, to the layers in the control post. In both command-posts, there were command switch-panels by means of which control posts, computers and guns could be switched without delay to another control system in order to concentrate fire against the more dangerous attacker. Each battery was represented in the two control posts by a rating acting as 'messenger'.

10·5 cm Ammunition Supply

The ammunition was transferred from the magazines below by electrically-driven endless chains. This conveyor system stopped automatically when the gun's supply requirement was satisfied. A stand-by facility was provided by normal hoists consisting of rope winches with attached baskets each holding six rounds.

The 3·7s

The 12 3·7 cm guns in six twin-turrets were mounted on both sides of the bridge structure, the after anti-aircraft command-post and the after control centre.

The normal centre-spread presentation has been reversed because the upper deck plan and profile elevation are based upon the original German drawings which used 'Third Angle' projection.

The Arado 96 twin-float seaplanes could be recovered only on the port side where the landing mat was stowed.

Boiler room control panel

Electrical power station control panel

in the torpedo-head magazine below deck. For the remaining parts, storage-lockers were fitted on either side of the funnel on the boat-deck. Before the Channel break-through, these 12 torpedoes were put ashore to avoid unnecessary risk to the ship. Large workshops and torpedo priming and checking areas were located on the upper deck forward of the cross-walk behind the funnel-shaft.

Torpedo Control

The torpedo armament was controlled by the First Torpedo Officer in the forward control post with the aid of torpedo target-directors. Of these, there were two in the forward, and one in the after control-post for the Second Torpedo Officer. It was possible to feed the target-bearing information from the gun's target-selectors in the foretop into the torpedo control-unit, so that the torpedo armament could be used even at very great ranges.

In addition there were two torpedo night-target columns on the bridge and two on either side of the after control post. The necessary computer and switch-gear were installed in the torpedo computer-centre beneath the armoured deck.

The Ship's Aircraft

The torpedo section, i.e. the torpedo crew, also had responsibility for the whole of the equipment concerned with the take-off, stowage and recovery of the ship's aircraft. The actual catapults were all of the same design.

The provision of additional storage and maintenance accommodation for the three aircraft on each ship was however arranged differently. On the *Admiral Hipper* and *Blücher*, the catapults were immediately forward of the mainmast and the aircraft hangar was forward again of this, that is between catapult and funnel;

Chart Room

Ship's aircraft, Arado 196, being manned for catapulting

Sketch of aircraft stowage

Aircraft stowage

however, on the *Prinz Eugen* the catapult was sited aft of the funnel and forward of the hangar.

The Cranes

The planes were hoisted on to the catapult or into the hangar by means of the ship's crane. In the *Prinz Eugen* only the port crane, lengthened by some two metres and sited some two metres further aft than the starboard crane, could be used for this purpose.

Aircraft Stowage

The aircraft stood one behind the other, the rear aircraft being placed on a carriage which then moved downwards to the rear.

In the *Prinz Eugen*, the hangar roof consisted of two sections, the forward section being pushed aft over the rear section to open right back under the after signal deck until it butted against the after anti-aircraft control post; to make this possible the after mast, i.e. the mainmast, had its foot stepped on a cross-bearer and, for the same reason, the after searchlight platform had splayed legs.

The Arado 196

(See Warship Profile No 4)

The three ship's aircraft were of the *Arado* 196 type: they were twin-float seaplanes for reconnaissance, gun-ranging observation and submarine chasing. Their engines developed 960 h.p., giving them a speed of 174 m.p.h., with a flight endurance of three and a half hours which required 600 litres of petrol. They had two fixed, built-in 20 mm machine-guns. The observer, seated behind, had a moveable 7·9 mm machine-gun and bombs to drop from the belly of the fuselage. As a rule, the aircraft were catapulted off at an angle, to port or starboard.

Recovery

All ships carried out the recovery operation on the port-side, because it was on this side that a landing-mat had originally been provided. This was originally fitted in the *Admiral Hipper*, but was removed in 1939 because it did not prove a success. The two other ships never had this landing-mat.

The landing of the aircraft and their recovery was decisively helped by appropriate ship's manoeuvres, particularly in bad weather. Depending on wind-strength, direction and the sea running at the time, the

Hoisting out the aircraft preparatory to unfolding wings

Diagrammatic sketch of retractable pole-mast

Hooked on! Note the steadying line, the snaking wake and the two torpedo mountings

The cruiser Leipzig *rammed by* Prinz Eugen. Leipzig *is low in the water*

ship smoothed the surface by swinging the rudder hard over, from side to side.

The Anchors

The sea-going equipment included anchor equipment and boats. The three bow anchors, weighing 6·5 tons each, were housed in hawse pipes and secured with short chains and tensioning bolts, one to starboard, the second to port and the third amidships in a stem hawse-pipe. In the course of the war, this last was removed as compensation for the weight of the additional anti-aircraft guns; up till then the port anchor had served as reserve anchor.

The anchor chains differed in length (port 250 m, starboard 275 m). The anchor capstans were driven by 50 h.p. electric motors, as was the capstan of the stern anchor, which was attached with a steel hawser 200 m in length.

The Ship's Boats and Rafts

The complement of boats included the following:

No.	Designation	Length	Size of engine	Capacity
one	captain's gig	9·0m	75 h.p.	22 men
two	liberty boat	11·5m	65 h.p.	80 men
one	pinnace	8·0m	52 h.p.	27 men

Pulling boats: two Class I cutters (with 10 oars), a barge for outboard work and two dinghies.

The boats were stowed on either side of the funnel on the boat-deck or on the boat-platform extension to this deck, which extended to the ship's side. The cutters on the other hand were slung in heavy rectangular frames which were lowered for hoisting the boats inboard or out-board but, when clearing away for action, were raised into the vertical position by threaded spindles.—In the course of the war many life-rafts were taken aboard, some of rigid manufacture, others of rubber and inflatable. They were distributed as space permitted and secured in place.

Booms and Accessories

When the ship lay at anchor, boats were made fast to the two lower booms; the captain's gig had its place at the stern-boom on the port quarter.

The ship had two or three accommodation ladders which, because of the great height of the ship's sides, were broken by a platform half-way.

To protect the propellers when lying at a jetty, a guard was attached on either side just above the water-line: this was folded back against the hull when the ship left port.

Masts and Rigging

The rigging of the ship, in addition to the jack-staff on the stem, a flag-staff on the stern-post, and a small staff on the after control-post, consisted of a fighting-mast in the form of a rectangular tower with rounded corners, and a mainmast with a tripod lower section. The fighting-mast carried at the rear a pole topmast which could be completely lowered until it rested on the funnel. The top was then on a level with the foretop control post. On the afterside of the fighting-mast, to starboard, was the shaft for the 2 cm ammunition-hoist.

Inside the mast, the individual decks were linked by companion-ways. The vertical centre-leg of the main-mast was hollow to accommodate the centre section of the upper mast, which could be lowered at need as far as the signal- and aerial-yard. The mainmast had to be shortened this way when the ship passed through the Kiel Canal.

Yards and signal halyards for visual signalling were located at the upper end of the lower section of the mainmast, and below the anti-aircraft control-centre on the turret-mast.

The Radio and Radio-Reconnaissance Equipment

The masts also carried the aerials for a very comprehensive radio installation, with transmitters and receivers each installed in separate rooms. The control of radio communications was centred in the operations information station, where the so-called *B-Dienst* groups were also accommodated (*B-Dienst*=Observation Service, nowadays 'Radio Reconnaissance').

Aircraft Information Centre

A special aviation information centre, for the collection of all reports on friendly and enemy aircraft movements, was located immediately below the foretop station in the turret-mast. It was linked to the anti-aircraft control-centre by telephone and speaking-tube.

The Bridges

Below lay the Admiral's bridge-cabin, below that the Admiral's bridge and below that again a signals centre for command of the formation. The signal bridge below this opened to the rear on to the storage racks for the signal flags and the operation area for the signal halyards. On the two bridge wings stood signal lamps. The lowest two decks of the fighting-mast, designated upper and lower bridge deck, contained living quarters for officers and warrant officers, the meteorological centre and, closest to the bridge, the captain's bridge-cabin.

The Forward Superstructure

The forward superstructure was divided into three decks. The uppermost was called the superstructure deck which, at the forward end, supported the control tower, the substructure of which was continued down to the next lower deck, the boat-deck. Within this substructure was located the operations information centre already mentioned.

The space between this centre and the front-wall to behind B turret held the chart room including the radio direction-finder.

THE CHART ROOM AND DIRECTION FINDER RECEIVER
The chart room and normal navigation wheelhouse—situated forward of the control tower—were linked by a companionway.

The Control Tower

The control-tower consisted of two parts, one part forward and slightly lower, with the navigational equipment (steering wheel, engine telegraphs, telephones, five telescopes: for captain, officer-of-the-watch, helmsman, navigating-officer, formation command) and an almost circular area, situated slightly higher and enclosed by the lower section at its forward extremity. One gun control and two torpedo controls were centred on this 'forward control station'.

On the roof was a rotating cupola with a range-finder of 7 m base. The control tower and control centre were linked by an armoured shaft. In this control shaft ran the most important telephone and telegraph cables. Metal rungs enabled it to be used as a rapid access route.

The Sick Bay

The remaining rooms in this bridge structure served as living quarters. In the lowest deck, that is the upper or main-deck level, was located the very large ship's sick-bay with all auxiliary accommodation such as operating theatre, investigation room, dispensary and dentist's surgery; and in the forward section the mess, with sleeping and living accommodation for 30 midshipmen.

Accommodation

Further aft on the main deck was the torpedo section already mentioned and, behind the crosswalk, the galley, preparation rooms for 10·5 cm ammunition, aircraft hangar and a large number of air-intake and ventilator shafts for boiler and engine-rooms; then came the after superstructure, which contained on the lowest deck the officers' mess with pantry, cabins for

The new bow section is outlined in white. Note mines spar protuberance

staff-officers and a large conference room. Above this, on the boat deck, right aft, was the cabin for common use of the Duty Commanding Officer and Captain; forward of this, on the starboard side, working and living quarters for the Admiral, on the port side for the captain; then a pantry and above that—in the substructure of the anti-aircraft control-centre—the bakery and galleys for officers and captain, which however were not used as such during the war, as the whole crew was served the same food.

The Decks

Within the hull, the decks, reading from top to bottom, were named as follows:
Battery deck
Lower deck (largely identical with the armoured deck)
Upper platform deck
Lower platform deck
Stowage

The starboard crane. The forward middle deck with set of torpedo-tubes: pillar under anti-aircraft control-post A, and under boat platform, the gangway fastened to the rail

In Kiel dry-dock, 1942. The camouflage netting and port propeller guard are visible

3·7cm gun in action. The target director and crew can be seen below the gun mounting

Target director equipment (*two in foretop, two in after anti-aircraft control-centre*)

Boiler and engine-rooms extended in height through both platform decks. All other compartments, well in excess of 200, all capable of being sealed off and made watertight, were only one deck high.

The battery and lower decks were above all the crew's living quarters. The ratings occupied the midship section, the junior petty officers the forward section, where they had pantries and refrigerators at their disposal, and the chief petty officers—mostly designated '*Portépéeunteroffiziere*'—in the after section, where a 'warrant officers' mess, with pantry was installed for their use. Individual, particularly important senior warrant officers, had living quarters in the vicinity of their battle- or duty-stations (senior coxswain, chief yeoman of signals, senior boatswain).

Workshops of the most varied types were distributed throughout the whole ship, though provision stocks and refrigerated storerooms were in the forepart. Even the compartments located on the sloping surfaces of the armoured deck, with almost triangular cross-section and mostly known on board as 'pockets', served as store-rooms.

The Armoured Deck

The armoured deck ran from the stern to forward of the 20·3 cm ammunition magazines for A turret at lower deck level, from there to the stem one deck lower, that is at the level of the upper platform deck. In this extreme, forward section the armour was not angled downwards at the sides. Above the rudder stock a

hemisphere provided protection for this important component.

Magnetic Mine Protection (De-Gaussing)

The ships were provided with MES-equipment (=autoprotection against mines) as protection against mines and torpedoes fitted with magnetic detonators. The cables needed for this purpose were attached on the outside of the hull under half-round covers bolted to the hull. These protective covers were located in the angle between the oblique hull-sides and the side-blister.

Gyro Compass, Flag-deck and Smoke Apparatus

The gyro-compass equipment consisted of two master-compasses to which up to 20 slave compasses could be linked.

A battle signal station for handling flag-signals was located below the signal-yard of the mainmast on the battery-deck. The signal halyards were therefore very long and were led in through the boat deck via apertures fitted with funnel-shaped guides.

At the stern was a 'smoke locker', accessible only from the upper deck, in which were several containers with smoke-making chemicals. The equipment could be switched on and off both from the forward and after control centres. To enable the ship to conceal itself behind a smoke-screen produced by a source independent of the ship itself, there were 20 smoke buoys

Interior of 20·3cm gun house: 'A' turret, left barrel

Brest: Prinz Eugen *camouflaged against air-raids*

20mm gun and range-finder crew

Aerial view of Prinz Eugen *in dry dock.*

on either side of the aft superstructure. These could be swiftly detached and thrown overboard.

Ship Handling

Opinions about ships of the *Admiral Hipper* class differ regarding their seamanlike handling qualities. This may in part be due to the fact that the two ships, *Admiral Hipper* and *Prinz Eugen*, on whom judgements are available, had differing underwater hull-shapes because of their varying dimensions; added to this, were also slight differences in the rudder arrangements. Both ships rode well, moved gently and were somewhat tender. They responded slowly to the helm, though their response could be accelerated considerably in the *Prinz Eugen*, if the speed was raised.

The turning-circle radius was some 450 m; for the *Prinz Eugen*, after losing her stern and standard rudder and after having two emergency rudders fitted, the turning circle was some 960 m. In this state the *Prinz Eugen* achieved 28 knots on trials. The testing of the emergency rudder was not continued further at the time, as the speed was adequate and there was no wish to risk the whole emergency rudder rig unnecessarily.

Strategic and Tactical Staff Requirements

The ships had been built with the aim, should it come to a war with France, of cutting off as far as possible the supply of French reinforcements and, above all, the transfer of French armies from Africa to Europe. For years on end these ships could have been opposed by only the heavy cruisers of the French fleet and some

of these would have been tied down in the Mediterranean by the Italian threat to the flank. With the exception of the *Algérie*, the French cruisers were considered by the German Navy inferior to their own heavy cruisers.

The author still has a very clear recollection, however, that the procedure in the event of an encounter with the *Algérie* had been thought out in great detail and that in many exercises, on clearing away the ship for action, such an encounter specified the hits assumed by those conducting the exercise.

The armoured de-gaussing cable which runs around the ship externally

Overall view of bridge. Men closed up at action stations, but not alerted for action. Captain Brinkmann on starboard wing of bridge, interested in something on starboard quarter, and all on his side looking in that direction. During cruise with the Bismarck

1943/45. The starboard well-deck. Note boiler-room intakes. Funnel fumes are obscuring the fighting mast and radar aerials

Bismarck *steams past* Prinz Eugen *off Bergen*

VERDICT OF HISTORY

From the moment that England had to be taken into account, first as a presumed and then as an actual enemy, any assessment of the ships must be less favourable. No doubt the German Naval Operations Staff still believed for a long time that they could maintain the ships in the Atlantic almost unhindered with the help of a wide-ranging supply network: an assumption that may well have seemed to be substantiated by the *Admiral Hipper* enterprise (November 1940 —March 1941).

This supposition was no longer justified a few months later, as was proved in May 1941 by the wholesale extinction of the supply ships which were to look after the *Bismarck* and *Prinz Eugen*. If a verdict on the ships is to be given, it must be said that they were outstandingly suitable for their original task but that they could hardly cope with the actual task imposed on them from May 1941 onwards: the demands which were made upon these superb cruisers exceeded their strength, which can be here expressed as *operational range*.

THE LIFE OF THE HEAVY CRUISER, PRINZ EUGEN

Main dates:

1939	From August until the end of 1939, the sale of the three still incomplete heavy cruisers *Prinz Eugen*, *Seydlitz* and *Lützow* to the Soviet Union was under discussion; on 8.12.1939 the decision was however reached to sell only the *Lützow* to Russia.
July 1940	Still not in commission, the *Prinz Eugen* received one bomb-hit in British air-raids on both 1 and 2.7.1940, while in the Germania yard at Kiel (in front of the main railway station).
1 Aug. 1940	Commissioned at Kiel.
April 1941	Training and exercises of all kinds.
23 April 1941	Damaged by magnetic mine in the Fehmarn Belt. Damage to optical sections of gun control directors and range-finders. Sailing with the *Bismarck* delayed.
18 May 1941	Sailed from Gotenhafen to break out into the Atlantic in company with the *Bismarck*.
21 May 1941	Both ships anchored south of Bergen in the Korsfjord and refuelled. While doing so they were detected by British aerial reconnaissance. The same evening both ships sailed again.
23 May 1941	0822 (CET), the British heavy cruisers *Suffolk* and *Norfolk* sighted the German ships north-west of Iceland in the northern reaches of the Denmark Strait. Both British ships shadowed the German pair. Short ineffectual exchange of fire between the *Bismarck* and the *Norfolk*. During the night the British cruisers lost contact for two and a half hours. The *Prinz Eugen* took up a position ahead of the *Bismarck* because, aboard the latter, the radar on the foretop had broken down.

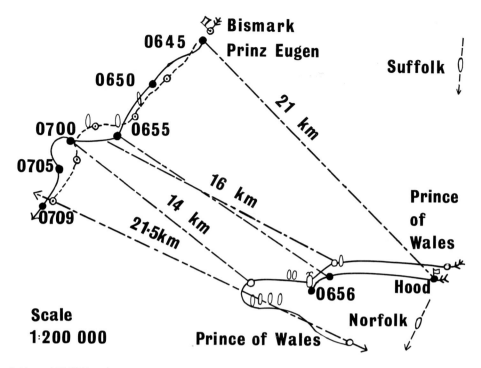

Plan of the sinking of HMS Hood

24 May 1941	0347 (CET), the *Suffolk* again made radar contact with the German ships. 0653–0713 (CET), engagement with the British battle-cruiser *Hood* and battleship *Prince of Wales*, under Vice-Admiral Holland. 0700, the *Hood* exploded and sank in 63° 20′N, 31° 50′W.

Both German ships had opened fire on the *Hood* at the beginning of the engagement. The *Prinz Eugen* scored the first hit of the engagement; the next five hits went to the credit of the *Bismarck*. After the *Hood* had been wiped out, the fire of the German ships was concentrated on the *Prince of Wales*, who received four hits from the *Bismarck* and three from the *Prinz Eugen*. The *Prince of Wales* broke off the engagement but maintained contact with the German ships, as did the *Norfolk* and *Suffolk*. The *Prinz Eugen* was ordered to maintain course and speed in order to draw the pursuit to herself. Between 1900–2000 the *Bismarck* then reduced speed and there was a short exchange of shots with the pursuers. By this manoeuvre the fact that the German ships were parting company was concealed. The *Prinz Eugen* was released by the Commander-in-Chief for commerce raiding in Mid-Atlantic.

26 May 1941	The *Prinz Eugen* refuelled from the supply-ship *Spichern* (former Norwegian prize *Krossfonn*).
26–29 May 1941	No merchant ships sighted.
29 May 1941	Damage to engines forced the cruiser to run for Brest. She reached port 1.6.1941.
July 1941	Bomb hits while in dock at Brest, during the night of 1–2.7.1941.
12 Jan. 1942	Hitler ordered the transfer of the battleships *Gneisenau*, *Scharnhorst* and *Prinz Eugen* through the Channel to Norway.
11 Feb. 1942	Sailing of group from Brest was planned for 2030 (CET). Postponed till 2345 on account of an air-raid.

Bismarck *from the quarter deck of* Prinz Eugen. *This photograph was taken shortly after the engagement in which HMS* Hood *was sunk: the German ships are disengaging at full speed*

Break through of Scharnhorst, Gneisenau *and* Prinz Eugen *from Brest to the Elbe, February 1942. In this photograph, the nearer ship is a destroyer of the escorting screen*

12 Feb. 1942   At 1120 (CET), the German force was detected by enemy air-reconnaissance. The ships at this time were already off the mouth of the Somme. 1319, passage of the Straits of Dover. Even now, still no enemy attacks or attempts at interference. 1325, unsuccessful attack by six British torpedo-bombers, which were all shot down. Between 1640 and 1900, various other attacks by torpedo-bombers and bombers; no success achieved by any of attacks. 1531, off the mouth of the Scheldt, the first damage, by a mine, suffered by the battleship *Scharnhorst*. The *Gneisenau* and *Prinz Eugen* steamed on. 1643, the British destroyers *Campbell*, *Vivacious*, *Mackay*, *Whitshed* and *Worcester*, out of Harwich, attacked the German force off Rotterdam. The *Prinz Eugen* drove off the *Mackay* and *Whitshed*. The German ships were able to evade all torpedo attacks. The *Worcester* was damaged by the *Prinz Eugen*, but reached her home port under her own steam. 2055, the *Gneisenau* damaged by a mine off Terschelling.

13 Feb. 1942   The *Gneisenau* and *Prinz Eugen* reached the mouth of the Elbe at 0800. As the two battle-cruisers were damaged, the Force Commander, Vice-Admiral Ciliax, transferred his flag to the *Prinz Eugen*. The heavy cruiser *Admiral Scheer* joined the force.

21 Feb. 1942   Various deception manoeuvres by the force in the North Sea to mislead the enemy. At 1210, the *Prinz Eugen*, *Admiral Scheer* and three destroyers on a northerly course off the Dutch coast. Contact was lost. Only in the afternoon of 22.2.1942 was enemy reconnaissance able to pick up the ships again, in Grimstadfjord.

23 Feb. 1942   Off the Drontheim Fjord, the British submarine *Trident* torpedoed the *Prinz Eugen* at 0700, and seriously damaged the ship. Vice-Admiral Ciliax transferred to the *Tirpitz*.

Feb.–Mar. 1942   Part of the ship's after section had to be cut away. Emergency rudder repairs.

16–18 May 1942   Transfer to Kiel (ship travelled under her own steam). Off Lister, 27 British torpedo-bombers and 19 bombers made a concentrated attack. No hit was scored.

October 1942   The *Prinz Eugen*, again ready for service, remained initially in home waters.

January 1943   In company with the *Scharnhorst*, on two occasions attempted to run through Kattegat and Skagerrak to Northern Norway. In both cases sighted by enemy aircraft and attempt abandoned.

May 1943   The *Prinz Eugen* joined the Fleet Training Squadron. The ship belonged

The Channel Breakthrough. At action stations

The Channel Breakthrough. Anxious bridge personnel conn the ship while station keeping at speed on the next ship ahead

to this Force, or to the Task Force derived from it, until the end of the war, chiefly as flagship.

Autumn 1943	Special tasks (development of equipment and weapons).
June 1944	From the heavy cruisers *Prinz Eugen* and *Lutzow* and the 6th Destroyer Flotilla, the Second Task Force was formed; after the break-up of the First Task Force in Northern Norway, the former was given the title, 'Thiele Task Force' after Vice-Admiral Thiele who was commanding the force. The cruiser was operating in the Eastern Baltic, north-west of Utö.
19–20 Aug. 1944	Advance into the Gulf of Riga and bombardment of Tukums.
15 Sep. 1944	The Task Force was at this time present in full strength in the Åland Sea and, by its presence, forced the unopposed passage of six German freighters coming from the Gulf of Bothnia with cargoes of heavy equipment of the German Lappland Army. The Task Force was shadowed by Swedish destroyers and aircraft. (The intervention of the Task Force was necessary because the German freighters had been fired on in the previous few days. Finland had capitulated at this time.)
October 1944	Employed in support operations for Army Groups in retreat, *inter alia* on 11, 12, 14 and 15 October near Memel.
15 Oct. 1944	On the retreat, the *Prinz Eugen* rammed the light cruiser *Leipzig*, north of Hela. The ships were interlocked for 14 hours.
Nov. 1944	
April 1945	Further support operations for the Army, *inter alia* 20 & 21.11. Sworbe Peninsula; 29–31.1. in Samland, March–April 1945 in the Bight of Danzig.
8 April 1945	In company with the *Lutzow*, the *Prinz Eugen* sailed to Swinemünde. The *Lutzow* remained there, while the *Prinz Eugen* sailed on to Copenhagen.
9 May 1945	Placed under British command.
27 May 1945	In company with the *Nürnberg*, and escorted by the British cruisers *Devonshire* and *Dido*, transferred to Wilhelmshaven.
13 Dec. 1945	The *Prinz Eugen* allotted to the USA and taken to Wesermünde.
13 Jan. 1946	Sailed for the USA. 22.1.1946 in Boston.
Summer 1946	In atom-bomb test (Bikini lagoon); slightly damaged but still afloat. Thereafter anchored near the Kwajalein Atoll; stranded and sank at Enubuj on 22 December 1947.

List of Serving Officers

Equivalent Ranks

Kapitän zur See	=Captain
Fregatten-kapitän ..	
Korvetten-kapitän ..	=Commander
Kapitän-leutnant	=Lieutenant-Commander
Oberleutnant zur See	=Lieutenant
Leutnant zur See	=Sub-lieutenant

After control-room for 20·3cm battery
Analogue computer. Gun-laying computer C/38K S.A. (S.A.=heavy armament)
Speed Prinz Eugen   The target course Speed
Firing direction
Rate of training finder   Rate of range finder

CAPTAIN:	
Kapitän zur See Brinkmann (Helmuth)	8.40—8.42
Kapitän zur See Voss (Hans-Erich)	9.42—2.43
Kapitän zur See Erhardt (Werner)	3.43—1.44
Kapitän zur See Reinicke	1.44—the end
SECOND-IN-COMMAND:	
Commander Stooss (Otto) (2.7.41)	8.40— 7.41
Commander Knoke (acting)	12.40— 2.41
vacant	7.41—10.41
(duties undertaken by N.O. &/or G.O.)	
Commander Neubauer	10.41— 1.43
Commander Beck (Wilhelm) (acting)	7.42— 9.42
Captain Beck (Wilhelm)	1.43—10.44
Commander Busse (Bernhard)	10.44—the end
NAVIGATING OFFICER:	
Commander Beck (Wilhelm)	8.40— 1.43
Commander Busch (Hans-Eberhard) (acting)	2.43— 3.43
Commander Brödermann	4.43— 6.43
Commander Frhr v. d. Recke	6.43—10.43
Commander Rost (Hansfrieder)	10.43— 6.44
Commander Bredemeier	6.44—10.44
Lt. Commander v. Salisch	10.44— 1.45
First Lieutenant Graf Saurma-Jeltsch (acting)	1.45— 3.45
Commander Wolf (Wilhelm)	3.45—the end
FIRST GUNNERY OFFICER:	
Commander Jasper (Paul)	8.40— 7.42
Commander Gohrbandt	8.42— 3.43
*Commander Schmalenbach	3.43—the end
SECOND GUNNERY OFFICER:	
*Lt.-Cdr. Schmalenbach	8.40— 3.43
Lt.-Cdr. v. Stülpnagel	4.43—the end
CHIEF ENGINEER:	
Eng. Commander Graser	8.40— 4.42
Eng. Commander Kurschat	4.42—11.43
Eng. Commander Hielscher†	11.43—the end

*Author of Warship Profile No. 6, *Prinz Eugen*.
† (Electrical engineer since 1939)

Series Editor: John Wingate, DSC

Prinz Eugen *capsized and awash on the reef at Enubuj,*
Kwajalein Atoll, 1947 U.S. Naval Institute

Bikini 1946: the end

OPERATIONS OF THE CRUISER PRINZ EUGEN

Serial No	Length of operation	Type of operation	Engagement fought with enemy reply. Date of action
1	18.5./1.6.41	Atlantic sortie	Action off Greenland with *Hood, Prince of Wales*; 24.5.41
2	11/13.2.42	Breakthrough English Channel	Air and destroyer engagements, including near-sinking of a destroyer at eastern exit from English Channel; 12.2.42
3	20/23.2.42	Advance to Drontheim and bringing in severely damaged ship	
4	16.5./18.5.42	Retreat from Norway, bringing in severely damaged ship	Fighting off aerial attacks off Lister
5	20.8.44	Advance and coastal bombardment	Support for Army's battles by bombarding land targets in Gulf of Riga
6	13/18.9.44	Forward thrust (Advance protection for group of net-laying barges)	Fighting off aerial attack
7	21/25.9.44	Advance protection for convoy	
8	10/13.10.44	Thrust and bombardment of land targets near Memel	Support of Army's battles by bombarding land targets near Memel
9	14/15.10.44	Thrust and coastal bombardment	As above
10	20.11.44	Coastal bombardment	Support for Army by bombardment of land targets on Sworbe peninsula
11	21.11.44	As above	As above
12	29.1/31.1.45	As above	Support for Army by bombardment of land targets on Samland

SUMMARY OF RESULTS OF LAND-TARGET BOMBARDMENT BY THE PRINZ EUGEN

Area of Operation	Dates	No of targets	Heavy Guns Ammunition Consumption Total	Average per target	Directed map, or unobserved fire (*)	Observed fire (**)	'On target' results for observed fire (***)
Tukums	20.8.44	3	265	88	—	265	?
Memel	11/12.10.44 14/15.10.44	28	1196	43	715	481	403=83·7%
Sworbe	20/21.11.44	12	514	43	—	—	?
Samland	29/31.1.45	35	871	25	871	—	—
Danzig Bight	10.3./4.4.45	132	2025	15	1026	999	808=80·8%
Heavy guns		210	4871				
Anti-aircraft guns		100	2644				
Total		310	7515				

(*) Bombardment, intended as map-directed (i.e. without observation), and bombardment during observation failed due to enemy interference (interruption of observation, of information links).
(**) Bombardment in which ranging and effective shots were observed, inclusive of individual unobserved salvoes or shots.
(***) Documentation inadequate for assessment.

Area of operation	Dates	Heavy Anti-Aircraft Guns Ammunition Consumption No of targets	Total	Average per target	Directed map, or unobserved fire (*)	Observed fire (**)	'On target' results for observed fire
Tukums	20.8.44	—	—	—	—	—	—
Memel	11/12.10.44 etc	—	—	—	—	—	—
Sworbe	20/21.11.44	2	198	99	Controlled directly from ship		
Samland							
Danzig Bight	10.3./4.4.45	98	2446	25	1704	739	634=85·7%
Total		100	2644				

MTB 66 *lying in Portsmouth during trials* (*Vosper Ltd*)

HM MTB/Vosper 70ft
by David Cobb ROI RSMA

The Motor Torpedo Boats

The British are not a martial race. Not relishing war, they seldom prepare for it; all too often the British serviceman by his conduct has had to make good the shortcomings of his material. In any case, his principal defence, the warship, is an unsuitable instrument for conquest, though a strong influence for curbing it in others.

In 1940, that traditional defence was disrupted by the new influence of air power. No longer could the conventional warship control the narrow seas now overlooked by a victorious enemy, whose plans for invasion were checked by the epic air battle of that autumn. The Navy found itself without vessels of the kind needed to re-exert its lost sea-power, even resorting to motor yachts and pilot-boats to provide anti-invasion patrols in the Straits of Dover.

The only craft suited (though not specifically designed) for such a task was an embryonic group of assorted MTBs negligible in numbers, without bases, operational experience or staff. Since all potentially-hostile coastlines lay apparently beyond their operational range, such craft had justified no tactical existence

145

Bow view of stemhead prior to planking-up.

(*Vosper Ltd*)

Engine bearers, looking forward. (Centre-engine shaft and coupling just visible in foreground) (*Vosper Ltd*)

Thornycroft C.M.B. 70 ft of World War I design, used also for cloak and dagger work in World War II

MTB 66 *showing back of unarmoured bridge*

(*Vosper Ltd*)

MTB 66 *0·5-inch turret, safety arc on forward side*

(*Vosper Ltd*)

in the Royal Navy. Now the Admiralty hurried to espouse what hitherto it had rejected; thus the nation reaped where private energy, capital and design skill alone had sown.

So it came about that the crews of these few, minute, complex warships were translated overnight from obscurity to offensive sea war. Their commitment to this undivided purpose was a distinction they shared with only one other branch of the Navy, the submarines, whose personnel, training and material were a byword of excellence. Nightly, in all possible weather conditions, the MTBs began to search the enemy coast in a wholly novel and specialised game of blind-man's-buff. In time the sum of experience slowly mounted. The dribble of improved material was turned to every aspect of skill in its use.

By 1943, a greatly expanded and, by now, sophisticated force had gained the initiative wherever it operated. The following year its competence was a major factor in the safe installation and guarding of the D-day fleet in one of the battle areas it had contested for so long.

This Warship Profile studies the one type of MTB which operated basically unaltered from 1939 to 1945, so it covers, if briefly, the complete pattern of this wholly novel type of sea war.

In retrospect, the MTB seems to have drawn its spirit from the fast vessels which have (if for diverse reasons) sought the cloak of darkness to conduct their business.

Inescapably, the activities of the boats of all types are linked in the minds of those that knew them with the distinguished services in various theatres of war of many men, not only from Britain, but from the Commonwealth and Allied Nations. The almost total omission of their names, if deeply regretted, is inevitable in a book of this size.

This short history is dedicated to the memory of those who gave their lives in this service.

Part I: THE WEAPON

The MTB Concept

With few exceptions, such as the use of fireships, throughout naval history it was axiomatic that a minor

MTB 66 *bridge controls. Torpedo firing levers and sight-base to port, later moved to starboard (C.O.'s) side*
(Vosper Ltd)

warship could pose no threat to a major one. The invention of the torpedo, whether delivered by boat or submarine, ended this era.

The submarine for long defied counter-measures, but the torpedo-boat led to the torpedo-boat-destroyer (TBD) with which it then merged identity to set the pattern of the small fast warship which carried a disproportionately destructive weapon.

If the early TBD was very small compared with a cruiser or battleship, it had both to defend and attack fleets of such vessels, and thus be large enough to keep to the open sea for long periods.

The Coastal Motor Boat of 1914-1918 (CMB) resulted from taking the torpedo to sea and mounting it on a minimal planing hull driven at very high speed by petrol engines. Like all its MTB successors, the boat had much more in common with an aircraft than

1939 Extension Programme boat. General view showing twin rudders and cavitation plates, also squared rudder-heads to carry hand-steering emergency tiller
(Vosper Ltd)

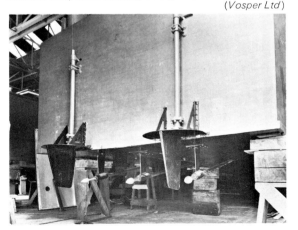

MTB 57 *wheelhouse showing original 'armoured conning tower' concept, with steering, E/R controls, torpedo firing levers, and armour-plate screens to cover windows* *(Vosper Ltd)*

MTB 66 *wheelhouse, all controls transferred to bridge*
(Vosper Ltd)

MTB 66 *E/R starboard side looking forward*　　*(Vosper Ltd)*

deep-draught naval vessels; but within the building and engine techniques of its period, it was an undoubted success, for it obtained sufficient power from the relatively heavy Thornycroft, Fiat and Green petrol engines to lift the hull and its torpedoes into a planing position. As with MTBs, aircraft engines also were adapted to this purpose, and the CMBs if less seaworthy were fully as fast as their successors.

Such activities as the CMB performed were crowned in 1918 by sinking a Russian battle-cruiser, which showed very clearly the boat's potentialities but, with the post-war reduction of armament, further British development petered out.

It was not until 1934 that the Admiralty re-considered at all the need for such small fighting craft, and 1937 before the first flotilla of six MTBs was formed. In that year the entire British Commonwealth had only these six boats, with seven building; in 1938 an Admiralty Fleet Order invited volunteers for service in MTBs.

The story of the *Vosper* 70' *MTB* began in 1937 when a 68' experimental boat, No. 102, built as a private venture, developed 40 knots while carrying two 21" torpedoes; in 1939, the first 70' boat was accepted, the unwitting progenitor of some 200 succeeding 70' boats which, built in the U.S.A. as well as in Britain, were to

be at the focus of the work for the next five years. In 1948, Vospers were awarded £35,000 by a Royal Commission in recognition of their contribution to the war effort. It might have been better invested in them 15 years earlier.

70ft VOSPER DESIGNS BUILT UNDER LICENCE

1940–43	201–212 246–251	S. White, Cowes
1942–44	275–306 363–378 396–411	Built in U.S., made available under Lend/ Lease to R.N. (363–370, 400–449, 661–730 transferred to Russia)
1943	347–362	Built by sub-contractors in U.K.

70ft VOSPER CLASS OF 1940:
Data & Equipment

Tonnage:	47
L.O.A.:	72' 6" (including rudders)
Beam:	19' 3"
Draught:	2' 9" × 5' 6"
Engines:	Isotta Frascini (3 bank 18-cyl.) 　　　BHP 3600/3450—40/42 knots Hall Scott (V-12 cyl.) 　　　BHP 1800　　　—27 knots Packard (V-12 cyl.) 　　　BHP 4050/3600—38/40 knots Sterling Admiral (V-12 cyl.) 　　　BHP 3360　　　—35 knots
Fuel:	2750 gallons 100-octane
Water:	50 gallons
Steering:	hydraulic, hydraulic-assisted hand
Crew:	2 officers, 9–13 men
Armament:	Torpedo Tubes (TT)　2×21" A.R.T.S. (angled outboard 7½°) Torpedoes MK IV**, V, XX**, VIII* (post 1943) *alternatively* 4 mines 'A' MK 1, 2, 3 or 4 dia. 18", length 9½'. Magnetic or acoustic pistols Vickers MK V M.G. 0·5" twin, in power-operated turret Fitted and supplied subsequently : Twin 20mm Oerlikon hand-operated (vice twin 0·5") Single 20mm Oerlikon (foredeck) Twin Vickers K 0·303" amidships, on tubes) Lanchester carbines Stripped Lewis M.G. 0·303" Hand grenades
Depth Charges:	4 × MK VII in single chutes aft
Smoke Apparatus:	C.S.A., Type B, 12 min., Total wt. 480 lb.
Illuminants:	2" Rocket Flare Projectors 1943 onwards, fitted on T.T. each side of bridge
W/T:	TGY/607—CW/RT 375–500kcs 1.2–8·3mcs
R/T:	TCS CW/RT 1.5—12mcs
R.D.F.:	Type 286 (fixed dipoles) Type 291 (rotating dipoles)
A.W./S.W.⎫ I.F.F.　⎬	Type 252
D/F Position- finding equipment:	QH1, QH2. Fr. 20/85 Mc/s. Range (appr.) 150m.

V-8 auxiliary drive with Isotta-Frascini marine engines
(Vosper Ltd)

Fire equipment:	Fixed Methyl Bromide in Engine Room (ER) and Tank Space, alternate operation Bridge/ER
	Portable : Foamite, Nuswift, Pyrene
Navigational:	Compasses (2) Pattern 11151A
	Kelvin Hughes E/S
Signals:	Naval Code signalling flags
	Aldis 24V
	Lamp patt 1038
	Verey Pistol 2-star cartridges
Hydrophone:	Rudimentary, various

SPEED TABLE
Approximate Speed Table—Packard

Revolutions per minute		Boost (lb/Sq")	Speed knots
1 engine	800	−8	7
2 engines	800	−8	9
3 engines	800	−8	12
	1000	−6	15
	1200	−4	18
	1400	−2	22
	1600	0	26
	1800	+2	30
	2000	+4	34
	2200	+6	36
	2400	+8	38–40

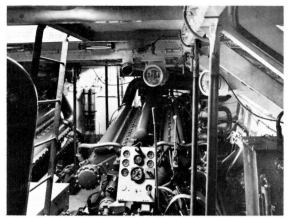

MTB 66 *E/R starboard side aft, looking forward*

(*Vosper Ltd*)

NOTES ON HULL, ENGINES AND EQUIPMENT

The Hull

The frames and planking of the double diagonal wood hull were strengthened longitudinally by a girder framework which included the metal engine bearers. The shape was evolved by a series of tank tests and the building of hulls in the early 1930s of increasing size for various utilitarian purposes.

The characteristic diamond-shape of the 70′ Vosper foredeck resulted from torpedo development trials, when the tubes were angled outboard and the foredeck each side pared away to ensure a clear launch.

The forward hull sections which affect so closely the behaviour of a fast planing boat, and also the overall length, were arrived at on the premise of use in service of very high or very low speed, as in the silent attack on, and swift escape from, a sheltered fleet anchorage; not as it turned out (and the difference is profound) the attack of escorted vessels in the open sea off a distant coast.

As used in service, the intermediate speeds of 12-18 knots proved frequently necessary, when the shape of the forward sections made the boats very wet. However no design change was permitted at a time of such need, and it was not until 1944 that the 73′ Vosper entered service with this much-needed modification. This boat had otherwise an identical bottom shape to permit the use of existing cradle facilities, but the bow sections were refined to improve sea-going throughout the whole range of speeds.

MTB 66 *W/T and Radar Office, looking aft down steps from wheelhouse* (*Vosper Ltd*)

MTB 66 *W/T installation* (*Vosper Ltd*)

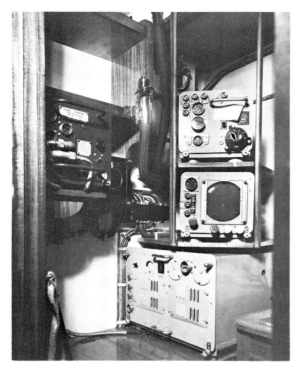

MTB 66 *Pattern 286 R.D.F.* (*Vosper Ltd*)

Engine Room

The high power of MTB engines was exceptional only in its economy of weight and space. No suitable British-made engine being available for Vosper development, three supercharged Isotta Frascini 1150hp marine engines were fitted. Italian entry into the war forced the robbery of the centre engine for the spares it could provide and the substitution of American supercharged Hall-Scott until 1250hp Packards became available. The effect was to reduce the top speed of boats so mutilated to a mere 26-27 knots.

Thereafter, as it became available, the Packard remained standard for the 47-ton Vosper short MTB. Each engine consumed roughly one gallon a minute at

MTB 66 *wheelhouse, aft starboard side, showing multi-purpose E/R telegraph to transmit a variety of orders. (Normal E/R voice-pipes would have been totally inaudible)* (*Vosper Ltd*)

MTB 66 *Wardroom, looking aft from galley hatch*
(*Vosper Ltd*)

a speed of 30 knots, giving a maximum range of some 400 miles on the 2725 gallons of fuel, some 16 hours of steaming. In effect, the longest passage to a patrol position would not exceed some 140 miles, or five-and-a-half hours running at 25 knots.

The Vosper 1942 programme was fitted with Ford V-8 wing auxiliary engines. At the cost of the delay needed to declutch the main engines and engage these auxiliaries, the boat could proceed economically and entirely silently at some 7-9 knots, but, to low speed and relatively poor control from twin rudders, was added the often embarrassing pause needed to re-engage main engines. To muffle the strident main exhaust, and for simplicity, at first only the centre engine was silenced but finally all three engines were similarly

MTB 66 *forward mess-deck, looking aft. Water-tight door open* (*Vosper Ltd*)

silenced at will. Use of these dumbflow silencers caused slight back pressure and loss of power, but the ability to use main engines continuously was a great advantage.

The sense of speed from three such engines at maximum power was an exhilarating experience not easily forgotten.

Wing-engines drove directly, with planet-type reverse gears, the centre engine through a V-drive. From rest, full speed could be reached in some 10–12 seconds, and in emergency the boat slumped to a stop almost instantly. The engines were maintained at sea and serviced in harbour by engine-room staff (and base staff when required) on a regular schedule entered in the engine-room register. More extensive maintenance took place at set intervals, until either some defect arose which required an engine to be changed, or the statutory 500 hour limit for replacement was reached. Being of aircraft origin, delicate and highly-tuned, the engines were not wholly suitable, and installed in small planing hulls driven at speed they performed a duty in adverse circumstances.

Major maintenance routines were planned to co-incide with periodic slipping of boats to clean and paint the bottom, and to give leave to the crew. The method of hauling out varied with the facilities available at different bases, but at each it was a matter of skill and care by the shore staff to settle the boat precisely upon the shaped supporting chocks of the cradle.

Whenever boats were in harbour, shore-lighting was connected to relieve the drain on batteries and consequent need to run charging auxiliaries.

Re-fuelling and re-arming was normally carried out immediately on return from sea, when the boats were restored to full readiness and their state reported to the operating authority.

The following questionnaire gives an idea of the specialised knowledge required of any Commanding Officer inspecting his engine room:

Engineer Training Officer,
H.M.S. 'BEE'
21st November 1943

ENGINE ROOM ROUNDS
Inspection Sheet for Commanding Officers
1. Bilges. Are they dry ? Are there any leaks ?
2. Bilge suction valves. Do they work freely ?
3. Echo Sounding Tank. Is it free from oil ?
4. Ventilators. Is the mechanism rusted ? Can the ventilators be rotated and blanked off ?
5. Fuel Tanks. Are the valves closed on the bulkhead ?
6. Petrol Filters. When were they last cleaned ?
7. Dumbflows. Are they in open position ?
8. Exhaust manifold drain cocks. Are they open ?
9. Main engine air filters. If exposed to open vent port or hatch, has the cover been placed over the filter ? Muster all air filter covers.
10. Check levels of fluids in :
    (a) Lockheed service tanks.
    (b) Main engine distilled water headers.
    (c) Main engine lub. oil service tanks.
    (d) Aux. Eng. sump and gearbox oils.
    (e) Distilled water reserve tank.
    (f) Lub. oil reserve tank.
    (g) Reduction gearbox oil tank or 'V' drive.
11. Gauges. Any faulty ?
12. Main engine starter batteries. Tops clean ? Terminals tight and greased ? Specific gravity O.K. ?
13. Inspection lights. Have they guards ? Is the wiring frayed ?
14. Muster tools.
15. Fire Extinguishers. Is there $\frac{1}{16}$" clearance between striker and knob ? Are the bottles full ? When were they last tested ?
16. Chain steering. Are chains and sprockets in after tiller flat lubricated daily ?
17. Slave steering mechanism. Are the steering rods bright ? They should be lubricated with Lockheed fluid only.

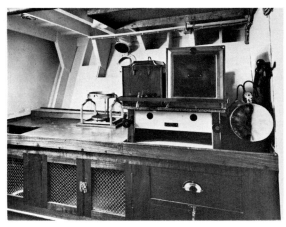

MTB 66 *galley* (*Vosper Ltd*)

18. C.S.A. Apparatus. Do the valves work freely ? Is the nozzle clear ? Are the bottles (air and acid) charged ? Is the set covered ?
19. Combustible material is to be safely stowed. Any rags or waste lying about ? Hand torches are not permitted. Are they being used ?
20. Are the alternative gun pump systems fully understood ?
    At the weekly inspection of Engine Room Registers, ask to see the daily registers for the previous seven days. Take special regard of hours run at speeds of 2000 R.P.M. and in excess. Is the average lubricating oil consumption increasing ?
    Fuel tank compartments should be inspected weekly.

Torpedoes

The torpedoes were fired (usually simultaneously unless ordered otherwise) by a 15 oz. cordite impulse charge released into an expansion chamber bolted to the tail of the tube. All had a safety range within which the firing pistol on the warhead was inactive, and in deciding a suitable firing range the torpedo had also to be given sufficient distance to assume its correct setting for depth. If launched at high speed it dived deeply, which limited the scope of firing conditions in shoal water.

Depth-settings could be altered with the torpedo in the tube, but normally these were selected prior to the commencement of the patrol at depths appropriate to the probable targets.

The correct running of the complex torpedo was naturally a matter of acute concern. While the majority ran true, due to prior damage or perhaps the shocks of sea-going, in early days there were a number of failures to hit in circumstances difficult to explain. Even in the worst conditions of sea, the torpedo track was revealed at night by phosphorescence.

An important item of torpedo maintenance was the internal dryness of the tubes. Only a small accumulation of oil in the tube, draining from the engine of the torpedo, could cause a bright flash at the moment of discharge.

MTB 73 *on trials in Solent. Observe draught-marks on stem and side amidships; also the easy planing attitude of a new boat at speed* (*Vosper Ltd*)

MTB 33 *at Flathouse, Portsmouth, her stern blown out and resting on the bottom at low tide. The watertight compartments appear to have kept the boat afloat at the oil-mark on the topsides* (Vosper Ltd)

Gunnery

The original Vosper armament consisted of a hydraulically driven, revolving HA/LA (High Angle/Low Angle) gun turret in which were mounted twin 0·5″ Vickers machine guns with an effective range of 500 yards. They fired belted ammunition of A.P. (Armour Piercing) tracer, each at 700 rounds a minute, controlled for elevation and training by the gunner seated in the turret, using a single control column and a cartwheel sight. The power was supplied from a mechanical pump in the engine room; maintenance called for the use of no less than 37 special tools.

Gunners were trained in surface action to fire only short bursts before re-sighting the target. Control of fire and shifts of target were indicated from the bridge, but necessarily much initiative lay with the gunners. Habitually, all guns were tested on leaving harbour.

As the war progressed and material shortages eased, further guns were fitted, both to strengthen the Vosper ability to defend itself and to acquire some offensive gun capacity, but the layout of the original design never allowed any radical re-distribution of weaponry, and the boat remained in essence what it was originally, a torpedo boat armed for self-defence.

The total weight of added armament and ammunition, the men to operate it, the heavy splinter-mats to protect them, plus the inevitable weight of water soaked into the hull combined in time to immerse the hull even more deeply, so that in time the short MTB (as with many other Naval craft) lost both the edge of its high performance and the cleanliness of outline which characterised the original design.

MTB 29 *Torpedo firing trials in HMS* Vernon (Vosper Ltd)

Mines

The original Vosper design allowed for the substitution of four ground mines for the two torpedoes. The chutes for these were fitted aft of the tubes, two on each side.

The weight distribution when carrying mines was located too far aft for satisfactory planing but, short of removing the tubes entirely, no other position was possible.

The mine clocks were set at the moment of release, which was timed to seconds between the boats concerned. On return to harbour the appropriate number of mine toggles was mustered to show that the mines were live when released.

Smoke

Smoke could be used both offensively and defensively. A strip could be laid through which to attack, or through which an enemy force would have to steam while the unit waited on the far side. Such use was very rare. It could be effective only in suitable wind conditions, and risked losing enemy contact altogether.

Defensive smoke was used frequently after an attack not only to hide disengaging craft, but also to provide short strips which showed up well under star-shell, and often diverted a high proportion of enemy fire.

C.S.A. was a strong acid in liquid form discharged as vapour by compressed air; this vapour was highly toxic if inhaled, but at times this drawback was regarded lightly compared with its advantages.

Illuminations

The faculty of night vision only develops fully after an average of some 20–30 minutes spent in total darkness. The moment the eye is exposed to light of any brilliance this faculty is lost; moreover, in such a condition the eye is easily, if temporarily, dazzled.

Hence, a volume of enemy fire-power consisting of well-placed star shell, mortars, variegated tracer shell, multi-barrelled automatic guns and heavy breach-loaded weapons could, and frequently did, blind an attacking force, or at least make it impossible to sight its target clearly.

Thus, from 1943 onwards, parachute rocket launchers (R.F.Ps) were fitted abreast the bridge astride the torpedo tube with which to illuminate enemy surface craft. Depending on the setting, these flares rose to 2000–2500 feet at a distance of $1\frac{1}{4}$–$2\frac{1}{4}$ miles and a series were fired usually in an arc to silhouette the enemy from the far side.

Naturally, their use removed the element of surprise, but frequently the need for them arose from prior detection of the attacking MTBs.

Depth Charges

Though these were seldom used by torpedo boats, once torpedoes had been fired they remained the one supply of bulk high explosive. As such they could be used to discourage pursuit, and in the event of a gun action at close quarters they could be dropped at shoal settings (sometimes with extra buoyancy attached) close ahead of an adversary to explode beneath it. They had the advantage that their release was virtually impossible to detect.

MTBs (*Fairmile 'D' coming alongside, Vosper 70 ft in foreground*) *working up at HMS* Bee, *Holyhead, 1943, after Weymouth was taken over for invasion preparations* (*Author's Collection*)

White-built Vosper with 20mm Oerlikon on foredeck, waiting to come alongside at Holyhead. Jan-Feb 1944 (*Author's Collection*)

Signals

Continuous W/T watch was kept by all boats at sea. A voice pipe linked W/T office and bridge, and the navigator in the wheelhouse was in easy reach of the W/T operator. Normal Minor War Vessels code-books were used, but at sea and on patrol W/T silence was maintained except for action reports and matters of operational urgency.

R/T (Radio Telephone) handsets came into use as the supply position eased, and units used plain language and the simple provisions of the Coastal Force Signal Pamphlet (C.F.S.P.) to direct and report their affairs.

Visual signalling was rare in a force which operated almost wholly by night, communication being confined to hoisting pendants leaving and entering harbour. Morse by lamp was customary, but only briefly and of absolute necessity when on patrol or outside friendly waters.

Navigation

With the early transfer of the controls to the bridge, the wheelhouse became the chartroom. The First Lieutenant, who was also the Navigator, kept track of the boat's movements while at sea by means of compass and engine revolutions. This was a skilled performance, particularly for the Senior Officer's navigator on whose accuracy the whole unit depended both for its landfall on the enemy coast, for intercepting a moving enemy and for return to the MTBs' home port, after, maybe, a night of continuous movement.

There could be no reliance on sighting coastal lights on the occupied coastline and, until the fitting of direction-finding equipment, the burden facing the navigator in thick weather was weighty.

An added duty, essential to the successful firing of torpedoes, was the methodical plotting on the chart of an enemy ships' course and speed, obtained either by visual or radar shadowing. The development of this technique was the first step which rationalised MTB firing tactics. Prior to its development, the best torpedo firing data could rest only on guesswork.

Camouflage

It was essential to minimise the sighting range at night of an MTB and early in the war a number of patterns of camouflage were adopted to distort their appearance. In time it was realised that they were most commonly illuminated by starshell from overhead, so it was desirable that the consequent shadows should, as far as possible, be artificially neutralised. Thus was adopted the pattern of camouflage shown in the coloured illustration of MTB 66 in which all upward-facing surfaces were painted darker, and all downward-facing spaces lightest of all.

Thus in 140 years the cycle of camouflage turned full circle, for it was well-recognised in the time of the Napoleonic wars that pale or white boats were exceptionally difficult to see at night, so such treatment for small craft suited for smuggling was prohibited by law, and all apprehended craft were forfeit.

The sighting range of a boat seen end-on was only about a third of that when seen on the broadside, so a boat kept almost stationary, pointing towards its target until the last minute, stood three times the chance

Early Vosper (*not yet fitted R.D.F. etc*) *practice firing in Weymouth Bay* (*HMS* Bee) *speed 15-18 knots checked momentarily by discharge of torpedoes* (*Author's Collection*)

Late Vosper at 35 knots, crossing leader's pressure wave to close station. Twin manual 20mm Oerlikon replaces 0·5-inch Vickers turret. Identification lights visible at starboard yardarm   (IWM)

Late Vosper off Harwich. Rocket flare projectors on tubes, rockets in racks visible on side of bridge. Oerlikon surrounded by bandstand. Loud-hailer at aft end of bridge. Fitted AW and SW   (IWM)

of remaining unperceived by eye against one which steered a broadly converging course and revealing its full length. Even if the boat itself was not visible, the white line of its stern wash against a dark sea drew the eye to its point of greatest intensity, namely the MTB herself.

Base Staff

To maintain such complicated craft at high efficiency required the continuous services of a large number of specialist staff at each base. They covered the entire scope of MTB equipment: engines, electrical gear, torpedoes, guns, radar, etc. and took a personal pride in the efficient working at sea of the material they cared for with such earnest attention in harbour. Any and every aspect of MTB activity relied on this basis of shore help, without which the boats could not keep running, still less fight successfully. Naturally it was no small support to the morale of a gunner, after an action, to have the performance of weapons and ammunition checked by an efficient and solicitous member of the W.R.N.S..

Part II: THE OPERATIONAL BOAT

THE 70′ VOSPER
Domestic Economy

All foreseeable events in the life of a British warship are provided for by a document called, The Watch and Quarter Bill, which lays down the various duties of each man. Compared with almost every other class of vessel, that of an MTB was of spartan simplicity. One point of difference made it unique: it issued no directions for 'Action Stations'; with only minor relaxations, the boats assumed this state on putting to sea, and retained it until return to harbour.

A second invisible point, not confined to MTBs but essential to their mode of life, was the practice of exercising ratings and officers in all capacities, so that no duty was unfamiliar. Gunners could handle engines, and engineers handle guns.

In general it was a volunteer branch of the Service, sought after by many. At times, particularly during the long nights of winter with its capricious weather, the physical strain merely of uneventful patrol work on a distant coast could be very great, so the average age of 'short-boat' crews was young.

The inability to work in sustained adverse weather contrasted with the heavy burdens which arose from prolonged conditions fit for patrolling. This could mean continuous wear and tear on both men and machinery, for normally no boat which could run remained in harbour, though naturally there was a limit to the number of consecutive nights which a boat and crew could spend at sea and yet remain efficient. It was a policy which, if it wore out boats, also wore out the enemy.

One consequence of this pressure was that flotillas were accustomed to sudden changes of pattern. A senior officer whose boat developed a major defect on passage transferred forthwith to another, often the junior boat present, where his experience could be of most benefit. Such instant flexibility had compensations. It welded a flotilla together, and no finer example could exist than the total inter-changeability of Allied and British units, between whom there was complete confidence.

A similar spirit was shown by the Base Staff who maintained the boats, engineer officers coming to sea to watch at work their delicate machinery, and occasionally, officers from other services who came for experience.

The severe physical strain of rough weather had its silver lining. Unlike, for example, the destructive weariness of watch-keeping aboard small convoy escorts at sea for two to three consecutive weeks in the fury of the North Atlantic winter, the short MTB could remain at sea only as long as its limited fuel permitted, perhaps 12 to 18 hours, and due to operational limitations, even less in summer. But, apart from fuel and operational factors, sustained vigilance also had very definite limits.

GENERAL FEATURES & PRACTICE
Handling

Throughout its life only two basic changes were made in the 70′ Vosper boat. Those boats of the 1939 programme were of 5′ less beam and were fitted with two hydraulically-operated linked rudders, sited between the three screws. Later boats were fitted with three rudders, each in line with a propeller, which improved control of direction at slow speed, and tightened the turning circle when planing. The vulnerable hydraulic operation was replaced by a hand/power-assisted system.

A minor change was the armouring of the open bridge instead of the wheelhouse, caused by the abandonment of the dual steering position down below. This original 'Armoured conning tower' conception never challenged the sensitive collusion of Coxswain and Commanding Officer standing side by side in the open bridge, the former at the wheel, the latter with engine-room controls and torpedo firing gear at hand. The ahead/astern telegraph settings of 'Stop', 'Slow', 'Half', 'Full' were used by the Commanding Officer in manoeuvring, to provide 'standard' revolutions agreed with the engine room. From the time a unit formed into station outside harbour, the Commanding Officer would usually ring up, 'Half Ahead', and thereafter assume personal control of the engine revolutions by means of his bridge throttles to adjust and maintain station.

The ambling gait of the Vosper at low speed was replaced at 1000–1200 revs by a labouring, bows-up attitude as power was increased. This created a heavy, broad wash, and brought thick spray aboard which continued until, at some 1600 revs and 22–23 knots, the hull began to plane, the supercharger boost checked in its rise and the hull took up its proper running trim. Thence upwards through its speed range, steering was positive, the plume of the power thrust dropped away, and the boat moved easily.

The performance of the three engines was indicated not only in the engine room by supercharger gauges and revolution counters but by their repeaters on the bridge for the Commanding Officer; and by a third set of rev. counters in the chart house for the information of the navigator. Each reading of revolutions had a theoretical correspondence with its boost gauge; if the boost was low, the performance was good; if high, it could presage some incipient defect.

To obtain proper performance, each engine had to deliver its full power. The loss of one engine cut performance by a third; and two, to a quarter. Wing engines only were used to manoeuvre, the centre engine being cut-in later, but all engines were warmed through and checked before leaving harbour for patrol. In emergency, it was possible to 'trail in' (or start) a third engine by use of two, or to relieve the starter-motor load of a second engine by steaming ahead on a single engine. (Engine room staff usually wore ear-plugs for they shared a compartment some 5′ × 15′ × 20′ with nearly 4000 horsepower.)

Sea-going Characteristics

Good station-keeping was an essential requirement of all units at sea, to retain both touch and flexibility of movement. In fine weather on patrol, distance was some 70 yards from stem to stem. In daylight after exercises or 'off-duty', boats sometimes closed up to an exuberant 5–6′. In rough conditions, station had to be opened. High atmospheric humidity caused the water-cooled exhausts to emit not only their normal unique flavour of 100-octane but also dense clouds of vapour which the Vosper discharged on each broadside to a distance of some 10–15 feet. In the dark this artificial fog commonly tended to obscure the shape of the wash, which was the most prominent feature used by those astern by which to keep station. The hull itself merged with night sky, but shaded sternlights were used when only absolutely necessary.

A patrol adopted the cruising formation decided by the Senior Officer, whose boat invariably led the unit. Boats in line ahead enjoyed directional flexibility, for a change of the leader's course was instantly evident and could be followed in succession by those astern, without altering the formation. But a major change of

Leaving for patrol (probably winter). Note emergency steering rigged aboard foreground boats, additional Carley rafts, and increased capacity C.S.A. container on nearest boat. S.O. is embarked, and undisturbed water suggests use of V-8 auxiliaries, i.e. boat is an early pattern prior to main engine silencing   (IWM)

the leader's speed was less easily observed, and, though it was customary on passage to signal such an alteration beforehand ('I' flashed for increase, 'R' for reduce) when on patrol or in contact, boats automatically followed any manoeuvre or speed change.

Line-ahead formation also suffered the drawback of an accumulated slip-stream thrust from the leading boats which required the third or fourth boat in line to run at unduly high engine revolutions to maintain the speed of the unit. To obviate this, station could either be opened to allow the thrust to dissipate between boats or a quarter-line or arrow-head formation could be adopted. This was an easier formation for following boats to sustain, as it allowed a better perspective view of those ahead, and was used commonly by boats on passage.

In any disposition, the sea conditions governed the labour of keeping station. Head seas of any kind caused pounding, and, above winds of Force 5–6 the use of high speed could cause hull damage and mechanical defects. Reduction in speed lowered to some extent the velocity, but not the volume of water which swept into, and over, the bridge. Keeping close watch and station in such conditions, particularly in winter, was a severe trial. Life below decks, if somewhat drier, was violent

Middle-period Vosper (armoured bridge) on cradle at Felixstowe   (IWM)

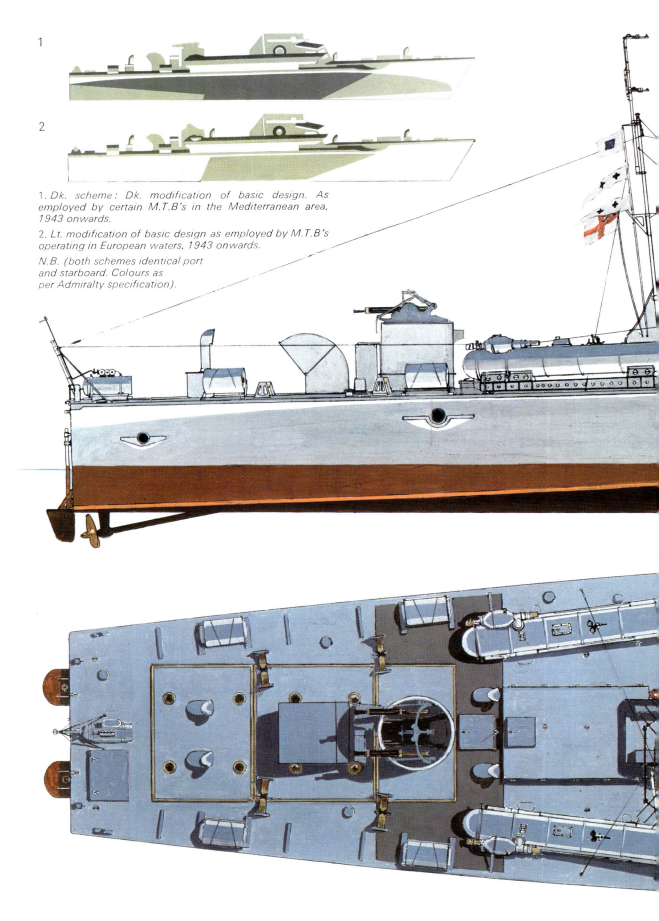

1

2

1. *Dk. scheme: Dk. modification of basic design. As employed by certain M.T.B's in the Mediterranean area, 1943 onwards.*

2. *Lt. modification of basic design as employed by M.T.B's operating in European waters, 1943 onwards.*

N.B. (both schemes identical port and starboard. Colours as per Admiralty specification).

MTB 66 is shown here in the camouflage colours devised to minimise the sighting range at night when illuminated from overhead by starshell. Various changes and additions were made to the armament, fittings and equipment of succeeding boats whose basic hull shape and outward appearance remained the same throughout the five years of their war service.

MTB 66 has hoisted the distinguishing flag of all MTBs (F̄LV for 'Victor') followed by her pendant numbers 66, a standard identification signal made by all H.M. Ships on entering or leaving harbour.

The boat is shown trimmed as she would lie when stopped in smooth water.

David Cobb ROI RSMA © Profile Publications Ltd

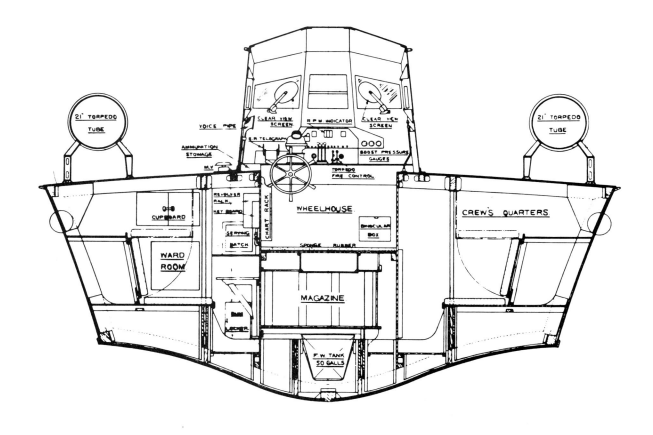

Labels on diagram:
21" TORPEDO TUBE (left)
21" TORPEDO TUBE (right)
CLEAR VIEW SCREEN
R.P.M. INDICATOR
CLEAR VIEW SCREEN
VOICE PIPE
E.R. TELEGRAPH
BOOST PRESSURE GAUGES
AMMUNITION STOWAGE
M.V.
TORPEDO FIRE CONTROL
RE-OILER RACK
KEY BOARD
CHART RACK
WHEELHOUSE
CREW'S QUARTERS
CUPBOARD
SERVING
HATCH
BINOCULAR BOX
WARD ROOM
SPONGE RUBBER
MAGAZINE
LOCKER
F.W. TANK 50 GALLS

Section through officer's wardroom and crew quarters, looking forward

and noisy, as well it might be under the impact of water hitting the bottom at some 50–70 lb. per square inch.

Beam seas were less troublesome. Big quartering seas made for wildness on the helm, particularly if boats came off the plane and dug a chine into the back of a wave, when they would career off against full helm, to recover course with equal violence. Following seas needed care to prevent a surf-ride into the next ahead. But torpedo firing required, above all, steadiness on the helm and, in sea conditions caused by winds above

MTB 80 at HMS Bee, Weymouth (one of the first group of Packard-engined boats). Moving up into quarterline at 40 knots, the boat is just coming down outside the leaders pressure-wave. R.D.F. 291 trained abeam. IFF aerial attached to foreside of mast. Single Vickers K on stanchion type mounting abreast wheelhouse   (IWM)

Force 4, precision in such small craft could not be achieved, however low the speed.

In very quiet weather it was sometimes possible for a following boat in quarter-line to run for hours without touching the throttles. The method was to put the boats inside quarter on the outside of the leader's pressure wave. Any tendency to gain station was checked by loss of its lift to the stern; any tendency to drop back was cured by a corresponding gain. A good coxswain knew this fact, and used it. Such calm conditions, at dusk and dawn, provided scenes of extreme beauty, with a taut group of boats carving effortlessly across a satin sea.

Formations and Tactics

Simplicity was the keynote of all formations adopted when in contact with an enemy force, whether or not action had been joined. The formations resulted from turns made by a line of boats either simultaneously, or in succession, depending on circumstances but most of all upon a high degree of mutual understanding between the Senior Officer and his Commanding Officers. As time went by, this developed to a marked degree, and the results were codified into flotilla standing orders. By 1943/44 such orders comprised an extremely sophisticated document.

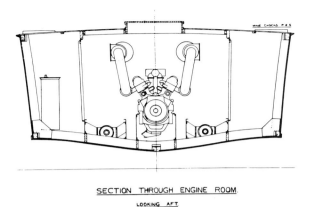

SECTION THROUGH ENGINE ROOM.
LOOKING AFT.

Section through engine room looking aft

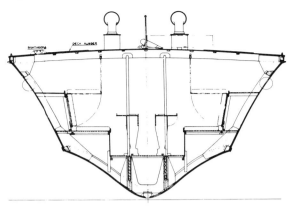

SECTION THROUGH FORECASTLE
LOOKING FORWARD.

Section through forecastle looking forward

Signals and Identification

Signals between a patrol at sea and its area C-in-C were exchanged by W/T but, since the source of transmission could be located by enemy direction-finding equipment, outgoing traffic from the boats was confined to essentials such as enemy reports and action details.

Signals between boats in company were made in daylight by Aldis, by shaded lamp at night and latterly by R/T. Simplicity was the keynote of the codes.

Recognition between friendly forces depended on two systems: a flashed challenge-and-reply, and on a system of vertical coloured lights hoisted on the yardarm, both of which altered character at fixed intervals to preserve security. All signal codes were contained in weighted books to ensure that they sank when jettisoned.

Despite these varied resources, wherever possible, boats stopped in close proximity, almost alongside, to settle domestic matters by using the one wholly infallible resource aboard—the human voice and a megaphone. Such a device had a two-way use, for the noise of the side exhausts of the Vosper boats made conversation difficult; the megaphone could then be held to the ear and so become a directional amplifier, and, on a quiet night, was also of service to detect the sound of distant engines, perhaps the first sign of the enemy.

Torpedo Attack:
The Mathematical Problem

Compared with the shell fired from a gun, the torpedo is abysmally slow—some 40 knots only. Against this, if it hits, the impact is decisive, and possibly final.

To achieve a hit, (i) the target's course and speed had to be estimated correctly, and set on the torpedo sight; (ii) the boat's firing course had to be held precisely in accordance with the sight, and (iii) the torpedo had to run precisely in accordance with its settings for direction, at a depth appropriate for the target.

The torpedo sight mounted on the bridge just in front of the C.O. was a device of arresting simplicity. It represented in a mechanical diagram the triangle of velocities and directions: the known torpedo speed and the estimated course and speed of the enemy; it could

also be set by feel in total darkness by counting the 'clicks' made by the passage of the speed sight along the enemy course bar.

But a hit depended also on the target maintaining the correctly judged course and speed, for, if either was altered, it would distort the triangle of velocities and the torpedo would miss. *Herein lay the whole thinking behind the MTB concept—the very small attackers whose presence might pass unnoticed, if not altogether, until it was too late for enemy evasive action to be effective. The ideal attack, therefore was undetected from start to finish.*

The fate of the whole operation depended on these few minutes prior to an MTB torpedo attack; whether made at the end of prolonged shadowing movements with their risk of premature discovery, or whether in a 'snap' attack made in the face of opposition to prevent the escape of a target.

The best position from which to fire was 60°–70° on the bow of the target. The desirable range was clearly as close as possible, consistent with the torpedo outrunning its safety range and with the target and torpedo meeting at right angles; but scarcely ever was it possible to remain unobserved at such very close proximity, say 200 yards, so hits were sought usually at two or three times this range. Special circumstances could

Boats alongside at Ferry Dock, Dover. Stoker in foreground is sounding fuel tanks. Note early type unarmoured bridge (probably an Isotta-engined boat) protected by splinter mats, and D/Cs attached to empty oil-drums to delay rate of sinking   *(IWM)*

produce hits at 1000–1500 yards, as will be observed in the action report which terminates this Profile.

Size of Patrols

In early years, the number of units on patrol was dictated by the number of available boats, and these were often only two or three; but if these small forces could be in the right place at the right time, their weakness was more apparent than real. Easily controlled, inconspicuous and flexible, their torpedoes were no less effective. Later, with more boats available, the early addiction to small patrols persisted, the extra boats separating into neighbouring areas whence they could stage movements in mutual support to provide diversionary or secondary attacks.

Contact with Enemy

Before it was possible to detect a distant enemy by radar, the chief operational constraint to contact was the very limited sea area visible to a lookout in a small boat on a really dark night. It was hide and seek on a titanic scale, over hundreds of miles of sea in which opposing forces could approach within a few hundred yards before sighting each other. The first visible warning might be the bow waves announcing, with only a few seconds notice, the arrival of a bellicose but worthwhile target. To attack immediately risked at best a miss due to inadequate data; yet to try to slide away unseen in order to gain bearing for a planned attack risked the loss of opportunity.

Targets ranged from fast destroyers and minesweepers, through merchant ships of all sizes, to escort vessels; and down to specially armed anti-MTB patrols sent out to destroy the MTBs before they could use their main weapon.

It was a popular illusion that the high speed of MTBs was connected with their methods of attack. In fact it was confined almost completely to disengagement after an attack, and only occasionally to the tactical requirements of gaining bearing on a distant fast-moving target.

Patrol Conditions

Clear, calm nights of full moonlight made an unobserved approach difficult. In such conditions the boats were often visible up-moon beyond torpedo-range—unusual phosphorescence was also a hazard. And when wind was a factor, it produced two effects. Enemy lookouts were less effective facing the wind, but they could hear more easily any sounds of engines it carried to them. To leeward, the factors were reversed. The ideal night had little or no moon, a light breeze, and a just-visible horizon.

At all times when approaching a patrol position, or when on patrol, speed was kept to a minimum. High speed meant conspicuous wash, and sacrifice of the ability to hear. Often patrols stopped at their patrol position (usually sited off a harbour, or on an enemy swept channel), moving only at intervals to compensate for the drift of wind and tide. When stopped, the boats lay beam to wind and sea, drifting to leeward at about 10% of the wind speed.

Detection of the Enemy

A simple hydrophone, lowered over the boat's side on a rod, was fitted in 1942 to detect distant propeller noise. The hydrophone was effective up to two–three miles, but only in relatively smooth sea conditions.

Radar, with dipoles rotated by hand from below decks, came in 1942–43, but its usefulness was sometimes offset by the enemy's introduction of search-receivers which registered the bearing of radar transmission, causing a patrol to be located much earlier than they would have been if preserving radar silence.

Action Conditions

The sudden translation of a pitch-dark night into a blinding firework display was characteristic of MTB action. The number of resulting hits might bear little relation to the awe-inspiring display of enemy firepower but, in turn, a single hit could, in such a small and fragile craft, do damage out of all proportion to the calibre of shell.

A boat disabled was at once the focus of enemy fire and the urgent object of succour, provided usually by a curtain of smoke laid by other boats of the unit behind which there was, if little else, a welcome sense of obscurity.

Early Vosper, preparing for practice shoot (all guns trained on Green 45). The heavy bow-wave formation at 12-15 knots is well shown (IWM)

U.S.-built lease-lend Vosper in Mediterranean 1943-44. Oerlikons fore and aft, tall and short R/F whip aerials P/S bridge, identification lights hoisted, modified type C.S.A. container, lifelines rigged aft (IWM)

U.S.-built lease-lend Vosper in Mediterranean 1943-44. Single Oerlikon, towing pendant fitted to starboard chine   (IWM)

Loading torpedoes at Felixstowe Dock. Note tackle on deck ready to launch torpedo into tube. Tow-rope stowed round E/R ventilators   (IWM)

The Tactical Battle

In 1942, an increasing scale of MTB damage without commensurate success brought about the development of varied diversionary tactics, including the co-operation of aircraft, and occasionally destroyers, but most often in conjunction with the recently-created forces of Motor Gun Boats (MGBs).

These units might attack the escort on one quarter of the convoy, to distract attention from the approach of MTBs from another direction.

Occasionally, at this period, the MGB would find itself with a torpedo target and attempt an attack with depth-charges dropped immediately under the enemy bow. This was a period of experiment and innovation, nourished by experience, which brought forth a high level of practical co-operation. It led also to added armaments to each class of boat to give it a dual role, gun *and* torpedo.

Damage Control

The control of damage consisted of first-aid to the wounded, and extempore repairs to the ship. The Vosper hull was divided into six watertight compartments, but the unarmoured boat bore a huge quantity

MTB and MGB flotillas in Felixstowe Dock. Packard-Vosper 70 ft in first trot, Packard and Isotta-Frascini in second trot, early B.P.B. 71 ft 6 in. MGBs in third and B.P.B. 70 ft MGBs in fourth   (IWM)

A deck scene at 30 knots. Oilskin overalls were standard wear for all deck personnel, with added quilted lining for winter work. 0·5-inch cartwheel sight is well shown
(Author's Collection)

of complex machinery, hydraulic and electrical circuits, armaments required for full efficiency and, moreover, her crew was largely unprotected.

Most vulnerable of all were the tanks of 100-octane fuel. These were coated with a self-sealing compound capable of expanding to fill a modest size of puncture. Should fire break out, there were methyl-bromide extinguishers operated by remote control for both tank space and engine room, but their use in the engine room was a decision of some gravity, for the gas obsorbed all oxygen, and meanwhile, however inconvenient it might be, all staff had to evacuate the engine-room and the boat was wholly immobilised.

There was little to obstruct any hits, which often went unhindered right through the boat, but more severe hull damage was repaired by quick thinking and extempore methods, the sole aim being to keep her afloat and get her home by any possible means.

Towing between boats was catered for by permanently rigged, strong wire pendants, fore and aft, which were stopped into position, ready for instant use.

If all efforts at salvage failed, demolition charges

Gunner climbing into 0·5-inch turret. Winter time, boat doing 30 knots
(Author's Collection)

could be operated from the bridge to sink the boat and prevent her falling into enemy hands.

A Carley raft was carried on the foredeck, and all members of crews wore inflatable life-belts when at sea on patrol. Each had also a small water-tight red light attached to his lifebelt to assist location in the dark. (When reminded, they also wore their 'tin-hats' when action was imminent.)

Small sealed packets contained such aids to survival and escape as money, a small compass, tablet food, benzedrine tablets, maps, etc, for use in the event of getting ashore undetected.

Part III: CAMEO OF MTB TACTICS

Enemy Tactics

In the Channel, the enemy was scarcely more prepared than the British for the tactical situation created in 1940. He had, however, a most effective and well-developed counterpart of the MTB in the fast diesel-engined E-boat. More relevant to this study, due to the nature of his own coastline and his special sea strategy, he had numbers of excellent small escort vessels, and a variety of destroyers and fast mine-sweepers which could be concentrated to defend the relatively small amount of shipping he wished to escort. (This contrasts sharply with the British scarcity of escorts for far too many ships.) Compared with the world-wide role demanded of any British warship, the enemy was able to specialise his naval architecture with excellent effect.

Exercise of Sea-power

Normally neither side was able to operate offensively with any warshp in daylight, due to the devastating effect of air-power.

The British could continue to wage war if a sufficient merchant tonnage reached the country from overseas, but they could not win it by offensive operations until they had sufficient force of all arms, and control of the waters and air-space which this invasion force must traverse.

The British purpose, therefore, was to exercise the maximum offensive sea-and air-power against the hostile force occupying the European coast, leading to total control of the Channel before any invasion could hope to succeed. It is against this simple fact that the five-year sea battle must be judged.

Enemy Defensive Measures

The first purpose of the enemy was to pass shipping along his greatly-extended coast so, faced with an increasing scale of MTB interference, his natural reaction was to increase massively the scale of his escort forces, both in numbers and fire power. However, the result was not so uneven as might appear, for a numerous flotilla of escorts surrounding one or two merchant ships carried with it the seeds of its own destruction. Such a force might be impossible to attack straightforwardly, but it was easily confused as to which was, and which was not, an MTB.

Not infrequently the result was that, by luck, judgment, or both, even an inconclusive encounter with attacking MTBs could develop into a brisk battle between the neighbouring screens of the escort; enlivened, if in range, by coastal batteries which certainly could not distinguish friend from foe. To an MTB patrol, such fruits, if they could not be precisely counted, tasted no less sweet.

Most intractable of all were the anti-MTB patrols. Scarcely of a type to justify torpedo attack, they were nevertheless of a size to carry an arsenal of automatic and other weapons. Happily, their arrival coincided with the full stature of the MGB, to whom they presented a suitable, if often ardent, opponent.

Various formations of enemy escort were adopted to provide early warning of torpedo attack, and these could be countered only by experiencing their nature and devising counter measures. To reconstruct an accurate picture of an involved action was never easy: the MTBs of two units, and the MGBs of two more might weave and turn, stop and start, glimpse and lose each other, or the enemy, among patches of smoke or shell bursts. Yet, if no clear narrative and pattern could be assembled from varying accounts, there could be no useful lesson for the future.

Tactically, the enemy torpedo targets developed one move which was most difficult to detect. It was simple. At the moment torpedoes were seen to be fired, the enemy stopped: all vessels *appeared* to be continuing in formation with the same course and speed, yet all torpedoes missed ahead—it was a puzzling result.

Surface Control of MTBs

To overcome the drawbacks of MTB radar, it was desirable to provide entire independent radar coverage for the battle area. Such coverage from the shore had existed prior to 1944 in the Dover area, latterly in the Channel, and was finally provided also by aircraft; but with the D-day landings in prospect, some effective surface system of MTB control was needed to guard remote beaches from seaborne attack.

This requirement was met by the excellent radar performance of the British-manned DE-type American A/S frigates, a number of these vessels being disposed to seaward, at intervals of some six miles along a continuous patrol line, and whose radar coverage entirely sealed off the area.

Each frigate had attached to her two or more groups of radar-silent MTBs or MGBs (by then the armament made them more or less interchangeable), under the R/T orders of a Control Officer who worked from the plot-room of the frigate. From this vantage point, any approaching enemy force was visible on the radar screen, and suitable forces could be detached to intercept, fully briefed with enemy course, speed, and numbers, and also with the inestimable advantage of surprise.

The existence of such an independent authority within the hierarchy of a warship was novel, for most Control Officers were ex-MTBs, often reservists and necessarily junior to the C.O.s from whose ships they issued orders. Moreover, occasions arose not infrequently when the control ship took action at the urgent behest of the Control Officer. In practice this ill-defined framework of authority worked flawlessly, much to the credit of the senior C.O.s of the controlling ships, who were nothing loth to join action if opportunity occurred, some of them being themselves ex-MTBs.

Torpedoman bringing port tube to the 'Ready'. Speed 30 knots   *(IWM)*

Exercises off Weymouth. D/C released from MGB exploding at shoal setting   *(P. J. Liddell)*

Early 1943, recovery of torpedo after practice firing. Portland. Smoke is from tell-tale Holmes light in dummy head. Pendant number (between 201-212) obscured for security reasons   (P. J. Liddell)

Mine-laying by short MTBs

A fact often overlooked is that the Vosper design from its inception provided for the replacement of the two torpedoes by four ground mines, and the total laid in the course of the war ran into hundreds. Often a mine-laying unit included one boat armed with torpedoes to cope with a suitable target should one appear.

Mine-laying was of two types, 'speculative' and tactical, both of which (like all mine-laying) required precise navigation to ensure that the mines were sited exactly in the chosen position where an enemy vessel was judged most likely to pass. Moreover the type of mine was selected to minimise the chances of its being swept. Such types had magnetic or acoustic pistols, and sank to the sea-bed.

A lay detected was almost certainly a lay wasted, which ruled out the most obvious places such as the very entrance to a harbour, however desirable it was. Hence the 'speculative' lay on the open coast in the centre of a known swept channel, in the hope of the mines becoming live in the interval between the passage of enemy mine-sweepers.

The tactical lay was aimed at a particular enemy convoy known to be on passage, and whose route was also

Passing tow-rope after recovering torpedo. Care was needed to prevent torpedo getting beneath chine, particularly in any sea at night, and holing the hull
(P. J. Liddell)

predictable within fine limits. If present, the customary minesweeping force ahead of the convoy would be allowed to pass, and in the very brief interval before the leading escorts of the convoy arrived, the minelaying unit, steaming close alongside each other to hear shouted directions, would release in succession their line of mines across the line of the approaching convoy.

This process, calling for no less skill than the use of torpedoes, required a flawless technique and co-ordination between boats to create undetected the geometrically regular pattern of mines on the sea-bed. As in torpedo tactics, the ideal was one of total inconspicuousness; the shadow in the dark corner, the stiletto behind the arras.

A mine-laying sortie which found itself involved with enemy surface forces had to decide quickly whether to jettison the mines and disengage, or whether to withdraw in the hope of making a fresh approach when the lay position was clear.

Tactical Skill

As well as tactical competence there were certain personal qualities which became identified with the successful handling of MTBs. Most important of these was a capacity to interpret swiftly the data obtained on the enemy, whether by visual sighting or other means, and thus to form quickly a complete and correct picture, the bird's-eye view on which to develop, delay or reject an attack. For example, small escorts such as R-boats sighted at 500 yards could be indistinguishable from major warships at five times the distance, yet the two different identifications created entirely different situations. It was a problem similar to that facing the Commanding Officer of a submarine, whose data was also restricted, but needed equally urgent and correct interpretation to make possible a successful attack.

Close to this talent, and a necessary adjunct, was the freedom enjoyed by the Senior Officer of a unit to develop and pursue his plan without necessarily issuing detailed orders to the following boats. These had often to be left to respond correctly on their own initiative to a wide variety of situations. But such co-operation could only be developed through contact with the enemy, and here there was no chance to rectify mistakes. No number of exercises and sessions on attack-teachers could represent the situations met at sea; and unlike, for example, the escorting of Atlantic convoys, there was no disengaged part of the friendly force to observe, deduce and later report on events which they could watch freely. The isolated operations took place on a distant coast, between dusk and dawn, unwitnessed except by the participants.

To allow a force to reform after the normal disengaging movements, a standard rendezvous position (usually 3–4 miles seawards from the action position) was included in the flotilla standing orders.

Cloak and Dagger

A further MTB duty was the delivery and collection of commandos and secret agents on the enemy-occupied coast. It was a secretive business carried out at night by single MTBs using dinghy and raft, in which the strained anxiety of those who waited long hours offshore, often at anchor, contrasted oddly with the high spirits of their passengers. When the stakes were so high, nobody asked questions, and even now, 30 years afterwards, there are remarkably few answers.

MTB Training

At first there was no traditional well of experience and expertise on which to draw. MTB personnel learned war solely by fighting it. But in time individual theory and practice were standardised, and training bases established. To HMS *Bee*, the training base at Weymouth (later moved to Holyhead), were sailed all newly-commissioned MTBs and MGBs to rehearse in every detail their future role; and into a comprehensive syllabus was fed a continuous stream of data from the operational flotillas, directed by officers of accomplishment and sea experience.

A SUMMARY

In Home Waters MTBs and MGBs of all types fought 464 actions; in other areas, 316. The 464 resulted in the sinking of 269 enemy ships, for the loss of 76 of our own, and in summarising this, as in any other campaign, it is tempting to dwell on the skill of the victor rather than the vanquished.

But MTBs had no monopoly of skill, and the enemy was rarely caught off guard. Yet no branch of any service can succeed without an experienced staff to plan and analyse its operations, and at first there existed no such staff. In the absence of any deeper understanding, the early boats were expected to exhibit the same clockwork precision as all other warships, and when it proved difficult to reassemble the disordered jig-saw of their chance encounters with the enemy, the inference too often drawn was one of costly and unreliable incompetence. Of no other warship in history, manned often by virtual amateurs and launched hurriedly into complicated and often violent night actions, was so little known, and perhaps so much expected.

Such interest as they attracted inside the Navy and among the public was of an uninformed type, evoking a picture on the one hand of operational haphazardness, and on the other, of a shell-torn midget manned by heroes hurling its torpedoes (which never misfired or

Torpedo staff. HMS Hornet *Gosport 1944. Torpedo withdrawn partially from tube for maintenance routines. Note R.F.P.s on boat astern* (P. J. Liddell)

ran off course) at an enemy force which invariably sank in a series of spectacular explosions.

In fact, the lessons were bought slowly at a high price. Even when learned, they could not guarantee success; only diminish mistakes.

Inevitably, at intervals, skilled and experienced units under excellent operational directions, could find themselves in trouble. Even the most promising situation could be reversed with devastating suddenness.

A single shell in the bridge of the leading boat could send it veering out of control to cross the firing line of its consorts. At times there seemed no limit to the disasters which piled upon one another, with successive boats crippled, knocked out or set on fire. In these conditions it required much concentration to exclude the surrounding distractions and continue the attempt to fire torpedoes; and perhaps even more resolution to withdraw prior to making a fresh attempt, knowing that the enemy was alert and shooting well.

Yet, time and again, an MTB which had been severely damaged or immobilised in the track of a passing convoy was found by its consorts and given succour, often, while still under fire. It was at such times that the Senior Officer, who carried total responsibility, suffered his greatest anxieties, adding, maybe, to the failure of his attack the virtual certainty of damage and casualties in his unit.

Even so, a number of boats which could well have sunk were nursed successfully home, perhaps under tow, but sometimes solo, with a crippled engine-room and bailing parties hard at work. If such events were

Four-tube 73 ft Vospers on passage to Dutch coast Christmas Eve 1944. Note the raised chine and easy flow of the bow-wave in these later pattern boats

(P. J. Liddell)

Four-tube 73 ft Vospers on passage to Dutch coast Christmas Eve 1944. Note the raised chine and easy flow of the bow-wave in these later pattern boats

Four-tube 73 ft Vospers on passage to Dutch coast Christmas Eve 1944.

not habitual, they seemed inevitable sooner or later, and posed the question of how long the luck could hold (and for many, happily, it never broke) but, if not, whose turn came next?

Naturally, there was no shortage of narrow escapes. Naturally, too, in such conditions of stress, perhaps the events lived on more for their comedy than for their drama. The report of the crippled MTB which, before making her escape, circled tightly at some 200 yards range within the turning circle of an enemy destroyer, whose outward heel alone prevented her guns depressing sufficiently to hit—this had a rueful humour which could be savoured best, and perhaps only, by those who felt they had earned the right to laugh.

At the end of every operation the Senior Officer wrote his report. Often it was a bare record of an uneventful night at sea, sometimes rough, sometimes smooth, leavened only by navigational data and observations of the enemy coast. Sometimes it was a complicated lengthy document reporting an action, which included track charts, narrative, signal log, action damage, recommendations, items of interest, casualties and torpedo firing records.

The following is an example of one of many hundreds of similar documents containing its meed of success, and disappointment, but notable for its thoughtful lucidity. Technical interest focuses on the very long range at which torpedoes were fired to hit, due primarily to the speed of the target being plotted by shore radar, and passed to the unit on patrol as it watched the approaching force being attacked from the air. This distracting factor also had its effect.

WARSHIP SERIES EDITOR: JOHN WINGATE, DSC

Appendix
MTB Action of Night of 23/24 May 1944

FROM   The Commander-in-Chief, Portsmouth.
DATE   21st June 1944.
TO   The Secretary of the Admiralty.
    [Copies to . . . etc.]

Be pleased to lay before their Lordships the attached reports of actions by units of Coastal Forces on the night of 23rd/24th May in amplification of Portsmouth 242006B/May.

2. Two distinct operations took place; the first an interception by Unit F of a group of E-boats 30 miles N.E. of Point de Barfleur, the second an attack on 8 enemy warships, consisting of 5 torpedo boats and 3 M-class minesweepers eastbound across the Baie de la Seine, by 4 MTBs divided into two units of two (M2 and M3).

3. In the first engagement . . .

4. In the second engagement it is considered that the Senior Officer of Unit No. 3, Lieutenant M. Arnold-Forster, D.S.C., R.N.V.R., showed good judgment in choosing his position for attack. The unobserved attack which resulted in the destruction of an enemy ship was a well deserved success.

5. The causes of the premature explosion of MTB 209's torpedo . . . are being fully investigated and will be the subject of disciplinary action.

CHARLES LITTLE,
ADMIRAL.

The Commander-in-Chief, Portsmouth

Reports of the Senior Officers, 14th and 13th MTB Flotillas of the action on the night of 23rd/24th May 1944, are submitted in accordance with C.A.F.O. 1734/43 and C.in-C. Portsmouth No. 0/9683/21.

2. I consider that it was a well executed torpedo attack, with MTB 208 scoring a hit on one of the enemy's ships.

3. With reference to paragraph 5(f) of the Senior Officer, 13th MTB Flotilla's report, the heavy explosion ahead of MTB 209 was probably caused by one of her torpedoes hitting the bottom. A report by the Torpedo Officer of this base is attached . . .

M. MURRAY,
CAPTAIN.

H.M.S. *Hornet*
1st June 1944.

HM MTB 212—25th May 1944

Sir,—I have the honour to submit the following report of the proceedings of Unit M.3 (MTB 209 Sub-Lieutenant J. Ferguson, R.A.N.V.R., with Senior Officer embarked, and MTB 208 Lieutenant P. J. Liddell, R.N.V.R.) under my command on the night of 23rd/24th May 1944. This report covers the period from 0138 onwards when Units M.2 and M.3 parted company.

Duty: Torpedo Attack.
Forces: Unit M.3, MTBs 209 (S.O.) and 208.
Orders: Covering Force for Operation KN8.
Weather: Wind 0, Sea 00. Fine and clear.
Narrative: Unit M.3 parted company from Unit M.2 in E.P. 128° TT 14.1 at 0138. Course was set for position 142° TT 18.8 at 10 knots. Unit stopped at 0159 and confirmed E.P. by bearings of C. de la Hève, Ouistreham and Pt. de Ver. At 0200 a number of starshell burst to the Eastward. It seemed likely that M.2s presence was suspected and it was decided not to proceed further inshore for the time being.

C.-in-C. Portsmouth's 0210 showed that Plot 2 would pass close S. of the Unit's position at about 0315. The prospects of an attack from inshore in this area did not seem good. Air attacks were taking place over the land as well as on Plot 2, and the flares and H.A. fire which resulted lit up the whole area between the Unit and the coast on several occasions between 0200 and 0300. It was therefore decided to attack from seaward, and a signal to this effect was made at 0321 for the benefit of Unit M.2. This was addressed to Portsmouth W/T to avoid the use of M.2's call sign.

At 0255 course was set for position 146: TT 14.9, i.e. one mile to seaward of the target's expected 0310 position. This was as far West as it was considered safe to go without entering the area in which air attacks were taking place. At about 0300 aircraft echoes were picked up to starboard by MTB 209, which soon faded between 8 and 10 miles. Several surface echoes were picked up from 0310 onwards on the anticipated bearing of the enemy, seven of which entered the ground wave at 0317. These were considered to be small craft—probably leading escort. The craft themselves were not sighted and it is now thought that these echoes may well have been spurious. However, the Unit stopped at 0308 to allow them to pass. In the meanwhile a group of three echoes was picked up at a range of 4200^x by MTB 208 and 6000^x by MTB 209, which were considerably larger. Both boats reported that only two of these echoes could be picked up after the attack. Mean plotted course of these echoes was between 080° and 100° but target's speed was difficult to assess. Range of the group had closed to 2000^x at 0321 and 1400^x at 0335.

Although the enemy's late arrival in the Unit's vicinity indicated a mean speed of less than 15 knots, it was considered that this speed (given in C.-in-C. Portsmouth's 0210) probably still held good, the delay being accounted for by the air attacks which had been seen. Both boats were therefore ordered to set enemy speed to 15 knots.

At 0319 MTB 208 reported enemy in sight, bearing S.5°E. at mean radar range of 3400^x. Neither the Commanding Officer of MTB 209 nor I had by then sighted the enemy. The visibility was too good to allow of any delay in carrying out the attack, and I instructed the Commanding Officer, MTB 208, to lead in at once. At 0320 MTB 208 proceeded to close the enemy on a mean course of S.15°E. While MTB 209 kept station on her in open order. Almost immediately the enemy vessels were sighted by the commanding officer of MTB 209 and myself and were seen to consist of one vessel, probably a large R-boat, followed at some distance by two larger vessels very close together. The latter were low in the water and appear to be at least 200 ft long. Other small craft were later sighted on the port quarter of the main group.

At 0325 MTB 208 fired both torpedoes at the combined silhouette of the two larger vessels from a radar range of 1400^x. Ship's head S.11°E. Mag., Track Angle set 112°, enemy speed 15 knots. MTB 208 then turned short round 180° to starboard and stopped to observe results. At 0327 a heavy explosion was seen, felt and heard on the second ship in the enemy line by both boats. This was accompanied by flame and a large cloud of black smoke which remained visible for a considerable period. This vessel was not seen again. At 0327½ MTB 209 fired both torpedoes at the third ship in the enemy line from a radar range of 1400^x. Ship's head S.10°E. Mag., Track Angle set 90°, enemy speed 15 knots. At 0328 a very heavy underwater explosion took place close ahead of MTB 209 which caused considerable damage below decks to electrics and pipelines and also to gun mountings, although main engines were not immediately affected. It is difficult to arrive at a conclusion as to the cause of this explosion, but it is considered probable that it was caused by MTB 209's torpedoes colliding or hitting the bottom. *(paragraph f)*

But in any case it is considered that the running of MTB 209's torpedoes must have been affected to a serious degree and had this explosion not taken place I consider that MTB 209's torpedoes stood every chance of hitting, as they were fired with virtually the same sight settings as those of MTB 208 and weather conditions were good enough to rule out any possibility of large sighting error. Owing to the explosion; and to the fact that the enemy had already opened fire, results could not be observed.

Enemy commenced firing into the air shortly before

Two-tube 73 ft Vospers, armed with power-operated 6-pdrs, in quarterline off Culver, 1945   *(P. J. Liddell)*

MTB 209 fired torpedoes. This was undoubtedly due to his recent experience of air attack, and it was some seconds before he realised his error.

MTB 209 altered course to starboard to N. mag. after firing, while MTB 208 made smoke to cover the retirement and took station on MTB 209 in ORDER 1, both boats increasing speed to 32 knots. The smoke screen provided good cover for both boats and an excellent target for the enemy who eventually concentrated a considerable volume of fire upon it, using 37mm and above. He also appeared to be using some form of mortar or other weapon with a low m.v. The projectiles showed white traces and appeared to burst with a white flash on hitting the water. A certain amount of A.P. shells or rockets burst above the unit during the withdrawal, but the enemy soon transferred his whole attention to the smoke screen, and neither boat was hit. Starshell continued to burst until daylight.

Unit proceeded to the R/V position which was reached at 0403. R/T contact was made with V.13 in Unit M.2 who reported that he was not in need of assistance and gave permission for M.3 to proceed. Course was set for E.A.3 buoy which was reached at 0627. Unit entered harbour at 0726.

It is submitted that the Commanding Officer, MTB 208, carried out his attack deliberately and well. His decision to attack from 1400^x while still unobserved was in my opinion the correct one in view of the excellent visibility, and the accurate information available as to the enemy's course and speed.

The attack carried out by the Commanding Officer, MTB 209, was equally deliberate and in my opinion would have stood an equal chance of success had the explosion referred to in para. (f) above not taken place. The same enemy speed settings were used by both boats and it is a source of some disappointment that further results were not obtained

The crew of MTB 208 (a sister ship to 246 illustrated) on paying-off. The insignia on the ensign refer to services in the Channel between October 1943 and September 1944. All but the Coxswain were civilians in peace time. MTB 208 features in the attached action report

(P. J. Liddell)

Able Seaman   Stoker 1st/Cl.   Telegraphist   Chief Motor Mechanic   Telegraphist   Able Seaman   Stoker 1st/Cl.
J. WARNER.   A. C. LANGDON.   T. CROWLEY.   P. DUNDAS, D.S.M.   T. DELVER.   R. COXON.   J. SLATER.
Able Seaman   Able Seaman   Sub Lieutenant R.N.V.R.   Lieutenant R.N.V.R.   Leading Seaman   Able Seaman
J. SCOTT.   H. E. HAMILL.   C. I. LUMSDEN.   P. J. LIDDELL, D.S.C.   L. S. STAPLEY, D.S.M.   F. WILLANE.
(Absent : Able Seaman D. M COLLIN, D.S.M.)

MTB 102—*the 68 ft experimental Isotta-engined Vosper MTB which in 1937 reached 40 knots loaded, and 48 knots light*
(*P. J. Liddell*)

for this reason. Both radar operators carried out their duties efficiently and provided accurate information throughout.
Casualties: Nil.

Damage: MTB 208: Nil. MTB 209: Turret pipe lines and oil pipes in engine room fractured by underwater explosion. Considerable damage to electric circuits (including both auxiliary ignition circuits), the full extent of which has not yet been ascertained. Port Vickers guns were blown off mounting.

Lights, etc. observed: C. de la Hève. Ouistreham. Pt. de Ver. Grandchamps. All showed normal characteristics. Two unidentified lights were sighted near the entrance to the port of Le Havre.

Items of interest: MTB 208's attack was unobserved, and the enemy were still under the impression that they were being bombed when 209 fired. After M.3 had withdrawn, the enemy kept up a very gratifying exchange of fire between themselves for a considerable period.

Recommendations and conclusions: MTB attacks carried out immediately after air attacks are bound to cause considerable confusion. It is suggested that a similar operation carried out in the reverse sequence would also stand a good chance of success.

List of signals: Appendices I, II, III, IV, V, VI, VII.

M. Arnold-Forster,
Lieutenant R.N.V.R.
Senior Officer, 13th MTB Flotilla.

DETAILS AND PENDANT NUMBERS OF VOSPER-BUILT 70ft MTBs (A total of some 200 were built)

Date	Numbers	Crew	Length ft	Engines	Torpedoes	Guns etc	Other
1939	29 and 30	9	70	3 Isotta Fraschini 2 Vosper/Ford V8s	2 × 21 in.	2 × Quad 0·303 in.	W/T
1939–40	31–40 218–221	10	71	3 Isotta Fraschini (31–40) 3 Hall Scott. 2 Vosper/Ford V8 (remainder)	2 × 21 in.	1 × twin 0·5 in.	W/T, radar or A/S
1939–42	57–66 347–363	10	70	3 Packard 2 Vosper/Ford V8	2 × 21 in.	1 × twin 0·5 in. depth charges	W/T, radar CAS smoke
1940	69–70	7	70	3 Isotta Fraschini (69) 2 Isotta Fraschini (70) 2 Vosper/Ford V8	2 × 21 in.	2 × quad 0·303 in.	W/T
1940 Royal Norwegian Navy	5 and 7 71 and 72		60	2 Isotta Fraschini 2 Vosper/Ford V8	2 × 18 in.	1 twin 0·303 in. 4 depth charges	W/T
1940–41	73			3 Packard 4M 2500		1 × twin 0·5 in.	CSA, Radar
	75–98 222–245	10	70	2 Vosper/Ford V8	2 × 21 in.	4 depth charges	W/T

LATER DEVELOPMENT

Date	Numbers	Crew	Length ft	Engines	Torpedoes	Guns etc	Other
1943	379–395	12	73	3 Packard 1 Vosper/Ford V8	4 × 18 in.	1 × twin 20mm Oerlikon 2 × twin 0·303 in. Vickers 2 Rocket projectors	CSA, Radar W/T
1944	510	24	100	4 Packard	2 × 18 in.	1 6 Pdr. 1 twin 20mm 2 twin 0·5 in. 1 rocket projector depth charges	CSA, Radar W/T
1944	523–530 532–533	16	73	3 Packard 1 Vosper/Ford V8	2 × 18 in.	1 × twin 20mm 2 × twin 0·303 in. 1 × 6 Pdr. 1 rocket projector	CSA, Radar W/T

70ft MTB WATCH & QUARTER BILL

	Part of Ship	Harbour Station	Prepare for sea	Boarding Station	Fire	Abandon Ship
Coxswain	Supervise work	Wheel	Test communications Check each man's duty	At wheel	As required	Carley raft
Telegraphist I	W/T gear W/T office Wardroom flat	Pendants	Test W/T, T.C.S. Echo/sounder Provide S.P.s and Recogs.	Remain closed-up	As required	Fire detonators Carley raft Ditch S.P.s
Telegraphist II	Cook/Galley	Fo'c'sle	Provide and test Aldis, Binoculars, 1038 lamp pistols and cartridges	Pistol	Responsible below forward	Assist Tel I mess-deck cushions
Seaman-Torpedoman	F. mess deck and heads	Fenders forward	Check T.T. and Torpedoes Test lights Detach shore-lighting	Provide hand grenades	E/R deck Foamite Stand by tubes	Star. Life-buoy Rubber dinghy
Trained man I	Star. Bunk space	Q.D.	Rig Lifelines Rig hand steering	Lanchester Carbine	E/R deck Nuswift I/C on deck	Port Life-buoy Rubber dinghy
Trained man II	Bridge and Wheelhouse	Fenders aft	Provide carbines and ammunition Place revolvers in Wheelhouse	Close up on 0·303" Vickers	Bridge messenger Bridge Foamite	Open W/T door Carley raft
Gunner I	Oerlikon Port Vickers	Fo'c'sle	Prepare Oerlikon magazines Prepare 0·303" magazines	Lanchester Carbine	Remain closed-up	Provide heaving-lines
Gunner II	0·5" turret Star. Vickers	Q.D.	Prepare 0·303" magazines Check R.F.P.s Test 0·5" turret with E/R	0·5" turret	Remain closed-up	Wooden lockers aft Rubber dinghy
Radar-Operator	W/R and W/R heads	Q.D.	Test 286 Test Q.H.2 Test Hydrophone	Remain closed-up on all-round sweep	W/T office Pyrene	Destroy set Supply mess-deck cushions
Motor-Mechanic	E/R	E/R	Set C.S.A. Warm through main engines	E/R	E/R gear as necessary	Detonators Rubber dinghy
Stoker I	E/R	E/R	E/R	Lanchester Carbine	E/R	Puncture tanks Carley raft
Stoker II	E/R	E/R	E/R	E/R	E/R	Puncture tanks Carley raft

A U-boat of the IX-B Class on patrol in the Atlantic   (BfZ/Dressler)

Kriegsmarine U-107

by Dr Jürgen Rohwer

The German U-Boat, U-107

U-107 has been selected as the Warship Profile of a German U-boat because, though not particularly well-known, she lays claim to special regard on several grounds. She belonged to the IX B class, the 14 boats of which, with a tally of more than 1·4 million GRT (Gross Registered Tons) sunk, scored roughly ten per cent of the total German U-boat successes and therefore represented the most successful class. With a total of 750 days at sea *U-107* was, among German U-boats, the submarine with the longest record of operational patrols during the Second World War; in addition, her score in the spring of 1941 of 14 ships sunk, totalling 86,699 GRT, represented the most successful achievement of a single patrol throughout the war period. A score of 38 ships and 217,751 GRT placed her in fifth place after *U-48, U-99, U-103* and *U-124* in the list of successful U-boats of the Second World War.

Eventually, in her 13 patrols from 1941 to 1944 she had participated in every type of U-boat operation known in the Battle of the Atlantic: attacks on convoys on the North Atlantic, Gibraltar and West Africa routes; successful individual operations off Freetown, the east coast of the United States and in the Caribbean

as far as the straits of Yucatan. She sailed on a mine-laying operation off the U.S. east coast and also played a part in bringing the first Schnorkel-fitted U-boats into action in this area. She was refuelled and replenished from surface vessels and submarine tankers, and participated in the first use of the 'Zaunkönig' ('Jenny Wren') guided-missile torpedo.

The U-boat Class IX B: Development

Before the Second World War, the German Navy developed three classes of U-boat to operational readiness:

(i) a small coastal U-boat (Class II A, B, C) of 254–291 tons;

(ii) a medium-sized U-boat (Class VII A, B) of 626 and 753 tons respectively, which, in a further development as Class VII C, was later to bear the main burden of the convoy battles;

(iii) for long-range patrols, a large boat (Class IA, IXA) of 862 and 1051 tons respectively.

The design of the large boat had its origin in a design for a 750-ton U-boat worked out in 1927 by the German U-boat design office 'Ingenieurskantoor voor Scheepsbouw' at the Hague; with German financial backing

Class IX was developed from Class I-A; here the Class-boat, U-37, who, between 1939 and 1941, achieved great success under her Captains: Lt-Cdr Hartmann, Snr.Lt Oehrn and Snr.Lt Clausen   (BfZ/Dressler)

A Class IX U-boat returns to her base from a successful operation in the Atlantic, with 8 pendants (BfZ/Dressler)

Bridge of a U-boat, 1943: Abaft the Captain, the opening for the LW-DF aerial (also MW); immediately behind the opening for rod-aerial. Aerial-target periscope retracted (middle opening); surface-target periscope raised. Behind, 2 MG 151. In front, opening for the retracted 'Hohentwiel' radar aerial (upper side of the beam aerial recognisable). Left of the Captain, round dipole aerial of the 'Naxos' radio-location apparatus
From 1943, the bridge of U-107 was similar (BfZ/Gröner)

From her antecedents: The Class-boat of Class I-A, U-25, developed from the U-boat Gür, built in Spain and bought by Turkey (BfZ/Dressler)

A 1XC U-boat at the surrender in May 1945.
The picture shows the final form of the tower, to starboard. On the lower open bridge, the 3·7cm AA M/42 with armoured shield; ammunition lockers behind. On the upper open bridge (hidden by people), two 2cm twin AA guns. The tube below the bridge is the connection from the snorkel-mast folded down in the upper deck to the diesel air inlet and outlet shafts under the upper open bridge. The upper deck has been levelled out forward to reduce diving time (sticking effect). (Probably no longer on U-107!) Otherwise in August 1944 the U-107 as on this U-boat; see also second photograph with port side (BfZ/Krulle)

U-805 is surrendered. Port side of tower: the armour-plating on front of open bridge is extended to take the 'Hohentwiel' radar apparatus; below, the extension for the cable-chute (BfZ/Krulle)

and material prepared in Holland, this design was then translated into the U-boat, *E1*, at the Spanish Echevarrieta shipyard in Cadiz; after completing her trials with a German crew in 1931. She was sold to the Turkish Navy under the name *Gür*.

The two German U-boats, *U-25* and *U-26* (Class IA), were built in 1935–36 in accordance with the improved plans of *Gür*. The results of trials with this class culminated in a demand for greater range. This was realised in the not inconsiderably enlarged Class IX A.

These boats showed improved sailing qualities, thanks to better lines and higher speed, in spite of the· increase in size due to the more powerful diesels installed. The difference between this Class IX A (*U-37* to *U-44*) and the following series of Class IX B consisted primarily of a further increase in the fuel supply from 154 cu. m to 165 cu. m and a consequent increase in the range at 10 knots from 10,500 to 12,000 sea miles.

The midship section of the Class IX U-boat. On the left the 3·7cm AA C/30; on the open bridge, a 2cm AA C/30, and below, the air inlet and outlet shafts for the diesel engines. On the bridge, is the centre forward spray deflector; above is the wind deflector. Above the bulwarks to the left is the attack periscope; to the right, the air-all-round periscope. Forward of the tower is the 10·5cm surface gun. Aerials for the radio-apparatus are mounted on the upper edge of the tower which served as net deflectors (BfZ/Dressler)

TECHNICAL DETAILS OF THE IX B CLASS

1 Dimensions

Standard displacement surfaced 1051 tons, submerged 1232 tons. Length overall: 76·50m; beam 6·76m; draught 4·70m; diameter of pressure-hull 4·40m; height from keel to upper rim of conning-tower 9·60m.

2 Propulsion:

Surfaced: 2 MAN, 9 cyl., 4 stroke diesel engines, each of 2200h.p. at 470r.p.m. on both shafts, max. speed 18·2 knots. Submerged: 2 SSW electric motors, supplied from 2 banks of accumulators with 62+62 cells, 740W at 11,300Ah. Range: surfaced: 12,000 sea miles at 10 knots; with diesel-electric propulsion 12,400 sea miles; 3800 sea miles at maximum speed. Submerged: 64 sea miles at 4 knots, 134 sea miles at 2 knots. Maximum oil supply: 165 tons; normal: 129 tons. Diving time 35 seconds. Diving depth 100m, with 2½ times safety factor (250m). From 1944, Schnorkel fitted on starboard side of conning-tower.

Forward deck of a Class IX U-boat. Alongside the tower are the rails for handling torpedoes from the on-deck tubes. Forward of the tower is the 10·5cm surface gun. On the bridge railings are the dipoles of the permanently-fitted GEMA-Seetakt 80cm radar apparatus (BfZ/Dressler)

After-deck of a Class IX U-boat. Under the side, removable upper-deck gratings housed the air-tight on-deck tubes for reserve torpedoes. The torpedoes were brought into the boat through the torpedo-hatches (rear centre). In the middle, in front of the lower structure, the 3·7cm AA gun C/30 was removed (BfZ/Dressler)

U-107 *(foreground)* and U-38 *(background)in the large construction dock of the Lorient shipyard*
(Grützemacher Collection)

3 Armament
Torpedoes: 4 bow and 2 stern torpedo-tubes, 53·3cm; 10 reserve torpedoes in boat, 9 more in pressure-tight on-deck compartments (from 1943 onwards, mostly no longer on board). TMA, TMB and/or TMC torpedo mines could be laid (2 TMA or TMC, 3 TMB per tube) from the torpedo tubes.
Guns: 1×10·5cm L/45 forward of the conning-tower; 1×3·7cm AA C/30 aft of the conning-tower; 1×2cm AA C/32 on the conning-tower (180, 2625 and 2125 rounds respectively). From 1942 (in some cases not until 1943) the 3·7cm and 10·5cm guns were removed and the AA guns reinforced; first, on the upper and lower open bridges one each 2cm AA C/38; 1943 on lower open bridge 1×2cm AA four-barrel gun; on upper open bridge, 2×2cm AA C/38 single-barrel; end of 1943/start 1944 in some instances, instead of 2cm four-barrel AA gun, 1×3·7cm AA M/42 or M/43 was mounted on the lower open bridge; 2×2cm AA twin-barrel guns on the upper open bridge; in some instances 4×MG-34 or Aircraft MG-151 were fitted on the bridge.

4 Communications Equipment:
Radio transmitters: 1 Short-wave transmitter, 200W, 3·75-15MHz; 1 Long-wave transmitter, 150W, 300-500kHz; 1 Short-wave transmitter, 40W, 5-16·7MHz. Radio receivers: 1 Short-wave receiver, 1·5-25MHz; 1 all-wave receiver, 15-20,000kHz, 1-2 broadcast receivers.
Radio Direction Finder: In some instances, rod aerial for reception submerged at periscope depth. The U-boats *U-103, U-104* and *U-124* were, under pre-war plans, intended as leaders for U-boat packs and therefore carried additional communication equipment on board (in part removed during the war).
Radar: Until 1943, individual boats were fitted with the 80cm wavelength GEMA equipment, dipoles (8-12) rigidly projecting from forward edge of bridge. These were not effective because of pounding in bad weather. From 1943, retractable aerial (mattress) 'Hohentwiel' on 556MHz, fitted to retract into a shaft on the port side of the bridge.
Radar Observation Equipment: From August 1942 to summer 1943, Metox R.600, after August 1943 replaced by Hagenuk wave-detector WANZ I, in part 'Borkum'. From November 1943, the fixed WANZ II covering the whole horizon. From the end of 1943 onwards, the 'Naxos' was installed for the 8-12cm band.

U-107 Dimensions:
Length overall: 76·50m; greatest width of the hull: 6·76m; average draught with keel: 4·70m; diameter of pressure hull/body: 4·40m; height from bottom of keel to top of standards: 9·40m.
Surface displacement: 1051 3/m; dive displacement: 1178 3/m; Total moulded displacement: 1430 3/m.

A Class IX U-boat returns to Lorient. In the foreground is the 3·7cm AA C/30. Alongside the deck, are the cover plates for the on-deck torpedo tubes (BfZ/Dressler)

Conning tower of a Class IX U-boat before the AA guns had been increased. On the open bridge is a 2cm AA C/30. Below the open bridge, are the air inlet and outlet shafts for the diesel engines. On the front of the tower, in the centre, is the spray deflector; above is the wind deflector (BfZ/Dressler)

Type IX B
Engines: 2 Diesel engines, 2200 h.p. 2 Main electric motors, 500 h.p. 2 Storage battery, 62 cells. No silent running electric motors. No diesel dynamo. Fuel oil: 165·45 tons. Fuel: Nil. Surface maximum cruising speed: 18·2 knots; dived maximum cruising speed: 7·3 knots. Surface range: 12,000 miles at 10 knots; dived range: 64 miles at 4 knots.
Armament: 4 Bow tubes with torpedoes. 2 Stern tubes. No side tubes. 16 Reserve torpedoes. Guns: 1×3·7cm HA; 2×2cm twin close range weapons.

U-107: Commissioning and Trials
On 8 October 1940, Senior Lieutenant Günter Hessler commissioned *U-107*, in Bremen. Until March 1940, he had been captain of the torpedo-boat *Falke* and in this ship had participated in mine-laying, trade-war and escort duties before he applied for transfer to the submarine branch, the Flag-Officer of which, then Rear-Admiral Karl Dönitz, was his father-in-law. Between April and October 1940, Senior Lieutenant Hessler attended the usual U-boat training course, before joining his new command.

U-107, like all her sister-ships was attached to the 2nd U-boat Flotilla. Her home base was Wilhelmshaven but, as early as June 1940, operational H.Q. staff had moved to the new base at Lorient and in June 1941, the remaining H.Q. personnel had followed. Those boats of the flotilla still in training were 'farmed off' on to the training flotillas stationed in the Baltic during their trials and training period. Until the end of 1940, *U-107* steadily completed her schedule of trials and work-up before she was declared fully operational at the beginning of 1941.

THE FIRST PATROL:
25 January to 1 March 1941 in the North Atlantic *(See map p. 177)*
Delayed by ice conditions, *U-107* finally sailed on 25 January 1941 from Heligoland in company with *U-48*, hitherto the most successful U-boat, with a score of 248,020 GRT. Three days earlier the battle-cruisers, *Scharnhorst* and *Gneisenau*, had slipped out of Kiel through the Kattegat and Skagerrak into the Atlantic. On their first attempt to break out south of Iceland, they had encountered the British cruiser, *Naiad*, during the night of 29 January, but were able to shake her off and make contact with the tanker, *Adria*, waiting in the North Sea.

The Group North responsible for Operation '*Berlin*' now strove to enlist *U-107* and *U-48*, at that moment

Alongside a lighter in Lorient, a Class IX U-boat is being fitted out for patrol. In the background is the hulk of the former cruiser, Strasbourg, *the one-time German,* Regensburg, *who went to France as reparations in 1920* (BfZ/Dressler)

CONSTRUCTIONAL DETAILS OF THE IX B CLASS BOATS

U-boat	Contract	Building No.	Keel laid	Launched	Commissioned	Operational	Lost
U-64	16 7 37	952	15 11 38	20 9 39	16 12 39	6 4 40	13 4 40*
U-65	16 7 37	953	6 12 38	6 11 39	15 2 40	9 4 40	28 4 41*
U-122 (ex U-66)	15 12 37	954	5 3 39	30 12 39	30 3 40	15 5 40	21 6 40*
U-123 (ex U-67)	15 12 37	955	15 4 39	2 3 40	30 5 40	21 9 40	19 8 44*
U-124 (ex U-68)	15 12 37	956	11 8 39	9 3 40	11 6 40	20 8 40	2 4 43*
U-103	24 5 38	966	6 9 39	12 4 40	5 7 40	21 9 40	1 44*
U-104	10 3 39	967	10 11 39	25 5 40	19 8 40	12 11 40	21 11 40*
U-105	10 3 39	968	16 11 39	15 6 40	10 9 40	24 12 40	2 6 43*
U-106	10 3 39	969	26 11 39	17 6 40	24 9 40	4 1 41	2 8 43*
U-107	10 3 39	970	6 12 39	2 7 40	8 10 40	25 1 41	18 8 44*
U-108	10 3 39	971	27 12 39	15 7 40	22 10 40	16 2 41	11 4 44*
U-109	10 3 39	972	9 3 40	14 9 40	5 12 40	8 5 41	7 5 43*
U-110	10 3 39	973	1 2 40	25 8 40	21 11 40	12 3 41	9 5 41*
U-111	8 8 38	976	20 2 40	6 9 40	19 12 40	5 5 41	4 10 41*

* Shipyard for all boats : Deutsche Schiffs- und Maschinenbau A.G., Bremen.

PATROLS, DAYS AT SEA AND SUCCESSES OF CLASS IX B BOATS

U-boat	Patrols	Days at sea	Sinkings	Sinkings shared with others	Damaged
U-64	1	8	—		
U-65	6	203	12/ 68,051 GRT	1/28,124 GRT	3/ 19,490 GRT
U-122	2	16	1/ 5911 ,,	—	—
U-123	13	703	1 Submarine 40/ 203,424 ,,	4/15,646 ,,	6/ 53,568 ,,
U-124	11	472	1 Corvette 46/ 218,275 ,,	—	4/ 26,167 ,,
U-103	11	595	42/ 220,060 ,,	—	3/ 28,158 ,,
U-104	1	9	1/ 8240 ,,	—	1/ 10,516 ,,
U-105	9	460	1 Sloop 22/ 126,876 ,,	—	—
U-106	10	483	21/ 131,703 ,,	—	1 Battleship 2/ 12,885 ,,
U-107	14	750	38/ 217,751 ,,	—	3/ 25,490 ,,
U-108	11	459	25/ 127,990 ,,	—	—
U-109	9	419	14/ 88,830 ,,	—	1/ 6548 ,,
U-110	2	41	3/ 10,056 ,,	—	2/ 8675 ,,
U-111	2	110	5/ 30,171 ,,	—	—
	88	3978	270/1,457,338 GRT	5/43,770 GRT	25/191,497 GRT

The Italian submarine Bianchi *who, with* U-107, *co-operated to sink the British Ocean Boarding Vessel,* Manistee, *on 24 February 1941*

sailing out north of the Shetlands into the open ocean, to help as scouts against a fresh attempt by the Home Fleet to check the break out. The 'B.d.U.' (Flag Officer, U-Boats) rejected this operation on the grounds that U-Boats were demonstrably ill-suited for such a task on account of their lack of manoeuvrability and their restricted horizon, particularly when air-reconnaissance could be employed in the same area. The battle-cruisers did in fact succeed in breaking out unnoticed through the Denmark Straits on 3/4 February and, after taking on fresh supplies south of Greenland from the tanker, *Schlettstadt*, began their operations on 7 February along the Halifax-England (HX) convoy route.

First Blood

In the meantime *U-107* and *U-48* when ordered to join forces on 29 January with *U-106*, *U-94*, *U-103*, *U-52*, *U-93* and *U-101* to the north-west of Ireland; the pack was to be ready for wide-ranging east-to-west aggressive sweeps to detect convoys, in conjunction with

aerial reconnaissance by the four-engined FW 200 (Condor) aircraft of the 1st K.G. 40.

On 3 February, shortly after midnight, while cruising at the north-western tip of the pack, *U-107* sighted the British steamship, *Empire Citizen* (4683GRT), the former German *Wahehe* of the German African line; she was steering a solitary course south-west in an attempt to link up with her convoy, OB.279. After an abortive approach run, one torpedo stopped the ship and a final hit sank her.

In the evening, Senior Lieutenant Hessler overtook the convoy. On receiving his report that he was shadowing, the B.d.U. brought the nearest boats, *U-52*, *U-103* with *U-96* and *U-123* (on weather duty) into action. During the night's shadowing, *U-107* fired a torpedo at the 'Ocean Boarding Vessel', *Crispin* (5051 GRT), who was steaming apart from the convoy which was under destroyer escort. Her boilers exploded and the ship disappeared. The convoy had now reached 20° W longitude and broke up—as was then the practice—before the other U-boats could arrive on the scene.

In the mist of the Newfoundland Banks, the battle-cruisers, Gneisenau *(forward, a 10·5cm AA tower) and* Scharnhorst *(an Arado* Ar-196 *ready to take off from the catapult), search for convoy HX in February 1941*

U-Boat Alert

The Admiralty issued a U-boat warning and the next convoys (e.g. SC.20 coming from the west) were diverted. At noon on 6 February one of the stragglers from this convoy, the Canadian, *Maplecourt* (3388GRT), steamed right ahead of *U-107* who had returned to her operational area; the first torpedo missed, but Hessler sank the ship in a submerged attack.

The U-boat attacks were not the only threat to force the Admiralty to divert the convoy traffic. The appearance of heavy German surface-units on the HX and HG/SL routes threw the North Atlantic convoy timetable into confusion. On 8 February, the battleship, *Ramillies*, sighted one of the two German battle-cruisers lying in wait to attack convoy HX.108. They turned away and *Ramillies* reported the enemy as a heavy cruiser.

The Admiralty immediately dispersed the Home Fleet in three groups to intercept the heavy cruisers presumed to be making for home (only *Admiral Scheer* or *Admiral Hipper*, in fact, passed through the area from 20 to 24 March). *Admiral Hipper*, after refuelling from the tanker, *Spichern*, had first hunted along the HX-route from 7–10 February and then been brought into action against convoy HG.53; this convoy had been reported by *U-37* who then attacked in combination with FW 200s of the 1st K.G. 40. *Hipper* had found only one straggler before the unescorted convoy SLS.65 steamed into her path on the morning of 12 February; the convoy lost seven of its 14 ships.

In the meantime, on 9 February the U-boat pack had moved off northwards towards Iceland but, including the Italian submarines operating to the south, the pack destroyed only stragglers from convoys HX.106 and SC.21; and then more stragglers from HX.107 after a further move close to the Icelandic coastline. No convoy-sightings were reported.

CONVOY BATTLE: OB.287

At last, at noon on 19 February, one of the FW 200s flying from Bordeaux to Stavanger reported convoy OB.287 north-west of the Hebrides; this consisted of 45 ships, two of whom the aircraft had bombed and sunk. The B.d.U. immediately ordered *U-73*, *U-107*, *U-48*, *U-96* and *U-69*, and the Italians, *Bianchi*, *Marcello* and *Barbarigo*, to form a line across the convoy's course. OB.287 succeeded in penetrating the line in the south, where the Italian submarines had not yet taken up their positions.

On 20 February, three FW 200s attacked the convoy and damaged four ships, but their position reports varied so widely that the patrol line could be directed

On 2 July 1941, U-107 returned to Lorient with 14 pendants. With white cap-cover, the Captain, Snr.Lt Hessler; in front, the 1st Officer of the Watch, Jnr.Lt Helmut Witte, who later had great success as Captain of U-159. On the tower is the ship's badge: 4 Aces
(Helmut Witte)

to a new position based only on estimates. On 21 February, a FW 200 scored bomb-hits on a tanker just west of the line, and *U-96* was then able to sink her. The U-boats did not find the convoy, though the destroyer, *Montgomery*, sank the *Marcello*.

Meanwhile another FW 200 had sighted west of Ireland the next convoy, OB.288, and had damaged two ships. *U-73*, *U-69*, *U-96*, *U-107*, *U-552*, *U-97*, *Barbarigo* and *Bianchi* formed a line of interception; the most northerly boat, *U-73*, made only a brief contact in the evening, so that on 23 February a new line had to be formed. Through this line on 24 February, the convoy duly steamed; *U-96*, *U-69* and the newly-arrived *U-95*

A Focke-Wulf FW200 C-1 (Condor of the 1st K.G.40) as used in February 1941 to reconnoitre convoys HG.53, OB.287 and OB.288 for the U-boats (BfZ/Eckert)

Through the morning haze, the Officer of the Watch and First Mate watch a freighter sink after a successful shot
(Bundesarchiv)

The transfer of on-deck torpedoes was hard work. Booms and cranes had to be set up and firmly lashed, so that with the help of blocks and tackles the heavy torpedoes could be lowered through the narrow, sloping hatch into the fore-ends, even when the boat was rolling in a swell

When the first torpedo did not have sufficient effect and other torpedoes had to be economised, the 10·5cm gun came into action, as seen here against the Eskdene. On the foredeck, aft of the jumping-wire, the T-shaped head of the underwater sound location device can be recognised   (Bundesarchiv)

sank four ships before the convoy dispersed in the morning at 20° W; *U-95*, *U-96*, *U-73* and *Bianchi* were each able to sink one more ship.

A Stubborn Adversary

Before midnight on 23 February Senior Lieutenant Hessler had sighted near the convoy the Ocean Boarding Vessel, *Manistee* (5368 GRT); shortly afterwards, *Bianchi*, commanded by Lt.-Cdr. Giovannini, also made contact from the other side. The first torpedo of a double fan shot from *U-107* hit the *Manistee* on the port side, but the crew succeeded in getting the ship under way again at 8 knots within 30 minutes. A hit by the *Bianchi* showed little effect and three fired shortly afterwards by *U-107* were duds. Only in the morning of 24 February, after a number of further attempted attacks by *U-107* and *Bianchi*, whom the skilfully handled British ship out-manoeuvred again and again, did Senior Lieutenant Hessler succeed in sinking the *Manistee* with a double fan salvo. Having fired all her ammunition, *U-107* had to return to base and sailed into Lorient on 1 March, with a tally of four ships sunk, a total of 18,490GRT.

THE SECOND PATROL:
29 March—2 July 1941 off Freetown
(See map p. 184)
The operational readiness of the first large series of Class IX boats; the near-peacetime traffic condition prevailing according to available reports; and the

favourable refuelling and provisioning situation existing as a result of the supply-ships sent out into the Atlantic in connection with operations of heavy naval forces; all these factors combined to decide the B.d.U. to dispatch operational Class IX boats from Lorient to the neighbourhood of Freetown, beginning in March 1941. In the summer of 1940, the *UA*, built in Kiel for Turkey, had returned from this area with a score of seven ships sunk (40,706 GRT) and in January 1941, *U-65* had sunk no less than eight ships (47,785 GRT) and one damaged by torpedo.

At the end of February, *U-105*, *U-124* and *U-106* sailed and, after refuelling from the German tanker, *Charlotte Schliemann* ('Culebra') lying in Las Palmas, set parallel courses southwards on longitude 20°, 21° and 22° respectively. After only two days, on 7 March, the report was received from the battle-cruisers *Scharnhorst* and *Gneisenau*, who were operating in this area that, after sighting the battleship, *Malaya*, they had broken off their attack on convoy SL.67, which they had sighted 300 miles north-east of the Cape Verde Islands.

U-105 and *U-124* were brought into the attack on the following night and sank five ships in the convoy. They did not sight *Malaya*, so that the German battle-cruisers could not renew the attack. A fortnight later, *U-106* succeeded in calling up *U-105* to attack the next convoy, SL.68, and, in a model joint operation —relieving each other in turn—they sank seven ships between them; *U-106* fired torpedoes at *Malaya* and damaged her in position 20° 02′N and 25° 55′W.

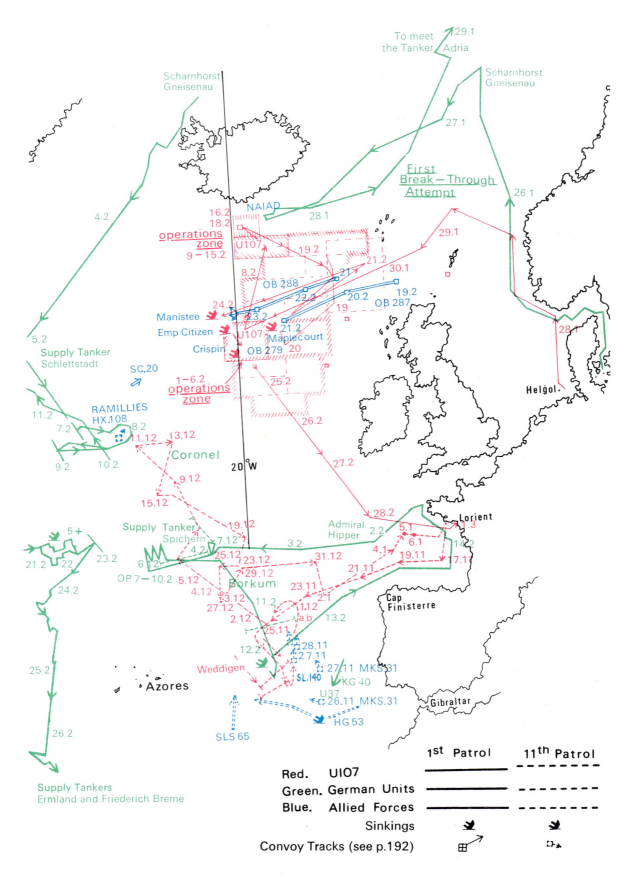

To meet
the Tanker Adria 29.1

Scharnhorst
Gneisenau

Scharnhorst
Gneisenau 26.1

27.1

First Break—Through Attempt

28.1

29.1

4.2

16.2
18.2
NAIAD
operations zone
9 – 15.2
U107

19.2

21.2

30.1

8.2
OB 288
21
22.2
20.2
19.2
OB 287

5.2

24.2
Manistee
Emp Citizen
U107
23.2
21.2
Maplecourt
19
Crispin
OB 279
20

Supply Tanker
Schlettstadt

SC.20

1 – 6.2
operations zone

25.2

28.1

Helgol.

11.2
RAMILLIES
HX.108
7.2
8.2
9.2
10.2
11.12
13.12
Coronel

26.2

20°W

27.2

9.12

15.12

28.2

Admiral Hipper
2.2

5.1

6.1

4.1

19.11

1.3

Lorient

14.2

17.1

5+
21.2
22
23.2

Supply Tanker
Spichern
7.12
4.2
25.12
23.12
29.12
3.2
31.12
21.11

24.2

6.12
OP 7 – 10.2
5.12
4.12
Borkum
3.12
27.12
2.12
11.2
1.12
25.11
a,b
23.11
2.1
13.2

25.2

12.2
28.11
27.11
27.11 MKS.31
SL.140
KG 40
U37
26.11 MKS.31

Cap
Finisterre

Weddigen

Azores

Gibraltar

26.2

SLS 65
HG 53

Supply Tankers
Ermland and Friederich Breme

		1ˢᵗ Patrol	11ᵗʰ Patrol
Red.	U107		
Green.	German Units		
Blue.	Allied Forces		
	Sinkings		
Convoy Tracks (see p.192)			

177

On the return from the most successful patrol, the Flag-Officer U-boats, Vice-Admiral Dönitz, decorates his son-in-law with the Ritterkreuz; to date Snr.Lt Hessler had sunk 22 ships of 105,189 GRT   (Bundesarchiv)

Success in Warm Waters

The next boat to sail, *U-107*, set course southwards at the beginning of April, west of longitudes 24° and 25°, hoping if possible to catch the next convoy making a wider sweep westwards. This disposition did not succeed, but, in compensation, Senior Lieutenant Hessler struck a trade-route north-west of the Canaries and, in underwater attacks on 8 and 9 April, was able to sink the British steamships, *Eskdene* (3829 GRT), *Helena Margaretha* (3316GRT), *Harpathian* (4671 GRT) and the British tanker, *Duffield* (8516GRT).

Two other attacks on 13 and 14 April further to the south, although failures, and several sightings, led Senior Lieutenant Hessler to radio the B.d.U. on 17 April, pointing out the favourable traffic conditions

In mid-Atlantic on 18 March 1941, U-124 (Snr.Lt Schulz, on the bridge, with forage-cap) met the heavy cruiser, Admiral Scheer (left), returning from the Indian Ocean, to hand over crystals for the cruiser's radar apparatus. In the background, the auxiliary cruiser, Schiff 41-Kormoran, from whom U-124 replenished her fuel and torpedoes
(W. Schulz)

north of the Cape Verde Islands, between 24° and 28° W, so the B.d.U. allowed the U-boat to operate in these waters.

But traffic now ceased and, apart from the British freighter, *Calchas* (10,305GRT), who was sunk by two submerged attacks, nothing more came into view. On 28 April Hessler was forced to leave his billet to reach the 'Andalusian' refuelling area punctually on 3 May, where he was due to replenish his fuel supplies at point 'Red' from the supply-ship, *Nordmark*. On passage, *U-107* encountered the British motor-vessel, *Lassell* (7417GRT), on 30 April, and sank her in a submerged attack.

On 5 May, *U-105* and *U-107* were able to report completion of revictualling and refuelling from the *Nordmark*. But while *U-105*, who had replenished her stock of torpedoes at the last refuelling returned to her billet between Freetown and Dakar, *U-107*, with only one torpedo unfired, had to await the arrival of the supply-ship, *Egerland*, on 9 May. On 11 May she too was able to sail for Freetown.

On 17 and 18 May, while still en route, she sank the Dutch tanker, *Marisa* (8029 GRT), and the British ship, *Piako* (8286 GRT), during night surface-attacks in which her guns also played a part. After *U-105* had also sunk five ships further to the north by 17 May, the C.-in-C., South Atlantic, halted the traffic and for a time sightings ceased.

Off Freetown

The B.d.U. ordered *U-105* and *U-107*, and *U-38*, *U-103* and *U-106*, who had sailed by 21 May from Andalusia, after refuelling from the *Egerland*, to intercept convoys off Freetown and to harry them over a considerable distance. The disposition was fruitless.

Reinforced by the *UA*, they were from 27 May allotted new operational areas in east-west patrols off Freetown against ships travelling independently. There was immediate success against the traffic which was beginning to build up again. *U-38* and *U-107* sank five ships each; *U-103* four, *U-106* three and *U-105* one; only the trouble-prone, *UA*, came away empty-handed.

Soon after midnight on 27 May, *U-107* sank the British ship, *Colonial* (15108 GRT), in a surface attack, the Greek ship, *Papalemos* (3748 GRT), in the afternoon of 28 May in a submerged attack: the British ship,

The Flag-Officer U-boats, Vice-Admiral Dönitz, awaits one of the boats returning from Freetown in July 1941; U-38 (Snr.Lt Liebe) with 8 pendants (Dressler Collection)

During the convoy action against HX.112, the destroyer, Bulldog, succeeded in boarding U-110, who had been forced to the surface by depth-charges and abandoned. Bulldog took the boat in tow. The secret information thus obtained was of the greatest importance in eliminating the German supply-ships in May and June 1941 (IWM)

After one hit amidships, the Piako was abandoned. Another hit aft caused her to sink by the stern
(Bundesarchiv)

On 18 and 19 June U-103, U-107, the Class VII-C boat, U-69 (centre), and the former Turkish boat, UA, wait in vain for the tanker, Lothringen, who four days previously had fallen a victim to British reconnaissance (Bundesarchiv)

A boat with survivors from the Marisa comes alongside. Lt Hessler (white shorts) questions the shipwrecked sailors and gives them course directions
(Bundesarchiv)

U.107

The 'Four Aces' was the insignia of *U.107* who, on her second patrol off Freetown, sank more tonnage than any other U-boat of the Second World War.

This Type IXB U-boat is shown here as she appeared after anti-fouling on return from patrol in 1941.

D. Johnson © *Profile Publications Ltd*

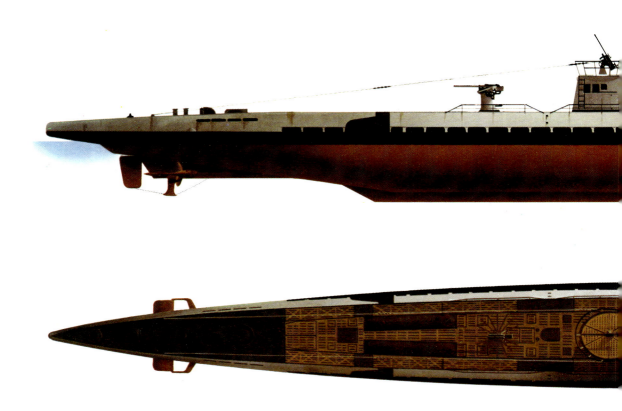

U.47 (Kl. Prien)
The Bull of Scapa Flow. This badge was carried not only by the *U.47* but by all the other submarines of the 7th U-flotilla.

U.108 (Kl. Schultz)
The coat-of-arms of Danzig.

U.106 (Kl. Rasch)
The Swordfish is white against the colour of the conning tower.

U.564 (Kk. Suhren)
'Three times black tom-cat' is painted against the standard colour of the conning tower.

To contest Coastal Command in the Bay of Biscay in 1943, extra close-range anti-aircraft weapons were mounted in the 'winter-garden' fitted abaft of the bridge. The two 10·5cm guns were removed at this time from the fore and after casing.

The W/T mast is obscured by the Schnorchel, depicted here in its raised position, which was fitted in 1944.

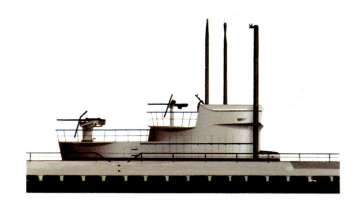

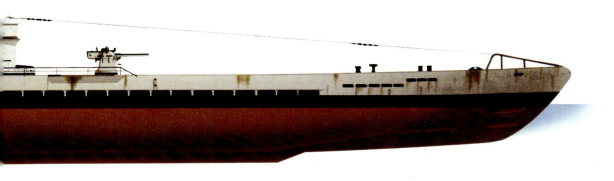

23 (Kl.Mochle.
degen)
el helmet, swords
laurel wreath were
ted in gold against the
r surround

U.552 (Kl. Topp)
The Black Devil.

U.130 (Kk. Kals 1941/3)
The Knight's Helmet.
The insignia is correct but
the colouring is an
assessment.

U.404
The Bows of a Viking Ship.
The insignia is correct but
the colouring is an
assessment.

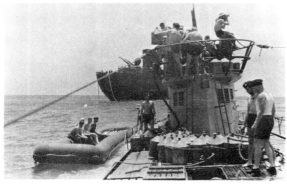

On 5 May 1941, U-107 *took on supplies in mid-Atlantic from the supply-ship,* Nordmark, *sister-ship of the famous* Altmark. *While fuel is taken aboard through fire-hoses, rubber dinghies bring cans of lubricant. The lookout must not be relaxed* (*Bundesarchiv*)

On 5 May 1941, in mid-Atlantic, U-107 *met the supply-ship* Nordmark, *sister-ship of the famous* Altmark, *to replenish fuel. The towing-hawser and the fire-hoses for taking on fuel are prepared* (*Bundesarchiv*)

In the summer of 1941, there was still no danger from the air in the open Atlantic. The crew of U-107 at physical training in the fresh air and sun. In the foreground, the 10·5cm gun (*Bundesarchiv*)

The British M/T Duffield, *had already been hit five times before she broke up and exploded after the sixth shot which hit on the port quarter* (*Dressler Collection*)

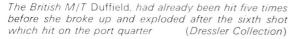

Sire (5664GRT), who sailed into sight on the morning of 31 May; at midday on 1 June the British motor-vessel, *Alfred Jones* (5013 GRT), who was thought to be an auxiliary cruiser and who sank only after the second finishing shot; and on the morning of 8 June the British ship, *Adda*, (7816 GRT). After taking on further supplies from the *Egerland* or the *Lothringen*, who were to arrive during the middle of June, U-38, U-103, U-107, UA and the Class VII C boat U-69, who had mined the ports of Lagos and Takoradi, all intended to carry on their operations off Freetown—but, this was not to be.

THE DEATH OF THE SUPPLY SYSTEM

On 7 May and 10 May, the destroyers, *Somali* and *Bulldog*, had succeeded in boarding the sinking German weather-ship, *München*, and U-110, respectively. The encoding and decoding documents captured in these actions enabled the British Y-Service to tap the German radio-traffic; this set-back provided the decisive foot-hold for mopping up the German supply system after the sinking of the battleship, *Bismarck*.

On 28 May, in the South Atlantic the blockade-runner, *Lech*; on 29 May, in the North Atlantic the weather-ships, *August Wriedt* and *Heinrich Freese*; on 3 June, in the Davis Straits the tanker, *Belchen*, while refuelling the U-93; on 4 June, north of Azores, the supply-ship, *Gonzenheim*; on 4 and 5 June, in the 'Andalusian' supply area, the supply-ships, *Esso Hamburg* and *Egerland*; on 6 June, near the Azores the blockade-runner, *Elbe*; on 12 June, north-west of Cape Finisterre the tanker, *Friedrich Breme*, and, on 15 June, while sailing out to the supply area in the mid-Atlantic, the U-boat supply-ship, *Lothringen*. All these vessels fell victims in these operations.

U-38 reported on 7 June the sinking of the *Egerland* before refuelling had been carried out; U-103, U-107, UA and U-69 waited in vain for the *Lothringen* on 18/19 June. The B.d.U. was then forced to break off the operations and to order the boats to return, using the 'Culebra' supply facilities as appropriate.

U-107, who, while sailing to the supply-rendezvous had still managed to sink the Greek ship, *Pandias* (4981 GRT), on 13 June, immediately set course for home; she was already lying too far to the north to take part in the operation against convoy SL.76 sighted by U-69 on the way to Las Palmas.

On 2 July Hessler sailed into Lorient after sinking 14 ships, with a total of 86,699 GRT. This was the most successful operational patrol of any U-boat during the Second World War.

THE THIRD PATROL:
30 August to 11 November off Freetown

The loss of the supply-ships and the diversion of the British traffic into the Pan-American Security Zone and its concentration (see Warship Profile No. 5) into convoys led in July to the complete failure of the operations of *U-123*, *U-109* and *U-66*. Even the attempt at the end of July to intercept SL convoys off the West African coast with a 'rake' composed of *U-124*, *U-93* and *U-94* met with no success.

The B.d.U. therefore dispatched stronger forces to intercept the SL convoys. *U-107* operated for six weeks in this area.

U-boats in company with U-107: U-68, 67, 66, 103, 108 and *125*.

Convoy: SL 87: first sighted by *U-107* on 21 September.

Escorts: Bideford, Gorleston, Gardenia, Commandant Duboc.

Sinkings: Silverbelle (5302)—*U-68; Niceto de Larrinaga* (5591)—*U-103; Edward Blyden* (5003)—*U-103; St Clair* (3753)—*U-67; Dixcove* (3790—*U-107; John Holt* (4975)—*U-107; Lafian* (4876)—*U-107*, (the last three all on 24 September).

At the end of patrol, Hessler was relieved by Junior Lieutenant Harald Gelhaus.

THE FOURTH PATROL:
10-26 December 1941, against Convoy HG.76

The development of the crisis in the Mediterranean (the heavy losses of supply ships for the German-Italian Africa Army and the offensive of the British 8th Army against Cyrenaica) had forced the German Naval Operations Command (seekriegsleitung) to re-inforce heavily the German U-boats transferred to the Mediterranean; and also, at the cost of temporary dislocation of the Atlantic operations, from the middle of November 1941 the B.d.U. was compelled to concentrate to the west of Gibraltar all available U-boats.

The Forces Gather

U-107, sailing from Lorient on 10 December, was directed to these waters where an HG convoy was

In the restricted Commanding Officer's cabin, the Captain, Snr.Lt Hessler, works on his patrol report before returning to base　　　　　　　　　　　*(Bundesarchiv)*

expected. On 14 December, German agents in Algeciras reported the departure of the convoy, which passed Cape Tarifa at 2045. This was HG.76 with 32 merchant ships, escorted by the 36th Escort Group under Commander Walker: the sloops *Stork*, *Deptford*, with the corvettes *Rhododendron*, *Marigold*, *Convolvulus*, *Pentstemon*, *Gardenia*, *Samphire* and *Vetch*. They were joined by the first escort-carrier, *Audacity*, and a Support Group, with the escorting destroyers *Blankney*, *Exmoor* and *Stanley*. Simultaneously, a U-boat hunting group of Force H, with the destroyers *Gurkha*, *Foxhound*, *Croome* and *Nestor*, had slipped out; to this force, *U-127* fell victim on 15 December. In addition a Near-East convoy was approaching, with four ships escorted by one destroyer and three corvettes.

On receipt of the agents' reports, the B.d.U. brought *U-107*, *U-127*, *U-574*, *U-67*, *U-108* and *U-131*, waiting west of Gibraltar, into action as the 'Seeräuber' ('Corsair') group, directing them to form a patrol line south of Cape St Vincent. At midnight on

The Free-French dispatch-boat, Commandant Duboc *who, with three British ships, escorted Convoy SL.87 that was attacked by U-107 in September 1941* 　*(IWM)*

The Commanding Officer of HMS Hesperus, *Commander D. G. F. W. Macintyre, DSO, RN, on the bridge*

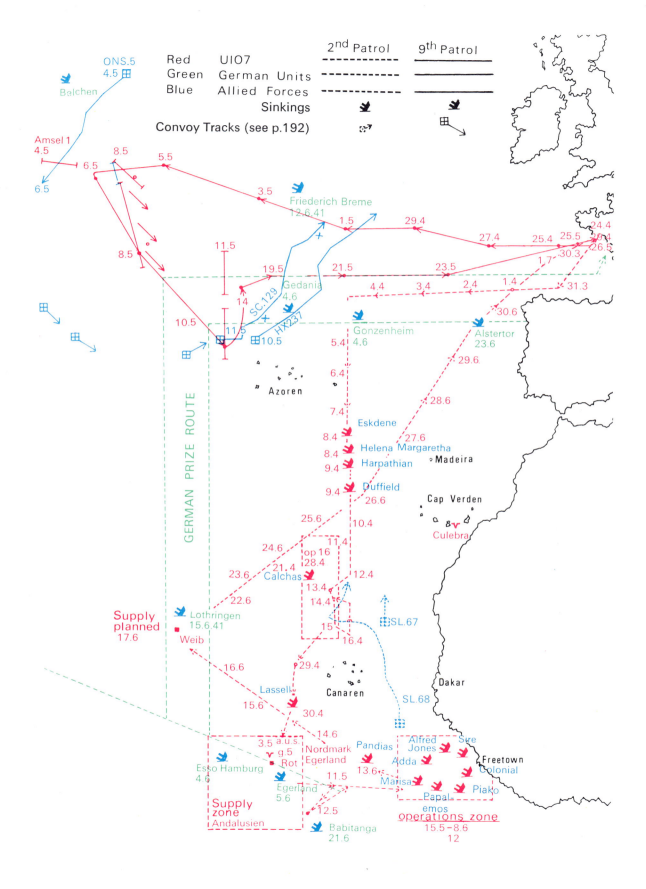

ONS.5
4.5
Belchen

Red   UIO7
Green   German Units
Blue   Allied Forces
Sinkings
Convoy Tracks (see p.192)

2nd Patrol   9th Patrol

Amsel 1
4.5
8.5
5.5
6.5
6.5

3.5
Friederich Breme
12.6.41
1.5
29.4
27.4
25.4   25.5   24.4
30.3   26.5

11.5
19.5
Gedania
4.6
21.5
23.5
1.7
31.3

8.5
14
SC.129
HX237

4.4   3.4   2.4   1.4
30.6

10.5
11.5
10.5

Gonzenheim
4.6
Alstertor
23.6

5.4
29.6

Azoren
6.4

28.6

7.4

8.4   Eskdene
27.6
8.4   Helena Margaretha
9.4   Harpathian   Madeira

9.4   Duffield
26.6

Cap Verden

25.6   10.4

24.6   11.4
op 16
28.4

23.6   21.4   12.4
Calchas
13.4
22.6   14.4
SL.67
15

Culebra

GERMAN PRIZE ROUTE

16.4

Supply
planned
17.6
Lothringen
15.6.41
Weib

16.6
29.4
Lassell
15.6
30.4
14.6
SL.68

Canaren

Dakar

3.5 a.u.s.
g.5
Rot
Nordmark
Egerland
Pandias
Alfred
Jones   Sre
Adda
Freetown
Colonial
Marisa
Papal-
emos
Piako
Esso Hamburg
4.6
Egerland
5.6
11.5
13.6

12.5
Babitanga
21.6

Supply
zone
Andalusien

operations zone
15.5 - 8.6
12

184

On 30 August 1941, Snr.Lt Hessler (*waving his white cap*) left Lorient with U-107 *for the third patrol*   (*Bundesarchiv*)

14/15 December *U-74*, on course for the Mediterranean, sighted the Near-East convoy and shortly afterwards one of its freighters, the *Empire Barracuda*, was sunk by *U-77*, also sailing under orders to the Mediterranean. On 15 December, FW 200 aircraft of the 1st/K.G. 40 were dispatched to reconnoitre in support of the U-boats; however, they did not find the convoy. Because of the concentration of U-boats that had been spotted, the British command had ordered the convoy to swing south, close under the Moroccan coast.

Only at 11·15 hrs. on 16 December did a FW 200 aircraft sight the convoy far to the south of the U-boat patrol line, which had meanwhile moved westwards and been reinforced by *U-434*. At 1731, *U-108*, the most southerly boat, reported contact and, after the arrival of *U-67* at 2030, attacked at 2119 hrs. After one quadruple and one double fan salvo, she heard several detonations, but these were probably depth-charges from the escorts because no ship was hit.

Battle is Joined

At 0645 on 17 December, *U-131* also reported contact but, after a number of attacks by *Swordfish* aircraft, one of which she shot down, the boat could not dive. After a long hunt by *Stork*, *Blankney*, *Exmoor* and *Stanley*, she was forced to scuttle. At 1008, *U-108* came up with the convoy once more and at 1347 summoned *U-107*, who shadowed until 0051.

In the morning of 18 December, *U-434*, the only boat still in touch with the convoy, was detected by the destroyers *Blankney* and *Stanley* and at 1055, after a long depth-charge counter-attack, she was forced to surface and abandon ship.

Although the Martlet fighters of the *Audacity* were continuously in action in an attempt to deter the German reconnaissance aircraft, between 1200 and 1500 on 18 December, four FW 200s were able to pass enemy reports of the convoy; this first brought up *U-107* at 2000, but the boat was immediately forced to dive by the corvette, *Pentstemon*. At 2132, *U-67* attempted to torpedo the *Convolvulus* but was driven off by the ship. During the night of 18/19 December, at 0315 *U-574* and at 0455, *U-108* made contact and were both able to work their way in to a firing course: at 0515 *U-574* sank the destroyer, *Stanley*, but in a counter-attack was rammed and destroyed by Commander Walker in the *Stork*. *U-108* sank the freighter, *Ruckinge* (2869 GRT), with a triple fan salvo.

SECOND ROUND: Loss of *Audacity*

At 1230 on 19 December, the first FW 200 shadowing aircraft was shot down by a Martlet; the second FW 200, before being driven away, at once passed her enemy report and transmitted a D/F signal at 1330; the third aircraft was shot down at 1700. At 1653, *U-107* had found the enemy convoy again, and Junior Lieutenant Gelhaus now hung on grimly, even trying—though without success—to sink a corvette with a quadruple fan salvo at 0617 on 20 December. Thanks to his running reports until 2330, *U-108* and *U-67*, and later *U-567*, *U-751* and *U-71*, who were on their way out and had been thrown into the battle on the same day, came up one after the other.

At 1010 on 21 December *U-67* was driven off by an aircraft from *Audacity*, and two others at 1632 and 2250 by the corvettes, *Marigold* and *Samphire*. In the meantime, Senior Lieutenant Endrass in *U-567* had closed and sunk the freighter, *Annavore* (3324 GRT), with a fan salvo. In the resultant confusion of the hunt, to which Endrass fell victim, Senior Lieutenant Bigalk in *U-751* managed to get in a shot at the detached carrier, *Audacity*, who sank after two hits from a fan salvo, finally and a finishing shot. An attack by *U-67* at 0008 failed.

U-71 (and *U-125*, who was on her way to America) shadowed during 22 December; *U-751*, who had missed a destroyer with a quadruple fan salvo, also maintained contact, but the last two boats were driven off by the corvette, *Vetch*, and the reinforcing destroyers, *Vanquisher* and *Witch*.

U-107 had broken off the engagement on the morning of 21 December when she turned for home; she sailed into Lorient on 26 December.

The Stork. *Bow view of the sloop*, Stork

HMS Audacity

With a 'cunning book', a volume of Talbot-Booth's Merchant Ships, *the experts try to identify a ship just sunk*

The depth-keeping panel of a U-boat. Two 'plane' wheels for the fore and after hydroplanes, with the hydroplane indicators and depth-indicator (to 250m). In the centre, the Papenberg trim-indicator and the depth-indicator for shallow depths, which was specially important for accurate trimming at periscope depth (*BfZ/Dressler*)

A Class IX U-boat returns to Lorient with empty bunkers

After the unsuccessful operation against Convoy SL.122, the boats of the 'Iltis' group reached the U-boat tanker U-460 (left) on 26 September 1942, to continue operations off Freetown with full tanks (*BfZ/Dressler*)

In the for'd tube space. In the foreground are the rear doors of the four torpedo-tubes; the spare torpedoes are stowed under the deck-plates. In these crowded, cramped quarters those off duty live and sleep while, alongside, the 'torpedo-mixer' adjusts a torpedo (*Bundesarchiv*)

The commander of the 2nd U-boat Flotilla, Lt-Cdr Schütze, formerly captain of U-25 and U-103, greets U-107 on her return from operations against Convoy HG.76; on the left is her second captain, Jnr.Lt Gelhaus (*Bundesarchiv*)

3) *Sumner/Gearing Class.* The 165 ships of this class were commissioned in 1944-45.

Charles Ausburne (DD570) was a ship of the *Fletcher* class. This class, with a standard displacement of 2050 tons was the fleet destroyer heavyweight until the last year of the war. Then the 2150 ton *Sumner* class, followed closely by their near sisters of the 2200 ton *Gearing* class, entered the war.

The first destroyers of the *Fletcher* class were authorised by the Vinson-Trammell Congressional Act of 27 March 1934. The later ships in this class were authorised by the 70% Expansion Act of 19 July 1940 —the '*Two-Ocean*' Navy Act.

Ausburne off Orange, Texas, as she appeared in late 1942 immediately after completion. Her initial gun fit included five 5in. main mounts, two twin 40mm mounts and four 20mm guns. The two twin 40mm are visible here—one between numbers three and four main mounts and one on the fantail. One 20mm gun can be seen in its tub on the main deck just below the after torpedo tube

(Photo: U.S. Navy)

The *Fletcher* was designed by Gibbs and Cox of New York and reintroduced the flush-deck destroyer into the US Navy. (All subsequent destroyer classes have been flush-decked.) A total of eight civilian shipyards and three Navy yards built the *Fletchers*. The average cost per ship was approximately $11,000,000. Numerous variations in detail, equipment and armament occurred between ships built in different yards and between the earlier and later ships. The later *Fletchers* had lower main battery directors on top of their bridge structures and flat-faced bridges vice the curved bridge faces of their earlier sisters. The building record for a *Fletcher* was established when USS *Dortch* was completed in 158 days.

The following data concerns the *Fletcher* class ships as they appeared during World War II. The various conversions to the *Fletchers* during the postwar era are discussed later in this Profile.

Hull

The hull, constructed of welded steel plate, was 376ft 5in in overall length, 39ft 7in extreme beam, with a maximum navigational draft of 17ft 9in. Standard displacement was 2050 to 2100 tons, full load displacement was 2940 tons. Fuel capacity for most of the *Fletchers* was 492 tons but varied between 301 tons to 525 tons in some ships of the class.

Machinery

Since the *Fletchers* represented a quantitative increase over the size of previous destroyers, an appreciable increase in power was required to propel these ships at their design speed of 35-37 knots. Designed shaft horsepower was therefore increased to 60,000.

To provide this power the *Fletchers* had four express-type water tube boilers installed in two fire rooms each served by its own funnel. The great majority of these boilers were Babcock & Wilcox but a few ships were equipped with Foster-Wheelers. At full power these boilers produced 565 p.s.i. of superheated steam at 850 degrees fahrenheit.

Each pair of boilers powered a double reduction geared turbine. Each engine was housed in its own engine room abaft their respective firerooms, the forward engine driving the port propeller, the after engine turning the starboard propeller. Through cross-connection, any combination of boilers could be set up to drive either turbine. The turbines were built by either General Electric, Westinghouse or Allis-Chalmers.

The distilling plant which converted sea water to fresh water was rated at 12,000 gallons per day.

Main Armament

The main battery consisted of five 5in/38 caliber dual-purpose, semi-automatic, rapid-fire guns in fully enclosed single-mounts—two each super-imposed fore and aft and the fifth located on the 01 level (the first deck above the main deck) just forward of the after deck house. There were two MK30 Mod 18 mounts, and one each MK30 Mod 19, 30 and 31 mounts. These were all basically the same mount with only minor differences based on their locations. The 5in guns fired semi-fixed ammunition (powder case separate from the

Another view of Ausburne *off Orange, Texas, just after completion. One of the 20mm gun tubs can be seen on the 01 level just below the starboard wing of the bridge. This view clearly depicts the fire-control radar mounted on top of the main director and the surface search radar on top of the mast. The false water line camouflage scheme was designed to confuse submarines in particular in computing the angle on the bow'*

(Photo: U.S. Navy)

The 'mothballed' Reserve Fleet at San Diego, California, in the late 1950s. Approximately two-thirds of the ships in this photo are *Fletchers*
(Photo: U.S. Navy)

projectile) with a projectile weight of 54lbs, a horizontal range of 18,000 yards and a vertical range of over 30,000ft. The gun could elevate almost to 90 degrees. Armor-piercing, general purpose illumination, or fragmentation shells could be fired with cut, V.T. (Variable Time), or contact fusing.

The mount was hydraulically driven in training and elevation and could be aimed, controlled and fired either remotely or locally. Each mount was located over an ammunition handling room with powered powder and projectile hoists to the mount. The hoist was provided with an automatic fuse-setting device.

Each mount had a gun crew usually composed of eight men: gun captain, trainer, pointer, sight-setter, fuse-setter, two loaders and a hot-case man. Projectile and powder case were hand loaded from the hoist into the gun housing and mechanically rammed into the breech. Empty cases were ejected out of the mount on to the deck. A firing rate of 15 rounds per minute was average but rates of over 20 rounds per minute for a short period were not unusual.

A single MK37 main battery optical director was fitted above the bridge with an MK22 fire control radar mounted on top. The director fed target information to the gun laying computer where all the other variables, such as ship's motion, wind and temperature were fed in and the firing solution was transmitted to the guns.

Secondary Armament

A variety of arrangements and numbers of 20mm Oerlikon and 40mm Bofors machine guns were provided for secondary armament. (Several early *Fletchers* were equipped with 1·1in quad. m.g.). The main purpose of these guns was anti-aircraft so, after the experience of the first months of the war, efforts were made to add more of these type guns to all classes of ships.

The closest to what might be considered a 'standard' fit for secondary armament on the *Fletchers* was five twin 40mm mounts and seven 20mm mounts. More of the class were equipped in this configuration than any other, but variations from two 40mm singles up to five twins and from six to eleven 20mm guns were built. Additional 20mm and 40mm guns were often added when a ship went through overhaul.

The usual placement of the 40mm guns in the 'standard' configuration was: two twins forward of the bridge, one on each side and slightly abaft the number two 5in mount; two twins amidships, one on each side of the after funnel; and one twin atop the after deck house between numbers three and four 5in mounts.

The 20mm guns were distributed: two each on both sides located on the main deck just below the after torpedo launchers, and three on the fantail.

40mm Bofors Machine Gun

The 40mm, a fully automatic gun, could fire up to 160 rounds per minute to an effective range of over 3000 yards. The single mounts were air-cooled—the twin and quad mounts were usually water-cooled. The usual mount on the *Fletcher* class was the MK1 twin con-

Ausburne *soon after commissioning. Note torpedo crane located beside after funnel: this was soon relocated to a similar position beside the forward funnel when a twin 40mm mount was installed in its stead. The two forward 20mm guns can be seen with barrels vertical just forward of the bridge. The odd shape tubing around the guns were physical restraints preventing the gun from being fired into any part of the ship* (Photo: U.S. Navy)

figuration. Either remote or local control could be selected. Drive was either powered or manual. Ammunition was fed into the gun loader by hand, four rounds per clip. The gun crew of a twin consisted of seven men: gun captain, trainer, pointer and four loaders.

To fire the Bofors by remote control, a MK51 slew type gun director was usually installed for each mount. These were normally sited in an area adjacent to and slightly above the mount it served. The two MK51s serving the amidships 40mm mounts were located on sponsons attached to the after funnel, a structure designed originally to house searchlights. The MK51 director contained a gyroscope that compensated for ship's motion and target relative movement was computed by the rate at which the director operator tracked the target.

20mm Oerlikon Machine Gun

Up to eleven 20mm machine guns were carried on the *Fletcher* class. An automatic, air-cooled gun, it was capable of firing ball, explosive or tracer bullets at a rate of 450 rounds per minute to a maximum range of 4000 yards. The gun was pedestal mounted and manually operated and fired. The gun crew consisted of five men; gunner, range setter, two loaders and a trunnion operator (who adjusted the trunnion up or down to correspond with the gunner's position).

Torpedoes

Most of the *Fletchers* were equipped with ten 21in torpedo tubes arranged in two quintuplet mounts

located one behind each funnel on the 01 level. The forward mount was a MK14 and the after mount a MK15, the basic difference being that the MK15 had a cupola type weather housing on top to protect the crew and aiming mechanism. Both mounts were equipped with a MK27 torpedo director and both could be trained through 360 degrees. There was no under-way reload capability.

The standard destroyer torpedo used during World War II was the MK15, 21in in diameter, weighing 2215lbs and costing approximately $10,000. Course, depth and speed were pre-set in the launcher. Maximum speed was 46 knots at a range of 4500 yards. Greater range could be obtained by running the torpedo at slower speeds. The torpedo was propelled by a gas turbine powered by an air, alcohol and water combustion system. The warhead varied from 500lbs of TNT in earlier models to 1100lbs of torpex in later models.

The US Navy had problems in the first year of the war with faulty torpedoes, the main difficulty being faulty depth-setting mechanisms and defective magnetic influence exploder mechanisms. Time and again destroyer and submarine crews were frustrated when seemingly perfect shots ran under the target, but did not explode or exploded before reaching the target. The problems were eventually solved—in the case of the defective exploder mechanism by reverting to the conventional contact exploder.

At no time during the war did the US Navy develop a torpedo comparable to the huge 24in, high speed, long range Japanese, '*Long Lance*'.

Anti-Submarine System
Depth Charges

Most of the ships of the *Fletcher* class were equipped with two depth charge launching tracks on the fantail. Each of these tracks had a capacity of six to eleven depth charges, depending on the size of depth charge and if extender rails were installed. In addition, on each side of the main deck beside the after deck-house, were located three MK6 depth charge projectors (K-guns). Usually four re-loads were positioned on pedestals around each projector with a davit type hoist to facilitate reloading. Roller racks were installed for each projector later in the war to make for easier handling. The depth charge was chained to a tray from which projected an arbor that was inserted in the K-gun barrel. An explosive cartridge provided the propellent which could be lanyard or electrically fired.

The standard 'ashcan' was the 720lb MK7 but later in the war the tear-drop shaped, faster sinking, 340lb MK9 was introduced. The depth charges were usually released in patterns of threes: one from each side and one rolled over the stern. The depth charge was set to explode at a pre-determined depth just prior to its launch.

A 20mm Oerlikon machine gun   (Photo: U.S. Navy)

Sonar (Asdic)

Sonar (Sound-Navigation-Ranging) could be used both passively and actively for detecting submerged objects. In the former mode the operator would listen for target generated noise; in the latter, the operator would send out a sound signal along a line of bearing and determine the distance an object was from him by the time it took for the echo to return.

Sonar was a great improvement over the World War I hydrophone. Shipboard experimental sets were in use in 1934 and by 1939 operational sets were being installed on US destroyers. By the outbreak of the war all fleet destroyers were Sonar equipped. By the time the *Fletchers* began sliding down the ways, the Navy had obtained from the British the *Sound-Range Recorder*. This device presented a graphic visual presentation of the sonar signals and greatly facilitated underwater fire control.

Ausburne *off Boston, Massachusetts 6 March 1943. Note the false water line camouflage has been painted out in favor of a solid dark grey color scheme. She fought in the Solomons with this color scheme and armament fit*
(Photo: U.S. Navy)

Superstructure

The forward deck house was built on three levels and housed the bridge, chart room, captain's sea cabin, Combat Information Center (C.I.C. was pioneered and developed in destroyers during the Solomon's Campaign) and signal bridge. The single pole mast was located abaft the bridge and supported the radio aerials. signal halyards and a search radar at its peak.

Radio communications equipment included low frequency and medium high frequency radio and very high frequency radio-telephone called the T.B.S. (talk between ships). The TBS with 'line of sight range' was a relatively secure tactical voice circuit that enabled instant communications between ships, to the shore, or in directing aircraft.

Two motor whaleboats were housed on davits abaft the forward deck house. Two raked funnels of equal size serviced the two boiler rooms and were oblong in cross-section except for Bethlehem built ships which were flat-sided. The funnel caps were smaller in diameter than the funnels themselves with a pronounced rake aft.

The after deck house usually supported a 40mm twin and was located between the number three and number four main batteries. Six *Fletchers* were planned to carry a scout plane each and the rotating catapult was located on the 01 level amidships. The after torpedo mount, number three main battery and after deck house were eliminated to make room for the catapult. Only four ships were actually so equipped—*Pringle, Stevens, Stanley,* and *Halford* but the arrangement proved impractical and the catapults were soon removed.

Armor

As with most destroyers the *Fletchers* were very lightly armored. Splinter shield protection was furnished around the bridge area, the main mounts and the secondary battery gun tubs. The small amount of armor carried varied in thickness from ·25 to ·50in.

CHARLES AUSBURNE (DD 570)
The Beginning

The contract for the second destroyer named *Charles Ausburne* was let to the Consolidated Steel Company, Orange, Texas on 9 September 1940 at a contract price (hull and machinery) of $7,315,000. The ship was authorised on 4 September 1940 under the 70%

A stern view of Ausburne *taken in late 1942 off Orange, Texas, where she was built by Consolidated Shipbuilding Company. The protruding frameworks on each side of the hull are propellor guards* (Photo: U.S. Navy)

Expansion Act of 19 July 1940 (Public Law No. 757). *Charles Ausburne's* keel was laid 14 May 1941 and she was launched 16 March 1942 by Mrs W. H. Cotten, foster sister of Charles Ausburne. The ship was placed in commission alongside the City Dock at Orange 24 November 1942 by Captain J. M. Schelling, u.s.n., retired, and was under the command of Lieutenant Commander Luther K. Reynolds, u.s.n..

Upon completion of fitting-out and dock trials, *Ausburne* sailed 29 December for New Orleans, thence to Guantanamo, Cuba, for her shakedown and work-up, where she arrived 6 January 1943. She headed

north for Boston arriving 6 February and, after a period of post-shakedown and final exercises in Casco Bay, *Ausburne* departed 24 March on her first combat assignment. For the first time, a majority of her crew and several of her officers would be at sea for an extended period. For, as was the case with most of the new ships in the fast growing US Navy in the early days of the war, only five to ten per cent of the crew were experienced navy hands.

First Cruise
On 1 April 1943, *Ausburne* escorted a convoy out of New York bound for Casablanca. The convoy made port 19 April and two days later she sailed again escorting a home-bound convoy, stopping in Gibraltar en route, and arriving back in New York 8 May without incident.

DesRon 23
The next day *Ausburne* was back in Boston to make preparations for deployment to the Pacific battle zone. On 11 May in a dress ceremony on the foredeck of *Ausburne*, Captain Martin J. Gillan, Jr, u.s.n., read his orders as commodore of the newly formed *Destroyer Squadron 23. Charles Ausburne* would carry the broad command pennant of ComDesRon 23 through most of the war.

DesRon 23 was composed of two Destroyer Divisions, (DesDiv) 45 and 46 with four destroyers each. The usual US Navy practice is to assign a captain in command of a DesRon with the honorary title of commodore and he also commands the senior DesDiv. A commander or, on occasion, the senior commanding officer in the junior DesDiv was assigned as that division's commander. In World War II, destroyer squadrons usually had eight ships assigned but this number could vary from four to twelve.

Only two other ships, *Foote* and *Spence*, of DesRon 23, were on hand in Boston harbor that May day. The other five destroyers of the squadron were elsewhere but all were under orders to rendezvous in the south west Pacific. All the destroyers of DesRon 23 were brand new *Fletchers*.

Pacific Bound
Ausburne departed Boston 17 May 1943 and headed south, stopping at Norfolk and Galveston. With oiler

U.S.S. Halford (DD480), *14 July 1943, shown carrying a catapult and a OS2U* Kingfisher *floatplane. Six* Fletchers *were originally planned in this configuration but the idea proved impractical and all six became standard* Fletchers.

(Photo: U.S. Navy)

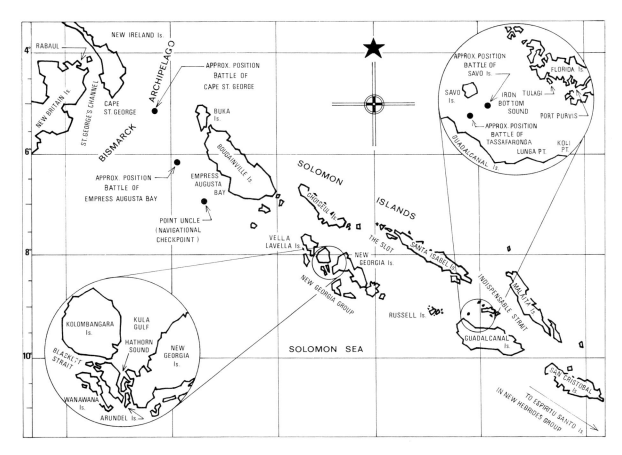

USS *Schuykill* under escort, she sailed for the Panama Canal which she transited 1 June.

Joining with her sister, USS *Foote*, and tanker *White Plains*, she crossed the Pacific arriving at Noumea, New Caledonia 28 June. The voyage was without significant incident, *Ausburne's* log indicating that, for economical fuel consumption, normal cruising was with one boiler on the line, cross-connected and the propellers turning about 140 revolutions per minute. *Neptunus Rex* made his ceremonial visit to initiate all the *Pollywogs* (persons who hadn't crossed the equator before) when *Ausburne* crossed the equator 6 June; it is also noted she took on 82,500 gallons of oil from *White Plains* on the 12th.

AUSBURNE GOES TO WAR

After two days of availability alongside destroyer tender USS *Whitney*, *Ausburne* sailed as part of the screen which was escorting the ships of Transportation Division 8 to Guadalcanal where they unloaded and returned to Efate. During the better part of the next four months this was to be *Ausburne's* lot: escorting convoys back and forth between Noumea, Espiritu Santo, Efate and the battle area in the Solomon Island chain, and seeing little combat in the process.

The bitter fighting around Guadalcanal was history by mid-1943 and the action was leap-frogging north-westward along the Solomons toward the big Japanese bastion at Rabaul, New Britain Island. So these first months proved dibilitating for *Ausburne* and her sisters in DesRon 23. Constant standing to general quarters, the continuing effort to keep the ships pro-

visioned and maintained for battle and a number of missed opportunities to come to grips with the enemy all contributed to the fatigue and low morale of the crew.

From 27 August 1943, *Ausburne* was based at Purvis Bay, Florida Island, where she became part of a strike force, under Commander Task Force (CTF) 31, designed to interdict the 'Tokyo Express'—the name given to the Japanese efforts to reinforce or evacuate, usually with destroyers at night, their garrisons along the Solomon chain. She made her first patrol 'up the Slot' (that wide channel formed by the Solomons on the north and the New Georgia Group on the south) the night of 27 August.

Radar: the decisive weapon

While escorting an LST convoy to Vella LaVella on 7 September, *Ausburne* made her first contact with the enemy when her group came under Japanese air attack. It was during this period that experimentation with night fighter direction was undertaken with the aid of radar. Radar would prove to be a critical element in the US Navy's defeat of the Imperial Navy. Although the Japanese had shown superior night fighting tactics in the opening battles in the Solomons, they did not have operational radars in any numbers until late in the war; this defect was to prove decisive.

Ausburne's first recorded 'kill' was the night of 27-28 September 1943, when she sank two barges in the waters off Vella LaVella.

Commander Luther K. Reynolds, USN (now Rear Admiral Reynolds, Retired) was the first commanding officer of Charles Ausburne serving from 24 November 1942 to 1 June 1944. Nicknamed 'Brute' because of his small stature Reynolds graduated from the U.S. Naval Academy in 1926. He commanded U.S.S. Barry (DD248), an old World War I 'four piper', before joining Ausburne and commanding her for a year and one-half of her illustrious career   (Photo: U.S. Navy)

When Commander Reynolds welcomed Burke aboard he added that the new Commodore had arrived a bit earlier than expected. One of the first remarks in Burke's new command was an example of the pace he would set for DesRon 23.

'You know, Brute', said Burke, 'I sometimes think the difference between a good officer and a poor one is about ten seconds. It's a fine rule to get going sooner than anticipated, travel faster than expected, and arrive before you're due. You'd be surprised how many fights you can get into that way and, after all, if you're ready, you can expect to win your share.'

Commodore Burke extended the thought of the preceding remark into three guiding principles for DesRon 23:

'*SPEED: move quickly while the other fellow is trying to make up his mind. LOOK FOR FIGHTS: if you look for them you'll probably find them. BE PREPARED: if you're ready for a fight you should win your share.*'

Ausburne, with the new commodore aboard, sailed for Purvis the next day arriving 25 October. For the first time all eight ships of the squadron were assembled in one place and for most of the next few months DesRon 23 would fight as a unit.

The destroyers in the squadron were: Division 45: *Charles Ausburne* (DD570), *Dyson* (DD572), *Claxton*

U.S.S. Spence (DD512) a sistership of Ausburne's and the only one of DesRon 23s 'Little Beavers' lost during the war. She was sunk in a typhoon off the Philippines 18 December 1944   (Photo: U.S. Navy)

Ausburne leads two of her sisters of Desron 23 in 'S' turns at speed somewhere in the Solomons. The first Fletchers were found to have little rudder effect below five knots. Subsequently, all ships of this class were fitted with a longer rudder which improved low speed handling
(Photo: Adm. A. A. Burke Collection, Naval Historical Foundation)

Burke Arrives

Ausburne returned to Espiritu Santo 3 October for replenishment and availability alongside tender USS *Dixie*. It was here on 23 October 1943 that Captain Arleigh A. Burke, a future Chief of Naval Operations, broke his pennant as the new ComDesRon 23 in USS *Charles Ausburne*. Under his command the 'Little Beavers', as he was to nickname his squadron, were to win their place in naval history—and to become the only destroyer squadron in World War II to win the Presidential Unit Citation.

Ausburne receiving mail from the cruiser U.S.S. Columbia *27 September 1943. That night she sank two Japanese barges off Vella Lavella*

(DD571) and *Stanley* (DD478); Division 46: *Foote* (DD511), *Converse* (DD509), *Spence* (DD512) and *Thatcher* (DD514). Of these eight destroyers all would survive the war except *Spence*—she sank with two other destroyers in a typhoon off the Phillipines 18 December 1944; only 23 of her crew survived.

Burke called a conference to discuss his doctrine with all his skippers as soon as he arrived at Purvis. In this respect Commodore Burke followed the same philosophy as Admiral Nelson and his 'Band of Brothers' concept, discussing thoroughly all phases of doctrine and lessons learned with his captains on every possible occasion.

DesRon 23 was combined with the four light cruisers of CruDiv 12 to form Task Force 39 commanded by Rear Admiral A. S. 'Tip' Merrill. On the morning of 26 October a portion of this force, Task Group 39.3, including *Ausburne*, moved out to provide a covering force for the diversionary landings against the Treasuries and Choiseul Islands—a prelude to the invasion of Bougainville. Their mission was accomplished with little interference from the enemy except for several light air attacks; the force then returned to Purvis to make ready for the main event—Bougainville.

BOUGAINVILLE PREPARATIONS

At 0200, 31 October 1943, all twelve ships of TF39 headed for Bougainville. Their mission was: first, in the darkness of the morning of 1 November, to bombard the enemy airfields along the Buka passage on the north coast of Bougainville; second, to do the same later in the day against his base complex on the Shortland Islands south of Bougainville; and lastly, to provide distant cover for the invasion force scheduled to land in the Cape Torkina area of Bougainville the morning of the 1 November.

Ausburne led the force in a single line. The destroyers' primary mission was counter-battery fire while the cruisers were to use their 6in and 5in batteries to blow up the airfields and base areas. At 0021, 1 November TF39, with the weather improving and temperature

Captain Arleigh A. Burke while serving as Commander Destroyer Squadron 23. Burke selected Ausburne *as his flagship and from 23 October 1943 to 26 March 1944 directed DesRon23 through much of the heavy fighting of the Solomons Campaign. A 1923 graduate of the U.S. Naval Academy Burke was a dedicated destroyer man throughout his naval career. From DesRon 23 he joined Admiral Marc Mitcher Commander Task Force 58, as his Chief of Staff. In 1955 as a Rear Admiral Burke was selected to become the Chief of Naval Operations jumping over 92 admirals above him on the lineal list. Admiral Burke served an unprecedented six years as CNO*

82 deg. F, the task force began its shore bombardment. 'Black Cat' (PBY Catalina patrol planes) were overhead spotting fire which appeared to achieve some degree of success. The Japanese reply was weak and erratic shore fire, harassment by several PT boats, and light air attacks.

Eight minutes after firing commenced, *Ausburne* completed her run and turned to retirement course

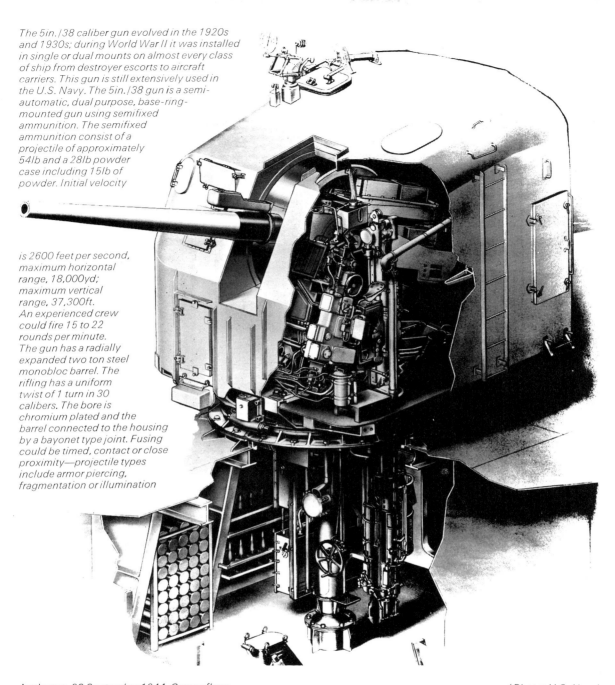

The 5in./38 caliber gun evolved in the 1920s and 1930s; during World War II it was installed in single or dual mounts on almost every class of ship from destroyer escorts to aircraft carriers. This gun is still extensively used in the U.S. Navy. The 5in./38 gun is a semi-automatic, dual purpose, base-ring-mounted gun using semifixed ammunition. The semifixed ammunition consist of a projectile of approximately 54lb and a 28lb powder case including 15lb of powder. Initial velocity

is 2600 feet per second, maximum horizontal range, 18,000yd; maximum vertical range, 37,300ft. An experienced crew could fire 15 to 22 rounds per minute. The gun has a radially expanded two ton steel monobloc barrel. The rifling has a uniform twist of 1 turn in 30 calibers. The bore is chromium plated and the barrel connected to the housing by a bayonet type joint. Fusing could be timed, contact or close proximity—projectile types include armor piercing, fragmentation or illumination

Ausburne, *30 September 1944. Camouflage*   (*Photo: U.S. Navy*)

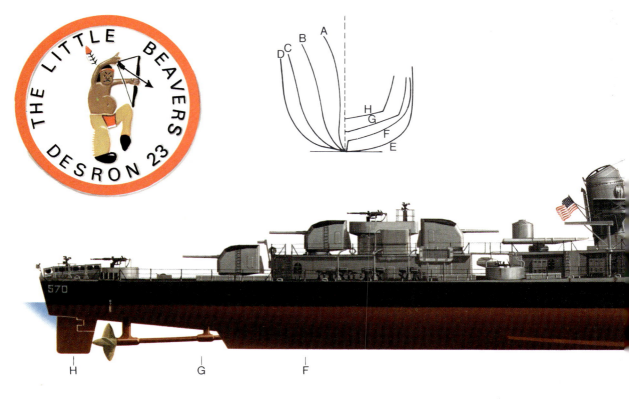

Ausburne in solid gray paint scheme, which she carried from February 1943 to September 1944. Secondary armament was increased to three 40mm twin mounts and ten 20mm single mounts.

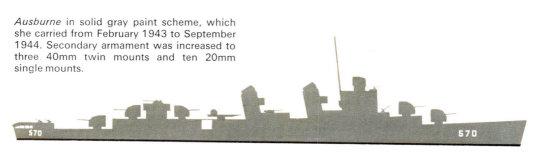

Ausburne's camouflage scheme from September 1944 until the end of the war. Secondary armament carried during this period included five 40mm twin mounts and seven 20mm single mounts.

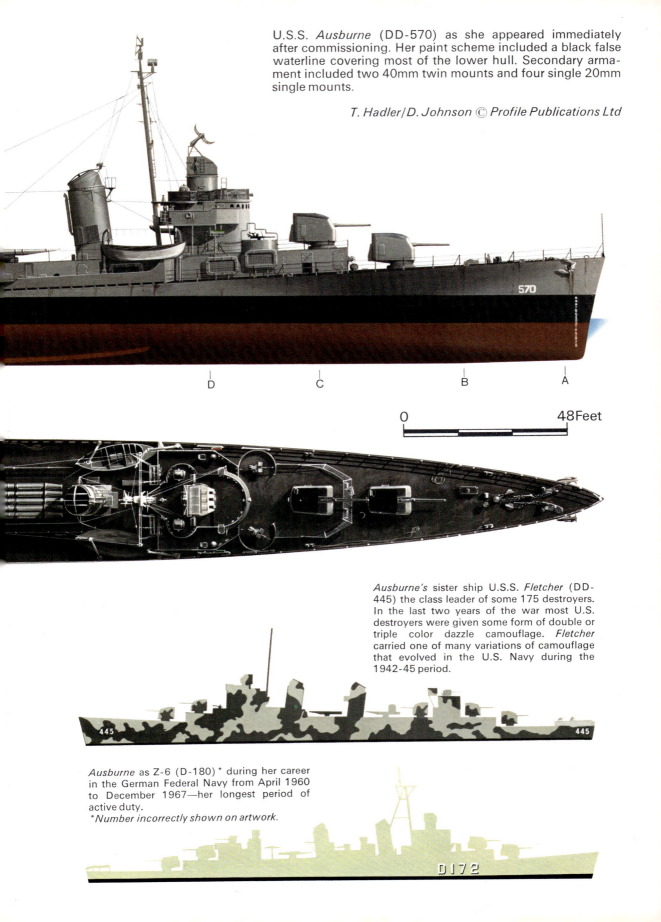

U.S.S. *Ausburne* (DD-570) as she appeared immediately after commissioning. Her paint scheme included a black false waterline covering most of the lower hull. Secondary armament included two 40mm twin mounts and four single 20mm single mounts.

T. Hadler/D. Johnson © Profile Publications Ltd

D   C   B   A

0   48 Feet

Ausburne's sister ship U.S.S. *Fletcher* (DD-445) the class leader of some 175 destroyers. In the last two years of the war most U.S. destroyers were given some form of double or triple color dazzle camouflage. *Fletcher* carried one of many variations of camouflage that evolved in the U.S. Navy during the 1942-45 period.

Ausburne as Z-6 (D-180)* during her career in the German Federal Navy from April 1960 to December 1967—her longest period of active duty.
Number incorrectly shown on artwork.

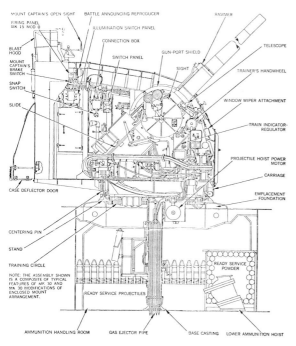

followed in turn by the rest of the force. As the task force headed south at 30 knots towards the Shortlands, enemy air attacks continued to harass it. *Ausburne* was raked by a low flyer which subsequently crashed—an apparent victim of '*Charlie' Ausburne's* anti-aircraft.

CTF39 passed the Bougainville invasion force heading into Empress Augusta Bay as it made for the heavily fortified Shortlands. Just after sunrise on 1 November, Japanese shore batteries opened fire on *Ausburne* as she led the force into its second mission of the day. For the next 43 minutes the US ships came under intense enemy fire as they zig-zagged on their bombardment courses. Leaving several large fires behind them, the US ships retired.

Ausburne was straddled several times with near misses and her fantail was sprayed with shell fragments. *Dyson* took a hit in the bow and numerous near misses were experienced throughout the force but its fighting efficiency was unimpaired.

Admiral Merrill now manoeuvred his force into position to intercept the inevitable surface challenge the Japanese would send down from Rabaul against the invasion force. CTF 39 had a two-fold mission: to interdict any such move by the enemy and to cover the transports of the landing force when they retired—his was the only sizeable US Naval surface force available to protect the beachhead at Cape Torokina.

The Battle of the Fuel

The Admiral's destroyers were in need of rearming and refuelling if they were to fight a major engagement. Over a day of steaming at high speeds, sometimes well above 30 knots, burned the *Fletchers'* fuel at a prodigious rate and large amounts of ammunition had been expended in the bombardments. The closest oil was in a barge at the advanced facility in Hathorn Sound, off the east tip of New Georgia Island. Needing to keep

some destroyers with his cruisers, Merrill ordered only DesDiv 45 to make the run for oil in all haste.

Ausburne and the rest of the Division departed at 0750 for Hathorn in what Burke called 'the battle for fuel'. Boiling along at 32 knots *Ausburne* and her 'mates' made Hathorn by 1115. *Ausburne* and *Dyson* moored to the barge first. *Claxton* and *Stanley* came in later, mooring alongside the first two and prepared to take over their sister ships' lines as they slipped them upon departing the barge, thereby saving minutes. Commodore Burke was living up to his doctrine of speed. At 1527 *Ausburne* and *Dyson* got underway at 15 knots: *Stanley* and *Claxton* were ordered to join up at 32 knots as soon as they were fuelled. They did so at 1800 and the division headed at 32 knots for the rendezvous with the cruisers and the Battle of Empress Augusta Bay.

BATTLE OF EMPRESS AUGUSTA BAY: Preliminaries

The Imperial Navy was not going to allow the American effort go unchallenged. From their intelligence, they had a fairly accurate picture of the composition of the US Naval Forces in the Solomons area. They felt, after the extensive bombardment effort of TF39 on the morning of 1 November, that the force would need to head south to replenish. The US Marine beachheads on Bougainville might be relatively unprotected later in the day.

At 1800, 1 November 1943, a Japanese force under Admiral Omori's command sortied from Rabaul. Its task was two-fold: to escort five high speed transport destroyers loaded with reinforcements to Bougainville and to sink any US force encountered in the area. This force consisted of two heavy cruisers, *Myoko* and *Haguro*, steaming in column, flanked on the right by light cruiser *Agano* followed by destroyers *Naganami*, *Hatsukaze* and *Wakatsuki*; and on the left by light cruiser *Sendai* followed by destroyers *Shigure*, *Samidare* and *Shiratsuyu*—fewer ships but more heavily gunned than TF39.

Because of late departure and a top speed of only 26 knots, the five APDs (Transport Destroyers) were ordered back to Rabaul and the reinforcement effort was postponed. Omori proceeded toward Bougainville at 32 knots.

CTF 39 Prepares for Battle

During the daylight hours of 1 November, while Burke's DesDiv 45 was off on the dash for fuel and the Japanese were preparing to sortie, Rear Admiral Merrill's cruisers and Commander B. L. 'Count' Austin's DesDiv 46 were patrolling near Vella LaVella and resting from their efforts earlier in the day.

Admiral Omori's force was sighted and tracked by US 'snooper' aircraft, so the decision was made to retire all the US shipping still at Bougainville beachhead, even though all the ships had not finished unloading. The four transports not fully unloaded would retire south for half the night, then turn around and head back to Cape Torokina in order to arrive at dawn.

At 2222 *Ausburne* made radar contact with a large formation of ships which turned out to be the main body of TF39 escorting the four transports. DesDiv 45 joined and TF39 detached itself from the transports and headed 355 degrees true at 20 knots to reduce the

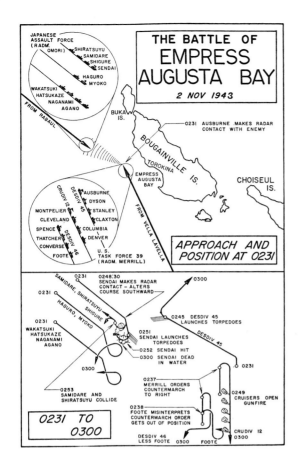

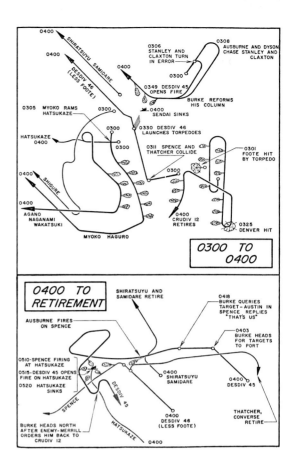

possibility of the ships' wakes being detected. The plan was to put TF39 between the oncoming Japanese force and the beachhead in the western waters of Empress Augusta Bay.

Merrill's force was disposed in line-of-bearing on unit guides. *Ausburne* was in the van and leading the other three destroyers of her division on the starboard wing and 6000 yards ahead of the guide (cruiser *Montpelier*). The cruisers then followed in column—distance 1000 yards between each. In the port column and to the rear were the four destroyers of DesDiv 46.

Plan of Battle

As the aircraft continued to track the more powerful Japanese force, it became clear that the enemy was heading for the invasion beaches. Admiral Merrill at 0100, 2 November, ordered his ships to increase speed to 28 knots to ensure they did not miss the enemy.

In pre-planning for this battle, Admiral Merrill had decided that the destroyers would open the battle with a torpedo run and, once action was joined, he hoped to edge the enemy westward away from Bougainville. He then planned to engage the enemy in a long range gun battle in order to avoid the Japanese torpedoes which even their cruisers carried. He hoped that the American radar advantage would offset the Japanese superior fire power.

Because of Japanese 'snoopers' in the area, TF39 slowed to 20 knots again. In fact, one of Omori's float planes sighted the US force but grossly underestimated it as one cruiser and three destroyers. It was a moonless, calm, overcast night, dark except for occasional flashes of heat lightning.

At 0227 'apple gadgets' (surface pips) began to appear on the flagship's radar at a range of 35,900 yards. Although several of the Japanese ships were equipped with rudimentary radar, it would be a crucial eighteen minutes later before the Japanese discovered the presence of the US ships.

Destroyer Torpedo Attack

As soon as the enemy was located, *Ausburne* led her division in for a torpedo attack on the Japanese northern flank, as the rest of the force counter-marched to allow DesDiv 46 to make a torpedo run on Omori's southern flank. At 0245, *Ausburne* launched a half salvo of torpedoes and was followed closely by the other three destroyers behind her; she then led the column in a circling course to the north to clear any torpedoes the Japanese may have fired at the attacking destroyers.

At about the same time, the Japanese detected the presence of the American force and altered course, manoeuvring themselves out of danger from the US torpedoes. Seeing the alteration, the American cruisers opened fire and with immediate effect. In the ensuing melée, confusion was experienced on both sides.

Four Japanese ships were damaged in two separate

U.S.S. Hazelwood (DD531) in 1960. This ship was badly mauled and almost sunk by Kamikazes off Okinawa in 1945; she is shown here with an experimental conversion to test the Dash drone helicopter concept. The hangar and landing pad predominate the area aft of the rear funnel. The triple torpedo launcher can be seen at the deck edge just forward of the hangar   (Photo: U.S. Navy)

collisions. *Spence* and *Thatcher*, both travelling at 30 knots on reciprocal courses, side-swiped each other in a shower of sparks and crumpled metal. *Ausburne* and *Dyson* became separated for a period of time from their two sisters and, at one time, DesDiv 45 was firing on DesDiv 46. At 0349, *Ausburne's* division got back into the battle by firing the *coup de grâce* into cruiser *Sendai*, already battered by the US cruisers.

First Light
As dawn approached, the Japanese headed back for Rabaul as fast as possible. TF39, with little ammunition left and four of its destroyers running low on fuel, 'licked its wounds' and prepared for the inevitable air attack.

TF39 had accomplished its primary mission in protecting the Bougainville invasion elements; in so doing, it had exacted from the Imperial Navy the loss of one cruiser, one destroyer, two cruisers damaged and one destroyer damaged. The US Navy had two cruisers and one destroyer damaged. The only casualties sustained were on *Foote* when she had her stern blown open by a torpedo. The above does not include the damage experienced on both sides due to collisions. During this action, the eight US destroyers expended 2596 rounds of 5in ammunition and 52 torpedoes of which only two were hits.

Claxton took *Foote* in tow, both being escorted by *Ausburne* and *Thatcher*. In the morning, the Japanese attacked with approximately 100 planes from Rabaul. They ignored *Ausburne's* formation with its cripple, and concentrated on the cruisers. The ships' guns and US fighters drove off the attack with little damage to the force, while accounting for 25 Japanese aircraft. TF39 returned to Purvis exhausted physically and materially after two and one half-days of concentrated action.

Bougainville Operations Continue
For the next three weeks, *Ausburne* and TF39 were engaged in escorting the re-supply echelons up to Bougainville: the force was harassed by continuing air

attacks but by little significant surface opposition. The night of 16 November, *Ausburne* took a near-miss bomb off her port side which showered her with shrapnel and dented her side.

The morning of 17 November, after fighting off a torpedo plane attack, *Ausburne* led her brood on another bombardment mission on the Buka installations.

THE BATTLE OF CAPE ST GEORGE
'31 Knot Burke'
DesRon 23 sortied from Hathorn Sound 1405 24 November heading for the now familiar waters around Bougainville. Only five destroyers of the squadron were operational: *Charles Ausburne*, *Dyson*, *Claxton*, *Converse* and *Spence*. *Spence* had a tube brush jammed in one of her boiler tubes so she could make only 31 knots. Admiral Halsey, who was then Commander Southern Pacific, queried Burke as to his ETA at his rendezvous, his composition, course and speed. The reply indicated 'The Little Beavers' were steaming at 31 knots. Halsey's next communication was addressed: 'For 31 knot Burke,' a title Admiral Burke carries with him to this day, even in retirement.

Commanding officers of the 'Little Beavers' of DesRon 23 enjoy 'a cool one' at the CLOOB DES-SLOT, Purvis Bay, Solomons Left to right: Cdr R. A. Gano (U.S.S. Dyson), Cdr L. K. Reynolds (U.S.S. Charles Ausburne), Capt. A. A. Burke (ComDesRon 23), Cdr. B. L. Austin (ComDesDiv 46), Cdr. D. C. Hamberger (U.S.S. Converse),unidentified officer, and Cdr. H. J. Armstrong (U.S.S. Spence). All the identified officers in this photo were destined to make admiral after World War II.
(Photo: Adm. A. A. Burke Collection, Naval Historical Foundation)

Destroyer Against Destroyer
Intelligence indicated that the Japanese were about to run a 'Tokyo Express' from Rabaul to the Buka-Bonis area. The enemy purpose was to bring 920 troop reinforcements and to take out 700 badly needed aviation rates from the now inoperative airfields there. The Japanese were in the process of doing this the night of 24-25 November. A force under Captain Kagowa consisting of three destroyers, *Amagiri*, *Yugiri*, and *Uzuki*, and two destroyers, *Onami* and *Makinami* acting as screen, had already accomplished the first part of its mission. It was now heading back to Rabaul as DesRon 23 raced north to intercept.

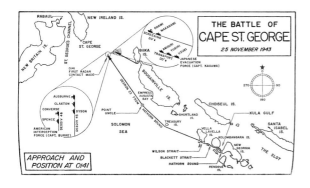

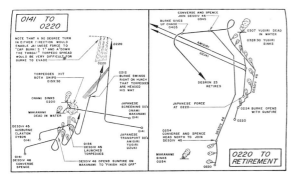

The night was overcast and moonless with intermittent rainsqualls, 'An ideal night for a nice quiet torpedo attack,' Burke noted. As DesRon 23 approached the line between Cape St George at the southern end of New Ireland Island and Buka passage, it slowed to 23 knots. *Ausburne* lead the squadron in a two column echelon formation. The Japanese, steaming 280 degrees true at 25 knots, were similarly disposed but with the two screening destroyers 13,000 yards in front. It was the American holiday of Thanksgiving and, at this early morning hour, several of the cooks in the squadron were already busy preparing the traditional turkey and pumpkin pie.

At 0141 *Dyson* picked up the Japanese screen at 22,000 yards. Again radar was to prove decisive: the Japanese would not know of the American presence until 30 seconds before the first torpedo struck. Burke closed his formation to within 5500 yards, 50 degrees on the port bow of the two enemy destroyers, and let fly 15 torpedoes from *Ausburne*, *Dyson* and *Claxton*.

While manoeuvring to avoid any counter-torpedo attack, radar picked up the second enemy column. Burke ordered *Converse* and *Spence* to take on the first two enemy ships while he took *Ausburne*, *Claxton* and *Dyson* after this new enemy force. No sooner had this order been given, when the American torpedoes ended their 210 second run in three large explosions. *Onami* sank almost instantly, while *Makanami* lay dead, afire in the water.

General Chase

Alarmed by the torpedo explosions, the three destroyers in the second Japanese column immediately turned north at top speed. *Ausburne* and her two mates followed at 33 knots in hot pursuit. At 0215 Burke on a hunch ordered a radical course change and, as his ships steadied on their original chase course, three enemy torpedoes exploded in their wakes in the water they had just vacated. At a range of 8000 yards, the pursuing destroyers opened fire and the three fleeing destroyers took three divergent courses in an 'every man for himself' move.

Yugiri, the northernmost destroyer, was finally stopped and sunk by *Ausburne* and her sisters at 0300. *Makinami* finally sank at 0254 and *Converse* and *Spence* raced north to join the other three 'Little Beavers'. The scene of the battle was now close to Cape St George, Rabaul's frontyard, and dawn was not far off. With the remaining two enemy destroyers damaged but now out of range, DesRon 23 reluctantly headed home. For some unknown reason, Japanese air did not molest *Ausburne* and her four sisters as they headed home that day.

The only damage received by the 'Little Beavers' was from the concussion of their own guns. *Ausburne*'s number one mount had to have its crew relieved several times because the muzzle blast of number two mount firing straight ahead, had torn the doors and other odd pieces off number one, thereby exposing its crew to a tremendous beating. The concussion from the guns had also disturbed the boiler mounts and the Thanksgiving turkeys.

As the gallant ships of DesRon 23 steamed into Purvis that night, the cruisers, in an unprecedented display of welcome and the flagsignal, 'Bravo Zulu' (well done) hoisted, illuminated and manned the rails. The Japanese reported they had been attacked by a 'cruiser division, a destroyer division and several PT boats'.

Solomon's Campaign Ends

Ausburne continued to support operations in the northern Solomons until March 1944. She escorted convoys and fought off enemy air attacks. She participated in bombardment missions against Tinputs, Ruri and Tsundawan 20 December; Buka-Bonis 23-24 December; and Sarime Plantation 4 February 1944. From 8-16 January 1944, *Ausburne* spent a well earned and needed overhaul period in Sydney, Australia.

On the night of 9 February 1944, *Ausburne* experienced the first effective use of 'window', radar jamming foil strips, by the Japanese.

From 13 to 17 February, TF 39, including *Ausburne*, provided cover for the landings on the Green Islands located north of Bougainville. The Japanese elected not to challenge the landings. On the 17th DesRon 23 headed north to raid the area around the Japanese port at Kavieng on the north side of New Ireland.

Ausburne and company, with an Army Air Force B-24 to spot their shots, opened fire on the harbor, airfield and base area at Kavieng at 0632 18 February. The B-24 reported the fire was effective and that a tanker was burning alongside a pier. The enemy's shore batteries scored a number of near misses but no serious damage was incurred.

Visit to Rabaul

After replenishing, the 'Little Beavers' were back in New Ireland waters on 20 February. This time their mission was to circum-navigate the island counter-clockwise, ending with a bombardment on Rabaul itself. It was hoped enemy shipping coming down from

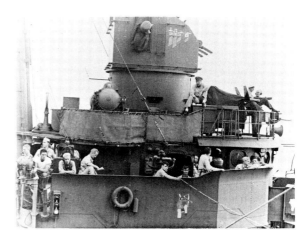

Captain Arleigh Burke, ComDesRon 23, leans against the torpedo director reading on the bridge wing of his flagship, Charles Ausburne, somewhere in the Solomons in early 1944. The hashmarks on the main battery director indicate from left to right number of aircraft shot down, shore bombardments conducted, warships and merchant ships sunk. Note 20mm canvas covered gun just forward of the director and 'Little Beaver' insignia on side of the bridge (Photo: U.S. Navy)

Ausburne, 27 September 1944. Detail left to right includes: the captain's chair, signal bridge with flag locker and signal halyards, forward torpedo tube, 40mm gun directors on after funnel immediately above their respective twin 40mm mounts and after torpedo tubes. Note DesRon 23 insignia on bridge wing (Photo: U.S. Navy)

Ausburne, 30 September 1944 with Golden Gate Bridge, San Francisco, in background. By the last year of World War II most new U.S. Navy destroyers and those going through major overhaul were given a camouflage scheme along the general lines as shown here. Variations included three color schemes, dappled or 'crazy quilt' effects (Photo: U.S. Navy)

Truk or Palau might be intercepted north of Kavieng. Nothing was sighted on the twenty-first.

About 1015 on 22 February the five ships pounced on a single Japanese ship of about 1500 tons. *Ausburne* hoisted the international signal to surrender which the enemy answered by opening fire. She was quickly sunk, *Ausburne* standing by to pick up survivors. Of the approximately 150 Japanese floating in the water, 75 were eventually rescued by three of the US destroyers including *Ausburne*. The rest of the Japanese refused to be rescued and a number committed suicide in a variety of bizarre ways.

Later that same afternoon, after the two ships of DesDiv 46 had departed to bombard Kavieng again, *Ausburne* and her two cohorts came upon an old type enemy destroyer. After a game chase and a heroic defense, the enemy ship sank with a tremendous underwater explosion as she went down near Tingwon Island.

U.S.S. Radford (DD446) in 1963, one of three Fletcher Fram II conversions. Most of the Fram conversions were made to the later Sumner/Gearing Class. Note that the Dash hangar is larger and the landing pad smaller than on the experimental Hazelwood. A variable depth sonar is installed on the fantail. Small circular funnel caps are installed   (Photo: U.S. Navy)

U.S.S. Boyd (DD544) in 1963. Note hedgehog launcher immediately below the port bridge wing. This weapon fired a 12 projectile salvo in a circular pattern ahead of the destroyer. These projectiles were contact fused and designed to puncture a submarine's pressure hull
(Photo: U.S. Navy)

That night at the mouth to Steffen Strait, a medium size cargo ship and several enemy barges were encountered and sunk. At 2247, the 'Little Beavers' started their run down narrow St George Channel. In driving rain, *Ausburne* and her friends fired some bullets at Duke of York Island and Rabaul as they rushed by; they were clear of the channel by dawn 23 February. En route back to Purvis, *Ausburne* picked up the crew of a downed B-24.

During March, *Ausburne* escorted a re-supply echelon to the Green Islands, made another run north of New Ireland looking for enemy shipping, and supported the Emirau Invasion 17-23 March.

On return to Purvis 23 March orders were waiting transferring DesRon 23 to CTF 58. Commodore Burke was also ordered as Chief of Staff to Commander Carrier Division 3 (who was the famous Admiral Marc Mitcher*) aboard the USS *Lexington*.

THE MARCH TOWARD JAPAN
CTF 58
Ausburne joined the Fifth Fleet on 26 March 1944 and, with an emotional goodbye, Commodore Burke was high-lined to the 'LEX' on the 27th. The greatest chapter in *Ausburne's* history had come to a close.

The United States had finally mobilized its great might and was now able to start island-hopping across the Central Pacific. Another year and one-half would go by and many battles would be fought before eventual victory, but *Ausburne* would not meet significant surface units of the Imperial Navy in combat again. From this point on, it would be his aircraft, kamikazes and shore installations that would feel *Ausburne's* fire. She participated in the following TF 58 operations:

1944

30 March—1 April	Palau-Yap-Ulithi-Woleai raid.
21-23 April	Supported Hollandia, New Guinea landings.
29 April—1 May	Truk-Satawan-Ponape raid.
6 June—3 July	Marianas operations: 12 June, on lifeguard duty for Pagan Island strike; rescued five aviators and destroyed two sampans. 15-16 June, screened for strikes on Bonins. 17-21 June, supported Saipan landings, and was in the carrier screen during the famous Marianas 'Turkey Shoot' of 19 June. 22-29 June, anti-shipping sweep and bombardment of Guam.

Ausburne received her second commanding officer 1 June 1944 when Lieutenant Commander Howard W. Baker relieved Commander Luther K. Reynolds at Majuro where she was based 4 May–6 June for tender availability and exercises. Baker would command *Ausburne* until she was placed in 'mothballs' in 1946.

Stateside Bound
After the Marianas Campaign, *Ausburne* received a well earned rest, departing Majuro 3 August 1944 for the United States. She arrived at Navy Yard, Mare Island, California 17 August for a much needed yard period and overhaul. While at Mare Island *Ausburne* received three additional twin 40mm mounts and various pieces of her machinery and electronics equipment were replaced with modern gear. *Ausburne* departed San Francisco 5 October, called at Pearl Harbor and Eniwetok en route, and arrived at the large fleet anchorage at Ulithi Atoll 5 November 1944.

Back to the War
Ausburne was back in the war and, until the capitulation of Japan in September 1945, she was to operate continually with elements of the Fifth and Seventh Fleets.

Ausburne's missions while operating out of San Pedro Bay with the amphibious forces of TF 78 were:

10-25 November 1944	Escorted carriers providing air cover to convoys to Leyte.
9 December—24 December	Escorted resupply LST convoy to Mindoro. Fought off heavy air attacks.
4-15 January 1945	Escorted transports for invasion of Lingayen Gulf and provided gun fire support for initial landings. *Ausburne* was credited with sinking destroyer *Hinoki* the night of 7 January 1945.
27 January—12 February	Escorted another convoy to Lingayen Gulf.
15-28 March	Supported the landings on Panay.
29 March—2 April	Supported the landings on Negros.
14-24 April 1945	Provided fire support for the landings at Parang, Mindanao.

Ausburne's missions while operating with TF 51 in the Okinawa area were:

16 May—22 June 1945	Antisubmarine patrol in Okinawa waters and participated in the Nansei Shoto occupations 3-9 June.
23-30 June	Radar picket duty.
1-24 July	Command ship for offensive screen.
25 July—10 August	Availability.
11-12 August	Radar picket duty.
23 August—10 September	An element of Task Flotilla 1, participating mainly in underway training.

Z-6 in its last form. Three single 40mm Bofors have replaced the three twin 3in. mounts

(Photo: Terzibaschitsch)

Homeward Bound

The War ended 6 September 1945. On 8 September *Charles Ausburne* reported to Commander First Carrier Task Force (CTF 11) and got underway 10 September from Okinawa with that force bound for Pearl Harbor. Escorting battleship *Idaho*, *Ausburne* steamed across the Pacific to transit the Panama Canal 8-12 October; she put in at Norfolk 16-17 October and passed up the Potomac River to the Navy Yard, Washington, D.C. 18 October.

In a ceremony on 19 October 1945, with four of the 'Little Beavers' (*Ausburne*, *Dyson*, *Converse* and *Claxton*) in attendance, Secretary of the Navy, James Forrestal, awarded Destroyer Squadron 23 the Presidential Unit Citation (see inside front cover). DesRon 23 was the only destroyer squadron so honored in World War II.

Ausburne opened her brow to the Washington public on Navy Day, 27 October. She departed for New York Harbor on 3 November and remained there until 5 January 1946. She arrived at Charleston, South Carolina 7 January and in preparation for her de-activation was thoroughly 'mothballed'.

Charles Ausburne was decommissioned 18 April 1946 and joined the Atlantic Reserve Fleet berthed in Charleston.

POST-WAR *FLETCHER* CONVERSIONS
Escort Destroyer (DDE)

Nineteen *Fletchers* were converted to escort destroyers under the programs authorized 1948-50. (See photo.) The DDE was designed to serve as a convoy escort and in hunter-killer ASW teams. The major changes were to electronics and armament. Two 5in main mounts were retained, numbers one and five. A Weapon ALFA, a trainable ASW 12·75in rocket launcher, was installed in the number two 5in mount position. Two twin 3in 50 caliber mounts were located in place of the number three and four 5in mounts. The forward 3in mount was offset to port and the after one to starboard. Two hedgehog launchers were placed one on each side of the bridge on the 01 level. The 40mm, 20mm, after quint torpedo mount and the depth charge K guns were removed. These 19 *Fletchers* were reclassified as DDs 1 July 1962.

Fram II *Fletchers*

Three *Fletcher* DDEs were further modified under the FRAM II (Fleet Rehabilitation and Modernization) program of 1960. Major changes in this modification were in electronics (improved CIC,* Sonar and radar) and armament. A tripod mast replaced the earlier pole mast. The funnels were top hat shaped caps. Two small triple torpedo launchers replaced the one remaining quint mount and were located one each side of the after funnel. The two 3in twin mounts were removed to allow the construction of a helicopter pad and hangar at the 01 level abaft the after funnel. Two torpedo carrying DASH drone helicopters could be stored in the hangar. A small trellis type mainmast was atop the hangar. Two FRAM II *Fletchers* were subsequently equipped with variable depth sonar, the transducer and hoisting gear being located on the fantail.

Additional Post-War Conversions

In the post-war period numerous *Fletchers* received various modifications besides those mentioned. Some 28 had their number three 5in mount and one of their torpedo mounts removed. The 20mm mounts were removed from most of the *Fletchers*. A number of the class had twin 3in/50 cal. mounts replace their twin 40mm. On others, the 40mm mounts were reduced in number of removed completely. Most of the *Fletchers* who remained on active duty had their pole masts replaced by tripods and eventually almost all of them had two of the smaller triple torpedo mounts replace the large quints.

Up to the present day, all the remaining *Fletchers* in the US Navy are in the Reserve Fleet except for six operational Naval Reserve Training ships.

AUSBURNE JOINS THE FEDERAL GERMAN NAVY
De-activation

Thirteen years after *Ausburne* joined the 'mothballed' Reserve Fleet at Charleston, South Carolina, she was called for service again. Under the provisions of the United States Military Assistance Program, *Ausburne* and five of her sisters, *Anthony* (DD 515), *Ringgold* (DD 500), *Wadsworth* (DD 516), *Claxton* (DD 571), and *Dyson* (DD 572), were loaned to the Federal German Navy as Z 6 (D 180), Z 1 (D 170), Z 2 (D 171), Z 3 (D 172), Z 4 (D 178), and Z 5 (D 179), respectively.

Charleston Navy Yard completely overhauled and modernized *Ausburne* and on 12 April 1960 she was commissioned as *Zerstörer* 6.

Representing the German Federal Navy at the commissioning was Vice Admiral Friedrich Ruge*, then *Inspecteur der Bundes-marine*, a position corresponding to that of Chief of Naval Operations in the US Navy. Returning to the familiar deck of *Ausburne* and representing the US Navy at the ceremony was Admiral Arleigh Burke, CHIEF OF NAVAL OPERATIONS.

Zerstörer 6: Modernization

Ausburne was the second ship in the German Navy named, Z 6. Her predecessor, Z 6, was named *Theodore Riedel*. She was commissioned 6 July 1937 and during World War II served in the North Sea, Northern Atlantic, English Channel and the Skagerrak. At the conclusion of hostilities she became a British war prize and later served in the French Navy as *Kleber*.

The modernization of Z 6 included an enlarged bridge area; a tripod mast with improved radar antenna installed; and a platform carrying additional electronics antennas was built on the after funnel.

Armament consisted of four 5in mounts, three twin 3in/50 caliber automatic open mounts, a single quint torpedo mount, two hedgehog launchers and one depth charge radar. Two of the twin 3in mounts were located on each side just forward of the after stack. Each of these mounts had its own director, both being installed in the area of the original forward torpedo mount between the two funnels. The third twin 3in mount was on top of the after deck house and its director was placed just forward, where the old number three 5in mount had been located. The two hedgehog launchers were on the 01 level, one on each side, just forward of the bridge. She carried a crew of 12 officers and 316 enlisted men.

Z 6, with Z 4 and Z 5, all ex-DesRon 23 destroyers, formed Destroyer Squadron 3 based at Flensburg. The primary mission of the squadron was to defend the Baltic approaches. During the course of her service Z 6 participated in numerous national and NATO exercises.

Z-6 passing under the Kiel Holtenauer Bridge. In the Federal German Navy she was fitted as most of her U.S. Navy sisters of the period: four 5in. main mounts, three twin 3in. mounts, a single quint torpedo mount, hedgehogs, tripod mast and glassed-in bridge
(Photo: Dressler Collection)

In a later overhaul, the two twin 3in mounts amidships were removed and two single 40mm mounts were installed in their place. The open bridge of Z 6 was also enclosed at this time.

It was decided to inactivate Z 6 and the US Navy subsequently sold her to the Federal German Navy to serve her five sisterships by providing much needed spare parts. She was stricken from the US Navy Register 1 December 1967.

On a cold and windy Friday, 15 December 1967, *Zerstörer 6* was de-commissioned. In a brief ceremony conducted by Kapitän zür See von Mutius, the Destroyer Type Commander, and in company with Kapitän zür See von Bulow (her first German skipper) and Fregattenkapitän Felmberg (the last skipper), her renowned exploits were recounted. It was noted that 2200 German officers and men had served in Z 6 during her seven and one-half years of service to the Federal Navy. As the band played *The Stars and Stripes Forever* and the *Alte Kameraden* (Old Comrades) the National Ensign was slowly lowered.

NOTES:
Builder Key:
Bath=Bath Iron Works Corp., Bath, Maine.
Bethlehem, S.F.=Bethlehem Shipbuilding Co, San Francisco, California.
Bethlehem, S.I.=Bethlehem Shipbuilding Co, Staten Island, N.Y.
Bethlehem, S.P.=Bethlehem Steel Co, SB Division, San Pedro, California.
Boston=Boston Navy Yard, Boston, Mass.
Charleston=Charleston Navy Yard, Charleston, S.C.
Consolidated=Consolidated Steel Corp., Orange, Texas.
Federal=Federal Shipbuilding and Dry Dock Co., Kearny, N.J.
Gulf=Gulf Shipbuilding Corp. Chickasaw, Ark.
Puget Sound=Puget Sound Navy Yard, Bremerton, Wash.
Seattle-Tacoma=Seattle-Tacoma Shipbuilding Corp., Seattle, Wash.
Todd Pacific=Todd Pacific Shipyards, Inc., Seattle, Wash.
Cancellations:
Percival (452) experimental ultra-high pressure steam plant, *Watson* (482) experimental with 24 GM 2500h.p. 32 cyl. diesel engines, *Stevenson* (503), *Stockton* (504), *Thorn* (505), *Turner* (506). Plus these unnamed serials: 523, 524, 525, 542, 543, 548, 549.

APPENDIX I

CHARLES AUSBURNE SPECIFICATIONS

Authorized:	4 Sept 1940—Under 70% Expansion Act of 19 July 1940 (Act of Congress 757 and Public Law 757).
Builder:	Consolidated Steel Co, Orange, Texas.
Contract Price:	$7,315,000·00 (hull and machinery).
Keel Laid:	14 May 1940.
Launched:	16 March 1942.
Commissioned:	24 November 1942.
Displacement:	Standard 2050 tons. Full 2940 tons.
Dimensions:	Length 356ft, beam 39ft 7in, mean draft 13ft, max draft 17ft 9in.
Engines:	Two General Electric Turbines with Falk double reduction gears (DeLaval design).
Boilers:	Four Babcock and Wilcox Superheated-water tube 565p.s.i. at 850° (F) at full power.
Shaft Horsepower:	60,000 through two propellers.
Trial Speed:	35·2 knots.
Fuel:	492 tons.
Accommodations:	20 officers, 309 men.
Directors and Radar (1945):	Main Battery Dir. Mk.37 Mod. 22.
	40mm Gun Dir. Mk.51 Mod. 01 (3).
	40mm Gun Dir. Mk.51 Mod. 02 (2).
	Torpedo Dir. Mk.27 Mod. 05 (2).
	Main Battery F.C. Radar Mk.12.
	Main Battery F.C. Radar Mk.22
	SG Surface Search Radar.
	SC Air Search Radar.

Armament:	Nov 42	Mar 43	Sept 44	Apr 60*
5in/38	5	5	5	4
3in/50 (twins)	—	—	—	3
40mm (twins)	2	3	5	—
20mm	4	11	7	—
21 'Torp. Tubes'	10	10	10	5
D.C. rails	2	2	2	1
D.C. launchers	6	6	6	—
Hedgehog launchers	—	—	—	2

*As Z 6 she carried an additional two ASW torpedo tubes, also had her three twin 3in mounts replaced by three single 40mm at a later date.

No.	Name	Builder	Date	Notes
571	CLAXTON	*Consolidated*	8/12/42	Transferred to W. Germany 15/12/59.
572	DYSON	*Consolidated*	30/12/42	Transferred to W. Germany 17/2/60.
573	HARRISON	*Consolidated*	25/1/43	Stricken 1/5/68.
574	JOHN RODGERS	*Consolidated*	9/2/43	Stricken 1/5/68.
575	McKEE	*Consolidated*	31/3/43	Reserve.
576	MURRAY	*Consolidated*	20/4/43	DDE conversion. Stricken 1/6/65.
577	SPROSTON	*Consolidated*	19/5/43	DDE conversion. Stricken 1/10/68.
578	WICKES	*Consolidated*	16/6/43	Reserve.
579	W. D. PORTER	*Consolidated*	6/7/43	Sunk on radar picket duty off Okinawa by *Kamikaze* 10/6/45.
580	YOUNG	*Consolidated*	31/7/43	Stricken 1/5/68.
581	CHARRETTE	*Boston*	18/5/43	Transferred to Greece 15/6/59.
582	CONNER	*Boston*	8/6/43	Transferred to Greece 15/9/59.
583	HALL	*Boston*	7/7/43	Transferred to Greece 9/2/60.
584	HALLIGAN	*Boston*	19/8/43	Sunk off Okinawa probably by a mine 26/3/45.
585	HARADEN	*Boston*	16/9/43	Reserve.
586	NEWCOMB	*Boston*	10/11/43	Badly damaged by three *Kamikazes* off Okinawa 6/4/45. Scrapped at end of war.
587	BELL	*Charleston*	4/3/43	Reserve.
588	BURNS	*Charleston*	3/4/43	Reserve.
589	IZARD	*Charleston*	15/5/43	Stricken 1/5/68.
590	P. HAMILTON	*Charleston*	25/10/43	Stricken 1/5/68.
591	TWIGGS	*Charleston*	4/11/43	Sunk by a *Kamikaze* off Okinawa 16/6/45.
592	HOWORTH	*Puget Sound*	3/4/44	Test ship 1958 atomic tests. Stricken 1/6/61. Expended as a target 8/3/62.
593	KILLEN	*Puget Sound*	5/4/44	Test ship 1958 atomic tests. Stricken 1/1/63. Expended as a target.
594	HART	*Puget Sound*	4/11/44	Reserve.
595	METCALF	*Puget Sound*	18/11/44	Reserve.
596	SHIELDS	*Puget Sound*	8/2/45	Active service as a Naval Reserve Training Ship.
597	WILEY	*Puget Sound*	22/2/45	Stricken 1/5/68.
629	ABBOT	*Bath*	23/4/43	Reserve.
630	BRAINE	*Bath*	11/5/43	Active service as a Naval Reserve Training Ship.
631	ERBEN	*Bath*	28/5/43	Transferred to Korea 1/5/63.
642	HALE	*Bath*	15/6/43	Transferred to Columbia 23/1/61.
643	SIGOURNEY	*Bath*	29/6/43	Reserve.
644	STEMBLE	*Federal*	16/7/43	Transferred to Argentina 1/8/61.
649	A. W. GRANT	*Charleston*	24/11/43	Reserve.
650	CAPERTON	*Bath*	30/7/43	Reserve.
651	COGSWELL	*Bath*	17/8/43	Transferred to Turkey 1/10/69.
652	INGERSOLL	*Bath*	31/8/43	Reserve.
653	KNAPP	*Bath*	16/9/43	Reserve.
654	BEARSS	*Gulf*	12/4/44	Reserve.
655	JOHN HOOD	*Gulf*	7/6/44	Reserve.
656	VAN VALKENBURGH	*Gulf*	2/8/44	Transferred to Turkey 28/2/67.
657	C. J. BADGER	*Bethlehem, S.I.*	23/7/43	Reserve.
658	COLAHAN	*Bethlehem, S.I.*	23/8/43	Stricken 1/8/66. Expended as a target.
659	DASHIEL	*Federal*	20/3/43	Reserve.
660	BULLARD	*Federal*	9/4/43	Reserve.
661	KIDD	*Federal*	23/4/43	Reserve.
662	BENNION	*Boston*	14/12/43	Reserve.
663	H. L. EDWARDS	*Boston*	26/1/44	Transferred to Japan 10/3/59.
664	R. P. LEARY	*Boston*	23/2/44	Transferred to Japan 10/3/59.
665	BRYANT	*Charleston*	4/12/43	Stricken 1/6/68.
666	BLACK	*Federal*	21/5/43	Reserve.
667	CHAUNCEY	*Federal*	31/5/43	Reserve.
668	C. K. BRONSON	*Federal*	11/6/43	Transferred to Turkey 14/1/67.
669	COTTEN	*Federal*	24/7/43	Reserve.
670	DORTCH	*Federal*	7/8/42	Transferred to Argentina 1/8/61.
671	GATLING	*Federal*	19/8/43	Reserve.
672	HEALY	*Federal*	3/9/43	Reserve.
673	HICKOX	*Federal*	10/9/43	Transferred to S. Korea 11/11/68.
674	HUNT	*Federal*	22/9/43	Reserve.
675	LEWIS HANCOCK	*Federal*	29/9/43	Transferred to Brazil 1/8/67.
676	MARSHALL	*Federal*	16/10/43	Stricken 12/7/69.
677	McDERMUT	*Federal*	19/11/43	Stricken 1/4/65.
678	McGOWAN	*Federal*	20/12/43	Transferred to Spain 31/11/68.
679	McNAIR	*Federal*	30/12/43	Reserve.
680	MELVIN	*Federal*	24/11/43	Reserve.
681	HOPEWELL	*Bethlehem, S.P.*	30/9/43	Stricken 2/1/70.
682	PORTERFIELD	*Bethlehem, S.P.*	30/10/43	Reserve.
683	STOCKHAM	*Bethlehem, S.P.*	11/2/44	Reserve.
684	WEDDERBURN	*Bethlehem, S.P.*	9/3/44	Reserve.
685	PICKING	*Bethlehem, S.I.*	21/9/43	Reserve.
686	HALSEY POWELL	*Bethlehem, S.I.*	25/10/43	Transferred to S. Korea 27/4/68.
687	UHLMANN	*Bethlehem, S.I.*	22/11/43	Active Service Naval Reserve Training Ship.
688	REMEY	*Bath*	30/9/43	Reserve.
689	WADLEIGH	*Bath*	19/10/43	Transferred to Chile 26/7/62.
690	NORMAN SCOTT	*Bath*	5/11/43	Reserve.
691	MERTZ	*Bath*	19/11/43	Reserve.
792	CALLAGHAM	*Bethlehem, S.P.*	27/11/43	Sunk on radar picket duty off Okinawa by a *Kamikaze* 29/7/45, one hour before due to depart for the US.
793	CASSIN YOUNG	*Bethlehem, S.P.*	31/12/43	Reserve.
794	IRWIN	*Bethlehem, S.P.*	14/9/44	Transferred to Brazil 10/4/68.
795	PRESTON	*Bethlehem, S.P.*	20/3/44	Reserve.
796	DENHAM	*Bethlehem, S.I.*	20/12/43	Transferred to Peru 8/10/61.
797	CUSHING	*Bethlehem, S.I.*	17/1/44	Transferred to Brazil 20/7/61.
798	MONSSEN	*Bethlehem, S.I.*	14/2/44	Stricken 1/2/63.
799	JARVIS	*Todd Pacific*	3/6/44	Transferred to Spain 3/11/60.
800	PORTER	*Todd Pacific*	24/6/44	Reserve.
801	COLHOUN	*Todd Pacific*	8/7/44	Sunk on radar picket duty off Okinawa by four *Kamikazes* 6/4/45.
802	GREGORY	*Todd Pacific*	29/7/44	Stricken 1/5/66. Serving as a non seagoing training ship at San Diego renamed *Indoctrinator*.
803	LITTLE	*Todd Pacific*	19/8/44	Sunk on radar picket duty off Okinawa by four *Kamikazes* 3/5/45.

APPENDIX II

Destroyers of the **Fletcher** class

Pendant No. Name and Builder *	Commissioned	Notes
445 FLETCHER *Federal*	30/6/42	DDE conversion. Stricken 1/8/67.
446 RADFORD *Federal*	22/7/42	DDE and FRAM II conversions. Stricken 15/7/69.
447 JENKINS *Federal*	31/7/42	DDE and FRAM II conversions. Stricken 2/7/69.
448 LA VALLETTE *Federal*	12/8/42	Reserve.
449 NICHOLAS *Bath*	4/6/42	DDE and FRAM II conversions. Stricken 30/1/70.
450 O'BANNON *Bath*	26/6/42	DDE conversion. Stricken 30/1/70.
451 CHEVALIER *Bath*	20/7/42	Sunk by destroyer *Yugumo*, Battle of Vella LaVella in the Solomons 7/10/43.
465 SAUFLEY *Federal*	9/8/42	DDE conversion. Stricken 1/9/66. Expended as a target February 1968.
466 WALLER *Federal*	1/10/42	DDE conversion. Stricken 15/7/69.
467 STRONG *Bath*	7/8/42	Sunk by torpedo in the Solomons 5/7/43.
468 TAYLOR *Bath*	28/8/42	DDE conversion. Transferred to Italy 1/7/69.
469 DE HAVEN *Bath*	20/9/42	Sunk by air attack off Guadacanal 1/2/43.
470 BACHE *Bethlehem, S.I.*	14/11/42	DDE conversion. Ran aground off Rhodes, Greece 6/2/68. Stricken 1/3/68.
471 BEALE *Bethlehem, S.I.*	23/12/42	DDE conversion. Stricken 1/10/68.
472 GUEST *Boston*	15/12/42	Transferred to Brazil 5/6/59.
473 BENNETT *Boston*	9/2/43	Transferred to Brazil 15/15/59.
474 FULLAM *Boston*	2/3/42	Test ship 1958 atomic tests. Stricken 1/6/62. Expended as a target 7/7/62.
475 HUDSON *Boston*	13/4/43	Reserve.
476 HUTCHINS *Boston*	17/11/42	Heavily damaged by suicide boat off Okinawa 27/4/45 and subsequently scrapped.
477 PRINGLE *Charleston*	15/9/42	Sunk by *Kamikaze* off Okinawa 16/4/45.
478 STANLEY *Charleston*	15/10/42	Reserve.
479 STEVENS *Charleston*	1/2/42	Reserve.
480 HALFORD *Puget Sound*	10/4/43	Stricken 1/4/68.
481 LEUTZE *Puget Sound*	4/3/44	Heavily damaged by *Kamikaze* off Okinawa 6/4/45 and subsequently scrapped.
498 PHILIP *Federal*	21/11/42	DDE conversion. Stricken 1/10/68.
499 RENSHAW *Federal*	5/2/42	DDE conversion. Stricken 1970.
500 RINGGOLD *Federal*	30/12/42	Transferred to West Germany 14/7/59.
501 SCHROEDER *Federal*	1/1/43	Reserve.
502 SIGSBEE *Federal*	23/1/43	Reserve.
507 CONWAY *Bath*	9/10/42	DDE conversion. Stricken 10/11/69.
508 CONY *Bath*	30/10/42	DDE conversion. Stricken 2/7/69.
509 CONVERSE *Bath*	20/11/42	Transferred to Spain 1/7/59.
510 EATON *Bath*	4/12/42	DDE conversion. Stricken 2/7/69.
511 FOOTE *Bath*	22/12/42	Reserve.
512 SPENCE *Bath*	8/1/43	Sunk in typhoon off Philipines, 18/12/44.
513 TERRY *Bath*	27/1/43	Reserve.
514 THATCHER *Bath*	10/2/43	Badly damaged and subsequently scrapped.
515 ANTHONY *Bath*	26/2/43	Transferred to W. Germany 17/1/58.
516 WADSWORTH *Bath*	16/3/43	Transferred to W. Germany 6/10/59.
517 WALKER *Bath*	3/4/43	DDE conversion. Transferred to Italy 7/69.
518 BROWNSON *Bethlehem, S.I.*	3/2/43	Sunk by air attack off New Guinea 26/12/43.
519 DALY *Bethlehem, S.I.*	10/3/43	Reserve.
520 ISHERWOOD *Bethlehem, S.I.*	12/4/43	Transferred to Peru 8/10/61.
521 KIMBERLY *Bethlehem, S.I.*	22/5/43	Transferred to Nationalist China 1/6/67.
522 LUCE *Bethlehem, S.I.*	21/6/43	Sunk by two *Kamikazes* off Okinawa 4/5/45.
526 ABNER READ *Bethlehem, S.F.*	5/2/43	Sunk by *Kamikaze* in Leyte Gulf 1/11/44.
527 AMMEN *Bethlehem, S.F.*	12/3/43	Stricken 1/9/60 after major collision.
528 MULLANY *Bethlehem, S.F.*	23/4/43	Active service as a Naval Reserve Training Ship.
529 BUSH *Bethlehem, S.F.*	10/5/43	Sunk by three *Kamikazes* off Okinawa 6/4/45.
530 TRATHEN *Bethlehem, S.F.*	28/5/43	Reserve.
531 HAZELWOOD *Bethlehem, S.F.*	18/6/43	Experimental ship for DASH helicopter. Reserve.
532 HEERMANN *Bethlehem, S.F.*	6/7/43	Transferred to Argentina 1/8/61.
533 HOEL *Bethlehem, S.F.*	29/7/43	Sunk by gunfire in the Battle off Samar 25/10/44.
534 McCORD *Bethlehem, S.F.*	19/8/43	Reserve.
535 MILLER *Bethlehem, S.F.*	31/8/43	Reserve.
536 OWEN *Bethlehem, S.F.*	20/9/43	Reserve.
537 THE SULLIVANS *Bethlehem, S.F.*	30/9/43	Reserve.
538 STEPHEN POTTER *Bethlehem, S.F.*	21/10/43	Reserve.
539 TINGEY *Bethlehem, S.F.*	25/11/43	Stricken 1/11/65. Expended as a target 1969.
540 TWINING *Bethlehem, S.F.*	1/12/43	Active service as a Naval Reserve Training Ship.
541 YARNALL *Bethlehem, S.F.*	30/12/43	Transferred to Nationalist China 1/10/69.
544 BOYD *Bethlehem, S.P.*	8/5/43	Transferred to Turkey 1/10/69.
545 BRADFORD *Bethlehem, S.P.*	12/6/43	Transferred to Greece 27/9/62.
546 BROWN *Bethlehem, S.P.*	10/7/43	Transferred to Greece 27/9/62.
547 COWELL *Bethlehem, S.P.*	23/8/43	Active service as a Naval Reserve Training Ship.
550 CAPPS *Gulf*	23/6/43	Transferred to Spain 15/4/57.
551 DAVID W. TAYLOR *Gulf*	18/9/43	Transferred to Spain 15/4/57.
552 EVANS *Gulf*	11/12/43	Badly damaged by four *Kamikazes* off Okinawa and scrapped at end of war.
553 JOHN D. HENLEY *Gulf*	2/2/44	Stricken.
554 FRANKS *Seattle-Tacoma*	30/7/43	Reserve.
555 HAGGARD *Seattle-Tacoma*	31/8/43	Badly damaged by *Kamikazes* off Okinawa 29/4/45. Scrapped at end of war.
556 HAILEY *Seattle-Tacoma*	30/9/43	Transferred to Brazil 20/7/61.
557 JOHNSTON *Seattle-Tacoma*	27/10/43	Sunk by Japanese cruisers in the Battle off Samar 25/10/44.
558 LAWS *Seattle-Tacoma*	18/11/43	Reserve.
559 LONGSHAW *Seattle-Tacoma*	4/12/43	Sunk after grounding on Ose Reef and subsequent pounding from Japanese shore batteries 14/5/45.
560 MORRISON *Seattle-Tacoma*	18/12/43	Sunk on radar picket duty off Okinawa by four *Kamikazes* 4/5/45.
561 PRICHETT *Seattle-Tacoma*	15/1/44	Transferred to Italy 10/1/70.
562 ROBINSON *Seattle-Tacoma*	31/1/44	Reserve.
563 ROSS *Seattle-Tacoma*	21/2/44	Reserve.
564 ROWE *Seattle-Tacoma*	13/3/44	Reserve.
565 SMALLEY *Seattle-Tacoma*	31/3/44	Stricken 1/4/65.
566 STODDARD *Seattle-Tacoma*	15/4/44	Reserve.

567	WATTS	29/4/44	Reserve.
	Seattle-Tacoma		
568	WREN	20/5/44	Reserve.
	Seattle-Tacoma		
569	AULICK	27/10/42	Transferred to Greece 21/8/59.
	Consolidated		
570	CHARLES AUSBURNE	24/11/42	Transferred to W. Germany 12/4/60.
	Consolidated		

Acknowledgements:

I wish to express my gratitude and thanks to the following without whose help this *Profile* would have never been written:

Admiral Arleigh A. Burke, USN (Ret.).

Rear Admiral Luther K. Reynolds, USN (Ret.).

Miss Anna C. Urband, Magazine and Book Branch, Office of Information, USN.

Vice Admiral Edwin B. Hooper, USN (Ret.) Director of Naval History and Curator for the Navy Department.

Captain L. G. Traynor, USN; Commander Earl Mann, USN; Mr H. A. Vadnais, Jr. and others of the Naval History Division.

Mr John Wingate, D.S.C.

Mr Raymond V. B. Blackman, M.B.E., C.Eng., M.I. Mar. E., M.R.I.N.A.

Dr Jürgen Rohwer, Bibliothek Fur Zeitgeschichte, Stuttgart.

Mr Jeremy Elms, Washington D.C.

The National Archives of the United States.

Selected Bibliography:

CRADLE OF SHIPS, HISTORY OF THE BATH IRONWORKS by Garnet Laidlaw Eskew, *G. P. Putnam's Sons.*

DESTROYER SQUADRON 23 by Ken Jones, *Chulton Company.*

DICTIONARY OF AMERICAN NAVAL FIGHTING SHIPS Office of the Chief of Naval Operations, *Naval History Division, Department of the Navy.*

FLUSH DECKS AND FOUR PIPERS by Commander John D. Alden, USN, *United States Naval Institute.*

HISTORY OF UNITED STATES NAVAL OPERATIONS IN WORLD WAR II by Samuel Elliot Morrison, Rear Admiral USNR (Ret.), *Little Brown and Company.*

JANE'S FIGHTING SHIPS (various volumes) edited by Raymond V. B. Blackman, *Sampson Low, Marston & Co. Ltd.*

THE SHIPS AND AIRCRAFT OF THE U.S. FLEET (various editions) by James C. Fahey, *United States Naval Institute.*

UNITED STATES DESTROYER OPERATIONS OF WORLD WAR II by Theodore Roscoe, *United States Naval Institute.*

Warship Series Editor:
JOHN WINGATE, DSC

* See Warship Profile No. 3.
* Combat Information Centre.
* Author of Warship Profiles Nos. 14 and 28.

2. Treasury-Bougainville Operation.
   Occupation and Defense of Cape Torokina.
   Bombardment of Buka-Bonis.
   Battle off Cape St George.
3. Bismarck Archipelago Operation.
   Bombardments of Kavieng and Rabaul.
   Anti-shipping Sweeps and Bombardments of Kavieng.
4. Asiatic-Pacific Raids.
   Palau, Yap, Ulithi, Woleai Raid.
   Truk, Satawan Ponape Raid.
5. Hollandia Operation (Aitape Humboldt Bay—Tanahmerah Bay).
6. Marianas Operation.
   Capture and Occupation of Saipan.
   First Bonins Raid.
   Second Bonins Raid.
   Capture and Occupation of Guam.
7. Tinian Capture and Occupation.
8. Leyte Operation.
   Leyte Landings.
9. Luzon Operation.
   Lingayen Gulf Landing.
10. Okinawa Gunto Operation.
    Assault and Occupation of Okinawa Gunto.
11. Consolidation of the Southern Philippines.
    Visayan Island Landings (including Lubang, Ticao-Burias, Panay Cebu Negros, Masbate and Bohol).
    Mindanao Island Landings (including Zamboanga Malaboang - Parang - Cotabato Davao Gulf-Digos-Santa Cruz-Taloma Bay-Luayon-Cape San Augustin-Macajalar Bay, Sarangani Bay-Balut Island).

Ausburne, *27 September 1944.* Detail shown left to right: *after torpedo tubes with warhead shields folded back, below on the main deck two 20mm guns, the torpedo hoist just forward of Number Three main mount, new VHF communications antenna and new roller type loaders for the three portside depth charge ejectors on the main deck immediately abaft the life raft*

(*Photo: U.S. Navy*)

Charles Ausburne (DD 570)

Charles Ausburne earned the Asiatic-Pacific Area Service Medal with 11 Battle Stars, and the Navy Occupation Service Medal Pacific, in addition to her Presidential Unit Citation during World War II. She was credited with or assisted in sinking nine warships, three merchant ships and six barges. Nine enemy aircraft were also shot down by *Ausburne's* guns. Through over two years of combat she received no major damage and came through the war without the loss of a man. *Ausburne's* 11 Battle Stars were for the following operations:

1. Consolidation of Solomon Islands.

Shark's Eye View of the quarterdeck: Illustrious *at anchor in the Solent in the late 40's*   (*MoD* (*N*))

HMS Illustrious
Lieutenant D. J. Lyon RNR, MA

No Uncertain Sound

> '*If the trumpet give forth an uncertain sound, who shall prepare himself to the battle?*': Saint Paul's First Epistle to the Corinthians, Chapter 14.

This verse was the inspiration for Captain D. W. Boyd's choice of a motto for the new aircraft carrier he was to command. 'VOX NON INCERTA' was emblazoned beneath the three crossed trumpets of *Illustrious's* badge. 'No uncertain sound' was certainly appropriate for the ship who launched the attack on Taranto. The ship also survived the attacks of *Flieger-korps X*, and perhaps, more action damage than any other allied ship. She also took part in the invasion of Madagascar, the first successful allied amphibious attack of the war, as well as serving at Salerno, and with the Eastern Fleet and the British Pacific Fleet. She was the first carrier to be commissioned after the outbreak of the war; she survived hits which would have sunk any carrier not possessing the armoured hangar which she introduced; and she continued to serve into the nineteen-fifties.

Arguably she had the most distinguished war record of any British carrier. Her story, and that of the aircraft she carried, will be told in Warship Profile No. 11, the second volume of this work. Although a carrier exists to operate her aircraft, and they are her chief weapon, she is herself a very complex ship. The purpose here is to tell the story of the design, construction and subsequent modification of one such vessel. Rather than

relate the technical history of the *Illustrious* in chronological sequence, the account is divided into sections on armament, protection, machinery etc., after following a summary of the main events in her story.

Design History

In the late 1930s the menace of the bomber loomed large, particularly to the Royal Navy, uneasily conscious that it would probably have to fight the large shore-based air forces of Germany and Italy. Aircraft carriers were one answer, but British naval aircraft design had fallen behind during the years of financial stringency and R.A.F. control. American and Japanese carriers, designed to fight an oceanic war and having better aircraft available, could afford to rely on their own fighters for defence. The British, anticipating a war in narrow seas dominated by hostile air forces, had to place greater reliance on anti-aircraft guns and more traditional means of protection.

The *Illustrious* began life as a set of staff requirements drawn up in early 1936. That year's programme of construction provided for two new aircraft carriers to follow into service the newly-ordered, *Ark Royal*. At first the naval staff favoured the idea of building two types of carriers, a larger one to carry 48 planes, and a smaller, 24 plane ship. During discussions of this latter project (design 'J') the idea of armouring the sides as well as the top of the hangar was put forward.

The final requirement had developed into a ship to

Captain D. W. Boyd DSC RN: the first Captain, he returned to the ship in June 1942 and flew his flag as Rear Admiral (Aircraft Carriers) Eastern Fleet in her until January 1943　　　　　　　　　　　　　　(IWM)

carry 36 torpedo/spotter/reconnaissance aircraft in a heavily armoured hangar. She was to have a powerful anti-aircraft armament, be highly manoeuverable, and reach a speed of 30 knots. This was all to be achieved within the treaty limitation of 23,000 tons standard displacement.

It might have been easier to use the already existing plan of the *Ark Royal*. The Third Sea Lord and Controller, in charge of design and construction, did not think so. He was Rear-Admiral R. G. Henderson, who had previously been the first Rear-Admiral, Aircraft Carriers. He was conscious of the importance and potentiality of carriers and also of the danger of air attack. It seems to have been his influence that forced the completion of the new design in an unprecedently short time.

1936 Staff Requirements

The DNC produced a sketch design to match the staff requirements in June 1936. The following table shows how it compared with the old *Courageous* and the as yet uncompleted *Ark Royal*:

	Illustrious Design	Courageous	Ark Royal
Length b.p.	670'	735'	685'
Length w.l.	710'	779'	725'
Length o.a.	745'	786¼'	800'
Breadth extreme	94'	90'	94'
Standard displacement	23,000 tons	22,500 tons	22,000 tons
Mean standard draught	24' 11½''	F23' 10½''	22' 11''
Deep draught	28' 1½''	27' 6''	27' 4''
Shaft Horse Power	111,000	90,000	102,000
Speed (deep)	30 knots	29¾ knots	30 knots
Oil fuel	4400 tons	3900 tons	4400 tons
Endurance at 14 knots	12,000 miles	6,900 miles	12,000 miles
Aircraft capacity	36 TSR	48 TSR 24 dive bombers	52 TSR
Freeboard to Flight deck	43' 4½''	60' 9''	60' 7''

This comparison, particularly with the otherwise similar *Ark Royal*, shows how much the new design

sacrificed to the armoured hangar. Machinery and armament were similar (though not identical) to the *Ark*, but freeboard and aircraft capacity were much less than the other vessel. The *Ark*, like all her predecessors and contemporaries, was armoured only around the magazines and machinery, with a waterline belt and an armoured main deck.

However, the Admiralty welcomed the design. The Assistant Chief of Naval Staff minuted: '*Concur with the design generally. The protection afforded is excellent and she should be a very fine ship.*'. The Board of Admiralty approved the sketch design on 21 July 1936. After much hard work and overtime by the DNC (Sir Stanley Goodall) and his subordinates, the detailed specifications and plans were passed by the Board on 14 December of the same year.

The Washington Naval Treaty

Under one of the articles of the Washington Naval Treaty, signatories were obligied to give the other participants certain details, including standard displacement and aircraft complement, of new aircraft carriers. These details had to be given four months before laying the ship down. The relatively low aircraft complement of the new design compared to the displacement might well give away the fact that the Royal Navy was adopting heavy protection for its carriers. The Staff had already determined to keep this secret for as long as possible. The armoured carrier was considered virtually a new type of warship. If the secret could be kept from leaking till the lead ship was one year from completion, Britain would have stolen a march on the rest of the world to the extent of six ships of the new type already on the stocks. The final decision on the declaration seems to have been to report only the displacement. The aircraft complement was stated to depend on type carried, and the decision on this was not yet made.

Order and Construction

On 28 November 1936 the Admiralty invited tenders for the construction of the two new carriers. The firms addressed were John Brown, Cammell Laird, Fairfield, Harland and Wolff, Hawthorn Leslie, Scott's, Swan Hunter and Vickers Armstrong. The final date for submission of the tenders was 4 January 1937. The lowest tender was from Vickers Armstrong. They would build one ship at their Barrow yard and the other at the Walker yard on the Tyne. The tender for the ship to be built at Barrow was for the hull to cost £1,690,000. The machinery would also be built at Barrow and cost £705,000. The total cost would be therefore £2,395,000, not counting £17,950 for insurance. The vessel was to be completed in 36 months. Both Vickers Armstrong tenders were accepted on 13 January 1937.

The keel of the new ship was laid at Barrow on 27 April. Her yard number was 732. Two years later she was launched by Lady Henderson, at 1100 on 5 April 1939.

After the war broke out she was given the code 'job' number, J.3986. Her real name, *Illustrious*, had been allocated before her keel was laid. Completion was delayed by the addition of radar. She did not leave Barrow till 20 April 1940, instead of the January delivery date originally specified. As she left the shipyard she accidentally sank the tug, *Poolgarth*.

From Barrow she sailed to Liverpool. In the Gladstone Dock she was tested, inspected, and final adjustments were made. The two cast iron four-bladed propellers with which she had been launched were replaced by three-bladed phosphor-bronze ones.

Trials

She ran her acceptance trials in Liverpool Bay on 24 May 1940. As she left the Mersey her displacement was 27,950 tons. She drew 25ft 10½in forward, 27ft 7in amidships and 28ft 11in aft. Her dimensions as built were:

Length b.p. 672′ 10″   length o.a. 743′ 6⅜″
Breadth, extreme 95′ 8″
Depth of hull (hangar to keel) 44′ 3¾″.

The trials were run with an escort of three destroyers,

A well-known drawing by an official war artist—Cdr Rowland Langmaid—depicts Illustrious *and her screen parting company with 3rd Cruiser Squadron shortly before sunset on 11 November 1940. The carrier group carried out the Taranto raid while the cruisers destroyed an Italian convoy in the Straits of Otranto* (IWM)

and paravanes (whose fittings gave some trouble) were streamed. Despite a certain amount of vibration, Captain Boyd was pleased with his ship. She was then handed over by her contractors.

The next day flying trials commenced at 0500. She then returned to Liverpool for work on her crash barrier to be completed. On 30 May she sailed to the Clyde for degaussing trials. Next she arrived at Devonport for her D/F (direction finding) equipment to be calibrated. She had been intended to work up at Dakar, but that programme was now in the hands of Vichy. Instead, she sailed to Bermuda, and was damaged by heavy weather on her voyage out.

Refits: World War II

On 28 June she returned from Bermuda, and was taken in hand for a ten day refit at John Brown's Clydebank yard. The original external degaussing coil, some of which had been carried away, was replaced by an internal one. Work was carried out on both catapult and arresting gear.

This was her last spell in dockyard hands before she suffered from the attentions of *Fliegerkorps X*. During the dive bombing attacks of 10 January 1941 six 250kg and 500kg bombs hit her. One hit the after lift and threw it up on the flight deck; another went through the armoured deck into the hangar. Others destroyed pom-pom mounts, whilst three near misses strained the hull. The steering gear was out of action; the after guns silenced; the aircraft lift was blown out bodily; and the hangar set on fire. No other carrier withstood anything like this scale of punishment. It was a supreme justification of her design, a tribute to her constructors and to the heroism and skill of her crew that she survived to limp into Malta.

In Valetta she was hit by more bombs, and further strained by the mining effect of near misses. Despite this she was patched together to sail for the U.S.A. via Suez on 23 January 1941. During most of 1941 she lay in Norfolk Navy Yard refitting. The still neutral U.S.A. was giving valuable assistance to the British

10th January 1941: Illustrious *burning and out of control. The shattered lift and the petalled rim of the hole made by the only bomb to penetrate the flight deck armour are wreathed in the smoke from the fires burning in the after lift and the steam rising from the hot flight deck* (IWM)

war effort. Drawings and parts were shipped from Britain. Armour plates were replaced, a new lift installed, machinery, guns and fittings refurbished. American built Oerlikons were added to the armament.

The refit over, she sailed for home in the company of her sister, *Formidable*. Unfortunately, *Illustrious* rammed her sister's stern (16 December 1941), and did considerable, though happily superficial, damage to her own bows. This damage was repaired and new radar installed at Liverpool. It was not until the spring of 1942 that she sailed for the Indian Ocean.

In January 1943 she returned from the Eastern Fleet. Her subsequent refit by Cammell Laird lasted from February to early June. Flight deck arrangements were modified. Further changes were made in those constantly-altering items, radar and light AA guns.

After more service in the Mediterranean, she rejoined the Eastern Fleet. Whilst in the Indian Ocean she was refitted at Durban in mid-1944. Extra Oerlikons, and a new homing beacon were added. Her boilers were re-tubed, and she was fitted to refuel destroyers at sea.

By the time she was serving with the British Pacific Fleet her machinery and hull were showing signs of strain. The central propeller shaft, in particular, had never fully recovered from the stresses of the 1941 bombing. Severe vibrations were causing hull seams to open, and she was becoming a liability. In April 1945 she left the fleet and limped home at 19 knots.

A long refit began at Rosyth. She was to be converted to a flagship, her machinery renewed, her accommodation enlarged. Her armament and radar were to be altered yet again. However, the end of the war with Japan caused a reappraisal.

Refits: Post-war

On 19 September 1945 it was decided that she should replace the *Pretoria Castle* as trials carrier. By the end of the refit in early spring 1946, her appearance had altered considerably. She was given new bows and stern, reminiscent of the new Light Fleet Carriers. Her island had been rebuilt and the flight deck altered.

So much equipment had been added to the ship by this time that her stability had suffered considerably whilst her displacement had grown alarmingly, as this table shows:

Displacement in tons	Deep	Light
designed:	28,620	22,840
completed:	28,210	22,440
1946:	31,630	25,940

The freeboard of the flight deck with the ship in deep condition had diminished from 38·4ft to 36·6ft. This accentuated the bad tendency of this class to ship water over the flight deck when steaming at high speed into a head sea. It was reported that on one occasion waves in the Bay of Biscay bent the plates of the forward end of the flight deck right back. Between 1940 and 1946 the GM was reduced 16%, the maximum GZ 29% and the maximum righting moment by 23%.

S1 Multiple pom-pom jammed at an elevation of 80° by the jib of the mobile crane. The bomb, which had demolished the crane, had impacted on S2 pom-pom ahead of the island, but the detonation had been of a low order (IWM)

The growth in displacement was calculated as consisting of the following increases in weight:

SPECIFICATIONS
Machinery = 150 tons.
Aircraft equipment (heavier aircraft, more aircraft because of the deck park and increased stowage of bombs and ammunition) = 350 tons.
General equipment (Complement up from 1280 to 2000) = 285 tons.
Armament = 50 tons
Structure, incidentals etc. (extra structure, electrical equipment, ventilation, paint etc.) = 990 tons.
Splinter protection = 85 tons.
Petrol and flooding water (extra tanks) = 300 tons.
Oil fuel = 260 tons.
Unaccounted for = 570 tons.
    TOTAL = 2520 tons.

This increase was the cost of improvements in armament, radar, aircraft stowage and handling capacity. Aircraft carriers are more liable than most ships to increase in weight, particularly topweight, and none more so than *Illustrious*. She had been designed under the restrictions of the Naval Treaties and was therefore less capacious than she might have been.

Newly painted and repaired, Illustrious *lies at a buoy off Norfolk, Virginia. Type 285 gunnery radar has been fitted to the HA Directors, but no air warning radar is fitted. The flight deck has been built up aft and sponsons have been added to the quarters* (MoD (N))

January 1942, at Cammell Laird's Birkenhead yard: two views of the 'superficial damage' incurred in the collision with Formidable on 16 December. The ship's company recreation space (2 Deck) and the Cable Deck (3 Deck) have been laid bare, but the damage is remarkably confined. The usable flight deck is not affected and flying would have been possible, although the aerodynamic turbulence would have been considerable. The three 20mm Oerlikons mounted on the top of the island are covered but can be made out clearly   (MoD (N))

She had two more refits, both at Portsmouth. One in 1948, the other in 1950-1. Armament, radar and flying arrangements were all changed (though full details are not yet available).

At the end of September 1954 she was reduced to Class Three demilitarised reserve. She arrived at Faslane at the beginning of November 1956, and her reduction to scrap began.

Sister Ships

The sister ship built at the Walker yard was the *Victorious*. Two more were ordered under the 1937 Programme, *Formidable* and *Indomitable*. The latter was converted whilst building to an interim standard, pending completion of the later *Implacable* and *Indefatigable*. These latter three ships were given an extra half hangar, a concession to the need for larger aircraft complements. Thinner side armour compensated for this increase. All these sister vessels differed so much after modifications and refits that each needs a history to herself.

HMS ILLUSTRIOUS: SPECIFICATIONS
Protection

The original staff discussions of armoured carriers only involved designs with three-inch armoured flight decks. The suggestion was then made that protection should be provided against bombs striking under the eaves of the flight deck. This was later expanded to include protection of the hangar against shellfire as well as bombs.

The final design made the hangar into an armoured box, completely enclosed within the hull. The 458ft of the flight deck above the hangar was of 3in NC (non-cemented) plate, proof against plunging fire from 6in guns. It was also proof against 500lb semi armour-piercing bombs dropped from below 7000ft, 250lb s.a.p. from below 11,500ft or 1000lb armour-piercing bombs from 4500ft, theoretically. The hangar sides and ends were to be of 4in armour capable of resisting 6in gunfire at ranges greater than 7000 yards. Unfortunately the lifts could not be armoured within the treaty displacement, but the hangar lift openings could be closed by armoured shutters. The floor of the hangar, outside the central citadel, was of 1in 'D' quality steel plating to protect against splinters coming from below.

The bridge was protected by bullet proof plating. The main armoured deck, protecting machinery, magazines and fuel stowage, was made of 3in armour. Extending from the hangar deck to 5ft below the standard water line, and 30ft along the water line at either end of the citadel was the main belt of 4½in plate. At the ends of the belt, protection was carried across the ship by 2½in armoured partial bulkheads. The steering gear was also protected by 2½in bulkheads. The 3in armour over the steering gear continued forward until overlapped by the flight deck armour in order to protect the central shaft.

Underwater protection was provided along the length of the citadel by empty compartments (to dissipate the effect of an explosion) next to the outside of the hull, and inside them wing tanks for oil fuel, which were to be kept as full as possible with oil or water. This protection was believed to be proof against a 750lb charge in contact.

The Bottle-neck: Armour Plate Production

Modifications during building were caused by the parlous state of British armour plate production. After the peak period of the 1914-18 war, the lack of orders during the period of disarmament and depres-

sion had nearly killed the industry. Vital plant and skills had all but vanished. The result was a series of delays which affected the *Illustrious* less than her sisters.

The worst bottleneck was caused by slowness in milling the edges of plates. To save plate and time, the *Illustrious's* transverse bulkheads at the end of the hangars, and the deck were to be thinner than originally planned. An alternative solution was also found.

The armour plate for the flight deck was ordered from Messrs. Vitkovice of Morava Ostrava in Czechoslovakia. The rest of the armour was ordered from the British firms, Beardmore, Firth and Brown. Fortunately, although ordered after the Munich Settlement, the Czech armour arrived before war broke out, though consignments for other carriers were not completed in time. It was this Czech armour which was penetrated by the German bomb.

The Fire Hazard and Damage Control

Despite the damage done by this and other bombs, the fires started on 10 January 1941 did not become uncontrollable. Similar fires in American and Japanese carriers sank the ships. *Illustrious* overcame her blaze, as

Contrasts I: *Two starboard bow views of* Illustrious, *taken in 1940 (L/8) and 1942 (L/9) show a number of differences in radar and armament fittings. The Type 79 radar has been replaced by the more compact Type 281 aerial array, and the angular MF/DF aerial 'basket' on the foremast has been suppressed altogether. Type 285 gunnery radar has been fitted to the HA Directors and and one of the single 20mm Oerlikon mountings, added during the American refit, can be seen atop the island, immediately in front of the HA Director* (L/8—IWM)
(L/9—Cdr T. L. M. Brander DSC RN)

much due to the sealed hangar design, which isolated machinery spaces from the affected area, and good fire fighting arrangements, as to the armoured hangar itself.

Petrol is not a safe cargo for a warship. In British carriers this risk was reduced to a minimum by storing the aviation spirit in cylinders built into tanks which were kept flooded with seawater. This arrangement could become worrying when seawater temperature rose in the tropics, but the system worked. No British-built carrier was lost by fire, just as no armoured hangar carrier was sunk by bombs, or any other form of attack.

Apart from the 1941 repairs to the flight deck, the only wartime additions to protection were the large quantities of splinter-proof screens supplied for the crews of the light AA. However, immense strides were made in the practice of damage control. *Illustrious*'s Damage Control centre was installed next to the chapel in 1943.

Armament
The 4·5s
The original 1936 suggestion for a larger carrier included a possible armament of 16 5·25in guns. This was too heavy for a ship of *Illustrious*'s size, so a lighter gun, the 4·5in was chosen. The 4·5in Mk. III was developed from an army AA weapon, and was taken into naval service because of obvious advantages in shared guns and ammunition between the services.

These guns were mounted in eight twin turrets. The mountings were in groups of two, each in a sponson. Though countersunk into these, the top of each BD Mk. II mounting protruded slightly above the flight deck; this arrangement improved the field of fire, but provided an obstacle to aircraft operations. The mountings were made by Vickers, the guns by Beardmore, or the Royal Gun Factory.

The HA Directors
Each group of turrets ('A' and 'X' to starboard, 'B' and 'Y' to port) were controlled by their own high angle director (Mk. IV, HA) though each director could control an entire broadside. Although chiefly anti-aircraft weapons, the guns were perfectly capable of engaging surface targets. The grouping of the guns was intended to leave the midships portion of the flight deck clear of blast as an aircraft park. The distribution of the directors could be organised with more flexibility. 'A' director above the bridge and the two after directors presented few problems, but 'B' director had to be raised during building to give it a clearer field of view. Its position forward and to port made it a potential obstacle to aircraft taking off. In later vessels of the class this director was given hydraulic lowering gear, but this was not available in time for *Illustrious*.

Close Range Weapons: The Pom-Poms
Mk. VIII two pounder pom-poms were fitted for close range fire. They were, mounted in six Mk. VIA eight-barrelled mountings. Two superimposed forward and two at the rear of the island were designated S1, 2, 3 and 4. P1 and P2 on the port side of the ship were moved down to the gallery deck during contruction, as experience in the *Ark* had shown that their original position would obstruct flight deck operations. All the pom-poms and the mountings were made by

The 'yagi' aerial array of the Type 285 range-finding gunnery radar mounted on an HA Director. Note the retention of the visual range-finder and also of the 'spider's web' close-range visual gun-sight (J. D. Brown)

A light cruiser crosses Illustrious's wake as the carrier, 'hockey sticks' lowered, prepares to recover aircraft, heeling as she turns into wind　　　　　　　(IWM)

Vickers. Circular screens were added to S1 and S2 mounts, partly for protection, but mainly to preserve the smooth airflow found the island.

0·5''s, Oerlikons, Bofors and Others
There was some debate about fitting four multiple 0·5in machine guns before the ship was built. Another weapon proposed for use in bow and stern positions was a six-barrelled 0·661″ machine gun which never progressed further than the project stage. There was even a suggestion that a twin two-pounder being developed by the army might be used, but none of these suggestions came to anything. Despite this, the ship had a very respectable AA armament for her day. This was especially so because she had an adequate number of directors (fitted from the start for the pom-poms as well as the 4·5s), and could engage several targets at once. A minor item of curiosity was that two of the multiple pom-poms fitted came from the mined cruiser, *Belfast*.

The carrier was designed for, and apparently carried at the beginning of her career, four three-pounder saluting guns. These were probably landed early in the war, not to be returned until the conflict was over.

Originally a number of Lewis guns were to be carried to be used against strafing aircraft. There were more urgent requirements for these elsewhere, so none was fitted. As the war progressed so the light AA battery was strengthened. During the American refit the ship was given 10 U.S. built Oerlikon 20mm guns. By the time of the 1943 refit, when the policy was to replace single Oerlikons by twins, she seems to have acquired 16 twins and two singles. In the same refit, the 4·5in directors and pom-pom mountings were modified, and Mk. VI pom-pom directors fitted. The forward searchlights were moved, and replaced by the single Oerlikons mentioned earlier.

At Durban in 1944 extra tubs for more Oerlikons were added. Also one 40mm Bofors gun was fitted, replacing S2 pom-pom, and two others replaced Oerlikons in twin-powered mountings.

When she went into dock in 1945, the after 4·5in were to be removed to provide extra accommodation. The light AA would be increased by two twin Bofors on austerity mountings. The after 20mm were to be replaced by single two pounders. This scheme never came to pass, however, and instead the 4·5in were all retained. The remaining Oerlikons (18 in all) were concentrated aft in stern and quarter galleries, whilst 19 single Bofors were disposed along the side of the ship and on the island. The forward 4·5in mountings were given remote power control, whilst 'A' director was moved down from the bridge to make way for radar, and replaced the Bofors in S2 pom-pom position.

In her final post-war refits, the ship lost her remaining pom-poms, and instead was armed with two twin Bofors as well as the already existing singles, and was reduced to six Oerlikons aft.

Illustrious, steaming at high speed, overtakes a battleship during exercises in the Indian Ocean during the summer of 1942 (IWM)

Its undercarriage flexing with the heel of the ship, a Martlet II taxies forward to line up for take-off. The Flight Deck Officer, green flag raised and red flag held down, stands ready to wave off the aircraft (IWM)

ARRANGEMENT OF MOUNTING MARK II

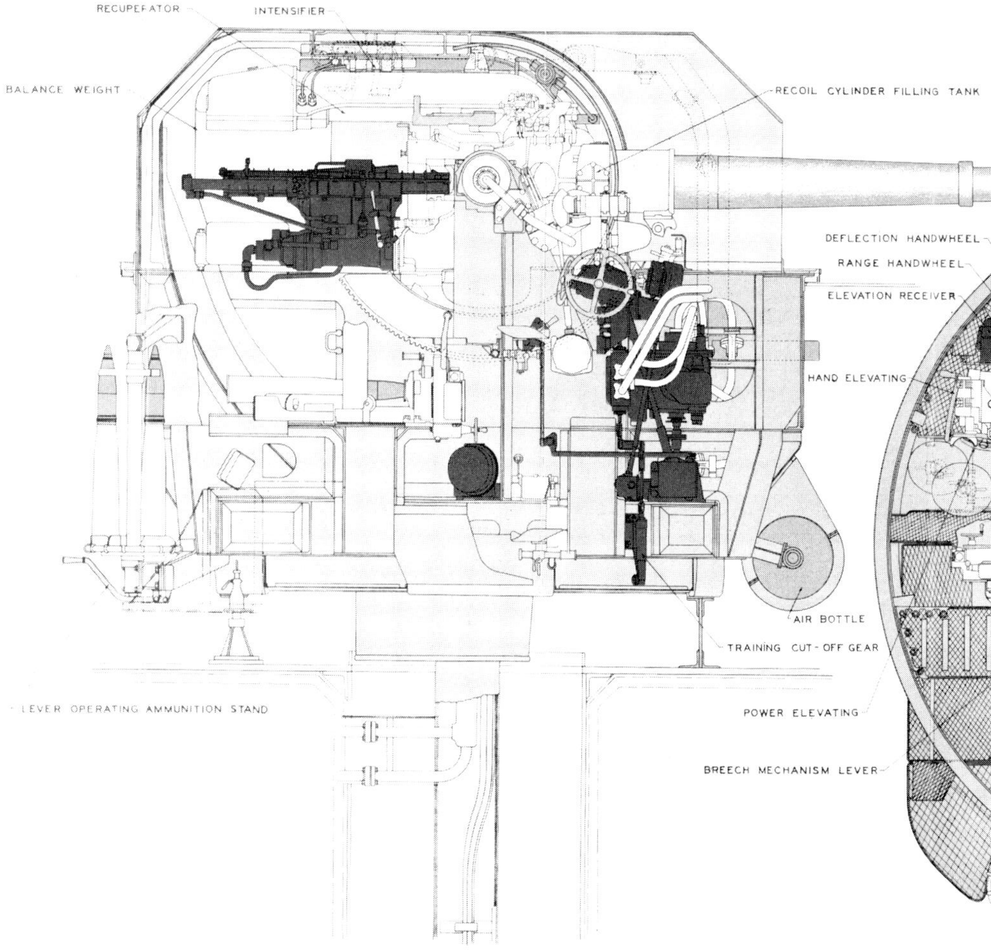

PLAN

RECUPERATOR

INTENSIFIER

BALANCE WEIGHT

RECOIL CYLINDER FILLING TANK

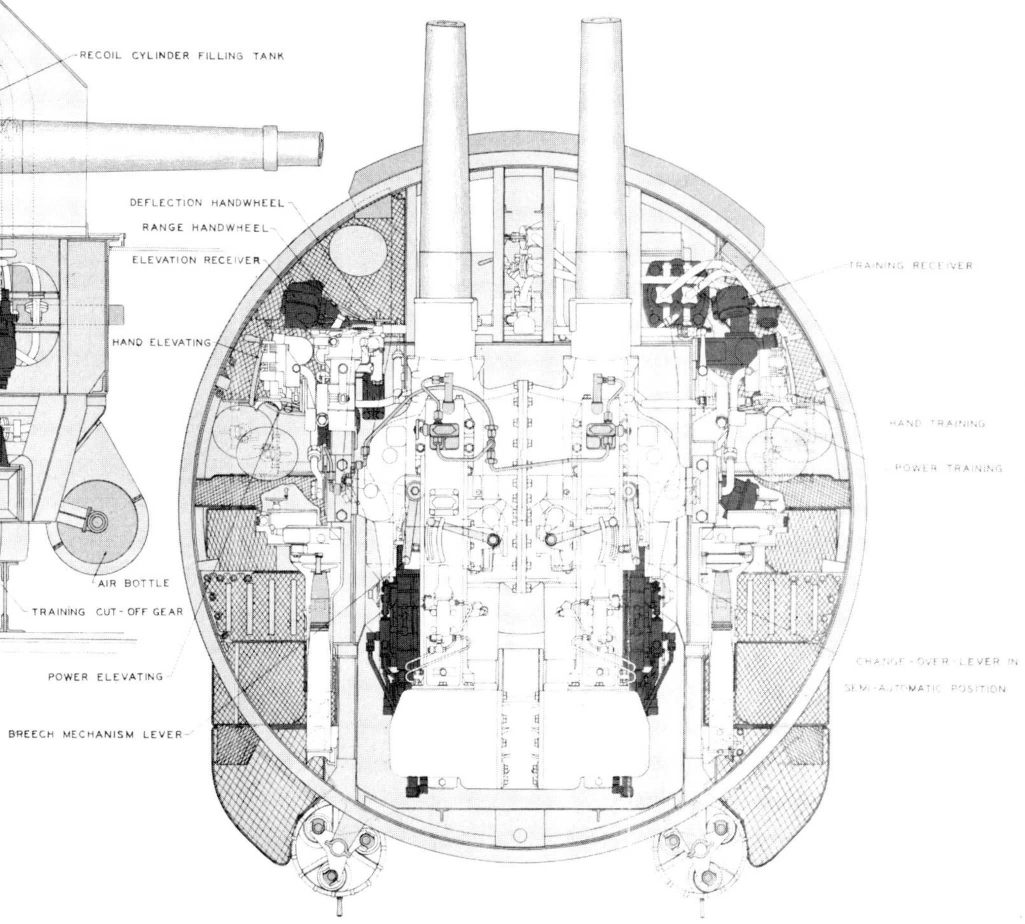

DEFLECTION HANDWHEEL

RANGE HANDWHEEL

ELEVATION RECEIVER

HAND ELEVATING

TRAINING RECEIVER

HAND TRAINING

POWER TRAINING

CHANGE-OVER LEVER IN SEMI-AUTOMATIC POSITION

AIR BOTTLE

TRAINING CUT-OFF GEAR

POWER ELEVATING

BREECH MECHANISM LEVER

LEVER OPERATING AMMUNITION STAND

RIGHT HAND SIDE ELEVATION

226

Ammunition Supply

Proposals to site the 4·5in magazines under the flight deck next to the guns had been ruled out on grounds of weight. Instead, shells were brought up from the conventionally-sited magazines by power hoists to the main deck. They were moved by power conveyor along that deck, and then by another power hoist to the gun deck. The magazines contained 400 rounds for each 4·5in barrel, 1800 for each pom-pom barrel, and also 200 star shell.

Radio and Radar

Radio

Originally *Illustrious* was intended to have a similar outfit of radio as the *Ark Royal*, though with two instead of four transmitting centres. A more satisfactory position was found for the cylindrical 72X (later 72DM) homing beacon. On the top of *Ark's* mainmast, it was moved down to the top of the tripod, thus freeing *Illustrious's* topmast for High Frequency Direction Finding (H/F D/F). A Medium Frequency D/F unit, type LM1 was also carried.

Wireless sets carried included types 56, 57, 52 L and 52 M, 405, 52 H and 49 C. Good radio communications to aircraft, other ships and to shore are particularly vital to a carrier.

Radar

In 1939 it was becoming increasingly obvious that the new invention, R.D.F. (radar), was equally important for warning of attack and for guiding her own aircraft. In November it was decided to accept a two-month delay in completion, and fit *Illustrious* with one of the first production SA radars. This type 79z equipment had separate transmitting and receiving aerials. The latter could be placed at the top of the mainmast, but a new mast had to be provided for the transmitter. It was placed just inboard of the after end of the island. Other members of the class were to have a telescopic mast in this position, but there was not time to fit such a refinement to *Illustrious*.

ARRANGEMENT OF MOUNTING MARK II

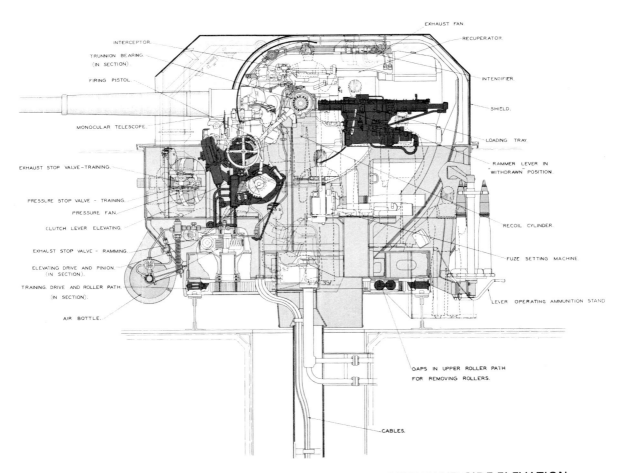

LEFT HAND SIDE ELEVATION

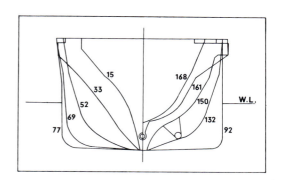

HMS *Illustrious* as she appeared when she launched the Fleet Air Arm attack on Taranto, 11 November 1940. She is shown wearing an overall medium grey, a colour used extensively by the Royal Navy from late 1940 until early 1941.

Deck colours and markings
Colour of the flight deck varied considerably at different times throughout the war as did the type and style of flight deck markings. The colour of the deck as shown applies to the 1940 period.

T. Brittain/M. Trim © Profile Publications Ltd

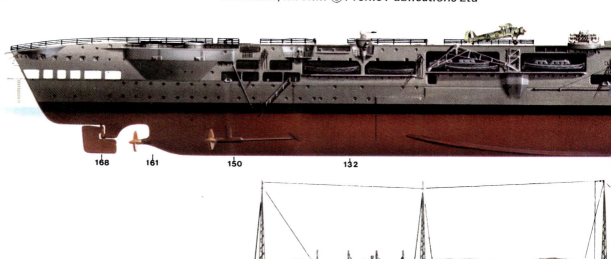

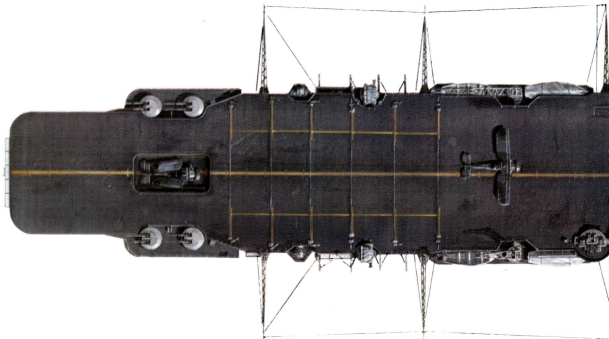

1. 'Flagship' of 819 Squadron, October 1940
2. Martlet II of 881 Squadron, Spring 1942
3. Fulmar I of 806 Squadron, October 1940

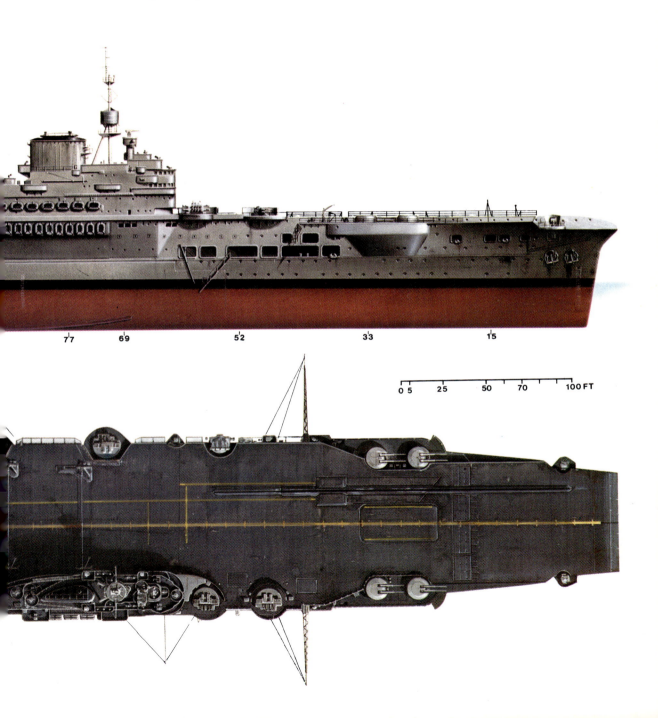

Tail-wheel just off the deck, a Martlet II passes the island. The detail of the Type 281 transmitting aerial can be seen clearly. The bandstand immediately abaft the funnel is a pom-pom director, while on the deck immediately below a single 20mm mounting fills the place designed for one of the 3pdr saluting guns (IWM)

Gunnery, Fighter Control, IFF Beacons and Jamming

At the end of the American refit (after the return to Britain) type 281 replaced the type 79 radar. Gunnery control type 285 radar was fitted to 'A' director (the other directors awaited a less bulky array which would not interfere with the flight deck operations). By early 1943 three out of the four directors were fitted with this device. The fourth was to be fitted with the improved mark IV radar, which was also to be retrospectively attached to the other towers. The pom-pom directors were given their own sets, 282M.

In the same 1943 refit, VHF fighter director radio sets and type 272 Mk. V target indicating radar were acquired. Type 281 was replaced by both 79M and 281M. Other additions included IFF (identification) sets, radar beacons and jamming sets.

At Durban in 1944 *Illustrious* was given an American YE homing beacon to supplement the old 72DM. The new beacon was mounted on a mast placed outside, and supported by, the funnel. It had been hoped to fit 277 (height-finder) and 293 (target indicator) at the same time, but this proved impracticable as the sets were not available.

The 1945-6 refit saw American SMI radar replacing 'A' director on the bridge, 293M, 281BQ and 961 were fitted on a new mainmast. VHF D/F was added, and the island was reconstructed with new radar rooms. Considerable changes were made to radar and communications equipment during the post-war refits, but full details of these are not yet available.

FLIGHT DECK, AIRCRAFT AND HANGAR ARRANGEMENTS

(*Note:* Details of changes in the ship's aircraft complement will be found in the second volume of this work.)

The Flight Deck

The original design of the ship was for a flight deck 745ft* long, divided in two by a single barrier 365ft from the bows. Six arrester wires were stretched across the deck. The 60ft wide hangar was divided into three by two steel fire curtains. Two electrically operated lifts at either end of the hangar measured 45' × 22'. These lifts, built by Frazer and Chalmers, were bigger and more powerful than any previously fitted to a carrier. They could lift six tons.

Stowage for 50,000 Imperial gallons of petrol was provided in the tanks already described (see under **Protection**). Bomb stowage was to be provided for:

250—500lb	216—250lb	432—100lb
576—20lb	4000—8½lb	54—18in torpedoes.

This outfit was later modified several times, the relative proportions of the different weapons being varied, but this list provides a good idea of the volume of stowage required. Two pairs of bomb lifts served both hangar and flight deck. A larger lift was provided for the torpedoes, the bodies being stowed in the hangar and the warheads in the bomb-room.

Alterations made to the design before the vessel was

---

*With a useful length of 620ft, the remainder being the curved round-downs.

launched included widening of the hangar to 62ft, and slightly increasing the length to 456ft. The overall length of the flight deck went up to 753ft 3in. Minimum width, abreast the island, was 69ft.

The Catapult, Windscreens and Crash-Barriers

One catapult was fitted, on the port side of the flight deck. Originally there was some question whether it should be an 'accelerator', which was fitted with a trolley to take the aircraft, or 'assisted take off gear' which could catapult the aircraft off on its own undercarriage. The latter was faster and easier to operate, caused less obstructions, and was chosen. The example fitted was a hydro-pneumatic device, which was capable of trolley-launching a maximum weight of 11,000lb at 66 knots. Three aircraft a minute could be catapulted. By 1943, the catapult was launching 14,500lb at 66 knots using the tail down method.

By the end of the early 1943 refit, all of *Illustrious*'s wires were double reeved, and two had been added abaft the after lift. The total number of wires was now eight. Number one wire was only 44½ft from the after end of the flight deck, thereby greatly increasing the effective area of the deck. The catapult was made more powerful during the refit to take the heavier aircraft with heavier warloads that were now operating from carriers. It could now launch a 20,000lb load.

The 1945/6 refit, with its modifications to bow and stern, reduced the number of obstacles preventing the efficient use of the flight deck. Two extra wires were fitted and another barrier. After the decision to convert her to a trials carrier she was given *Pretoria Castle*'s camera boom, and was also fitted with television to record landings. The lifts were enlarged to 48′×22¾′ and strengthened to take the new generation of naval aircraft.

In front of the forward lift were four 10ft high windscreens which were normally stowed flush with the flight deck. They could be raised to shelter aircraft parked on deck but they were not totally effective in giving shelter, and tended to flex and distort when aircraft ran over them in the stored position. Despite some complaints they were retained.

Illustrious on completion had two crash barriers fitted in place of the original one. Wires number 4 and 6 were double reeved (and found to work much better

The discrepancy in levels between the Type 281 radar transmitting (aft) and receiving aerials resulted in a disappointingly poor detection range against aircraft throughout the ship's second commission   (IWM)

than the others). Before going to Bermuda an extra 'trickle' wire was fitted 70ft short of number 1 barrier. This soon proved its worth, stopping aircraft which would otherwise have damaged themselves in the barrier.

Despite initial mistrust, the pilots soon accepted the new-fangled barrier with enthusiasm, but found that more wires were needed further aft, though nothing was done immediately.

Fire Precautions

Whilst at Norfolk Navy Yard, the steel fire curtains which had splintered and caused casualties when the bomb exploded in the hangar, were replaced by Fearnought curtains. These asbestos curtains would give way to blast, but fall back to their original position to prevent fire spreading afterwards. Experiments before 1930 had proved the superiority of these curtains to steel ones, and *Furious** had been fitted with them. By the time *Ark Royal* and her successors were designed, the experiments seem to have been forgotten.

On 2 April 1942 a fire in 'B' Hangar was caused by a naked light bulb setting some netting ablaze. This resulted in the fitting of additional sprinklers to spray

*See Warship Profiles Nos. 23 and 24.

Looking a little weather-beaten, Illustrious *proceeds at slow speed off the South African coast as she returns to the United Kingdom in January 1943*
(IWM)

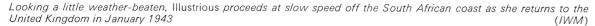

On return to the United Kingdom in February 1943, the ship was used for flying trials of certain new aircraft types. Here the prototype Seafire FIII (MA970) is folded. The slot of the HIII hydraulic catapult track can be seen at bottom right
(*IWM*)

De-ammunitioning in the Clyde, February 1943: 2pdr pom-pom ammo boxes being loaded on to a pallet for hoisting into a lighter. The arrester wires have been unrigged. Note the raised HA Director behind the slings of the crane. (*The carrier on* Illustrious's *port quarter is the old* Argus, *in use at this time as the deck-landing training carrier*)   (*IWM*)

the deckhead, and to supplement the main system which had shown its worth in January 1941.

Aircraft Handling Machinery

As *Illustrious* was commissioning in May 1940, she acquired a mobile crane. This was diverted from a Canadian order and rushed from Loughborough, where it was made, to Liverpool. 'Jumbo' was a $2\frac{1}{2}$ ton petrol-electric crane, weighing $6\frac{3}{4}$ tons and could not be used on some parts of the deck. Destroyed during the 1941 bombing, an American replacement was provided; *Illustrious* left the States with two small tractors as well, which proved very useful in marshalling the deck park. By 1944 she had four tractors on charge for this purpose.

Complement and Habitability

Although a carrier is a large ship, it is difficult to find space for the large numbers of hands required to operate the ship and her aircraft. As the numbers of guns, radar sets, and aircraft embarked increased, so it became progressively more difficult to find room for more men on the already crowded mess decks of the *Illustrious*. A further complication was the creation of a special deck-handling party which rapidly grew to 80 from 30 hands, and which was not available for other duties while at 'Flying Stations'. The size of the problem grew as follows:

Unfused 4·5in. rounds arrive on the flight deck via the bomb/torpedo lift on the starboard side (aft) of the flight deck. The Sergeant RM is leaning on the armoured hatch which was lowered when the lift was not in use
(*IWM*)

	Aircraft	Crew		
1936 design	36	1256 (including 425 F.A.A.)		
1937 estimate	36	1274	,,	?	,,
1940	33	1229	,,	?	,,
1941 after refit	—	1326	,, ·	500	,,
1943 after refit	46	1831	,,	?	,,
1944 with B.P.F.	57	1997	,,	?	,,
1948 trials carrier	—	1090	,,	157	,,

All figures are shown as a private ship: when she

acted as a flagship she carried about 20 more personnel.

As her complement grew all recreational spaces were taken up as accommodation. By 1945 the Captain's day cabin had been turned into offices; all officers' cabins were double-bunked; and ratings' accommodation was at such a premium that all the after 4·5in guns were to be sacrificed for extra messes. Many of the boat flats had already been taken over for this purpose.

The fact that the ship was far below peacetime standards of habitability was one reason for the length of the 1945-6 refit. Having her as a trials carrier meant that her complement could be reduced to a reasonable number. The addition of electrical cooking equipment

General view of the de-ammunitioning process; handling canisters litter the deck as the 4·5in. rounds are brought up for packing. At top right the bomb lift can be seen and, at top centre, the uncovered top of the lowered HA Director can barely be discerned
(*IWM*)

in the galley, and a laundry capable of coping with 2000 men would have made the cramped life a little more comfortable for a full complement.

During the long time she spent in tropical waters, life in her crowded mess decks must have been very unpleasant. The officers had a little extra room, and some pilots were known to have indulged themselves by using the open space of the wardroom as an ideal place to fly cordite powered model aircraft.

As in all ships at sea, there was always the chance of an accident, possibly fatal, from moving aircraft on slippery flight decks, or merely from falling off the flight deck during a game of deck hockey.

At the end of her career, *Illustrious* knew crowding again when she made two voyages carrying troops and their equipment to Cyprus at the time of the Canal Zone troubles.

Added electronics brought their problems too. To maintain the many compartments with their black boxes at the required temperature and humidity, air-conditioning plants had to be installed, thus cutting into the already cramped accommodation and stowage space without benefiting general habitability.

Captain R. L. B. Cunliffe RN, Captain of Illustrious *from August 1942 until May 1944* (IWM)

Lying at anchor in the Clyde in the summer of 1943, Illustrious *displays her third camouflage scheme. The flight deck has been lengthened yet again, this time by building up the forward round-down.* (IWM)

A port bow view of Illustrious *in the Clyde in July 1943 showing the revised air warning radar installation. The combination of Types 79 (foremast) and 281 (pole), each with a combined transmit/receive aerial, not only overcame the problem of poor performance but also improved the volumetric radar coverage by reducing the gaps in the beam radiation pattern* (IWM)

Illustrious *refuels an R-class destroyer en route for the second attack on Sabang, July 1944. The connection point in the carrier is located in the starboard midships boat stowage and the cable can be seen lying across the boat crutches before being slung outboard over a trough slung from the starboard crane. Approximately 70 tons per hour could be passed to a destroyer using this method* (IWM)

Machinery

Carriers have to be fast in order to create a high relative wind speed over their decks, a factor vital for efficient aircraft operation. These ships also have to be man-oeuvrable in order to turn into wind quickly. To fulfil these requirements *Illustrious*, like *Ark Royal*, was given a triple-screw installation. Six three-drum type boilers, placed in three groups of three in separate boiler rooms, supplied steam for three sets of geared Parsons turbines. All the machinery was built at Barrow.

Probably because of the lack of time available for design work, the three-shaft installation was only a qualified success. Although the Germans had used such an arrangement for capital ships and liners since the First World War, it was new to the Royal Navy.

In her sea trials *Illustrious* reported a certain amount of vibration, particularly of the island superstructure. This was not serious, and it was not until the end of the war that the problem became acute. By then the delayed results of hard usage and action damage were becoming apparent.

In 1944 *Victorious* was given a new rudder, when she became almost impossible to steer. It appeared that the rudders of all the class were over-balanced. Modifications were made to *Illustrious* during the 1945-6 refit to cure this.

Vibration, Handling and Speed

Worse problems, both of vibration and subsequent leakage, were experienced by *Illustrious* in early 1945. The chief cause was the deteriorating state of the gland packing of her central shaft. Before the Sakishima Gunto operations, the central propeller was removed. She operated for a time with a maximum speed of 24 knots, and could only rid herself of serious vibration by steaming at 19 knots or less.

The USN had found similar problems in the 1930s. The American solution was to fit a five-bladed propeller, which would increase the frequency, but greatly reduce the intensity of the vibrations. One was fitted to *Illustrious*'s centre shaft in 1945/6. It was apparently successful. In 1947, increasing vibration was recorded, this time caused by wear of the wing shafts.

Performance in trials is summarised in the following table:

	s.h.p.	r.p.m.	knots
Design	111,000	—	30
24/5/1940	113,700	234·2	about 30
1948	110,600	227½	29
1950	111,450	225·1	29·2

In her acceptance trials, she was streaming her paravanes, and had no accurate method of telling her speed, She could probably reach 31 knots under full power.

On the same occasion she turned at full speed with 35° of rudder and only heeled 6°. Her helmsman said that she was not very hard to steer, but he would not like to keep the effort up for too long. Her design speed was 30 knots in deep condition; operational speed was 29 knots with one boiler shut down. In deep condition at half power she could make about 25 knots.

The hangar, looking forward. The Corsair's wingtips had to be cropped to give a maximum folded height of 15ft 6in. in order to fit it into an armoured carrier's hangar. The capacity of the hangar varied considerably, depending upon the types of aircraft embarked, but up to 20 Corsairs and 16 Avengers could be stowed *(IWM)*

Contrasts II: *Not only the types of aircraft and styles of 'batting' have changed between the summer of 1942 and 1944. Top—a Swordfish of 810 Squadron taxies forward as the batsman, festooned with cabling for the lighted bats, awaits astern. Below—the batsman watches an Avenger I of 851 Squadron bounce after picking up a wire. On the deck, the domes supporting the wires at the swivel shackles have been removed, and the wires are held up by centre-line bow-springs. The radar arrays on the island have undergone further change: now that the transmitter and receiver can be incorporated in the same aerial, a 281 is mounted on a pole-mast moved to a position immediately abaft the funnel. Above the 281 is the 'hayrake' aerial of the Type 243 IFF interrogator. At the foremast-head is the Type 79B aerial, surmounted by its 243 IFF* (Both IWM)

Oil Fuel, Electrical Power and Inter-flooding

Stowage was provided in wing tanks and double bottoms for 4460 tons of oil fuel.

Electric power was provided by six 400kW generators, two in the wing engine rooms, the other four on the main deck. As the war continued so the size and number of pumps grew.

The *Indomitable* was hit by a torpedo in 1943, and probably only saved from disastrous inter-flooding of the boiler rooms via the boiler uptakes by the calmness of the sea. After this painful reminder of how the *Ark Royal* was lost, the Admiralty ordered the heightening of uptake bulkheads in all carriers. This was not, however, carried out in *Illustrious* until the 1945-6 refit.

Structure

The armoured hangar and flight deck of the *Illustrious* formed an integral part of the hull, and provided a large part of the strength of that hull. This was very unlike contemporary American and Japanese practice, in which the hangar was an exposed box on top of the hull, and the flight deck a platform on top of that.

The British ships had built up bows and sterns, merging with the flight deck into a clean aerodynamic shape, which was all the more necessary because of the relatively low height of the flight deck above the water. *Illustrious* had been designed with careful attention to aerodynamic considerations. The aerofoil shape of the island smoothed the airflow round it, and only caused turbulence over the flight deck when the airflow was at more than 15° to the ship's head.

This was in great contrast to American carriers, which were aerodynamic misfits, almost designed to create turbulence. The Americans could afford this: their stronger aircraft could land faster, and therefore cope better with turbulence.

Alterations made to *Illustrious's* structure early in her existence included stiffening of the superstructure and of the forward searchlight sponsons, which were vulnerable to storm damage, in an attempt to obviate vibration.

There was little novel about the construction of the hull below the armoured hangar. The assymetric moment due to the weight of the island to starboard was countered by making the port side wing oil tanks 15in wider than those to starboard. With additions to the superstructure this was soon no longer adequate and, in 1941, 400 tons of permanent ballast were stowed in the port wing compartments.

Boats

The original complement of boats was: one 35ft admiral's barge, two 35ft fast motor boats, one 35ft crash boat, two 32ft motor cutters, one 25ft fast motor boat, two 32ft lifeboat cutters, one 16ft fast motor dinghy, two 27ft whalers, and two 14ft sailing dinghies. This list changed from time to time, generally by reduction in the numbers to make way for items of equipment, extra messing space, or guns. The main life-saving equipment of the ship was not the boats, but the two rows of Carley life rafts outboard of the island.

The boats were hoisted in and out by two large electric cranes, which could also be used for loading or off-loading aircraft or stores.

In 1945, the *Illustrious* carried a 25ft motor boat which had originally belonged to the *Hood*.

Other Fittings

The ship was equipped with three 160cwt anchors. She was commissioned with four 44in searchlights in bow and stern sponsons, but these soon made way for anti-aircraft guns, and were moved to less exposed positions.

When the ship was based in Alexandria in 1940, and communications with the squadrons based on shore was difficult, two motor bicycles were unofficially acquired. They proved so useful that the Captain

Illustrious after her 1945/46 refit. The most significant alterations to the hull have been made at her extremities; the flight deck has been lengthened, the forward round-down completely re-shaped and the Oerlikon sponsons aft have been extended to meet the 4·5in. sponsons, with plating at the 'corners' (MoD (N))

As well as the alterations to the structure, the close-range AA armament has also been changed, with 40mm Bofors sprouting from the top of the island and from the port-side sponsons. S2 pom-pom mounting has been suppressed and in its place the HA Director has been installed, replaced on top of the island by the Type 277 height-finding radar. A single Type 960 air warning radar is mounted on a new tripod mast abaft the island, with a Carrier-Controlled Approach talk-down radar on the vertical leg of the tripod. Outboard of the funnel is the characteristic 'hayrake' aerial of the YE beacon (MoD (N))

recommended them to the Admiralty for issue to all carriers.

There is not the space here to deal with the full complexities of the internal arrangements of a carrier, the tools of the repair shops, the immensely complicated business of running the victualling, or the naval stores, of so large a ship. However, the author has attempted to demonstrate that the carrier was more than a convenient flat-top on which aircraft could land, central to her existence though that function was.

Conclusions

Were the armoured hangar carriers a successful design?

Certainly they succeeded in surving the war despite heavy attacks and damage. *Illustrious* in 1941, and her sisters with the British Pacific Fleet at the end of the war, gave conclusive proof of their ability to survive and come back fighting after attacks which would have sunk or devastated any other carrier.

Both Americans and Japanese paid the design the compliment of copying many of its features. Both the *Midways* and *Taiho* had armoured decks and built-up bows. However, neither of the other two main builders of aircraft carriers copied the full armoured hangar, for the very good reason that circumstances were different. Though America was at one stage, late in the war, so impressed by our design; and we, in our turn, by theirs, that equal numbers of *Illustrious* type vessels and *Essex* class ships were swapped between the two navies, this interesting mutual abandonment of

principles never took place.

For the Royal Navy in 1940, the *Illustrious* was the best type of carrier. Germany and Italy had air superiority, our own aircraft were obsolescent or worse, radar was a new and untried invention. A carrier capable of putting up a good anti-aircraft barrage and of absorbing heavy punishment was vital.

Later, during the offensive in the Pacific, British carriers compared badly with those of her American ally. The Americans had better aircraft, superior flight deck organisations and doctrines, and larger aircraft complements (this was the stage when the *Ark Royal* might have come into her own had she not been sunk). An armoured flight deck was far less suitable on which to marshal aircraft than the American wood-covered deck. Deck edge lifts serving the American type of open hangar (in which aircraft could warm up their engines before coming on deck) made the swift preparation of a strike far easier. (Though, after the war, experiments were made with aircraft warming up inside *Illustrious*'s hangar: it was possible but unpleasant.)

It was not until the onslaught of Japanese Kamikazes that the Americans appreciated what had already been demonstrated by *Illustrious*'s ordeal in 1941. This was that the sacrifices involved in building an armoured hangar carrier sometimes paid off. A smaller and more awkward deck, and fewer aircraft was better than a smashed and blazing deck, or a carrier at the bottom of the ocean.

DIMENSIONS & PARTICULARS

Length	1940	1942	1945
Overall	740ft	740ft	748ft 6in
Flight deck *	620ft	670ft	740ft
Beam (flight deck at island)	95ft 9in	95ft 9in	95ft 9in
Draught (Aft)	28ft 10in	29ft	29ft 3in
Lifts	45ft long × 22ft wide, to carry 14,000lb aircraft weight		
Hangar Overhead Clearance	16ft	15ft 9in	16ft
Furnace Fuel Oil	4850 tons	4850 tons	4839 tons
Range	—	—	6300 nautical miles at 25 knots
Aviation Fuel	50 660 Imp. gallons	—	50,540 Imp. gallons
Ship's Armament	16×4·5in DP (8×2)	16×4·5in DP (8×2)	16×4·5in DP (8×2)
	48×2pdr (6×8)	48×2pdr (6×8)	40×2pdr (5×8)
		10×20mm (10×1)	3×40mm (3×1)
			52×20mm (19×2, 14×1)
Aircraft Complement	15 Fulmars	25 Martlets	36 Corsairs
	18 Swordfish	6 Fulmars	16 Avengers
	(September)	15 Swordfish	(March)
		(September)	
Aircraft Torpedoes	42 18in (British)	42 18in (British)	30 22·4in (American)
Depth Charges	72	72	144
Mines	24	24	—

*Flight deck length is from the top of the forward to the top of the after round-down.

Commanding Officers
Captain D. W. Boyd DSC RN — January 1940
Acting Captain G. S. Tuck RN — February 1941
Captain A. G. Talbot DSO — October 1941
Captain R. L. B. Cunliffe — August 1942
Captain C. E. Lambe CB CVO — May 1944
Captain W. D. Stephens — July 1945

Flag Officers
Rear Admiral A. L. St G. Lyster CVO DSO, (RA (Aircraft Carriers) Mediterranean Fleet) — August 1940—January 1941
Rear Admiral D. W. Boyd OBE DSC, (RA (A) Eastern Fleet) — 1942
Rear Admiral C. Moody (RA (A) Home Fleet and RA (A) Eastern Fleet) — May 1943—June 1944

Comparison between this 1940 starboard beam view and later photographs will show the successive alterations to the effective length of the flight deck. As built, the usable deck extends from the after end of the 4·5in. sponson forward to a point above the searchlight sponson
(MoD (N))

The last big occasion: Illustrious *moored off Spithead for the Coronation Review in June 1953. Little further change was incorporated during her final refit in 1952 apart from the complete suppression of the pom-poms, the removal of all Oerlikons, and the fitting of a modernised Type 277*
(G. A. Osbon)

Acknowledgments:

I particularly wish to thank the Curator of Naval Drawings, Bath, and his department for their assistance. My gratitude is also due to Mr Squires and other members of the Staff of the Imperial War Museum.

Mr Judd of Vickers Limited provided much useful information, for which I am most grateful.

J. D. Brown, Alan Raven and John Wingate have all been most kind and helpful.

I would also like to thank the friends and colleagues at Greenwich who have helped, particularly George Osbon, and, as ever, Antony Preston.

Last, but not least, to one Martlet pilot of 881 Squadron who flew from *Illustrious* and made her name and shape familiar to me: *Leo Etiam Alatus Est.*

Bibliography:

I found the following books useful:

Polmar N.: AIRCRAFT CARRIERS (*London 1969*).
Popham H.: INTO WIND (*London 1969*).
Brown J. D.: CARRIER OPERATIONS, Vol. 1 (*London 1968*)
Poolman K.: ILLUSTRIOUS (*London 1955*).
JANE'S FIGHTING SHIPS (*London, various dates*)

Warship Series Editor: JOHN WINGATE, DSC

These two pictures show Illustrious *after her 1945/46 refit. The most significant alterations to the hull have been made at her extremities: the flight deck has been lengthened, the forward round-down completely re-shaped and the Oerlikon sponsons aft have been extended to meet the 4.5in sponsons with plating at the 'corners'.*

Flying trials, June 1940: A Skua is lined up between the parallel white lines (the span of a Swordfish) used to position aircraft for take-off and to assist with line-up when landing. Nine arrester wires are fitted and the two lowered barriers can be seen abreast the rear end of the island. The catapult trolley is at the forward end of the track and, at the after end, more white line-up markings can be seen, these being used as guides to align the aircraft with the trolley

(Cdr T. L. M. Brander)

Another view of Illustrious *before she became operational. The indentations in the port side of the flight deck, between the 4·5in. batteries are, from for'd to aft: a lowered HA Director, two multiple pom-pom mountings, the port crane, another HA director, and a pom-pom director. The shadow of the after (transmitting) Type 79 radar antenna can be seen on the deck*

(MoD (N))

HMS Illustrious
by David Brown

Work-up

Illustrious's flying trials were probably the shortest on record—a single day sufficing to test arrester wires and accelerator in conjunction with the current and soon-to-enter-service aircraft types—the Swordfish, Fulmar and Albacore. The trials went well and the pilots commented favourably on the deck, comparing her with previous carriers: the deck was no wider than *Ark Royal's* but the difference in the height above the water —some 16ft—gave the illusion that *Illustrious* was beamier.

Final contractor's and dockyard modifications occupied the ship between 3-21 June 1940, additional delays having arisen from generator defects. The delay was sufficient to occasion the political decision to change the work-up area from Dakar to the safe waters of the western Atlantic.

With *Illustrious* went the 21 Swordfish of her two torpedo-spotter-reconnaissance squadrons—815 and 819, and nine fighters of 806 Squadron. The latter was

in the process of re-arming with Fairey Fulmars after a short but hectic three-month life flying Blackburn Skuas and Rocs from shore bases; three Fulmars were all that could be spared, together with four Skuas and two Rocs. The aircrew were nearly all experienced personnel and the work-up off Bermuda progressed without major incident. The lack of a night-flying airfield ashore meant that the Swordfish pilots became night-qualified aboard the carrier much earlier than they would normally have done, and this in itself shortened the work-up period.

Two innovations marked *Illustrious's* flying work-up —the safety barrier and the deck-landing control officer (the 'batsman'). Both had been used before, but not in conjunction by the Royal Navy since May 1939 or by the Fleet Air Arm before that date. The barrier was intended to preserve aircraft parked in the forward deck park from an aircraft which missed the arrester wires on landing: its effect was to speed up flying opera-

An early casualty—A Swordfish I of either 815 or 819 Squadron comes to rest in the safety barrier during the work-up off Bermuda. Note that only the six after arrester wires have been retained, three forward units being suppressed and the 'trickle wire' added in their place, rove to the barrier retardation unit   (MoD (N))

tions, as aircraft landing could do so at much shorter intervals than under the previous 'clear deck' system, in which the aircraft ahead had to be struck down and the lift returned to flight deck level before the next could land. The appointment of a designated batsman brought a degree of standardisation to the hitherto somewhat intuitive art of landing control. In the course of 300 deck-landings during the trials and work-up programme, only six accidents occurred and in only one of these was the aircraft badly damaged.

Illustrious returned to the United Kingdom on 23 July. She spent three weeks storing ship and setting her defects to rights before proceeding to Scapa Flow for flying exercises with her full aircraft complement. During her time off Bermuda, the Admiralty had decided to deploy her to the Mediterranean Fleet, based on Alexandria; only the old, small *Eagle* was there, with an *ad hoc* fighter complement of three Sea Gladiators, with which she had to defend herself and the Fleet against the much faster Italian bombers. *Illustrious's* fighter complement was adjusted accordingly: 806 Squadron embarked with 15 Fulmars while 815 Squadron was reduced by three Swordfish. All 33 aircraft were stowed in the hangar—the possibility of a permanent deck-park of fighters had already been considered, but there were just not enough naval aircraft to permit this.

⤳ MEDITERRANEAN 1940-41 ⤳

Rear-Admiral A. L. St G. Lyster shifted his flag of Rear Admiral Aircraft Carriers (Mediterranean) to *Illustrious* on 19 August 1940, sailed from Scapa three days later and headed east from Gibraltar on 30 August, in company with the battleship *Valiant* and two C-class AA cruisers. Also in company was the full might of Force H, built around *Ark Royal*, and the two forces remained in company until dusk on 1 September, when Force H turned to the west leaving *Illustrious*,

who had that afternoon launched her first operational sorties, and her consorts to head for the rendezvous with the Mediterranean Fleet, to the south of Malta.

The Fleet had been covering the reinforcement of Malta and when all units had concentrated early in the afternoon of 2 September, it turned towards the Dodecanese for the first offensive operation by carrier-based aircraft in the Eastern Mediterranean. 806 Squadron had already drawn blood—two shadowers and a bomber had been shot down and two others damaged in the first full day of combat for the Fulmar. The experience was obviously salutary as far as the Regia Aeronautica was concerned, for no shadowers bothered the Fleet on 3 September, as it headed for the strike on Rhodes.

At dawn on 4 September, eight Swordfish of 815 and 819 squadrons bombed Calato airfield, setting aircraft and buildings on fire with 250lb bombs. All returned safely, but four of the dozen Swordfish launched by *Eagle* to strike the neighbouring Maritza airfield were shot down by Fiat CR42 fighters—the only occasion on which enemy fighters interfered with a Mediterranean Fleet carrier strike. Italian bombers which attacked the Fleet as it retired to Alexandria were met by the Fulmars, which shot down one and damaged three others. Three Savoia-Marchetti SM 79-IIs broke through the patrols but missed the ships: this did however give *Illustrious's* 4·5in batteries the chance to open fire in earnest for the first time.

Benghazi
The carrier had only 10 days in Alexandria to allow her aircrew to become acclimatised. Four spare Fulmars which had been brought out were disembarked and a

Illustrious goes to War. Valiant and Illustrious seen from Ark Royal, on the afternoon of 1 September 1940, as they steam through the Mediterranean towards Malta
(MoD (N))

Swordfish was embarked to replace one lost in an accident, and *Illustrious* sailed on 15 September to attack Benghazi. This was to be a diversion for a cruiser bombardment of Bardia, but the 15 Swordfish which were flown off shortly after midnight on 16/17 September achieved one of the greatest successes enjoyed by any of *Illustrious's* air groups.

Nine aircraft of 815 Squadron dive-bombed shipping in the harbour, while all six of 819's Swordfish laid a mine apiece in the entrance, unobserved by the defences which were busy missing the dive-bombers. 815 Squadron sank the destroyer *Borea* and two merchant ships totalling 10,160 tons—a considerable feat with 250lb bombs, but the effect of the mines was not immediate. Over the next few days the six mines claimed four victims, sinking the destroyer *Aquilone* and two smallish ships (1700 tons) and damaging a modern motor ship. All 15 Swordfish returned safely.

Malta Convoys

The Fleet was out again at the end of September, covering Malta reinforcements. On 29 September, SM 79s again broke through the fighter patrols and a gaggle of torpedo-bombers delivered the first attack on *Illustrious*. On the next day a reconnaissance Swordfish sighted the Italian battlefleet—five battleships and seven cruisers—150 miles to the south-west. The enemy were also protecting a convoy, bound for Tripoli, and as only nine Swordfish could be mustered for a torpedo strike which could not be followed up by battleship

action before nightfall, it was decided to shadow but not to take offensive action.

Another convoy operation was followed in the early hours of 14 October by an attack on Port Laki, Leros. Fifteen Swordfish set fire to workshops and a seaplane hangar without loss to themselves and the riposte by the SM 79s gave *Illustrious's* AA crews their first success. 806 Squadron's tally now stood at 11 destroyed, one 'probable' and a dozen damaged; one Fulmar had been shot down by return fire and two others had force-landed. With normal wear and tear others were temporarily unserviceable: sufficient reserve Swordfish were on hand to make good the losses, but the 19 Fulmars which *Illustrious* had brought out represented the total stock in the Mediterranean.

TARANTO 1940

On return from the second convoy mission, all the serviceable aircraft were flown ashore to the RN Air Station at Dekheila. This was fortunate, for a serious hangar fire broke out in *Illustrious* shortly after arrival. As it was, only fittings and equipment suffered damage and the carrier was fit for operations by 29 October, when the Fleet sailed with despatch to cover Commonwealth forces occupying Crete.

The Fleet returned on 2 November and *Illustrious* prepared for the attack on the Italian main fleet base at Taranto—Operation JUDGEMENT. This attack had

A running range of Fulmar Is prepares for take-off from a wet deck. Note that one aircraft does not have the canvas strip pasted across its muzzle apertures—indicative of the haste needed in re-arming between sorties (MoD (N))

Four Sea Gladiators were embarked in early November 1940, attached to 806 Squadron. On 8 November, one of these aircraft, flown by Lieutenant O. J. R. Nicholls, destroyed a CRDA Can. Z.501 flying-boat (MoD (N))

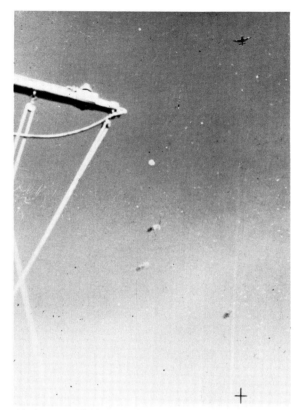

10 January 1941: A Ju 87R pulls out of its dive at the height of the attack *(IWM)*

been intended for 21 October, but the fire had forestalled the sortie. Now *Eagle* had developed faults in her aviation fuel system—the legacy of bomb near-misses on 12 October. Five aircraft and eight experienced crews were transferred to *Illustrious* and, with another aircraft from the pool, 24 Swordfish were embarked in *Illustrious* for the strike. The fighter complement was brought up to strength by the temporary addition of four Sea Gladiators, flown by 806 Squadron pilots and maintained as a permanent deck park. During the operations before the strike—another Malta 'run'—three more Fulmars were embarked from *Ark Royal* via Malta, to give *Illustrious* her largest aircraft complement to date—22 Swordfish, 14 Fulmars and four Sea Gladiators.

Two Swordfish had already been lost, and another was to be lost, through contamination of the fuel, so that for the actual attack on Taranto on 11/12 November there were only 21 strike aircraft, and of these one had to turn back before reaching the target. The raid has been amply described elsewhere and space does not permit repetition here. The battleship *Conte di Cavour* was sunk outright, *Littorio* and *Caio Duilio* were put out of action for months and considerable damage was inflicted on shore installations. At the price of two Swordfish and one crew, the Royal Navy had eliminated half the Italian battlefleet with 11 18in torpedoes.

A programmed re-strike on the night of 12/13 November was cancelled due to the deterioration of the weather, and the Fleet returned to base. The enemy had had no knowledge of the exact position of *Illustrious* since 10 November, thanks to the efforts of 806 Squadron, whose Fulmars destroyed eight shadowers and bombers during the three days before and the two days after the strike.

Malta Convoys

Illustrious's next two outings were both connected with Malta convoys, one in late November and the other, half way through December. The first saw her Swordfish attacking Port Laki again: little damage was inflicted and one of the 15 dive-bombers lost. The second was a little more successful and was more varied. On 12 December the Swordfish bombed enemy transport laagers near Bardia, in support of the 8th Army's invasion of Cyrenaica. *Illustrious* returned briefly to Alexandria to top up with fuel and then sortied once more to protect convoys and strike at three objectives. The first*, really two targets, was ruined by bad weather and little damage was inflicted at either Rhodes or Stampalia. The next was brilliantly successful, with nine torpedo-armed Swordfish from the two squadrons sinking a refrigerator ship and a freighter (totalling 8437 grt) off Kerkenah Is, achieving seven hits and losing no aircraft. The last strike* was against Tripoli, where 15 Swordfish set fire to warehouses and dumps in the most important Italian port in North Africa. For the first time since *Illustrious* had

*Rhodes/Stampalia—17th; torpedo strike 21st; Tripoli 22nd.

commenced Mediterranean operations, her Fulmars were not called into action throughout the 15 days spent at sea (15-25 December).

Little time was allowed in harbour for *Illustrious*. On 3 January her aircraft provided fighter and A/S protection for a force bombarding Bardia, and on 7 January she sailed again for what was to be her last operation with the Mediterranean Fleet.

Once again a convoy was the major reason for the operation—'EXCESS'. Four fast merchant ships were to be 'collected' from Force H and escorted through to Alexandria. The rendezvous position was 60 miles to the west of Malta and less than 100 miles from the Trapani complex of airfields which now housed the Luftwaffe's *Fliegerkorps X*. This small self-contained air force was a specialist anti-shipping formation which had cut its teeth during the Norwegian campaign in the spring of 1940 and whose advance elements had arrived in Sicily at much the same time as *Illustrious* had joined the Mediterranean Fleet. The backbone of the force was the Ju 87R with *Stukagruppe* 1 and the Ju 87B with St G 2, these two units possessing 54 Ju 87s in Sicily on 9 January 1941. Their main objective was the armoured carrier and their training had been orientated to her destruction.

The Reckoning—10 January 1941

Shadowers had followed the Fleet since 8 January, but although the Fulmars failed to make any interceptions there were no air attacks until four hours after the rendezvous with the convoy had been effected. What happened thereafter was a well-drilled set-piece action whose success stopped short of actually sinking the main target.

The five Fulmars which were airborne when the raid was detected just after noon on 10 January had been drawn to low level by a pair of SM 79 torpedo-bombers; neither they, nor the four additional fighters that were scrambled before the attack began, were able

Illustrious, steering by main engines and still on fire aft, is near-missed as she heads for Malta during the afternoon of 10 January (IWM)

to climb to 12,000 ft in time to disrupt the Ju 87s before they could deploy for their attack.

It was all over in 10 minutes. *Illustrious* was hit by

Parlatorio Wharf provided no sanctuary. Here, bombs fall in the creek and ashore while the ship herself is unharmed, although down some 10 feet by the stern due to the flooding of the steering gear and adjacent compartments (IWM)

six bombs of varying sizes, as well as three near-misses and one out-of-control Ju 87. She was very fortunate, all things considered, for the three bombs which hit forward inflicted little serious structural damage and the three bombs which struck further aft, while putting the ship out of action as a carrier and causing many casualties, did not affect either the functioning of the main machinery or the watertight integrity. Two bombs hit the lightly-armoured after lift and these caused the majority of the immediate damage, and one bomb barely defeated the flight deck armour forward of the lift and exploded above the hangar deck.

The situation was complicated immediately after the attack was over by a steering failure. This was not rectified until mid-afternoon, when she commenced the 75-mile journey to Malta, still on fire aft but maintaining a minimum of 18 knots despite almost unbearable conditions in the machinery spaces, which were filled with thick smoke and fumes from the fire-fighting chemicals. Subsequent dive-bomber attacks added another hit and two near-misses: the hit landed in the after lift well, where it caused little additional damage and even blew out some of the fires.

Illustrious arrived alongside Parlatorio Wharf at 2215 on 10 January, but not until 0300 the next morning were the fires finally extinguished. Of her ship's company, 126 were dead and 91 wounded.

Repairs to the steering gear were of the highest priority, to enable her to return to Alexandria. The damage to the flight deck and area around the after lift well would require full dockyard attention which was unobtainable in the Mediterranean. The period at Malta was enlivened by further air attacks, in which another direct hit was scored abaft the after lift on 16 January, and a near-miss on 19 January caused shock damage to the turbines.

Eight of her Fulmars had landed ashore on 10 January, with nine Swordfish airborne at the time of the attack. The fighters flew alongside RAF Hurricanes in defence of the island until 23 January, by which time two had been shot down and all the others rendered unserviceable. In the meantime they had been credited with eight enemy aircraft, to add to the five claimed on 10 January.

Illustrious left Grand Harbour at dusk on 23 January and arrived (undetected by the enemy) at Alexandria on 25 January, after a 23-knot passage. Further repairs, to fit her for the long ocean passage ahead, were carried out at Alex. until 10 March; mines delayed her southward passage through the Suez Canal, but on 20 March she left Port Suez for Aden. It was decided that she should be re-fitted at Norfolk Navy Yard, Virginia, and she was docked at Durban in early April, to enable the constructors to ascertain the extent of the underwater damage so that the US Navy authorities could be forewarned of the scope of the repair task. The passage was resumed, via Capetown, Freetown and Trinidad.

Repairs

Norfolk was reached on 12 May 1941, four months after the bombing. The highest priority was accorded to work on *Illustrious* and, six months later to the day, she was undocked. The major work had been the virtual re-building of the after end of the ship, weakened by blast and gutted by fire. In addition, the Navy Yard

added an extension to the flight deck aft, adding 50ft to the effective length of the deck; the catapult was modified to permit tail-down launches, using a bridle in the American fashion as opposed to the British trolley. A greater 'end-speed' could be achieved, for a given aircraft weight, with the bridle, but only American aircraft could be launched by the bridle method, although American aircraft built to British specifications had to use the trolley.

Leaving Norfolk on 28 November, *Illustrious* proceeded to the Jamaica area to undergo trials and to collect the 12 Swordfish of 810 and 829 Squadrons. She then returned to Norfolk to join *Formidable*, under repair since August 1941, and the two sister-ships left American waters on 12 December, *Illustrious* with 23 Lend-Lease Martlet IIs embarked for delivery in the United Kingdom.

The passage was made in heavy weather, both carriers flying Swordfish for A/S protection when possible. There was one major incident. A little after midnight on 15/16 December, while steaming in low visibility and heavy seas, *Illustrious* 'nudged' *Formidable*. The former's port forward 'corner' hit the latter's starboard quarter, causing superficial damage to both ships but without impairing seaworthiness. An amusing aspect of this collision was that when dawn broke, *Illustrious's* flight deck was seen to be strewn with oranges, which had broken out of their temporary stowages in *Formidable's* overhang when she was holed.

Illustrious arrived at Greenock on 23 December 1941 and a few days later continued to Birkenhead, where Cammell Laird Ltd repaired the collision and weather damage and installed Type 281 radar. She did not leave until the end of February and she began to work up her air group at the beginning of March 1942. 810 and 829 Squadrons were retained, with 21 Swordfish between them, but one fighter squadron, 881, was a new unit, armed primarily with nine Martlet IIs but also possessing a couple of Fulmar IIs until more of the superior single-seaters became available. 882's six Martlets joined from *Archer*.

DIEGO SUAREZ 1942

The work-up was cut short on 19 March to prepare *Illustrious* for an earlier deployment than had been planned. Japan had now joined the war and the Eastern Fleet needed carrier reinforcements. *Illustrious's* first role would be to support an amphibious assault on the Vichy-controlled island of Madagascar, where the excellent port of Diego Suarez could not be allowed to fall into the hands of an enemy.

Illustrious left the Clyde on 23 March, joined Force F under Rear-Admiral E. N. Syfret CB at Freetown* and on 22 April arrived at Durban, the assembly port for Operation 'IRONCLAD'. A relatively slow speed of advance from Freetown, in company with a troopship convoy, had allowed her to progress the work-up of her squadrons, which were at a high state of efficiency by the time that she left Durban on 28 April, heading for the Diego Suarez assault.

---

*Just before entering Freetown, fire destroyed 10 Swordfish and one Fulmar: the damage was made good in Freetown.

Martlet IIs of 881 and 882 Squadrons, with 881's Fulmar and three Swordfish of 810 and 829 Squadrons parked forward after the pre-IRONCLAD rehearsal on 3 May 1942 (IWM)

'IRONCLAD'

According to the original plan for the operation, *Hermes* was to have joined *Illustrious* off Diego Suarez, but she had been sunk by Japanese carrier dive-bombers on 9 April, off Trincomalee, and so the larger *Indomitable* had been substituted. The latter joined Force F on 3 May, giving her staff and air group less than 48 hours in which to assimilate the plan and to prepare flying programmes.

The tasks were divided between the two carriers. Broadly, *Illustrious* was to neutralise any naval forces and give tactical support to the troops, while *Indomitable* attacked airfields and protected the invasion shipping and Force F.* 200 miles to the east, *Formidable* guarded against any attempt by the Japanese Fleet to interfere. Had such interference materialised, then *Indomitable* would have joined *Formidable*, leaving

*Consisting of Admiral Syfret's Force H, supplemented by units from the Home and Eastern Fleets.

Illustrious to subdue the defences alone, using her 21 Swordfish, 20 Martlets and one Fulmar.

At 0344 on 5 May 1942, *Illustrious* launched 18 Swordfish, followed by eight Martlets, to attack Vichy warships at Diego Suarez. It was the first offensive launch since 22 December 1940, when Tripoli had been the target.

The operation was successful and Diego Suarez was firmly in British control by the evening of 7 May. *Illustrious*'s aircraft had flown 59 Swordfish and 114 Martlet sorties during the three days. The one Fulmar sortie had ended in the aircraft being shot down by small-arms fire. Other combat losses amounted to four Swordfish and a Martlet, but in return an Armed Merchant Cruiser—*Bougainville*—and two submarines —*Beveziers* and *Le Héros*—had been sunk by 829 Squadron; 881 Squadron had shot down three Potez 63.11 reconnaissance aircraft and four Morane Saulnier MS406C fighters; and all three squadrons had

Illustrious (*right*) *and* Indomitable *in the Diego Suarez roadstead, May 1942; beyond* Indomitable *can be seen the battleship,* Resolution, *and the AA cruiser,* Hermione, *lies, between the carriers* (IWM)

made a significant contribution to the troops' success by flying tactical reconnaissance, close support and bombardment spotting missions.

Following this first successful carrier-supported amphibious operation, both *Illustrious* and *Indomitable* entered the captured harbour on 9 May and remained until 20 May, when the threat of attacks by Japanese midget submarines forced the withdrawal of all heavy units to Durban and Mombasa.

The latter was to be the main base for the Eastern Fleet until early 1944, and *Illustrious* was based there for the eight months she spent with the Fleet. From it she undertook three major sorties, two of which took her to Ceylon and the third back to Madagascar.

Ceylon and the Indian Ocean

At the end of May she and *Indomitable* proceeded to Colombo, where the island's air defences were tested by the carrier aircraft. Searches were flown on the way out and during the return passage, and Addu Atoll, in the Maldive Is, was investigated to ensure that the Japanese were not attempting to infiltrate. The Fleet returned to Mombasa on 1 July, only to leave again three weeks later, bound once more for Ceylon. *Indomitable* had been recalled to take part in the 'PEDESTAL' Malta convoy, so *Formidable* took her place.

On this occasion, the carriers made a diversionary sortie to the east of Ceylon, towards the Andaman Is. This operation was intended to distract Japanese attention from the Solomons, where the US Marines were about to land on Guadalcanal Island. The carriers were sighted by reconnaissance aircraft and, on 2 August, Martlets from *Formidable* destroyed a Kawanishi H6K5 'Mavis'. The Eastern Fleet returned to East Africa on 18th August. Six days later, *Illustrious* was on her own as the only carrier in the Indian Ocean: *Formidable* had been recalled to replace the damaged *Indomitable*—the third armoured carrier to be hit by Ju 87s in the Mediterranean.

In the light wind conditions experienced in the Indian Ocean, even the Swordfish was likely to sink below flight deck level after take-off (Cdr T. L. M. Brander)

In the Indian Ocean in 1942, 806 Squadron's Fulmar IIs were used as reconnaissance aircraft, searching out to as far as 250 miles from the ship in half the time taken by a Swordfish and with a better chance of returning in the event of meeting the enemy. This aircraft is fitted with a jettisonable 'slipper' tank beneath the centre-section (IWM)

Martlet at the 'cut', a mandatory signal from the batsman ordering the pilot to throttle back. Illustrious's *top-scoring Martlet pilot was Sub-Lieutenant J. Waller RNVR, of 881 Squadron, who destroyed a Potez 63.11 and two Morane Saulnier MS 406Cs during the Diego Suarez operation* (IWM)

During the summer months there had been changes in *Illustrious*'s Air Group. Three Sea Hurricane IBs had been allocated when 803 Squadron was disbanded, but these had never been embarked; 806 Squadron had rejoined in late May, their half-dozen Fulmars being used for long-range reconnaissance. For the second trip to Ceylon, 810 Squadron had been reduced to nine Swordfish and while at Trincomalee on 3 August, the four Martlets of 882 Squadron transferred to *Formidable*. For the last major operation, *Illustrious* embarked 881 (21 Martlets) 806 (6 Fulmars) and 810

A Martlet II lined up (but not yet running up) for take-off. A feature found on this Mark of Martlet was the pair of spigots on either side of the lower fuselage (one on an arm just behind the pilot's ventral window and the other below and behind the 'J' of the aircraft's code). These were the attachment points for the catapult trolley. By the time that the Lend-Lease Martlet IV entered service, the Fleet carriers' catapults had been modified to allow launching with a bridle (or 'strop')
(IWM)

Her deck unusually clear, Illustrious *is seen during an air defence exercise. The combination of shadow and reflected light from the bow wave gives a false impression of her port side camouflage pattern*   *(IWM)*

and 829 Squadrons (9 Swordfish each); 41 of these aircraft could be stowed in the hangar, leaving four Martlets as a permanent deck-park.

Operations 'STREAM' and 'JANE'

On 5 September 1942, *Illustrious* left Kilindini Harbour, Mombasa, to take part in the final tidying up of Madagascar, the southern part of which was still occupied by Vichy forces. Landings at Majunga were covered on 10 and 11 September, but the carrier aircraft's part in Operation 'STREAM' was restricted to demonstrations of strength and tactical reconnaissance, the latter by Fulmars. 'JANE' followed on 18 September, with more demonstrations and tactical reconnaissances around Tamatave. Only 57 sorties

Seen during another Indian Ocean sortie in the summer of 1942, Illustrious *prepares to fly off a fighter patrol while in company with* Warspite *and* Formidable   *(IWM)*

Seven Martlets, five Fulmars and a single Swordfish parked on deck, Illustrious *crosses the Indian Ocean at nearly 20 knots*
(IWM)

were flown on the three days and *Illustrious* left the Tamatave area on 18 September to proceed to Durban for a short refit. En route she provided distant cover for the unopposed occupation of Vichy Reunion and her Swordfish located a merchant ship attempting to escape from the island.

Not until 20 October did *Illustrious* return to Mombasa. The appearance of U-boats in the Indian Ocean led to the use of the Fleet destroyers with convoy escort groups and the resulting lack of screening vessels prevented the carrier from undertaking any more operations with the Eastern Fleet. The Swordfish squadrons had been amalgamated to form 810 Squadron with 15 aircraft in October 1942.

The ship was in need of modernisation when she finally left Mombasa on 13 January 1943, leaving the Eastern Fleet without a carrier; not until she returned a year later was the deficiency made good.

Refit 1943

Illustrious arrived at Cammell Laird's Birkenhead yard on 26 February 1943 and refitted until 7 June. The flight deck was extended once again so that the effective length was 75 feet greater than when she had been completed. Sixteen power-operated twin 20mm AA mountings were installed, with two singles, to replace the 10 single manually-operated mountings which had been fitted by Norfolk Navy Yard. Radar ranging (Type 282) was added to the pom-pom directors and to complete the armament additions, the aircraft depth-charge stowage was doubled in capacity to 144 charges.

After the refit, at the end of June, *Illustrious* proceeded to the Clyde to conduct flying trials with Barracuda, Tarpon (Grumman TBF-1 Avenger), Firefly, Seafire, and Martlet V aircraft. Two additional arrester wires had been installed, aft of the after lift and these proved to be of considerable value, adding an extra 45 ft to the effective landing space.

The work-up began on 12 July. Only one squadron

had been retained since the last commission—810—and this had been re-armed with Fairey ·Barracudas. The fighter complement was provided by 878 and 890, with 10 Martlet Vs each, and 894 Squadron, with 10 Seafire IICs. The latter had to be maintained as a permanent deck-park, on outriggers and forward of the island, as these were non-folding aircraft and their wing-span was too great to permit their being struck down the 22ft-wide lifts.

A pre-production Fairey Barracuda II *takes off from* Illustrious *during the same series of trials, conducted in the approaches to the Clyde in late February 1943* (IWM)

Home Fleet

Illustrious relieved *Furious** in the Home Fleet in mid-July and little time was allowed for a full work-up. A diversionary sweep was to be carried out off Norway, to persuade the enemy that Sicily was not the only Allied objective for the month. *Illustrious* was deployed

*See Warship Profiles Nos. 23 and 24.

250

Flying trials 1943: The third prototype Firefly I (Z1828) lifts its tail wheel with 470 feet of deck still available ahead of it. Behind, a Blackburn Firebrand I interceptor prototype (DD810) awaits its turn for launching. Note the bow-springs under the wires are lowered (IWM)

In company with Unicorn, Illustrious *sails for Gibraltar in August 1943, on her way to join Force H for the Salerno operation. Her radar installations varied little after this photograph was taken: a Type 79B is at the foretop, a Type 281 on the pole aft of the funnel, and a Type 272 surface warning radar is fitted on a bracket below the compass platform. Three of the 10 Seafire IICs of 894 Squadron are stowed on outriggers, but the other seven constitute a permanent deck-park, necessitating continuous movement up and down the deck for launch and recovery serials* (MoD (N))

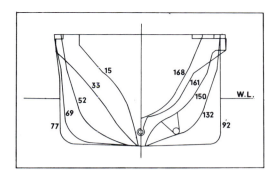

HMS *Illustrious* took part in the Salerno landings in September 1943. The port side profile as depicted below, shows her in her Admiralty dark disruptive camouflage design which she wore from mid 1943 to mid 1944. Camouflage of Admiralty mottled disruptive type worn from the time of the American refit in January 1942 until it was changed to Admiralty disruptive type: 1942 design in mid 1942.

T. Brittain/M. Trim © *Profile Publications Ltd*

A

B

Illustrious in war paint:
Views A, D: Admiralty Disruptive Pattern—March 1942-January 1943

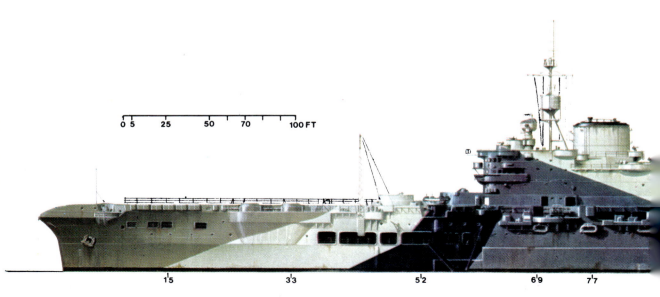

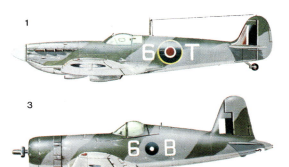

1. Seafire IIc of 894 Squadron, September 1943
3. Corsair II of 833 Squadron, January 1945

2. Avenger I of 832 Squadron, May 1944
4. Barracuda II of 810 Squadron, April 1944 (non-standard SEAC roundel and over-large code lettering)

C

D

Bottom view and B: Admiralty Disruptive Pattern—May 1943-August 1944
View C: Admiralty Standard Scheme Type B—October 1944-February 1945

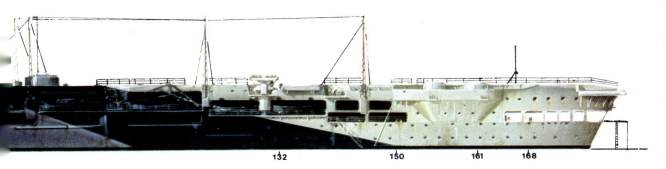

132   150   161   168

to Iceland, and on 26 July 1943 she left Hvalfjord with the battleships *Anson* and USS *Alabama* to trail the Home Fleet's coat 150 miles off Norway. Operation 'GOVERNOR' *did* cause a flutter in the enemy camp, their search aircraft identifying a cruiser force as 'transports'; the Blohm and Voss Bv 138s paid for their mistake. On 28 July three were shot down by RAF Beaufighters and two more fell to 890 Squadron's Martlets.

All the Scapa-based forces which took part in 'GOVERNOR' returned to Scapa on 29 July. This was *Illustrious's* one and only operation with the Home Fleet throughout the war, for on 5 August she sailed for the Mediterranean to replace the again-damaged *Indomitable* in Force H. En route, she escorted the *Queen Mary* to a position outside the range of Luftwaffe long-range attack aircraft; the 'monster liner' was carrying the Prime Minister to Quebec for the 'QUADRANT' conference and she arrived without hindrance.

SALERNO 1943

Illustrious joined Force H at Gibraltar and, with *Formidable*, returned to Malta on 21 August—31 months after she had left on the last occasion. The Mediterranean situation was vastly different. The Sicilian bases which had accommodated the Stukas now held Allied aircraft and Allied troops were about to gain their first foothold on the mainland of Italy. To support the drive from the toe, an assault was to be made just below the knee, at Salerno. The beaches were too far from the Sicilian fighter airfields for complete shore-based air cover and five small carriers—Force V—were to be supported by Force H while they flew defensive patrols over Salerno. Fighters from *Illustrious* and *Formidable* would protect Force V and Force H, while the Barracudas and Albacores would stand-by for action against the Italian battlefleet. *Illustrious* had embarked eight more Martlets for 878 and 890, bringing her aircraft complement to 50 for the first time.

As the Force approached the combat area on the night of 8/9 September 1943, about 30 Luftwaffe torpedo-bombers attacked but were beaten off by the intense AA fire from the two carriers, the battleships *Nelson* and *Rodney*, and the powerful screen. During the operations itself—'AVALANCHE'—there was no attempt made to attack Force H, or indeed Force V, and the only real excitement was the surrender of the Italian Fleet. One 890 Squadron patrol did accept the surrender of an Italian aircraft and took it all the way to Sicily to establish 'ownership', but this was the only notable event as far as *Illustrious's* air group was concerned. Two hundred and fourteen sorties were flown on 9, 10 and 11 September, all by the fighters and without a single deck-landing accident—a remarkable achievement.

Force H retired on the evening of 11 September, but six of 894 Squadron's Seafires were flown to the repair carrier *Unicorn*, acting as a Light Fleet carrier with Force V, to provide temporary replacements for her heavy non-combat losses. Four of these aircraft went on to operate from beach-head airstrips until 14 September, when they flew back to join the ship at Malta.

Consideration was given to using *Illustrious* to support the amphibious operations in the Aegean in late September, but this was decided against and both she and *Formidable* returned to the United Kingdom via Gibraltar. While the latter went to Scapa Flow to join the Home Fleet, *Illustrious* returned to Birkenhead on 29 October. During the next month she was modified for operations with the Eastern Fleet and for handling Chance-Vought F4U-1B Corsair IIs. The catapult was 'beefed up' to launch fully-loaded Barracudas and the flight deck was extended yet again, this time to 740ft; another pair of 'twin-power Oerlikon' mountings were also added.

Return to the Eastern Fleet

Illustrious arrived in the Clyde to commence her work-up on 28 November 1943. Another air group had been allocated, but again continuity was provided by 810 Squadron. The strike and fighter aircraft had been organised into 'Wings' to enable the most to be made of their capabilities in combat. Each was led by an experienced officer who was responsible for the tactical doctrine, training and combat efficiency of their Wing, leaving the individual squadron commanding officers the responsibility for the administration of their units.

No. 21 Torpedo-Bomber-Reconnaissance Wing—12 Barracudas of 810 Squadron and nine of 847—embarked in early December, but No. 15 Naval Fighter Wing—28 Corsairs of 1830 and 1833 Squadrons—had not yet completed their initial work-up ashore and they did not join the ship until later in the month.

Early in January 1944, *Illustrious* left Greenock for Gibraltar and the Eastern Fleet. On this occasion she passed through the Mediterranean and made her second (and last) south-bound transit of the Suez Canal. The Eastern Fleet was now based at Trincomalee, where she arrived on 31 January. Only the escort carrier, *Battler*, had been available during the months preceding *Illustrious's* deployment, and she had been fully occupied in trade protection operations.

The work-up was progressed at Trincomalee, and on 8 March *Illustrious* sailed with heavy units of the Fleet on her first operation. Three Japanese heavy cruisers had made a brief foray into the Indian Ocean from Singapore and had sunk two unescorted merchant ships near the Cocos Islands; the carrier aircraft searched for three days for the enemy who had returned to his base almost immediately. *Illustrious* put to sea again on 21 March, this time to meet the US Navy carrier, *Saratoga*, attached to the Eastern Fleet for operations against the occupied East Indies.

After the rendezvous, while returning to Trincomalee, the two carriers exercised together, with *Saratoga's* veteran Air Group 12 imparting the benefit of their hard-won experience to the untried Royal Navy Wings. The rehearsals continued in Ceylonese waters until 16 April, when 27 warships of six Allied Navies sailed for Operation 'COCKPIT'.

SABANG 1944

The target for the strike was the island of Sabang, at the northern extremity of Sumatra. The Japanese had established a small naval base and there were supply and workshop facilities at the port. On 19 April, *Illustrious* flew off 17 Barracudas—each armed with two

The Corsair IIs of No. 15 Naval Fighter Wing (6-1833 and 7-1830) on deck during the Eastern Fleet's period of exercising with USS Saratoga *(seen heading in the opposite direction). Aircraft are being ranged up the after lift, which is at hangar-deck level, showing the thickness of flight deck armour. The trough of an unshipped outrigger stowage can be seen in the foreground at the deck edge* (IWM)

17 May 1944: Illustrious *and* Saratoga *head towards Exmouth Gulf after their combined strike on Soerabaya* (MoD (N))

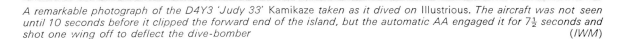

A remarkable photograph of the D4Y3 'Judy 33' Kamikaze taken as it dived on Illustrious. *The aircraft was not seen until 10 seconds before it clipped the forward end of the island, but the automatic AA engaged it for 7½ seconds and shot one wing off to deflect the dive-bomber* (IWM)

'L' of 1833 Squadron roars off on 25 July 1944—the fact that only one other aircraft, out of the eight visible in the range, is running suggests that the launch is of a fighter patrol. Points of interest include the batsman's platform behind the nearest stationary Corsair, the lowered barrier and the protective fairing built up around the port stanchion, and the revised arrester wire raising arrangement—two bow-springs replacing the single centre-line spring and the supports at the swivel shackles (IWM)

500lb and two 250lb bombs—and 13 escorting Corsairs. *Saratoga*, with a much larger aircraft complement, launched 29 Avengers and Dauntlesses, escorted by 16 Hellcats, while another 16 Hellcats were to attack neighbouring airfields. The American aircraft attacked the shipping—what there was of it—in Sabang harbour, while the Barracudas dropped their bombs on the shore installations; no fighter opposition was encountered and all aircraft landed safely.

Soerbaya and Port Blair

The carriers and their followers returned to Trincomalee on 21 April. *Illustrious* then exchanged her Barracudas for the Avengers of 832 and 851 before the next operation—an attack on the oil refineries at Soerbaya, Java. For this strike, the aircraft would have to fly across the breadth of Java; the mountainous spine of the island averages 10,000ft in height, and this minimum height, coupled with the distance to be flown—about 240 miles—prohibited the use of the essentially low-altitude Barracuda.

Soerbaya was attacked on 17 May 1944. The distance of the launching point from Trincomalee, 1800 miles, obliged the force to put into Exmouth Gulf, Australia, to fuel the destroyers both before and after the attack. The strike itself was a partial success. *Illustrious* lost two of the 18 Barracudas launched shortly after take-off and, though none of the aircraft which continued, nor their escort of 16 Corsairs was intercepted, targets were few in the harbour; and the US Navy strike, by 31 bombers, failed to inflict permanent damage on the oil installations. *Saratoga* detached from the Eastern Fleet during the second fuelling visit to Exmouth Gulf, and *Illustrious* returned to Trincomalee, flying searches and A/S patrols on passage.

Alone, the carrier's value was much lessened. The standard complement of 21 strike and 28 fighter aircraft was sufficient either to strike the enemy or to defend the Fleet, but not both. To support *Illustrious* and provide a spare deck, the Fighter escort carrier, *Atheling*, joined the main body of the Fleet for the next operation: a sweep towards the Andamans to divert Japanese attention from the forthcoming US Pacific Fleet assault on the Marianas. The experience proved to be unfruitful and when *Illustrious* left Trincomalee on 19 June 1944 (the day of the 'Marianas Turkey Shoot')* she was alone. To provide extra fighter defence, the 14 Corsairs of 1837 Squadron were added to No. 15 Wing, and the number of Barracudas was reduced to 15.

Illustrious's only solo strike was delivered against the airfield and harbour of Port Blair in the Andamans. Apart from a couple of aircraft strafed on the airfield and a small craft sunk offshore, there was little to show for the effort of the 15 Barracudas and 23 Corsairs despatched. As the strike returned, there were no fewer than 51 of the 57 aircraft embarked airborne, and of these all but 18 required immediate recovery. Had one of the early landings resulted in an accident, then over half of the air group might have been lost through loss of fuel—well within range of Japanese airfields. This experience, on 21 June, was not repeated by carriers in the Far East.

---

*See Warship Profile No. 9.

Sabang Again

At the end of June 1944, *Illustrious* was joined in the Fleet by *Victorious* and *Indomitable*. Their arrival meant that further offensive action could be taken against the enemy as soon as the fresh air groups could be acclimatised. *Victorious*'s squadrons had already seen service with the Home Fleet during the spring and were thus ready for action within a fortnight of arrival.

On 25 July, the battleships of the Eastern Fleet bombarded Sabang. While *Victorious*'s Corsairs protected the Fleet and blanketed the local airfields, No. 15 Fighter Wing covered the battleships and spotted for the fall of the 301 15in. shells fired, terminating the operation with a photographic mission to determine the results of the shelling. Late in the afternoon, enemy aircraft reacted for the first time and *Illustrious*'s three squadrons all opened their scores, with four kills between them. The Japanese did not even sight the carriers.

Only nine Barracudas had been embarked in *Illustrious* and they were not employed on 25 July. In fact, this was No. 21 TBR Wing's last full operation; it had already been reduced to just 810 Squadron (by amalgamation) with 15 aircraft. It was now apparent that the armoured carriers were destined for Pacific operations and that the day of the short-ranged and relatively slow 'Barra' was past.

Refit at Durban, 1944

Illustrious herself needed a refit before sustained operations could be undertaken and, on return from the Sabang operation, she proceeded to Durban. The refit took from 14 August to 10 October, and yet another armament alteration was made, with one multiple pom-pom mounting giving way to a pair of 40mm Bofors and another couple of twin powered-Oerlikons. The remainder of the work had been devoted to making good the many defects which had arisen since her arrival in the Indian Ocean. It had been hoped originally that the refit could have been carried out in the United Kingdom, but the dockyards and all suitable major shipyards were already fully occupied.

Illustrious returned from refit on 2 November 1944. 810 Squadron had been embarked for protection during the passage but they now left the ship for the last time, after an association which went back to March 1942. To take their place, the 21 TBM-1C Avengers IIs of 854 Squadron were working up ashore; with 857 Squadron in *Indominable* they were to form No. 1 Naval Strike Wing in the coming operations.

∽ PALEMBANG 1945 ∾

By 17 December 1944, the air groups of the First Aircraft Carrier Squadron (*Indomitable*, *Illustrious*, *Victorious* and *Indefatigable*) were ready for action, after a prolonged re-training period ashore. *Illustrious* and *Indomitable* sailed for the first of a series of strikes on the oil installations in Sumatra.

The first strike, on 20 December, was not propitious. Low cloud obscured the primary target, the refinery at Pangkalan Brandan, and the 16 Avengers of 854 Squadron made an inconclusive attack on the port of Belawan Deli. Four Corsairs dropped bombs on the Medan airfield—their briefed objective, and during the

The only damage immediately apparent—the cracked radome of the 272 radar antenna

afternoon another eight fighters strafed Kota Raja airfield.

Pangkalan Brandan was successfully re-attacked on 4 January 1945, but *Illustrious* was not with the Carrier Squadron for this operation. She had to wait until 16 January before leaving Trincomalee again, this time en route for Sydney and the Pacific.

As the Fleet, including all four carriers of 1st ACS, passed Sumatra, two attacks were launched against the Palembang oilfield complex. The operation, 'MERI-DIAN', stands as high in Royal Navy lore as the Taranto and *Tirpitz* strikes: by halving the output of the Pladjoe refinery on 24 January 1945 and entirely stopping the Soengi Gerong refinery on 29 January, the British Pacific Fleet made its greatest contribution to the final victory over Japan.

Illustrious's contribution to the offensive missions consisted of 24 Avenger and 52 Corsair sorties. Individual bombing claims cannot be assessed, but the fighters destroyed four enemy aircraft while losing five of their own number to flak and interceptors, and an Avenger claimed a fifth victory. Three Avengers were lost to enemy action. On 29 January, seven enemy aircraft attacked the Fleet and although all were shot down before they could inflict damage, *Illustrious* was hit by 'friendly' AA fire, one shell damaging a port side pom-pom and another hitting the port side of the island; 12 men were killed and 21 were wounded.

The damage was repaired at Sydney, where the Fleet had arrived on 10 February. *Illustrious* was simultaneously docked to investigate defects in her centre shaft. These turned out to be more serious than had been thought and to enable her to join the Fleet for the forthcoming operations off Okinawa the centre propeller had to be removed, making her a two-shaft ship in effect and reducing her speed to a maximum of 24 knots.

OKINAWA 1945

Illustrious rejoined the 1st ACS at Manus, Admiralty Islands, on 15 March 1945, leaving with the Fleet soon after, bound for the operating area off the Sakishima Gunto. The Royal Navy carriers were to interdict the airfields in the island group while the Americans landed on Okinawa, 200 miles to the north-east.

Task Force 57, as the main body of the BPF was designated, began to fly strikes against the islands of Ishigaki, Miyako and Mihara on 26 March. Airfields, coastal defences, barracks and small shipping provided costly and barely-worthwhile targets for the Avengers and fighter-bomber Hellcats and Corsairs, but the Americans' left flank was held secure by attacks on 27 and 31 March, and on 1, 2, 6 and 7 April.

Enemy aircraft shadowed Task Force 57 while the carriers were 'on the line', but not until 1 April did the Kamikazes make their first appearance, one bouncing off *Indefatigable's* armoured deck. *Illustrious* was the target for a surprise attack on 6 April, but the ship's

Lieutenant P. S. Cole, Senior Pilot of 1830 Squadron drops a wing as his Corsair bounces over the after barrier and pitches on its nose between the two barriers. This was one of Illustrious's *last war-time deck-landing accidents, occurring on her last day of combat—13 April 1945*

automatic weapons fired 700 rounds of 2pdr, 75 rounds of 40mm, and 600 rounds of 20mm AA to tear the port wing off the D4Y3 'Judy', deflecting it so that only the starboard wingtip scratched the dome of the Type 272 radar forward of the bridge. The explosion of the bomb in the water caused the carrier to whip severely, but it was believed at the time that damage was restricted to the radar dome and the two Corsairs which had been written off on deck by the splash from the bomb.

On 8 April, *Formidable* was ordered up from Leyte to relieve *Illustrious* in TF 57 but, before the latter left, she took part in the two-day strike serial against north Formosa, her Avengers and Corsairs striking at Kiirun harbour and nearby airfields. On 13 April 1945, her last day in action, the Corsairs scored their final two victories. At dusk on the next day *Illustrious* left the Fleet to proceed to Leyte, escorted by two destroyers. During her nine days of participation in Operation 'ICEBERG' her aircraft had flown 234

November 1946: Firebrand trials again. Redesigned as a torpedo fighter, the Firebrand, in its TF4 version, returns to continue the 1943 type trials. Here one aircraft is positioned on the catapult while the other is spotted for a free take-off
(MoD (N))

A Firebrand is arrested during flying trials in the English Channel
(MoD (N))

offensive and 209 defensive sorties, losing two Avengers and three Corsairs in action and one Avenger and six Corsairs operationally.

Withdrawal, Japanese Surrender and Post-War Refit

At Leyte, divers examined the carrier's hull. The near-miss on 6 April had caused more damage than had been realised: the outer plating was split and internal transverse frames were cracked on both sides of the ship, approximately in line with the forward lift. Temporary repairs were effected and *Illustrious* left Leyte on 1 April. Recently-joined fighter pilots remained to reinforce the other two Corsair Wings still with the Fleet and their aircraft were transferred to *Unicorn* as spares, while the Avenger squadron returned to Sydney. *Illustrious* was non-operational and was limited to 19 knots because of her hull damage.

Little time was spent at Sydney, for on 24 May she departed for the long, unescorted return to the United Kingdom, where she was to undergo a four-month refit at Rosyth. She arrived in the Forth on 27 June 1945 and was promptly taken in hand but events overtook her programme. The war came to an abrupt end on 15 August and the effect on *Illustrious* was to delay the completion of her refit until June 1946.

It was an extensively altered *Illustrious* which recommissioned into the post-war Fleet. The successive extensions to the flight deck were made permanent by the re-modelling of the entire 'front-end'. The catapult was modernised to launch heavier aircraft, the aviation fuel stowage was increased by 30 per cent, and the armament was changed again. She was intended for use as a trials and deck-landing training ship, but successive problems, material and personnel shortages principally, prevented this until mid-1947.

She operated in Home Waters on trials until the end of 1947, when she underwent a short refit, in which her catapult was modified yet again and her close-range armament was altered to consist of 40 2pdr pom-poms, 17 40mm Bofors, and 16 20mm Oerlikons. Her full-load displacement rose to 31,790 tons. The refit ended in the spring, but with naval manpower shortages it was not until September 1948 that she could be returned to sea duties.

Last Years

From the autumn of 1948 until the end of 1954, *Illustrious* remained in service as the trials and training carrier in Home Waters. As the training carrier, she provided experience for the student pilots undergoing operational flying training at RN Air Stations, Eglinton (Naval Air A/S School) and Culdrose (Naval Fighter School), as well as for the periodic embarkations of the RNVR Air Squadrons. Additionally, the Deck Landing Control Officers' Courses underwent carrier training aboard *Illustrious*, 'batting' for the Seafires, Sea Furies and Fireflies which were the then-current front-line types.

This was a period of evolution in the sphere of carrier operations, the advent of jet propulsion bringing problems in its wake. *Illustrious*, in her capacity of

Flying Trials 1950: *The Vickers Armstrong* (Supermarine) *Type 510 research aircraft* (VV106) *lines up for a Rocket-Assisted Take-off from* Illustrious *during November trials in the English Channel; the RATOG 'bottles' can be seen above and below the wing root. A Type 277 height-finding radar has replaced the HA Director on top of the island, a YE homing beacon is mounted on a mast attached to the funnel, and the Type 960 Warning Air radar is mounted on a tripod at the rear end of the island* (IWM)

A fine shot of Illustrious *running for flying trials in 1947. A Sea Fury 10 prototype is being ranged aft for take-off and forward of the island, on an outrigger, one of the Seafire 45s of 778 Squadron, the Trials and Development Squadron. Only two of the three barriers are rigged* (MoD (N))

Last Look. *As* Illustrious *steams into the sun towards the end of her career, the alterations to her arrester wire layout can clearly be seen. The pair of wires aft of the lift were installed during the refit in the spring of 1943, but the wire across the lift is a post-war addition. The batsman is barely visible against the dark background of the palisades on the port quarter, but the bats can just be discerned as two white discs. The barriers are not only lowered but are also unrigged*

(MoD (N))

Illustrious *at Portland in July 1949 with the Seafires of either 1831 or 1833 RNVR Squadrons and Fireflies of 1830 RNVR Squadron, undergoing annual deck-landing training. The forward Firefly is resting on its belly and its mainplanes have been removed, in preparation for the aircraft's removal by crane and lighter*

(G. A. Osbon)

trials carrier, was the ship in which most of the initial deck-landing acceptance trials of new naval aircraft were conducted, together with the new handling and servicing equipment required for their operation. One of the more interesting trials conducted during 1949 involved the flying of a glider, tethered to the flight deck, to investigate airflow over the deck.

Occasionally, *Illustrious* 'escaped'. In 1951 she was used to carry troops out to Cyprus in November, while the crisis in the Canal Zone was growing. For this brief Mediterranean cruise she had embarked the eight Firefly AS6s of 824 Squadron; on her way home she embarked 827 Squadron's Fireflies for passage. A year later, in September 1952, *Illustrious* took part in

Exercise 'MAINBRACE' in the North Atlantic. For this she embarked 824 Squadron and No. 4 Squadron Royal Netherlands Navy with 20 Fireflies between them, and 860 Squadron R Neth N, with eight Sea Furies.

In December 1954, after an Autumn cruise in which trials and training aircraft had carried out 2160 fixed-wing and 483 helicopter deck landings in three months, *Illustrious* proceeded to the Gareloch, where she was laid up in reserve. Of her immediate sister-ships, *Formidable* had been scrapped already and *Victorious* was to be taken in hand for modernisation. The hull and machinery of *Illustrious* had been hard-worked for more than 14 years and modernisation was not considered economical.

On 11 October 1956 approval was given to dispose of *Illustrious* and on 3 November she was sold to the British Iron and Steel Corporation for scrapping.

Illustrious *turns into wind to launch a pair of Royal Netherlands Navy TBM-3E Avengers of 860 Squadron RNN and a single Royal Navy Firefly AS6* (MoD (N))

Warship Series Editor:
JOHN WINGATE, DSC

APPENDIX I

Illustrious 1940-45
AIR GROUPS
September 1940—January 1941
806 Squadron : 15 Fulmar I—29 confirmed victories
815 Squadron : 9 Swordfish !
819 Squadron : 9 Swordfish I

March-May 1941
700 (*Dorsetshire*) Flight : 1 Walrus I

February 1942—February 1943
881 Squadron : 12 Martlet II   increasing to 25 in September 1942—7
                              confirmed victories
882 Squadron : 6 Martlet II   (to *Formidable* August 1942)
810 Squadron : 9 Swordfish I increasing to 15 in October 1942
829 Squadron : 12 Swordfish I reducing to 9 in September and disban-
                              ding in October 1942
806 Squadron : 6 Fulmar II   (joined late May 1942)

July-October 1943
878 Squadron : 10 Martlet V   increasing to 14 in August
890 Squadron : 10 Martlet V   increasing to 14—2 confirmed victories
894 Squadron : 10 Seafire IIC
810 Squadron : 12 Barracuda II

December 1943—July 1944
1830 Squadron : 14 Corsair II   —1 confirmed victory
1833 Squadron : 14 Corsair II   —2 confirmed victories
 810 Squadron : 12 Barracuda II (not May 1944)
 847 Squadron : 9 Barracuda II (not May 1944) disbanded June
 832 Squadron : 9 Avenger I   (May 1944 only)
 851 Squadron : 9 Avenger I   (May 1944 only)
1837 Squadron : 14 Corsair II   (June and July)—1 confirmed victory

December 1944—May 1945
1830 Squadron : 18 Corsair II   —5 confirmed victories
1833 Squadron : 18 Corsair II   —3 confirmed victories
 854 Squadron : 21 Avenger II reducing to 16 in March 1945—1 con-
                              firmed victory

Illustrious spent approximately 120 days in the various combat areas, excluding time spent on passage between Fleets. During this time she launched nearly 2000 operational sorties. Strike missions were launched on 33 days, for a total of 725 Swordfish, Avenger, Barracuda, Martlet, Fulmar and Corsair sorties—22 were lost to enemy action. The enemy paid dearly for the destruction of these aircraft, and for the 11 aircraft lost on the two occasions on which she was damaged by air attack.

'Game Bag'

Aircraft	Merchant Ships		Warships			
	Sunk		*Sunk*		*Damaged*	
51 destroyed, 9 'probables'	6 of 20,399 grt		6 of 37,110 grt		5 of 81,567 grt	
2 destroyed by AA	*Gloria Stelle*	(b)	*Cavour*	(t)	*Littorio*	(t)
	Maria Eugenia	(b)	*Borea*	(b)	*C. Duilio*	(t)
25 Italian	*Intrepido*	(m)	*Aquilone*	(m)	*Trento*	(b)
14 Japanese	*Verace*	(m)	*Bougainville*	(t)	*Libeccio*	(b)
7 German	*Norge*	(t)	*Beveziers*	(d)	*D'Entrecasteaux*	(b)
7 Vichy	*Peuceta*	(t)	*Le Héros*	(d)		

(m)=*mined*   (b)=*bombed*   (t)=*torpedoed*   (d)=*depth charged*

Acknowledgements:
The author would like to express his appreciation of the assistance received from Lieutenant Commander F. J. Dodd RN (Retd), D. J. Lyon MA, A. L. Raven, Captain J. F. H. C. de Winton RN, and C. F. Shores ARHS.

Kongo *under full power trials in Clyde Bay on 8 May 1913. With displacement of 27,580 tons, she registered 27·54 knots with a total of 78,275s.h.p.*

IJN KONGO / Battleship 1912-1944

by Masataka Chihaya and Yasuo Abe

ARMOURED CRUISERS AFTER 1905

In the Russo-Japanese war of 1904-5, the Russian Pacific and Baltic Fleets were defeated by the Imperial Japanese Navy and its Combined Fleet, the nucleus of which consisted of six battleships and six armoured cruisers. These latter had slightly different features from their counterparts in other navies of the world at that time.

These armoured cruisers had greater gun power; greater protection—although this was inferior to that of their battleships—and slower speeds, these cruisers being not more than two knots faster than the battleships. These specific features of the Japanese Navy's armoured cruisers were to be incorporated in the design of battle-cruisers of later days.

In this Russo-Japanese war, the Japanese employed the armoured cruisers to supplement the battleships' strength in many decisive battles with enemy forces. Because of their ships' superior speed the Japanese Fleet was able to take up advantageous positions against the enemy. Their victory in the battle of Tsushima Strait in particular contributed greatly to the eventual destruction of the Russian Baltic Fleet.

Based upon lessons learned in that war, the Japanese Navy made it a basic policy to provide all future battleships with heavier guns and faster speeds than those of its potential enemies but at the same time it saw the need of having more powerful armoured cruisers. These would be known as 'Battle-Cruisers'.

The Japanese capital ships that fought against the Russians in the 1904-5 war had all been constructed in overseas yards, the Japanese yards at that time being unable to build ships of the requisite size. However, so much pressure was brought to bear by the need of

more and more warships, and such was the advance made in industrial technology that, during the war, home yards began the construction of capital ships. The first two (the armoured cruiser *Tsukuba* and her sister ship *Ikoma*) were completed in 1907 and 1908 respectively. The *Tsukuba* was equipped with two twin turrets, mounting 12in guns/45 calibre as her main battery, an equivalent gun power to that of any battleship at that time. Eventually she was the forerunner of the 'Battle-Cruisers' of later days.

Crack Ships

In the wake of their completion, two battleships, *Satsuma* and *Aki*, and two armoured cruisers *Ibuki* and *Kurama*, were constructed in local yards. The *Ibuki* and *Kurama*, who were completed in 1908 and 1911 respectively, were improved versions of the *Tsukuba*. In addition to four 12in guns in twin mountings, they carried eight 8in guns as their secondary battery. The *Ibuki* became the premier ship of the Japanese Navy, the installation of steam turbine engines enabling her to produce a maximum speed of 22.5 knots—two knots faster than her sister ships. Thus she paved the way for the eventual improvement of speeds in all capital ships.

The superiority which the newly-built Japanese armoured cruisers boasted over their counterparts immediately after the war was rudely shattered by the appearance in 1908 of the revolutionary battle-cruiser HMS *Invincible*.

The study of ship design by the Royal Navy during the war had been more thorough than that of the

The Kongo *being launched at Vickers' Barrow shipyard on 18 May 1912. Note the chrysanthemum emblem at her bow which symbolised a warship of the Imperial Japanese Navy*

Japanese, who found it difficult to discard traditional thinking.

The Japanese Navy was to have a hard time matching the strength and power of British and German warships of the future.

BUILDING PLANS OF BATTLE-CRUISERS : THE BIG GUN RACE

In order to outrange the *Invincible* battle-cruiser class, the Japanese culled all the experience at their command. As many as thirty plans were drafted before a final decision was made, the details of which have never been made public.

Before information on the *Invincible* was made available, the Japanese Navy produced a plan of a prototype capital ship whose displacement was to be:

Displacement:	18,650 tons.
Length (b.p.):	541′
Beam:	80′
Draught:	26·5′
Main Machinery Output.	44,000 h.p.
Maximum Speed:	25 knots.
Armament:	4×12″ guns/45 calibre.
	8×10″ : 10×4·7″ guns : 8 small guns.
Torpedo Tubes:	Five.
Waterline Belt:	7″ plates.
Deck:	2″ plates.

At first it was suggested that the main battery should follow that of the *Invincible*, but when the Royal Navy produced the *Indefatigable* with its improved arrangement of two midship turrets en-echelon, studies were made on this design, on the superimposed-turret arrangement and on the possibility of mounting ten 12in guns/50 calibre. Design details are not available

but they are considered by the Japanese School of Warship Design Study to include the following specifications:

Displacement:	18,725 tons.
Length (b.p.):	495′
Beam:	82·5′
Draught:	27·5′
Main Machinery Output:	44,000 h.p.
Maximum Speed:	26·5 knots.
Armament:	10×12″ guns/50 calibre.
	10 (approx.) ×6″ guns/45 calibre.
	More than 4×4·7 guns/40 calibre.
Torpedo Tubes:	Five 18″

Kongo: first conception

The turret arrangement plan of her main battery called for one twin-mounting turret forward, two twin-mounting turrets amidships in en-echelon and two superimposed twin-mounting turrets aft, similar to the Kriegsmarine *Moltke* class. Later the design was changed to have two superimposed twin-mounting turrets fore and aft, while one twin-mounting turret was positioned on the centre line amidships. This plan of the main battery arrangement eventually produced the prototype of the *Kongo*.

In 1909, soon after the prototype of the *Kongo* was drafted and the necessary financial arrangements for its production were made, the Royal Navy began building the *Lion* class battle-cruisers. As a result, the Japanese Navy was once again outranged by the Royal Navy. The Japanese Navy was obliged to change the construction plan of *Kongo* and decided to seek the technical co-operation of the Royal Navy in transforming her into a 27,500 ton class battle-cruiser, an improved type of the *Lion*.

The world's first 14in gun warship, Kongo, takes to the water at Barrow yard

Soon after launching, Kongo is secured in the yard basin underneath the big crane. On her starboard side is HMS Princess Royal, the second sister ship of the Lion who, incidentally, is being fitted out in the same yard

ORDER PLACED WITH VICKERS

Since Japan and Great Britain had signed a treaty of alliance at that time, the Royal Navy rendered much technical assistance to the Japanese Navy. Moreover, the Japanese Navy had been a good client to major shipbuilding firms in Great Britain before the Russo-Japanese War. Knowing the Japanese Navy's new policy of building its latest warship overseas, British shipbuilders were very eager to win the new order. Vickers (who were incidentally building the *Princess Royal*, the second ship of the *Lion* class) submitted to the Japanese Navy a new design based upon the *Lion* class battle-cruiser, as did Armstrongs who had previously built warships for the Japanese Navy.

After much deliberation, the Japanese Navy decided to adopt the Vickers' design. By ordering the construction of *Kongo* from Vickers, the Japanese Navy hoped to bring into Japan the latest advances in British shipbuilding technology, machine manufacture and weapons. The construction contract with Vickers was signed on 17 October 1910.

When ordering *Kongo* from Vickers, heated discussions took place in the Japanese Navy on what size guns should be installed. The main point at issue was whether she should carry 12in guns/50 calibre or larger. The argument was finally won by the group advocating 12in guns and a decision was made to install these as her main battery.

Vital Inside Information and Change of Policy

This decision as to the size of guns to be installed in *Kongo* had to face an entirely unexpected 'about-turn', however. Thanks to the very friendly relations maintained through the Anglo-Japanese alliance treaty, a Japanese naval attaché in London availed himself of very confidential information on the precision and lifetime of big guns. According to data from the Royal Navy's firing trials, the 12in gun/50 calibre had a shorter lifetime and a larger spread of salvoes than those of the 13·5in gun/45 calibre, which had been scheduled by the Royal Navy as the main battery of new capital ships to be built in the future.

Kongo *being fitted out at Vickers in mid-January 1913. Note her tripod mast and three funnels already installed. The Japanese characters read: 'The* Kongo *in mid-1913. Weight: 18,000 tons.' This photograph was sent by the then Sub. Lt. Shinchiku Kondo to a friend in Japan with his own inscription. Kondo became captain of* Kongo *in 1933 and was Senior Officer of the Southern Invasion Naval Force, including* Kongo *and* Haruna, *in December 1941*

The Hiei *soon after she was completed in 1914. Based upon the design of* Kongo *her keel was laid at Yokosuka Naval Yard ten months after that of the* Kongo. *She was completed in 1914. Compared with* Kongo, *her first funnel was made taller and the distance increased between the first and second funnels*

The Kongo *in about 1926. The DCT (Director Control Tower) had been installed on top of the foremast, while a searchlight platform had also been mounted between the first and second funnels. (Her three sister ships had a searchlight platform for'd of their first funnel.) Her first funnel, with a large cap fitted, was made taller than before to prevent smoke and fumes from coming over the bridge*

In view of this surprising information, the Japanese Navy suddenly changed its mind and decided to adopt the 14in gun for the *Kongo*. Since the 14in was an entirely new gun in the world, the Japanese Navy ordered Vickers to manufacture its prototype. When completed, it was tested at the Royal Navy's firing range at Shoeburyness in March 1911. After confirming satisfactory results in the test, the formal decision was made to adopt the 14in gun for the *Kongo*.

Soon after this decision was made, the U.S. Navy made public that it had decided to adopt the 14in gun for her new battleships *New York* and *Texas*. Had not that attaché's vital information reached the Japanese Navy, it would have lagged behind the U.S. Navy in the big gun race.

KONGO CHARACTERISTICS
The basic design of the *Kongo* was executed by the Japanese Naval Construction Department and consisted of the requirements stipulated by the Japanese Navy with the Vickers' draft plan for an improved *Lion* class.

As a result, her displacement increased to 27,500 tons, some 1000 tons more than that of the *Lion*, and 6500 tons greater than the largest warships—*Kawachi* and *Settu*—that the Japanese Navy was constructing at that time.

Hull Shape
Her hull was similar to that of the *Lion* but her stem was clipper type and her flare larger than that of the British ship, in accordance with the Japanese Navy's policy of providing their ships with the best possible design for sea-worthiness. In furtherance of this, the underwater portion of her bow was built straight as opposed to the protruding stem of the *Lion*. This decreased the *Kongo's* length by approximately 5ft. Her beam however was wider by about 3·5ft. The reason for this will be explained under the next heading.

Main Armament
Major differences between:

KONGO	*LION*
Four twin-mounting turrets of 14in guns/45 calibre (two mounted forward, *one abaft her third funnel* and one aft).	Four twin-mounting turrets of 13·5in guns/45 calibre (two mounted forward, one amidships between second and third funnels and one aft).
Third turret between boiler rooms and engine rooms.	Boilers divided into two groups fore and aft (third turret between two groups).
Eight 21in torpedo tubes.	Two 21in torpedo tubes.

In order to maintain high speeds, battle-cruisers needed ample space amidships for powerful boilers. It was difficult therefore to find enough magazine space, if two superimposed gun turrets were situated aft.

As can be seen from the diagram, both *Kongo* and *Lion* positioned one gun turret amidships and the other aft. This meant that in the case of the British ship which had two groups of boilers—one fore and the other aft—the turret was sandwiched between the second and third funnels with the result that its firing traverse was limited and the effect of the blast on the bridge was very heavy. In addition, her cutters and boats had to be positioned in two groups—also fore and aft—causing great inconvenience.

Kongo, however, had her third turret positioned between her boiler rooms and engine rooms and thus the three funnels were concentrated in one area. Because of this position the traverse of her guns was greatly increased. This battery arrangement is considered to have been the reason why the beam of the *Kongo* was wider than that of the *Lion*; in fact, this arrangement was adopted by the Royal Navy in its design for the battle-cruiser *Tiger*.

Secondary

For the *Kongo*'s secondary armament, the Japanese Navy decided to mount sixteen 6in guns in her casemates: the 4in guns mounted by the Royal Navy were considered insufficient for the repulsion of enemy destroyers. Later, the Royal Navy also adopted this policy.

This decision to mount larger guns on warships such as the *Negato* and *Yamata* classes eventually led to the Japanese gaining the ascendancy over other navies.

Protection

By reducing the thickness of her waterline belt by one inch, the designers hoped to strengthen *Kongo*'s protection because, due to the increased range of firing, shells were landing at steeper angles than ever before.

For her waterline belt, armour plates of 8in thickness were used; above the waterline plates 6in thick were extended up to her weather deck. Barbettes were protected with 9in plates, while the roof of the turret was made of 3in plates. The below-deck section of the four main battery turrets was protected with 3in armour. This protection of the main turrets was much heavier than that of the *Lion*, the aim being to supplement the weak protection of the main battery inherent in the battle-cruiser.

Over such vital parts as magazines, boiler rooms and engine rooms (on the lower deck), covering by armour plates of ¾in thickness was provided, while the weather deck was protected with 1·5in plates. This protection was normal for battle-cruisers at that time, but later the armour was discovered to be weak against bombs and shells hitting with plunging fire.

The protection of the steering gear room was also improved and plates of 1in and ¾in thickness were provided over it.

Machinery

The *Kongo*'s main machinery consisted of four Parsons steam turbines with a total output of 64,000 s.h.p. Steam was supplied by 36 Yarrow coal and oil-burning boilers. With this main machinery the *Kongo* logged a maximum trial speed of 27·5 knots.

An aerial photograph of Kongo *in about 1926. A rare aerial view to depict so clearly a Japanese capital ship of those days*

The Kongo *in 1928. Note that her foremast was now a complicated shape, a typical pattern of the large Japanese warships. A cap of the inflated type to prevent the entry of rain was fitted atop the second funnel for experimental purposes. The booms of the anti-torpedo netting had also been removed*

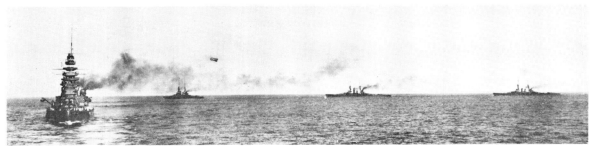

A scene in the major naval manoeuvres of 1924 taken from the battleship Nagato. *In her wake is the battleship* Mitsu, *while the three identical ships seen near the horizon are, from left to right,* Kongo, *towing an observation balloon, the* Kirishima *and the* Hiei

Kongo *under her first reconstruction in No. 3 dry dock, Yokosuka Naval Yard in 1928. The former first funnel has been removed from her and is seen on shore in the background*

Rigging

Her foremast and mainmast were of a tripod type. The position of the foremast was better than that of the *Lion* as the latter had a defect inasmuch as smoke and fumes from her funnels blew back continually to her bridge.

Even the Kongo, *in spite of her powerful armament and protection, had one great weakness. She did not mount a director control tower until World War I, although warships of most other navies had done so earlier.*

Construction

The keel of the *Kongo* was laid on a slipway in Vickers' Barrow shipyard on 17 January 1911. The yard was also building the *Princess Royal*, the second ship of the *Lion* class whose launching was scheduled for three months later.

Launching Day

After the *Kongo* was launched on 18 May 1912, she was secured for several months alongside the *Princess Royal* for fitting-out. The Japanese battle-cruiser was completed and turned over to the Japanese Navy on 16 August 1913, some ten months after that of the British battle-cruiser. The fitting-out of *Kongo* went on very smoothly, partly because the Japanese naval officers in charge of the work were able to observe the fitters working on the British battle-cruiser close by!

Immediately after delivery, *Kongo* steamed to Plymouth where she prepared for the long voyage to her homeland. On 28 August 1913 she left Plymouth on her home-bound trip and arrived at Yokosuka on 5 November of that year to become a poweruI addition to the fast-growing Japanese Navy.

The *Kongo* was the last Japanese warship to be imported from abroad and the forerunner of her three sister ships to be built at local shipyards.

DEVELOPMENTS BEFORE FIRST MODIFICATION

She had only just completed her 'shakedown' cruise, when World War I started in 1914 and Japan went to war with Germany. *Kongo* sailed from Yokosuka on 26 August 1914 for escort duty in the Central Pacific and subsequently returned to Yokosuka on 12 September of that year. Except for this duty, however, she did not take part actively in the war.

In the latter part of the war, the Royal Navy asked the Japanese Navy for the lease of the four *Kongo*-class battle-cruisers, a request the Japanese Navy refused. Had this lease been permitted, the Jutland Sea Battle might have had a different outcome.

During this period minor refits were carried out on

Kongo *during her first reconstruction. With her boilers newly installed, two new funnels are mounted. This photograph was taken on 20 February 1931.*

the *Kongo*. In 1917 the long-desired DCT (Director Control Tower) was installed atop the foremast and, to accommodate it, the top of the foremast was enlarged by 3ft in length and 2ft in width. At this time, a searchlight platform was newly mounted between her first and second funnels, upon which 110cm searchlights were installed. In 1918 the former four 8cm AA guns were replaced by four 8cm AA guns/40 calibre, two each on both sides amidships.

Funnel Smoke and Fumes

Although *Kongo*'s first funnel was better positioned than *Lion*'s, she still could not completely eliminate smoke and fumes coming over the bridge because the funnels were all of the same height. In order to remedy this situation, the first funnel was made taller in 1920. As this step proved to be still insufficient, a large cap was mounted at the fore part top of the first funnel. In 1921, seaplanes were first installed on board.

In 1924, fire-command and searchlight-directing equipment, as well as devices determining enemy speed and course, were mounted on her foremast, with the result that her profile started to take on a complicated shape, a feature specifically typical of large Japanese warships.

This refitting was soon followed by work involving the increase of elevation of the 14in guns. A maximum elevation of 25° was increased to 33°, resulting in the increase of the maximum range from 25,800m to approximately 29,000m.

In 1926, three single-mounting 8cm AA guns/49 calibre were added, bringing the total to seven. Out of the three newly-added AA guns, one was positioned on each side amidships, while another was mounted above the after secondary bridge.

In the following year, *Kongo*'s bridge was replaced by the so-called 'pagoda' type bridge, similar to that of the *Nagato*, in order to accommodate various fire-command and other equipment that had in the meantime become larger and larger.

In 1928, an inflated type of cap, to prevent the entry of rain, was fitted on top of the second funnel for experimental purposes. This cap, after further improvements, was widely used in the Japanese Navy in later days. The booms of the anti-torpedo netting were also removed at the same time.

FIRST RECONSTRUCTION

During the latter part of 1920, the Japanese Navy began reconstructing the *Kongo* class ships within a limit of 3000 tons increased displacement (as was allowed under the Washington Naval Armament Limitation Treaty) with a view to strengthening the protection of decks and magazine rooms, modernising boiler rooms and installing anti-torpedo bulges.

The first ship of this class to be given these modifications was the *Haruna*, followed by the *Kirishima*. Work on the *Kongo* herself was begun in September 1929 and finished on 31 March 1931.

As a result of this reconstruction, her displacement increased from 26,300 tons to 29,330 tons; her beam widened and her maximum speed was reduced to approximately 26 knots. The Japanese Navy then changed the *Kongo* class warships from battle-cruisers to battleships and the reconstruction was continued.

Protection

The protection of her decks was strengthened so that they could withstand the impact of 14in shells fired from a range of 20,000m to 25,000m. The middle deck above the magazine rooms and the engine rooms was covered with plates of 2·5in to 4in thickness, in addition to the ¾in armour plate already fitted.

For even greater protection of the magazine rooms, the circular portion of the main battery below the middle deck was also strengthened by fitting additional plates of 3in thickness over the existing plates of 2·5in to 3in thickness.

The roofs of her main battery turrets were strengthened by fitting additional plates of 3in thickness over the existing 3in thick plates.

In addition, circular plates of the following thicknesses were added to parts of her armour deck to strengthen protection: 6·5in at funnel outlets, 7in at ventilation passages for the boiler rooms, 4in to 5in at ventilation passages for the engine rooms and ammunition passages.

Underwater Protection

In order to provide her with underwater protection, her magazine rooms and the engine rooms were protected so that those parts could withstand the impact of explosion of 200 kg explosives. For that end, three to four layers of 1in high-tension steel plates were extended either inside her outer hull or directly over her outer hull plates. Underwater protection longitudinal bulkheads of approximately 3in thickness were also installed in parts of her boiler rooms.

In addition, bulges were newly installed on both sides with the aim of increasing her buoyancy to meet any weight increase due to the reconstruction, as well as increasing her underwater protection. Water-tight steel tubes were fitted in the bulges so that buoyancy might be maintained even if damage occurred. This fitting of watertight steel tubes was completed just before the outbreak of World War II.

Machinery and Reduction to Two Funnels

The *Kongo*'s machinery department was also largely reconstructed. Her 36 Yarrow coal and oil burning boilers were replaced by six 'Ro'-type Naval Construction Department's large capacity coal and oil burning boilers and four smaller capacity oil burning boilers. Her fuel capacity was accordingly changed from the former 1000 tons of heavy oil and 4200 tons of coal to 3292 tons of heavy oil and 2661 tons of coal. Her radius of action, therefore, increased from 8000 miles at 14 knots to 9500 miles at the same speed.

The replacement of her boilers resulted in a reduction of space needed for the boilers to produce the same output as before. Her three funnels were replaced by two funnels.

Fire Control and Spotting

The maximum elevation of her main battery was raised from 33° to 43° to increase its maximum range to 33,000m. This increase of her 14in guns' range enabled her to enter the battle line with the 16in gun-mounting *Nagato* class battleships. With the increase in her maximum range of firing, her pagoda-type foremast was enlarged and modernised so that more

Kongo *under full power during her preliminary trials held off Tokyo Bay on 4 August 1931. With a displacement of 33,800 tons, she logged a top speed of 25·7 knots with 73,850s.h.p. Note the thin smoke fumes emitted as she still had a few coal-burning boilers*

Kongo *immediately after her first reconstruction, seen from her bow*

Kongo *after her first reconstruction seen from her bow*

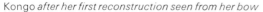

Kongo *in the naval review held off the port of Yokohama on 25 August 1933. The carrier seen behind her bow is the* Akagi. *About six months later* Kongo's *mainmast was lowered*

A scene taken from the bridge of the Kongo *in the major naval manoeuvres in 1933. On deck between third and fourth turrets are three seaplanes. In her wake are the* Haruna *and the battleship* Fuso *who had just completed refit*

Kongo soon after the second reconstruction. By virtue of this second reconstruction, Kongo was reborn as a modern high-speed battleship equipped with eight 14in guns, 14·6in guns and eight 12·7cm AA guns, but still capable of a maximum speed of 30 knots. The photograph was taken in January 1937

Kongo, taken from HMS Birmingham, *off the port of Amoy in China on 21 October 1938. A tall pole on her fourth turret is a support stand for the W/T aerials so that the operation of the plane-hoisting crane may not be hindered*

complicated fire-directing devices for long-range gunnery could be mounted there.

Attention was paid also to increasing the accommodation for seaplanes which were being used more and more at sea. The deck space between her third and fourth turrets was used to accommodate three 14-Type seaplanes.

Four underwater torpedo tubes were removed, leaving four tubes still mounted onboard.

Many improvements were also made to her ventilation system and to other equipment during this reconstruction period.

Minor Changes Before Second Reconstruction

Despite the large-scale reconstruction, the *Kongo* still had to undergo a series of minor refits in order to keep up with the rapid developments of naval weapons and technologies then taking place in the world. In 1932, only one year after the first reconstruction was completed, two large searchlights of 150cm in diameter were mounted to improve her fighting capacity at night. Almost simultaneously, her single-mounting 8cm AA guns/40 calibre were replaced by four twin-mounting 12·7cm AA guns, two units on both sides amidships.

In early 1933, two twin-mounting 40mm AA machine-guns were installed, while a catapult was mounted on her seaplane accommodation deck.

During the following year, the barrels of her 14in guns were replaced by new ones for the first time since she was commissioned, while 91-Type armour-piercing shells were provided for her. The three

seaplanes were also replaced by new 90-Type seaplanes of the same number. Her mainmast was lowered about this time, because improvements in wireless equipment no longer necessitated having such a high mast which could be sighted at long ranges by enemy ships. Two quadruple-mounting 13mm AA machine guns were also mounted on board.

A New Tactic

The Japanese Navy by tradition favoured a night engagement before a decisive battle. By such tactics they aimed to destroy some of the enemy capital ships with torpedo attacks by their destroyers, thus neutralising the enemy's superiority of big gun power before the decisive battle. In order to accomplish this, it was necessary to be able to penetrate the outer defence ring which protected the main force.

Had their speed been as high as that of cruisers and destroyers, the *Kongo* class ships would have been ideal for the execution of these tactics. They could—together with light men-of-war—have destroyed the enemy cruisers with their big guns, thus enabling destroyers to penetrate the defences as required.

The maximum speed of the *Kongo* class warships was therefore raised to 30 knots.

SECOND RECONSTRUCTION

The second reconstruction of the four *Kongo* class ships started with the *Haruna* in 1933, followed by that of the *Kirishima*. The second remodelling of the *Kongo* herself started at Yokosuka Naval Yard on 1 June 1935 and

IJN Kongo *and her sister ships*

Kongo *as completed in 1913*

Hiei *in 1936 (Y turret removed)*

The battleship *Kongo* is depicted as she appeared in 1944, at the peak of her operational life in the Pacific. Her reconnaissance aircraft, a Jake floatplane, is on the catapult which is trained fore and aft.

Warships of the Imperial Japanese Navy wore no ships' badges; instead, the national emblem, a chrysanthemum, was fitted to the stemhead of their ships.

The Imperial Standard is shown on the left, between the ensign of the Imperial Japanese Navy (left) and (right) the Admiral's flag which was so often worn by *Kongo*.

Gordon Davies © *Profile Publications Ltd*

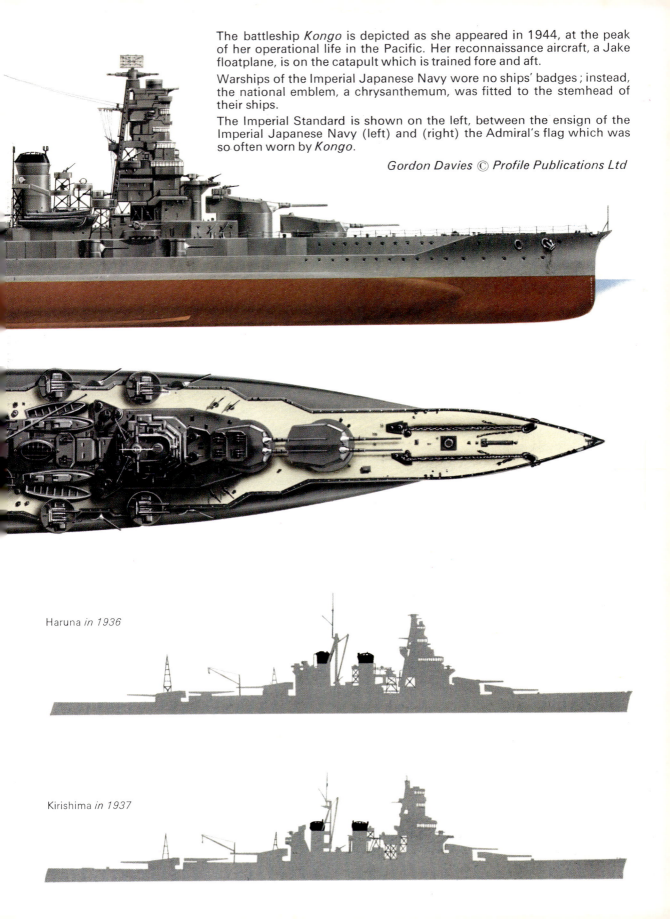

Haruna *in 1936*

Kirishima *in 1937*

Kongo (*right*) *and* Kirishima *in 1938*

HMS Prince of Wales   (*H. C. Timewell*)

HMS Repulse   (*H. C. Timewell*)

The Japanese carrier task force steaming in the Indian Ocean in March 1942, taken from the carrier Zuikaku. *Ahead are four* Kongo *class battleships and three flat-tops. Immediately ahead is the* Kongo. *This was the first* and *last time that the four* Kongo *class battleships operated as one unit during World War II*

was completed on 8 January 1937. As their maximum speed increased up to 30 knots, the Japanese Navy now classified them as high speed battleships.

New Machinery and Hull Shape

Because the second reconstruction aimed at, among other improvements, giving the *Kongo* a maximum speed of 30 knots, her machinery was entirely replaced by new, powerful plant. Her old boilers were replaced by eight oil-burning boilers of a greater power, each of which was housed in a separate watertight compartment. The four Parsons direct-connecting steam turbines were replaced by four Naval Construction Department Type reduction geared steam turbines with a total output of 136,000shp, more than double that of the original 64,000shp.

Her fuel capacity was increased to 6000 tons of heavy oil by adding new oil tanks. Installation of additional oil tanks required a considerable amount of refitting to her hull, but the alteration contributed to the increase of her radius of action from 9500 miles at 14 knots to 10,000 miles at 18 knots.

In order to reduce her propulsion resistance, her stern was lengthened by 25ft to 720ft (bp), while her beam of 95·3ft remained unchanged. On the other hand, her draught was deepened from 28·4ft to 31·9ft. Her displacement increased from 31,780 tons to 36,610 tons.

Armament

In this second reconstruction, there was little alteration to her armament except for the elevation of the 6in guns being raised from 15° to 30° to increase their range. In order to achieve this, the ring platforms of those guns in the casemates were raised. Twin-mounting 40mm AA machine guns were replaced by ten twin-mounting 25mm AA machine guns.

To compensate for an increase of weight due to the refit, two 6in guns in the foremost casemates on both sides and all torpedo tubes were removed.

Rigging and Upperworks

Her foremast was considerably altered, emphasis being placed on improving capacities of the long-range gunnery and also of the night action equipment. A 10m range-finder was installed atop the foremast, whilst various kinds of command posts, fire-directing devices, devices for determining the enemy course and speed, searchlight-directing equipment and lookout posts were mounted in it. Because most of this equipment required a wide field of observation, her foremast became very large and complicated to fulfil these requirements. The lower portion of her mainmast was also re-built to house the secondary director control tower. Six 110cm searchlights were additionally installed around her first funnel to improve her night fighting capacity.

Damage Control

Another feature of the second reconstruction was that she was at last equipped with a damage-control system. On both sides of the hull, 20 compartments with a total capacity of 500 tons were newly built for quick flooding, and 26 compartments with a total capacity of 1500 tons for ordinary flooding. By means of quick flooding of all compartments the ship's list could be

adjusted by 5·5° while by means of ordinary flooding it could be adjusted by 7·7°.

By virtue of the second reconstruction, the *Kongo* was thus reborn as a modern high-speed battleship equipped with eight 14in guns, fourteen 6in guns and eight 12·7cm AA guns and yet having a maximum speed of 30 knots.

Minor Changes Before World War II

After the second reconstruction, *Kongo* engaged in some hard training with the Combined Fleets as one of its important main units. As the world international situation became tense, however, she had to undergo minor refits from time to time to prepare her for any emergency. About 1939, the air-defence command post was added to the top of her foremast. In early 1941, armour was added to the barbettes of her main battery to reinforce her vertical protection, while anti-flash equipment in the main turrets was improved. In the autumn of the same year, degaussing was fitted to her outer hull to neutralise the magnetic effect of the ship.

Although *Kongo's* protection was, as stated earlier, reinforced to withstand the impact of 14in shells fired from ranges between 20,000m and 25,000m, it must be admitted that this protection was not sufficient. Especially was this so with her vertical protection, which was her weakest point, as little reinforcement had been added since she was first completed.

The Japanese Navy had concluded, in fact, that her side protection could be penetrated by shells of the U.S. capital ships at any range. This weakness of her side protection was later proven in the so-called Guadalcanal Sea Battle in November 1942, when the *Kirishima*, her sister ship, was sunk by gunfire from USS *Washington* and *South Dakota*, both armed with 16in guns.

ACTIVITIES IN WORLD WAR II: WORK HORSE OF THE FLEET

When Japan entered the war in December 1942, the four *Kongo* class high-speed battleships found themselves much in demand. While other battle-ships of the Combined Fleets vainly waited in the Inland Sea for the chance of a decisive battle with the U.S. Fleet (a chance that never came) the *Kongo* and her three sister ships were given multiple and unusual assignments.

They were destined to play many roles, not only in the initial stages but in almost all stages of the war. They eventually became the main 'work horses' among the big-gun men-of-war of the Japanese Navy. Taking full advantage of their excellent mobile capacity, they steamed east, south and west to their various assignments. It is little exaggeration to say that the Japanese Navy would have had a much harder time in the war had it not possessed the *Kongo* class high-speed battleships.

Prince of Wales and Repulse

Before the outbreak of war, the *Kongo* and *Haruna* were deployed in the South China Sea as the sole big-gun force under the command of the Southern Invasion Naval Force. The main mission was to support an

Kongo on her homeward trip, off Tokyo Bay in May 1942, after the successful completion of the Southern Invasion Operation. Note the rising sun mark painted atop her second and fourth turrets for identification purposes

invasion of Malaya by the Japanese Army, one of the major objectives of Japan's war strategy. When news reached them of the arrival of HMS *Prince of Wales* and HMS *Repulse* at Singapore, the Japanese were grimly determined to challenge them, an ambition that eventually failed to be realised since both powerful men-of-war of the Royal Navy were sunk single-handed by aerial attacks from the land-based Air Force of the Japanese Navy.

Pearl Harbour

The *Kongo* class then assisted in the Japanese invasion of British Borneo and the Dutch East Indies. From late February to early March 1942, they joined the powerful carrier force which followed up the successful attack on Pearl Harbour—by launching a sweeping operation south of Java Island conducted in conjunction with the landing there. During this operation the *Kongo* opened fire for the first time in the war, when she bombarded Christmas Island in the Indian Ocean in order to destroy enemy installations there.

The *Hiei* and the *Kirishima*—sister ships of the *Kongo* —had a particularly disappointing experience when they encountered a British destroyer on 1 March 1942. They opened fire with their 14in guns, but although the *Hiei* fired a total of 210 rounds and the *Kirishima* a total of 87 rounds, they failed to score a single hit on the enemy warship. This incident caused the gunnery experts to have serious second-thoughts on the effectiveness of firing big guns.

In late March the *Kongo* class four high-speed battleships left Sterling Bay in the Celebes Islands as a powerful element of the carrier task force to launch a new operation in the Indian Ocean, during which time it raided Colombo and Trincomalee in Ceylon, while destroying the Royal Navy's one carrier, *Hermes*, and two heavy cruisers, *Cornwall* and *Dorsetshire*, at sea. After this operation, the battleships returned to the homeland in late April.

The Battle of Midway Island

The four *Kongo* class ships joined the Combined Fleet when in June 1942 it attempted to capture Midway Island in the Central Pacific with all available forces— the *Kongo* and the *Haruna* as the main force of the invasion force and the *Hiei* and the *Kirishima* as part of the carrier task force. This time the gods of war were no longer with the Japanese: the Japanese carrier task force was ambushed by the U.S. Fleet and all four powerful carriers were sunk by enemy bombing. The four *Kongo* class high-speed battleships were not hurt however, and made port in Japan safely.

After the defeat at Midway, the tide of the war flowed apparently against the Japanese. The Japanese

As a result of the London naval treaty, the Hiei, who was then under her first reconstruction at the Kure Naval Yard, was ordered to be converted to a training battleship. With her fourth turret and also waterline belt removed, her speed was limited to 18 knots because the number of her boilers was also reduced. Her foremast however was modernised like her sister ships. Since the number of her boilers was reduced, her first funnel was made slim. Photographed in 1933, soon after completion of the conversion

Navy, which had taken the initiative, was now denied it and had to stand on the defensive. When the Allies made a surprise landing on Guadalcanal Island in August 1942, the Japanese armed forces fought back fiercely. They did not hesitate to throw as many combat men, ships and planes as possible into the fight night and day, resulting in a series of battles in the air, and on land and sea.

Guadalcanal Island : Bombardment

The four *Kongo* class men-of-war also took their turn in actions centring around the 'Bloody Island', in the most risky manner ever conducted in the war. When their reinforcement attempts to the islands were frustrated by superior enemy air forces, the Japanese saw the urgency of neutralising the enemy air strip on the island, even if only for a while. To achieve this, the Japanese Navy planned to use the 14in guns of the *Kongo* class high-speed battleships. They were to bombard Henderson air field with their big guns at night, after closing in at high speed in the face of enemy air interceptions. It was a very hazardous challenge to superior enemy air forces by single men-of-war.

Kongo and her sister ship, *Haruna*, were detailed in mid-October 1942 for this bombardment, when a large-scale reinforcement attempt was made on the island. Taking advantage of their high speed, they successfully closed the island shore on the night of 13 October and bombarded the enemy air field with their 14in guns for more than an hour. A bombardment result of 14in guns with a total of 920 rounds was even more effective than anticipated: most of the enemy airfield was set on fire and approximately two-thirds of more than 80 planes there were destroyed. It was indeed the highlight of *Kongo's* activities in the war.

Battle of the Solomon Islands : Sinking of USS *Hornet* *

Although the Japanese were on the defensive, the Japanese Navy strength and that of the Allied Powers were still well balanced, with the result that frequent engagements took place between them. In less than two weeks after the successful bombardment on Guadalcanal Island, a fierce sea battle between the carrier force of both sides took place at sea off the Solomon Islands in the South Pacific on 26 October 1942. The Japanese fleet sank USS *Hornet* and heavily damaged

---

* Warship Profile No. 3.

The Hiei *under full power trials after her major reconstruction in December 1939. The conversion was similar to that of her sister ships. In addition, her foremast was further modernised as the prototype of the* Yamato *class battleship, with the result that her profile was slightly different from that of her other sister ships*

The Hiei *homeward-bound off Tokyo Bay in May 1942 after the successful completion of the Southern Invasion Operation. Her DCT is painted white as an identification mark*

The Haruna *after her second reconstruction, which was completed in September 1934, ahead of her sister ships. Her foremast is slightly taller than those of the others*

The Haruna *in 1935. The range-finder atop her foremast was 8m, to be replaced later by a 10m instrument like those of her sister battleships*

USS *Enterprise* without losing any of its own ships. The four *Kongo*-class ships also took part, although they were divided into two groups—one consisting of *Kongo* and *Haruna*, the other of *Hiei* and *Kirishima*.

The battle situation around Guadalcanal Island had in the meantime deteriorated in spite of desperate efforts on the part of the Japanese to recapture the 'Bloody Island'. The Japanese then planned to launch a larger-scale reinforcement attempt than that of mid-October in order to turn the tables once and for all. This time, also, a bombardment by big guns on Henderson airfield was planned and the *Hiei* and *Kirishima* were detailed. They were not, however, so lucky as *Kongo* and *Haruna*.

No Surrender : the Battleship *Hiei*
When they closed the shore of Guadalcanal Island on the night of 12 November, they were ambushed by the U.S. fleet. The fiercest night engagement in World War II was then exchanged between the Japanese and U.S. fleets. The *Hiei*, flagship of the Japanese bombardment force, was subjected to concentrated

gunfire from enemy heavy cruisers. Her protection was strong enough to protect her turrets, engine and boiler rooms, but unfortunately one 20cm shell hit her steering compartment, throwing her out of control. She dropped out of the action not far from Guadalcanal Island. When daylight came, she was subjected to aerial attacks which lasted all day long. Although several bombs and torpedoes struck her, she still remained almost intact except for the damage in her steering compartment. Since there was no way to save her, she had finally to be sunk by friendly torpedoes after darkness came over the scene. She was the first battleship of the Japanese Navy to be lost during the war.

Battleship versus Battleship
On the night of 13 November, two heavy cruisers and one light cruiser bombarded Henderson airfield without mishap. The following night, another attempt to attack the island was made with the *Kirishima* (who was not damaged in the engagement of 12 November) and two heavy cruisers as nucleus. This

The Haruna *under full power in battle training held on 21 May 1936*

force was again ambushed by the U.S. fleet which included USS *Washington* and USS *South Dakota*. The first engagement between battleships of the two fleets then followed. The *Kirishima* was out-classed by the new 16in gun battleships of the U.S. Navy and, after being hit by more than six 16in shells, she went down, following the fate of her sister ship, *Hiei*.

With this costly yet unsuccessful reinforcement attempt as the turning point, the battle situation around the Solomon Islands went from bad to worse. The Japanese finally had to give up large-scale reinforcements to Guadalcanal Island toward the end of that year. As the Japanese, as well as the Allied Powers, had been greatly exhausted after long and desperate fighting, a lull came over the battle scene for a while. The *Kongo* and the *Haruna*, together with other ships, headed for the homeland in early 1943 to undertake repairs and maintenance, which they needed very badly, because they had not been docked since the autumn of 1941.

MAJOR REFITS 1943-1944 : LESSONS LEARNT

Main refits undertaken at this time and also in early 1944 were as follows:

1. Two twin-mounting 12·7cm AA guns were additionally installed, one on each side, thus making a total of twelve. Ten twin-mounting 25mm AA machine guns were replaced by six triple-mounting 25mm AA

machine guns and eight twin-mounting units with a total of 34 machine guns.

2. Type 21 radar for air lookout and Type 22 radar for surface lookout were installed with their antennae mounted on her foremast.

3. In view of the fact that the *Hiei* was hit in her steering compartment by an enemy shell which led to her doom in the sea battle in November 1942, the following measures were undertaken to strengthen the *Kongo's* protection of the steering compartment.

The former steering compartment was separated by a watertight bulkhead into a steering gear room and a rudder stock room, both of which were to be shielded by a thick layer of concrete to withstand the hitting of a 20cm shell. In addition, an emergency hydraulic steering device to be operated by a diesel-driven generator was installed. A unit of jacks with a capacity of 50 tons was also provided on either side to push back the rudder to the midships position in case it jammed at 'hard-over'.

4. To compensate the increase in weight due to the additions mentioned above, six 6in guns were removed from her sides.

As the Japanese Navy's main fleets remained relatively inactive during 1943 while rebuilding their strength, the *Kongo* and the *Haruna* did not participate in any action. With the continuance of the war into 1944, the Allied intention of breaking through the island chain in the Central Pacific became apparent:

The Kirishima *after her second reconstruction. This photograph was taken in May 1937 in Sukumo Bay off Shikoku, one of the four major islands of Japan proper*

The four Kongo *class battleships in April 1942, when they participated in the carrier operation in the Indian Ocean. From the forefront are the* Kongo, Haruna, Kirishima *and* Hiei. *The carrier at the extreme left is the* Soryu

the Japanese Navy planned to meet the enemy challenge with all air and sea forces available once and for all.

Battle of the Philippine Sea : Gallant but Defeated

The showdown took place in the Philippine Sea in mid-June 1944, when the Allies landed on Saipan in the Mariana Islands. Although the Japanese air and sea forces fought very fiercely and with grim determination, the battle ended in their complete defeat. Their three carriers were sunk and most of the land-based air forces destroyed by the powerful enemy carrier strength. The balance between the Japanese Navy and the Allied Navies was now entirely upset. The remnant of the Japanese fleet, including the undamaged *Kongo* and the *Haruna*, made port in the homeland toward the end of June.

Emergency Refit and Desperate Work-up

Immediately after arrival at her homeland, *Kongo* was refitted. In addition to six triple-mounting 25mm AA machine guns and eight twin-mounting units of the same type, 12 triple-mounting units and 24 single-mounting units were installed to make the total of machine guns 94. Type 13 radar for air lookout was also added, while Type 22 radar was improved so as to be used also for fire control. These alterations and additions had to be carried out in a hurry because the next Allied assault, somewhere along the Philippines, Formosa, Okinawa and the Japanese homeland, seemed imminent.

Immediately after the refit, *Kongo* proceeded in late July to the Linga anchorage, south of Singapore, where she underwent vigorous training in preparation for the forthcoming showdown with the Allied Powers. She did not, however, succeed in improving her gunnery radar fire control.

Fleet Strategy : Battle of Leyte Gulf

When the Allied Powers landed on Leyte Island in the Philippines in mid-October, the Japanese fleets converged from north and south on Leyte Gulf, while its land-based air arms and the Army air forces attacked enemy forces from the Philippines or Formosa. Since the Japanese Navy was no longer able to launch a carrier-borne air attack, its basic strategy called for the surface force, including *Kongo* and *Haruna*, to make a daring dash eastwards through the island chain, while its carrier group acted as a decoy to lure the powerful enemy carrier task force away from the main battle fleet.

This unorthodox strategy succeeded very well. When the surface force broke forth east of the island chain in the early morning of 25 October, 1944, it encountered no enemy, but at dawn found itself unexpectedly within fighting range of the enemy carrier groups which the Japanese Navy had long wanted to attack. Though the Japanese surface force identified them as enemy regular carrier groups, they were actually escort carrier groups.

Battle off Samar : October 1944

Then occurred the Sea Battle Off Samar, in which the Japanese attacked the enemy fleet. Taking full advantage of their high speed, the *Kongo* and the *Haruna* proceeded ahead of the force to open fire with their 14in guns. This was the first time in the war that either had fired with their big guns on enemy ships.

The Japanese force sank one escort carrier and one destroyer. Japanese ships also received serious damage, but the *Kongo*'s was very slight. Despite desperate fighting, however, the Japanese Navy not only failed to prevent the enemy invasion of Leyte Island, but

HMS Hermes   (*H. C. Timewell*)

suffered irretrievable damage. Most of the remaining Japanese force, including the *Kongo* and the *Haruna*, returned to Brunei Bay in Borneo.

HOMEWARD BOUND : DISASTER, 21 NOVEMBER 1944

Since Brunei Bay was no longer a safe anchorage for the Japanese fleet because of intensified air raids by the Allied Powers, the Japanese ships decided to return to the homeland in separate groups. The *Kongo* and the *Haruna* left with an escort of destroyers on 6 November on their homeward trip. On the night of 20 November, when steaming northwards in the Formosa Strait, the *Kongo* was suddenly hit by torpedoes fired by the U.S. submarine *Sealion*. At about 0530 in the morning of 21 November, there was a loud explosion, whereupon she settled into the sea and sank.

Kongo's Three Sister Ships

Hiei: Completed at the Yokosuka naval shipyard on 4 August 1914. Reconstruction to convert her into a training battleship as a result of the London naval treaty began in September 1929 at the Kure naval shipyard and was completed on 31 December 1932. A large-scale reconstruction to transform her into a high-speed battleship started on 26 November 1936 at the Kure naval yard, and was completed on 31 December 1939.

Activities in World War II: Took part in the air-raid upon Pearl Harbour; the air-raid upon Port Darwin in 1942; the invasion operation of Dutch East Indies; the mobile operation in Indian Ocean in 1942; the Midway Sea Battle, and a series of sea battles around Guadalcanal Island in the autumn of 1942. In the night action on 12 November 1942, she was seriously damaged and finally sunk by friendly torpedoes.

HMS Cornwall   (*H. C. Timewell*)

HMS Dorsetshire   *(H. C. Timewell)*

USS Washington   *(H. C. Timewell)*

Haruna: Completed at Kawasaki Dockyard in Kobe City on 19 April 1915; the first reconstruction began at the Yokosuka naval yard on 1 March 1924 and was completed on 31 July 1928; the second reconstruction started at the Kure naval yard on 1 August 1933 and was completed on 30 September 1934. Activities in World War II: Took part in the invasion operations of Malaya, the Philippines, British Borneo and Dutch East Indies; the mobile operation in Indian Ocean; the Midway Sea Battle, the bombardment of Guadalcanal Island, the Sea Battle off the Solomon Islands in October 1942, the Sea Battle in the Philippine Sea in June 1944, the Sea Battle Off Samar in October 1944. She was sunk near Kure on 28 July 1945 due to air raids by enemy carrier borne air forces on 27 to 28 July.

Kirishima: Completed at the Nagasaki shipyard of Mitsubishi Heavy Industries in Nagasaki City on 19 April 1915; the first reconstruction started at the Kure naval yard in March 1927 and was completed on 31 March 1930; the second reconstruction began at the Sasebo naval yard on 1 June 1934 and was completed on 8 June 1936. Activities in World War II: Same as those of the *Hiei* except that the *Kirishima* was sunk in the night engagement of 14 November 1942 near Guadalcanal Island.

Series Editor: JOHN WINGATE, DSC

CHARACTERISTICS OF KONGO

	When first completed	First reconstruction	Second reconstruction
Normal displacement:	27,500 tons	—	—
Standard d/t:	26,330 tons	29,330	32,156
Trial d/t:	27,900 tons	31,780	36,610
Length (oa) ft.:	705	705	730
Length (bp) ft.:	695	695	720
Beam (ft.):	92	95·3	95·3
Draught (trial) ft.:	27·5	28·4	31·9

Engines:

Boilers:	Yarrow		
Type:	Coal & Oil	Coal & Oil	Oil burning
Number:	36	6 Oil burning 4	8
Machinery:	Parsons turbines	Parsons turbines	Reduction geared turbines
Number:	4	4	4
Number of Shafts:	4	4	4
Max. Output (s.h.p.):	64,000	64,000	136,000
Speed (knots):	27·5	25·9	30·3
Radius of action:	8000 miles at 14 knots	9500 miles at 14 knots	10,000 miles at 18 knots

Fuel Capacity:

Coal (tons):	4200	2661	—
Heavy oil (tons):	1000	3292	6330

Armament:

14″ guns/45 cal.:	8 (elev. 25°)	8 (43°)	8 (43°)
6″ guns/50 cal.:	16 (15°)	16 (15°)	14 (30°)
AA guns:	nil	7×8 cm. (40 calibre)	8×12·7 cm.
AA machine guns:	nil	nil	20×25 mm.

Torpedo tubes:

21″ submerged:	8	4	nil
Seaplanes:	nil	3	3

USS South Dakota   (*H. C. Timewell*)

Weight distribution:

Protection (*tons*):	6502	*10,478	10,311
Armament (*tons*):	3812	3962	5443
Machinery (*tons*):	4750	3943	2737
Complement:			
Officers:	} *1221	*69	*73
Men:		*1118	*1364
Completion:	Aug. 1913	March 1931	Jan. 1936

Note: * marks represent those of the *Haruna*, a sister ship of the *Kongo*.

Acknowledgements

Profile Publications Ltd, wish to express their gratitude to H. C. Timewell, Esq., Hon. Secretary of the Naval Photograph Club, who kindly contributed photographs.

Enlargement of picture appearing on page 270. Kongo *as she was in 1928*

Another enlargement this time from page 275. Kongo January 1937 after the second reconstruction

288

Index